speaker's encyclopedia

of stories
quotations
and anecdotes

by

JACOB M. BRAUDE
JUDGE OF THE MUNICIPAL COURT OF CHICAGO

Englewood Cliffs, N. J.
PRENTICE-HALL, INC.

82404

contents

introduction

Somewhere in the "innards" of this book, a diligent search will turn up a young man who insists that capital punishment in most states means death by elocution. To those of you who go along with such a theory, this book becomes a mission of mercy. Its purpose is to outlaw forever death by elocution and substitute instead life by anecdote.

Some sage student of after-dinner speaking once commented that speeches are like steer horns—a point here and a point there, and a lot of bull in between. The points, for the most part, you will have to dredge from your own conscience; but in this book, carefully indexed, categorized, and annotated, you will find the bull.

On the pages to follow are some 2961 separate and distinct stories, jokes, proverbs, quotations, philosophies, poems, definitions, and comments on life in general and the human race in particular. It would be difficult to conceive a situation in which at least one reference from this book couldn't be used with telling effect. I feel that I know what I'm talking about. I've been using this material in speeches for more than 40 years. I couldn't even begin to estimate how many days and weeks and months of work it has saved me in preparing for talks — and how many audiences it has saved from aggravated cases of boredom.

The material that follows did not come into being as a result of any deliberate effort to make a book. Rather it is the product of a natural process of accumulation that began back in a college public speaking course at the University of Michigan in 1915. There an instructor named Immel — whom I shall always remember with affection and gratitude — introduced me to the card file method of collecting material for use in extemporaneous talks. He so impressed on me the value of salting away every piece of grist that might sometime be useful that I've been doing it ever since.

When I finished college, I had only a few hundred cards bearing bon mots in my file collection. But today, that number has grown to more than eight thousand! The material included on the pages to come is only a fraction of the total number I have accumulated. Those selected for use here were chosen for two reasons: they are the best of the lot, and they have the broadest general application.

Unlike most similar accumulations, however, this one was selected and is being offered to you now with a definite purpose in mind: to make it easier for you to put together and for your audience to digest a talk or a piece of writing. People unfortunately insist on things being capsuled and sugar-coated these days. In the extremity, this book might conceivably be used in the same fashion as a numbered joke book was once used in a penitentiary. A new convict there was puzzled when, every night after dinner, his fellow prisoners would stand up, one at a time, and call out a number — whereupon the other convicts would prostrate themselves with laughter.

"What," asked the newcomer, "is going on?"

"We're telling jokes," he was informed. "But instead of going to all the trouble of telling them, we just call off a number from our joke book, and the fellows know the book so well that they remember the joke."

Anxious to be one of the boys, the newcomer studied up on the joke book, and, when he was ready, got hesitantly to his feet one night after dinner and called out, "27." There was dead silence. "113," he offered. Nothing. Desperately he called out his favorite, "222." No response. Humiliated he sat down, and later asked his cellmate what had been wrong with his jokes.

"There was nothing wrong with the jokes," pointed out the cellmate. "It was the way you told them!"

To belabor a moral, if you don't get a response from the material contained herein, it isn't because of the material, but rather the way you use it. I can say that with impunity because practically none of it is my own. It represents the combined talents of some of the world's greatest writers, lecturers, philosophers, and public servants at their pungent best. I have dipped into them freely, and I'm sure they would have no objection if you should do likewise. If you become a pundit in the process, so be it. As Irvin S. Cobb pointed out, a raconteur is merely a person who has a good memory—and hopes other people haven't.

what this book can do for you

There are four areas in which the contents of this book can be especially useful to you by serving as a ready source in speaking and writing for (1) illustrative anecdotes; (2) over-all themes; (3) the framework of entire talks; and (4) just plain entertainment of the reader.

(1) First and foremost, it provides an excellent reference work for the right story at the right time. Every talk or manuscript can be spiced by an appropriate anecdote or philosophical tidbit — keyed to fit an audience, a situation, and a point that is being impressed. Here, in this volume, can be found *that* story.

There must be ebb and flow in a speech. Too much of anything — whether it be serious or comic — becomes monotonous. The most responsive audience is the one to which the speaker permits a constant emotional rise and fall, even though the changes may be almost imperceptible. A few well-chosen anecdotes or pieces of pilfered philosophy can quite easily make the difference between a thumpingly successful talk and a complete flop. In this book are the audience-stoppers, the frosting on the cake that makes the company at your particular table eat through the top layer and come upon your basic thought-food still alert and bright-eyed.

Thus, the first way this book can work for you is to provide a handy source of adrenalin for a speech that appears a little weak-in-the-knees. A few shots, injected painlessly in the right places, will restore a robust measure of health to your talk. Used in this fashion, the book permits you to take a completed speech manuscript or outline, select the places where it needs buoying up, and then look in these pages under the most likely categories for the one or more anecdotes that you need.

In selecting your material, though, always remember that it's a poor story if —

> some woman blushes with embarrassment;
> some heart carries away an ache;
> something sacred is made to appear common;
> a man's weakness provides the cause for laughter;
> profanity is required to make it funny;
> a little child is brought to tears;
> everyone can't join in the laughter.

(2) Every speech should have some kind of theme, one "big idea" to help it hang together and give each member of the audience a thought to carry home with him. Oftentimes, the effectiveness of a

speech is in direct relation to the care with which its theme is selected and its thought-images implanted in an audience.

This volume is full of theses around which talks can be built. The themes can be found in many forms and shapes; you need only find the one that sparks you and extract it from the anecdote, poem, joke, or other form in which you find it.

For example, when seeking a theme around which to build a talk to be given at the dedication of a new building for a Boy's Club, I was browsing through my files and came on the story of a sidewalk-superintendent who was watching a building going up and asked several of the workmen what they were doing. One said he was laying brick, another mixing mortar, a third installing plumbing. Finally, one said "I'm helping to build a cathedral."

Here was my theme: the importance of keeping a proper perspective — of having vision — of seeing the forest beyond the trees. And I'll bet that nine-tenths of that audience took this thought home with them.

These files can provide you the same service. They're literally crawling with themes — of every nature and description for almost every occasion.

(3) Every speaker starts with a subject. From that point, he's usually on his own. Using his subject and allied topics as reference points, a speaker might actually research most of the framework of his talk within these pages.

This book makes no pretense of being a substitute for factual reference works. But by offering the capsuled thoughts, comments and stories of outstanding people on just about every subject imaginable, it gives the seeker after speech material ample ammunition to construct the outline of his talk, along with anecdotal material to illustrate it.

It remains, then, only for the speaker to add the factual data — either out of his own knowledge or from factual reference sources — and he has his talk.

(4) A night club marquee once proclaimed to the world: "Good, clean entertainment — every night except Monday." In these pages you can find entertainment even on Monday. The stories collected here are just about the best of the best. I selected for my files in the first place only those nuggets that in my opinion are unusually

informative, interesting, or amusing; and the best of those have been selected for this volume.

If you never make a speech or write an article, you can have a wonderful time entertaining yourself in the pages to follow.

how to use this book

Once you've decided in what area you want the book to work for you, the next problem is how to go about it.

One of the great advantages this volume has to offer the seeker after spoken or written ammunition is its Index. To quote again from later pages, "The best book in the world would owe the most to a good index, and the worst book, if it had but a single good thought in it, might be kept alive by it."

This volume has been thoroughly endowed with a topical index. You'll have no difficulty running down whatever subject matter interests you — and in following up through the index any tangents that researching the original idea might take you upon.

Assuming then the efficient index, perhaps the best way to demonstrate how this book can be used to your best advantage is by example.

Suppose I'm scheduled to speak three months hence before a high school teacher's association on the subject, "Let's Look at Youth." I addressed the same group last year on a somewhat similar subject.

I go to my card files (as you, using this book, would go to the Index) and look up every category I can think of which might be remotely applicable. For example, I check Youth, Education, Success, Ambition, Delinquency, Advice, Teachers, and Parents. I find a wealth of material from which to build the framework of my talk. I can pick and choose and cull until I have just what I want.

Now I need a theme. I know the thought I want to get across — that we must broaden our viewpoint in considering the problems of youth, that too often we myopically see only the insignificant and overlook the important. But how to illustrate this for maximum impact on the audience? In my search through the files, I find the ideal story to get across my point: the story about a man who tacked up a huge sheet of white paper before a group of business men, and then made a tiny black dot in the middle of it.

He asked a man in the front row what he saw, and the listener answered promptly, "A black dot." The speaker then asked the same question and got the same answer from each of the other members of the group. Then with deliberate emphasis, the speaker said: "All of you have noticed the tiny black dot. But not one of you mentioned the huge sheet of white paper which surrounds it."

With my theme and framework selected, I find one other need. I have addressed this group before, and my audience will certainly include many of the same people. Therefore, it would be to my advantage to acknowledge this in some clever way in the opening of my talk, and at the same time reassure the repeaters that they won't be bored to death with exactly the same speech.

So I go back to the collection and discover an anecdote about a farmer who assigned a new hand to the job of milking the cow and returned a few minutes later to find him pouring a pail of milk down the cow's throat. When asked what he was doing, the farmhand answered, "It came out so thin the first time, I'm running it through again."

There's my opening gambit! I've already established my theme and the superstructure of my talk from the collection. I need only to put the material I've selected on file cards, add some current factual material from newspapers, draw on my own knowledge of the subject to fill in the body, and I have what I think is a good talk.

In addition to the items in my card file — some of the best of which are reproduced for you here — I have a rather specialized shortcut that might be helpful to you in preparing a speech.

As soon as I accept an invitation to speak, I take a little 4" x 6" paper notebook and note all the pertinent information, such as date, subject, length of talk, and location, on the cover. Then, from that time until the speech is to be given, I clip anything on that or related subjects that comes to my attention and put them in my little notebook. A few days before the talk is scheduled, I go through my card file collection (the contents of this book), as described earlier, and add this material to the notebook. Then I sort carefully through the whole mass of material, select what I want, arrange it in a logical order, and I have my talk. If the speech is to be given out of town, I also always pick up a copy of the local newspaper on the day of the talk and use something from it to bring in a local angle that makes it sound up-to-the-minute. It's really as simple as all that.

Another area in which this collection can be of particular help is to provide you with a wealth of material if ever you find yourself maneuvered into serving as chairman of a meeting or toastmaster at a dinner where you are required to introduce the speakers and say clever things in between the talks. In this book, you will find stories directly and admirably suited to every such occasion.

how to collect your own files

It's conceivable that the contents of this book may inspire you to start a collection of your own. If so, I heartily endorse the activity for you; and I can assure you the effort will be rewarding in a number of directions.

First of all, if you do a lot of speaking or writing, your own collection will be invaluable in supplementing this collection. Second, because it's *your* collection, it will reflect *your* specialized interests, just as *my* collection is heavier in the subjects of primary interest to *me*. And, finally, it will give you a great deal of satisfaction and provide a constructive activity while broadening your outlook and keeping you constantly alert to what the world is saying, doing and thinking. Every time you read a book, magazine, or newspaper, you will also be on a hunting expedition.

If all this sounds pretty ambitious as the result of a simple file collection, just try it for awhile. After years of working together — my cards and I — it seems that the right ones almost jump out of the file and clamor for attention when I'm looking for the solution to a particular speaking problem.

The best way to start collecting is to select a dozen or so categories in which you are especially interested and put them on tab cards in a file index card box. Then add categories for "General," "Anecdotes," and "Miscellaneous." Eventually, these latter three groups will have to be broken down into other specific headings, but this is a satisfactory way to begin.

Then carry a pocket-knife and a few blank cards with you all the time. When you see a printed item of interest, clip it. (This is not recommended in libraries nor with respect to the newspaper of the man sitting next to you on the train.) When you hear something on the radio or television or in conversation worth preserving, jot it down on your omnipresent file card or any other scrap of paper you can lay your hands on at the moment. You can throw these notes and clippings into a drawer at home, and whenever you have a few spare minutes, mount or transcribe them on the cards and add them to your collection. It's easy, productive, and satisfying.

If you do decide to have a try at your own collection, the two biggest obstacles you'll have to overcome are a tendency to put things down later and the feeling that you don't have the time to maintain your collection properly.

I can report from experience that it actually takes very little time. Such a collection is an activity that can be pursued effectively in odd moments — while waiting for the wife to get dressed, the children to wander home for dinner, or a long-distance phone call to go through.

Procrastination is something else again. Refusing to let a thought get away at the moment you see or hear it requires a great deal of will power — and you'll have to work at it, as I did. You should always be on the lookout for material that you can stow away and use on some future occasion. Don't wait until you have to make a particular speech or write a particular article. You'll never know when and under what circumstances a significant item — on whatever subject — might come in handy.

some tips on speechmaking

It would not be inappropriate, at this point, to offer some suggestions on speechmaking in general. Although I do not pose as an authority qualified to give advice on this subject, I do offer some forty years of platform experience and a good many thousands of speeches as justification for my trying to be helpful.

Even more convincing is the happy fact that I have, on a number of occasions, been invited back to address, again, the same groups. When this happens, you can be reasonably sure that: (1) they can't afford anyone else; (2) no other speaker is available; (3) they prefer to have a known, measured quantity; (4) the program chairman likes your wife; or (5) you gave such a compelling speech the first time that they just had to have you again.

I prefer to think it's reason Number (5). Hence, the following advice on speaking.

1. A speaker *must* have some specific idea he wants to get across to his audience. Only a fool speaks under any other circumstances. There is nothing more pathetic than an empty speaker pouring himself forth to a full house.
2. Natural language and a sincere manner will convey a speaker's point much more effectively than bombast.
3. A speaker who is able to weave matters of special or local

8

interest into his talk has a great advantage. As I have already indicated, I always read the current issue of the local newspaper wherever I make a talk, and try to refer to local issues in the body of the talk. It brings the subject close to home.

For example, in speaking at a high school that may be involved in a tight race for an athletic championship, a comment on this situation at the beginning of the talk will put the audience solidly behind you. The subject of the comments should, however, be non-controversial. Christmas, motherhood, and football are normally safe issues.

4. Speaking arrangements should be checked and rechecked several days in advance. This will often save a great deal of pain. I once got the wrong date down on my speaking calendar, failed to check it, and wandered leisurely into the town where I was to speak — a day late. As usual I picked up the local newspaper to look for items of interest and found one on the front page — a headline that read: CHICAGO JUDGE DISAPPOINTS LARGE AUDIENCE. A college professor of my acquaintance once drove from Chicago to Menominee, Michigan, to make a talk that was supposed to be given in Menomonie, Wisconsin. Even if the talk is to be given in your own office building, you should check the arrangements carefully and well ahead of time to make sure you have them right.

5. It is normally a poor policy to lunch with a segment of an audience you are scheduled to address later in the day. One reason is gastronomic: a big lunch normally forbodes an uncomfortable speech, for both speaker and audience. When your brain and stomach compete for a limited blood supply on the lecture platform, the audience usually gets the worst of it.

The other reason is that you usually find yourself making the same speech twice: first, at lunch in conversation and later before your real audience. Elbert Hubbard was once negotiating with a woman's group on a lecture fee. When they had agreed on a figure, the program chairman said, "Of course Mr. Hubbard, you'll take dinner at my home, won't you?"

"In that case," said the redoubtable Mr. Hubbard, "the fee will be $50 more!"

6. Oftentimes, an electrifying start will keep an audience alert throughout a talk — especially during a long and unnecessarily boring group of speeches. A preacher, without premeditation,

once accomplished such a start when he found himself without his carefully prepared manuscript as he started to deliver his morning sermon. "As I have forgotten my notes," he began, "I will rely on the Lord for guidance. Tonight, I shall come better prepared."

7. Don't worry about nervousness; it is perfectly natural to be nervous and sensitive before delivering a talk. Mark Twain once advised a very frightened speaker: "It may help if you keep one thing in mind — just remember, they don't expect much!"

8. Work at looking individual members of your audience straight in the eye. It materially increases your communication with them. One thing that helped me master this was repeated practice in front of a large group photograph in which I singled out individuals and addressed myself directly to them.

9. The advent of the microphone and public address systems has completely outmoded the full-throated, stentorian, William Jennings Bryan type of oratory, which comes through a p.a. system like a low-level air raid. Today's most effective speakers talk in a conversational tone with a well-modulated voice.

10. When quoting, always give full credit to the source being quoted. My conscience forces me to point out, here, that in preparing this foreword, I have borrowed occasionally — without credit — from material that appears later in the book. I justify this on the ground that I am merely plagiarising what is already a legalized sort of plagiary. But in the interest of building for yourself a reputation for fair play with an audience that may recognize pilfered material, try always to give credit where it is due.

11. Deal with audience distractions promptly and effectively; otherwise you may lose your audience and never regain it. These distractions can range from the cry of a child to a bird in the auditorium to a heckler, which is just about the meanest form of animal life to a speaker.

A fussy baby once gave a speaker of my acquaintance a hard time, and the mother finally got up to take the child out. "Never mind the baby, lady," said the speaker, "It's not bothering me a bit."

"The baby may not be bothering you," said the mother, "but you sure are bothering the baby."

There are two effective ways to deal with a "sleeper" in your audience. The immediate antidote is to stop, wherever you happen to be in the speech, look directly at the offender, and wait. He'll come to and be embarrassed — and you won't have any more trouble with him. The other, and more effective, method is to examine the content of your talk and the style of your delivery a little more closely to find out what about them is putting people to sleep — and then do something about it.

As for hecklers, there are two ways to handle them. Withering them with a reply may stop some of them. It will also probably alienate a large portion of the audience who, consciously or subconsciously, may sympathize with the heckler. The better method of handling them is to treat their wise crack as a sincere inquiry. A serious reply to a heckler's question puts him in his place and disarms him without offense.

12. Keep within the time limitations prescribed for you. In the early days, it was always difficult for me — and I assume is for others as well — to keep my mind on the time while concentrating on the subject matter of my talk. This trick may help you as it did me. Jot on a card in large figures the hour and minute indicating about five minutes prior to the time you want to quit. Keeping this card in front of you provides a solid reference point, which makes checking with a clock or watch meaningful. I now use an alarm watch, which alerts the audience, as well as me, to the fact that it's time to quit. When all is said and done, too many people keep on talking. Just as in the horse and buggy days, so today, the longer the *spoke* the bigger the *tire*.

13. Don't subject the audience to a series of false climaxes. Nothing is more wearying. The perfect speech is one which builds up to a natural climax, at which point the speaker quits. It's all right for you to have a train of thought, but you must also have a terminal. Voltaire said: "The secret of being tiresome is to tell everything."

14. If you use visual aids, make them enhance — not retard — the impact of the talk. Visual aids that become mere distractions are worse than worthless. If you pass a visual aid through an audience, there should be a break in the speech for this purpose. Exhibits in the hall where the speech is being delivered should be displayed after — not during — the speech.

15. Generally, a speech should *not* be read. To do so is the shortest cut to boredom — in speaker and audience alike. Speeches should be read only when they are of a highly technical nature

11

where pinpoint accuracy is absolutely mandatory; or when the speaker is talking in an official capacity for publication on a subject on which it would be dangerous to extemporize. But even in these instances, the speaker can take some of the curse off the reading by leaving his manuscript to drop in an occasional illustrative anecdote — like those to be found in this book.

16. Certain precautions should be observed in throwing a meeting open to a post mortem question-and-answer session. If written questions are submitted, the speaker should read all of them before he starts to answer any. This will enable him to put them in the order of their importance or his ability to answer them. It will also prevent him from stumbling into a situation similar to the aftermath of a speech on juvenile delinquency I gave, entitled "I Like Bad Boys." Without realizing what I was reading, I shared with the audience a question, sent to the platform, which asked succinctly, "Do you like bad girls, too?"

Written questions also effectively eliminate declamations from members of the audience who are much more interested in expounding their own point of view than in asking a legitimate question. There are invariably some of this type when oral questions are sought.

And I feel, quite strongly, that an audience that has just put up with me for an hour or so shouldn't be subjected to someone else's unscheduled speechmaking the same evening.

conclusion

Now, supplied with the know-how and armed to the teeth with the best possible material, you should be able to go out and wow 'em in Altadena, Peoria, or West Farmington.

If you're at all dubious about how easily the material in the pages to follow can be worked into a manuscript or a talk, consider this: as mentioned earlier, I've used references from the collection a number of times in writing this introduction. For example, on page one, I used Nos. 2155 and 2174 and on page four, No. 2767 and on page three, No. 2825. You can do it, too.

Before I turn you over to the collected thoughts of a great many people much more talented than I, let me steal one more epigram from what is to follow. This one says: "If a speaker doesn't strike oil within ten minutes, he should stop boring."

This is good advice — for writing as well as speaking.

ability

1. A book agent came to sell one of the combination farmer-mer-chant-bankers of southeast Arkansas a set of books on scientific agriculture. The old man thumbed through them:

"No, I don't want to buy them."

"You ought to buy them, sir. If you had these books you could farm twice as good as you do now."

"Hell, son," he replied, "I don't farm half as good as I know how now."

— JONATHAN DANIELS, *A Southerner Discovers the South.* (Macmillan)

2. Ability is a poor man's worth.

— MATTHEW WREN

3.
You've got to have the goods, my boy,
    If you would finish strong;
A bluff may work a little while,
    But not for very long;
A line of talk all by itself
    Will seldom see you thru;
You've got to have the goods, my boy,
    And nothing else will do.

The fight is pretty stiff, my boy,
    I'd call it rather tough,
And all along the routes are wrecks
    Of those who tried to bluff —
They could not back their lines of talk,
    To meet the final test,
You've got to have the goods, my boy,
    And that's no idle jest.

— *Author Unknown*

4. Never stand begging for that which you have the power to earn.

— CERVANTES

5. Brains and capacity are different. One is a gift, the other is acquired. Were I asked to choose between them, I should select capacity, because it represents human efforts and not merely something which came by inheritance. If we shall honor people for what they receive, then there may be an aristocracy of brain; but for capacity there will never be anything but democracy. Brains represent inherent power; capacity represents developed force. Brains are the dynamo which may or may not be put at work; capacity is the current that controls and illuminates.

Aaron Burr had brains; John Marshall had capacity. Gazing around, we find on every hand that those who wrought for the ages, who produce constructive ideas, who gave utilities and conveniences to the world, had capacity as representing the inherited brain power, whether it was large or small, put to its maximum speed. We cannot conceive of useful performances, of helpful productions emanating from brains alone. They come from the concentration of effort, the development of skill, from the qualities which we sum up in the one word — capacity.

— Source Unknown

6. There is great ability in knowing how to conceal one's ability.
— LA ROCHEFOUCAULD

absence

7. Judicious absence is a weapon.

— CHARLES READE

achievement

8. The most gladsome thing in the world is that few of us fall very low; the saddest thing that, with such capabilities, we seldom rise high.
— JAMES MATTHEW BARRIE

9. It is not the critic who counts; not the man who points out how the strong man stumbled, or where the doer of deeds could have done better. The credit belongs to the man who is actually in the arena; whose face is marred by dust and sweat and blood; who strives valiantly; who errs and comes short again and again because there is no effort without error and shortcoming; who does actually strive to do the deeds; who knows the great enthusiasm, the great devotions, spends himself in a worthy cause; who at the best knows in the end the triumph of high achievement; and who at the worst, if he fails at least fails while daring greatly, so that his place shall never be with those cold and timid souls who know neither victory nor defeat.

— THEODORE ROOSEVELT

10.   YOU MAY COUNT THAT DAY

If you sit down at set of sun
And count the acts that you have done
    And counting, find
One self-denying deed, one word
That eased the heart of him who heard —
    One glance most kind,
That fell like sunshine where it went
Then you may count that day well spent.

But if, through all the livelong day
You've cheered no heart, by yea or nay —
    If, through it all
You've nothing done that you can trace
That brought the sunshine to one face —
    No act most small
That helped some soul and nothing cost —
Then count that day as worse than lost.

— GEORGE ELIOT

11.   Henry Thoreau, the poet who invented a lead pencil and refused to patent and cash in on it, knew all the birds and enjoyed looking at them with a spyglass. He said: "A gun gives you the body, not the bird."

12.   He was nobody's fool, this Henry Thoreau, who said: "Sometimes we class those who are one-and-a-half witted with the half-witted because we appreciate only a third of their wit."

13.   *Observer to ditch digger:* "How do you like your job, my good man?"

"I don't like it. The harder I work, the lower down in the world I get."

14.   There are two tragedies in life. One is not to get your heart's desire. The other is to get it.

— GEORGE BERNARD SHAW

15

15. There's a man in the world who is never turned down, wherever he chances to stray; he gets the glad hand in the populous town, or out where the farmers make hay; he's greeted with pleasure on deserts of sand, and deep in the aisles of the woods; wherever he goes there's a welcoming hand — he's the man who delivers the goods.

— WALT MASON

16. The man who rows the boat generally doesn't have time to rock it.

17. Difficult — That which can be done immediately.
Impossible — That which takes a little longer.

— GEORGE SANTAYANA

18. Doing little things well is a step toward doing big things better.

19. "If you have built castles in the air, your work need not be lost. . . . Now put the foundations under them."

—OSA JOHNSON

20. Think that day lost whose low descending sun
Views from thy hand no noble action done.

— JACOB BOBART

21. The world is not interested in the storms you encountered, but did you bring in the ship?

— WILLIAM McFEE — *Tales of Hoffman*

action

22. When a man hasn't a good reason for doing a thing, he has a good reason for letting it alone.

— SIR WALTER SCOTT

adolescence

23. Adolescence: the period in which the young suddenly begin to feel a great responsibility about answering the telephone.

24. Adolescence: that period when a boy refuses to believe that someday he'll be as dumb as his father.

25. Adolescence: that period when children feel their parents should be told the facts of life.

advertising

26. Mark Twain once edited a paper in Missouri. One of his subscribers wrote him he had found a spider in his paper and wanted to know whether it meant good luck or bad. This is what Mark answered:

"Old Subscriber: Finding a spider in your paper was neither good luck nor bad luck for you. The spider was merely looking over our paper to see which merchant is not advertising so that he can go to that store, spin his web across the door and lead a life of undisturbed peace ever afterward."

27. "Do you find that advertising brings quick results?"
"I should say it does. Why, only the other day we advertised for a night watchman, and that night the safe was robbed."

28. "I put an ad in the paper asking for a wife."
"Any answers?"
"Any? The first day I got 400, and two from men asking me to take theirs."

29. A restaurant owner with plenty of advertising ideas and little money for advertising purchased the largest fish bowl he could find, filled it with water and put it in his window, with a sign reading:
"This bowl is filled with invisible Paraguayan goldfish."
It required two policemen to keep the pavements in front of the window cleared.

30. "Mother," said little Bobby, bursting into the house all out of breath, "there's going to be the deuce to pay down at the grocer's. His wife has got a baby girl and he's had a 'Boy Wanted' sign in the window for a week."

31. "Why don't you advertise?"

Town Storekeeper: "No, siree. I did once and it pretty near ruined me."

"How was that?"

"Why, people came in and bought dern near all the stuff I had."

32. A shop in New York was advertising the famous people who came in and what they bought. They mentioned a certain man who bought an expensive vanity case. The next morning he rushed in breathlessly to buy one for his wife.

33. Honesty in Advertising — *For Sale:* Automobile-Buick-Sport. Best looking job in city; this car won't last long; best offer takes it. ?211 South Michigan. Open Eves.

34. Americans, probably because of the stiff competition for their attention, have a way of listening with only one-half, or maybe one-third, of their minds. Foreigners repeatedly point this out. In this connection, an advertising man tells us a story about the advertising of a certain tooth paste over the air. The company which made it used to have its broadcasting hour, in which it issued stern and grave warnings against "pink toothbrush." It seems that somebody made a checkup and learned that 300 odd persons went to drugstores of a certain chain and asked for pink toothbrushes. Discouraging, isn't it?

— *Readers Digest*

35. People expect canned salmon to be pink, and it is not easy to sell white salmon, even though an expert taster could hardly detect any difference. Some years ago, when pink salmon in the Columbia River were late in arriving, a canner successfully took his chances on selling the white. On each can he placed a label: "This salmon is guaranteed not to turn pink in any climate."

— FRED C. KELLY, *The Saturday Evening Post*

36.
> He who has a thing to sell
>   And goes and whispers in a well,
> Is not so apt to get the dollars
>   As he who climbs a tree and hollers.

37. Sign in restaurant window: Pies like mother makes — 5¢. Pies that mother tried to make but couldn't — 10¢.

adversity

38. I love the man who can smile in trouble, who can gather strength from distress, and grow brave by reaction. 'Tis the business of little minds to shrink, but he whose heart is firm, and whose conscience approves his conduct, will pursue his principles unto death.

— THOMAS PAINE

advice

39. No vice is so bad as advice.

— MARIE DRESSLER

40. We ask advice, but we mean approbation.

— C. C. COLTON

41. No man's advice is entirely worthless. Even a watch that won't run is right twice a day.

42. It is not necessary to take a person's advice to make him feel good — all you have to do is ask it.

— RICHARD ARMOUR

43. Advice is seldom welcome. Those who need it most, like it least.

— SAMUEL JOHNSON

44. Advice is like snow; the softer it falls, the longer it dwells upon and the deeper it sinks into the mind.

—SAMUEL T. COLERIDGE

45. A good scare is worth more to a man than good advice.

46. This was the advice of Noor ad Deen Ali to his son in "Arabian Nights."

"Oppress no one, lest Fortune oppress thee, for the fortune of this world is one day for thee and another against thee, and its goods are but a loan to be repaid. Be merciful to all, as thou on mercy reckonest; for no hand is there but the hand of God is over it, and no oppressor but shall be worse than the opprest. Keep therefore thy wealth, that it may keep thee and watch over it, that it may watch over thee. Squander not thy substance, or thou wilt come to need.

19

When a rich man grows poor, his lustre dies away, like to the setting sun that pales with ended day. Absent, his name is not remembered among men; present, he hath no part in life and its array. He passes through the streets and fain would hide his head and pours out floods of tears in every desert way. By Allah, when distress and want descend on men, strangers midst their kin and countrymen are they."

47. *Speaker:* I realize that giving advice is usually a thankless business, and I assure you that I shall not venture far in that direction. I have always kept in mind the unconsciously profound summation written by a small school girl:

"Socrates," she wrote, "was a Greek philosopher who went about giving people good advice. They poisoned him."

48. Wm. Feather told of an Indian who was converting a log into a canoe. A man came along and said, "Chief, I think she's too wide for her length." So the Indian narrowed her down. Another said, "Chief, the stern's too full." So he cut down the stern. A third said, "The bow's too sheer, Chief." So he fixed up the bow. . . . When he launched the canoe it capsized. He hauled it back on the beach, found another log and began again. Once more a stranger offered advice, but this time he answered: "That's everyman's boat over there," pointing to the monstrosity that wouldn't float. Resuming his work, he mumbled, "This will be Indian's boat."

— M. BACON, *Thirty Years With Dotted Lines* (E. O. Painter)

49. He who gives advice to a self-conceited man stands himself in need of counsel from another.

— SAADI

50. It is always a silly thing to give advice, but to give good advice is absolutely fatal.

— OSCAR WILDE

51. "Be yourself!" is about the worst advice you can give to some people.

— JOHN MASEFIELD

52. To profit from good advice requires more wisdom than to give it.

— JOHN C. COLLINS

age

53. You've reached middle age when your wife tells you to pull in your stomach — and you already have.

54. You are as young as your faith, as old as your doubt; as young as your self-confidence, as old as your fear; as young as your hope, as old as your despair.

55. Forty is the old-age of youth, fifty is the youth of old-age.
— VICTOR HUGO

56. I am not afraid of tomorrow, for I have seen yesterday and I love today.
— WILLIAM ALLEN WHITE, on his 70th birthday

57. At a reception in Washington, a young man was asked by a widow to guess her age. "You must have some idea," she said as he hesitated.

"I have several ideas," he admitted with a smile. "The only trouble is that I hesitate whether to make you ten years younger on account of your looks, or ten years older on account of your brains."

58.   It's sad for a girl to reach the age
          Where men consider her charmless,
          But it's worse for a man to attain the age
          Where the girls consider him harmless.

59. A man is young if a lady can make him happy or unhappy. He enters middle age when a lady can make him happy, but can no longer make him unhappy. He is old and gone if a lady can make him neither happy nor unhappy.
— MORITZ ROSENTHAL in *Time*

60. "Men," says one sage, "seem to fall into two groups. They're either old and bent or young and broke."

61. To me — old age is always ten years older than I am.
— BERNARD M. BARUCH

62. Marlene Dietrich saw the first week's rushes of a new picture and complained that they didn't suit her. The cameraman had also photographed her in The Garden of Allah, one of the star's favorites; so they went to a projection room and had The Garden of Allah shown. When it was over Miss Dietrich said, "I looked gorgeous in that picture. Why can't we get the same result in this one?"

"Well, you see, Miss Dietrich," said the cameraman, "I'm eight years older now." — LEONARD LYONS, *Readers Digest*

63. One theatre has discovered an effective means of making women remove their hats. Just before the performance, this notice appears on the screen:

> The management wishes to spare elderly ladies any inconvenience. They are, therefore, invited to retain their hats.

All hats come off.

64. "A man is never older than he feels," declared the ancient beau bravely. "Now I feel as a two-year-old."

"Horse or egg?" asked the sweet young thing brightly.

65. A man's as old as he looks when he needs a shave, a woman is as old as she looks just after washing her face.

66. The Stone Age is about 20. And the bigger the stone, the better she likes it.

67. It's not how *old* you are but *how* you are old.

68. A Santa Monica woman has at last become the champion of her sex. She had been subpoenaed as a witness and the court, before she began her testimony, instructed her as follows:

"You must be very careful madam, to state only what you actually saw and know. There must be no hearsay evidence."

He then signaled for the prosecutor to go ahead.

"What is your age?" asked that worthy.

"I cannot answer," cooed the lady, "I have only hearsay knowledge on that point."

69. And the Pulitzer prize for diplomatic journalism should go to the Arkansas editor who printed the following item:

"Miss Beulah Blank, a Batesville belle of twenty summers, is visiting her twin brother, aged thirty-two."

70.   Inscription on Tombstone:
This man died at 30;
He was buried at 70.

71.   *Husband to wife:* "How do you expect me to remember your birthday when you never look any older?"
— *The Saturday Evening Post.*

72.   Don McNeill tells about the woman who was filling out an application for credit. When she came to the space for age, she hesitated a long time. Finally, the clerk leaned over and said: "The longer you wait, the worse it gets."

73.   I have found no differences that are absolute between Eastern and Western life except in the attitude toward age. In China, the first question a person asks the other on an official call is: "What is your glorious age?" If he replies apologetically that he is 23 or 28, the other generally comforts him by saying that he still has a glorious future, and that one day he may become old. Enthusiasm grows in proportion as the gentleman is able to report a higher and higher age, and if he is anywhere over 50, the inquirer drops his voice in humility and respect. People actually look forward to the celebration of their 51st birthday.
— LIN YUTANG, *The Importance of Living.* (John Day Company)

74.   Beautiful young people are accidents of nature. But beautiful old people are works of art.   — MARJORIE BARSTOW BREENBIE, *Be Your Age.* (Stackpole)

75.   A man is young as long as he looks.

76.   Never say you are too old. You do not say it now, perhaps; but by and by, when the hair grows gray and the eyes grow dim and the young despair comes to curse the old age, you will say, "It is too late for me." Never too late! Never too old! How old are you,— Thirty, fifty, eighty? What is that in immortality?
— LYMAN ABBOTT
Reprinted by permission of Dodd, Mead & Company from "Problems of Life."

77.   Growing old doesn't seem so bad when you consider the alternative.

78. A woman begins to realize her age when people comment on how young she looks.

79. The old believe everything; the middle-aged suspect everything; the young know everything.

— OSCAR WILDE

80. Many of us are at the "metallic" age — gold in our teeth, silver in our hair — and lead in our pants.

81. Middle age is the time when a man is always thinking that in a week or two he will feel as good as ever.

— DON MARQUIS

82. If you want to know how old a woman is, ask her sister-in-law.

— EDGAR W. HOWE

83. To be seventy years young is sometimes far more cheerful and hopeful than to be forty years old.

— OLIVER WENDELL HOLMES

84. *Mrs. No. 1:* "That's a lovely coat you're wearing, Mrs. Jones."
Mrs. No. 2: "Oh, thank you. My husband gave it to me for my 35th birthday."
Mrs. No. 1: "It certainly wears well, doesn't it!"

85. "Teacher, if Shakespeare were alive today, would he be considered a remarkable man?"
"Indeed he would! He'd be three hundred and fifty-seven years old!"

86. Middle age: when you begin to exchange your emotions for symptoms.

87. I'm old enough to know how and young enough to do it.

— ALBEN W. BARKLEY, (at the age
of 76 telling the voters of Kentucky why they should elect him
United States Senator)

88. Youthful figure: something you get when you ask a woman her age.

alcohol

89. There was the Montreal drunk who was found muttering, "It can't be done, it can't be done, it can't be done," as he looked up at a big sign that read, "Drink Canada Dry."

90. It is when a man gets as tight as a drum that he makes the most noise.

91. You can't keep both yourself and your business in a liquid condition.

92. Early in 1842 Lincoln entered into the Washingtonian movement organized to suppress the evils of intemperance. On Washington's birthday, in the Presbyterian Church, he delivered an address in which he said:

"In my judgment such of us as have never fallen victims have been spared more from the absence of appetite than from any mental or moral superiority over those who have. Indeed, I believe, if we take habitual drunkards as a class, their heads and their hearts will bear an advantageous comparison with those of any other class."

— HERNDON, *Life of Lincoln*

93. Walking into a bar optimistically and coming out misty-optically accentuates the inevitable.

94. Cocktail: an ice cube with an alcohol rub.

95. A "blind" beggar sat at the subway entrance with a tin cup in his hand. A passer-by, somewhat under the influence of alcohol, took out his pocket flask, and started to pour a drink into the old man's cup.

The beggar peered from behind his black glasses suddenly, saw the flask, and yelled — "Nix! Nix! None of that stuff. Do you think I wanta go blind?"

96. Absinthe makes the heart grow fonder.

— ADDISON MIZNER

97. *Youngster (at night):* "Daddy, I want a drink."
Daddy: "Aw, go to sleep. I've wanted one for two years."

98. Modesty has ruined more kidneys than bad liquor.
— DR. S. MORRIS, West Virginia University

99. In a cheap little side street saloon, the sailor had suddenly picked up an empty whiskey bottle and banged it resoundingly upon the bartender's head. Now he stood in court to answer for his offense.

"My client admits he struck the bartender," said the sailor's lawyer, "but he acted under the influence of liquor, and pretty poor liquor at that."

"But he does admit assaulting the man," insisted the court.

"Yes," replied the attorney, "but your honor, consider this fact — the man first assaulted my client with its contents."
— *Wall Street Journal*

100. Hangover: something to occupy a head that wasn't used the night before.

101. Champagne: a beverage that makes you see double and feel single.

102. *He:* "And who made the first cotton gin?"
Young thing: "Heavens! Are they making it from that, too?"

103. Intoxication: to feel sophisticated and not to be able to pronounce it.

104. A deputy sheriff was sent to take an inventory of the property in a house. When he did not return for three hours, the sheriff went after him, and found him asleep on a lounge in the living room of the house. He made a brave effort with his inventory, however; he had written down, "Living room — 1 table, 1 sideboard, 1 full bottle whiskey." Then the "full" had been crossed out, and "half full" substituted. Then this was overlined, and "empty" put in its place. At the bottom of the page, in wobbly writing, was written: "1 revolving carpet."

105. One day, so an Arab legend goes, the devil presented himself to a man and said, "You are about to die. I can save you from death under any one of 3 ways — kill your servant, or beat your wife, or drink this wine."

"Let me think," said the man. "To kill my faithful servant is impossible; to mistreat my wife is ridiculous. I will drink the wine."

He drank the wine, and being drunk, he beat his wife and killed his servant who attempted to defend her.

— Home Missions

106. *Mrs. Blake:* "Husbands are strange creatures."

Her Friend: "Aren't they? John has to ask his garage man a hundred questions about the brand and manufacture before he puts a drop of oil into the car, but he never asks the man from whom he buys his liquor a single question for fear of hurting his feelings."

107. Smith was definitely neurotic and was generally a source of irritation at home to his wife and family. His wife attributed his difficulty to his excessive use of alcohol, but the husband insisted that that was not the source of his difficulty at all, and refused to listen to her counsel that he abandon it. She did, however, finally prevail upon him to see his doctor. He made an appointment with the medico, which he kept. Much to his chagrin, the doctor told him just what his wife had told him — that the excessive use of alcohol was responsible for all of his difficulties and told him if he hoped for relief, he would have to discontinue its use.

On leaving the doctor's office, Smith was terribly upset. He hated to go home and have to admit to his wife that she was right. That would merely make things even less tolerable for him than they had been. As he sauntered homeward, he kept trying to think up something he would be able to tell his wife without having to admit the truth. Suddenly he saw before him a sign hanging in front of the entrance to a music hall. "Syncopation," it read. And there he found the answer to his problem. On his arriving home, his wife inquired of him as to whether he had visited the doctor and if so, what he had been told.

"The doctor says I have 'syncopation,' my dear."

"Syncopation!" she said. "What's that?"

"Well, I don't know how to tell you," he said, "but the best thing for you to do is to look it up in the dictionary."

"His wife did — and there it was: "Syncopation — Intermittent progress from bar to bar."

108. Dignity is something that can't be preserved in alcohol.

alimony – See *Marriage*

ambition

109. When a man is no longer anxious to do better than well, he is done for.

110. There was once a bank cashier who wanted to be one of the 400 and now he is No. 387.

111. A shoe manufacturer's ambition is to perfect for women some shoes that are larger inside than they are outside.

112. There are two things to aim at in life: first to get what you want; and after that, to enjoy it. Only the wisest achieve the second.

113. Ambition has its disappointments to sour us, but never the good fortune to satisfy us. Its appetite grows keener by indulgence and all we can gratify it with at present serves but the more to inflame its insatiable desires.

— BENJAMIN FRANKLIN

114.
Some fellows stay right in the rut
    While others head the throng.
All men may be born equal but –
    They don't stay that way long.
There is many a man with a gallant air,
    Goes galloping to the fray;
But the valuable man is the man who's there
    When the smoke has cleared away.
Some "don't get nuthin' out of life"
    But when their whines begin,
We often can remind them that
    They "don't put nothin' in."

— *Author Unknown*

115.
You are the fellow that has to decide
Whether you'll do it or toss it aside.
You are the fellow who makes up your mind
Whether you'll lead or linger behind –

Whether you'll try for the goal that's afar
Or be contented to stay where you are.
Take it or leave it. Here's something to do,
Just think it over. It's all up to you!
What do you wish? To be known as a shirk
Known as a good man who's willing to work,
Scorned for a loafer or praised by your chief
Rich man or poor man or beggar or thief?
Eager or earnest or dull through the day,
Honest or crooked? It's you who must say!
You must decide in the face of the test
Whether you'll shirk it or give it your best.

116. He lives who dies to win a lasting name.

— HENRY DRUMMOND

117. Good, better, best; never let it rest, till your good is better, and your better best. — *Readers Digest*

118. If begging should unfortunately be thy lot, knock at the large gates only. — *Arabian Proverb*

America

119. "This face of America is many faces. Many races molded it, many weathers seasoned it. The eyes are blue or brown or gray, Indian-black, almond-shaped. But the light in the eyes is the same. Freedom put it there. It rains down carelessly out of the high skies arching over our forty-eight united states, and our children catch it in their eyes as soon as these are opened."

—*Source Unknown*

120. A mosaic is a design of some kind formed by every minute piece of glass, stone or something else which is inlaid in a ground of stucco or metal, all of which are different, yet they blend into making a complete whole. Thus the symbol of our nation is rather that of a mosaic than a melting pot. A melting pot enforces conformity and our rule, as a nation, should be and is to make use of differences to create a worthy whole.

— Editorial, *Alabama Baptist*

121. America never lost a war nor won a conference.

— WILL ROGERS

122. America — a place where they lock up juries and let defendants out.

123. A nation is made great, not by its fruitful acres, but by the men who cultivate them; not by its mines, but by the men who work in them; not by its railways, but by the men who build and run them. America was a great land when Columbus discovered it; Americans have made of it a great nation.

— Reprinted by permission of Dodd,
Mead & Company from *Problems
of Life* by LYMAN ABBOTT

124. Our British cousins don't eat *candy;* they call it *sweets.* They don't play *checkers,* but *draughts.* Their *counterfeiters* are *coiners, elevators* are *lifts* and *peanuts* are *monkey nuts.* American men may wear *undershirts* but English men wear *vests.* We *shine* our *shoes;* Britons *polish* their *boots. Garters* are *sock-suspenders* — and *suspenders* are *braces.*

125. An Englishman having returned to his native land from a visit to our shores was commenting on the terrible abuse of the English language in America. "Why," said he, "I heard one of those blooming Yankees say, 'where am I at' — 'where am I at!' when what he really meant was, 'where is my 'at?'"

126. American — a man who likes to discuss the United States Constitution despite the fact that he has never taken the time to read it.

127. I do not choose to be a common man. It is my right to be uncommon — if I can. I seek opportunity — not security. I do not wish to be a kept citizen, humbled and dulled by having the state look after me. I want to take the calculated risk; to dream and to build, to fail and to succeed. I refuse to barter incentive for a dole. I prefer the challenges of life to the guaranteed existence; the thrill of fulfillment to the stale calm of utopia. I will not trade freedom for beneficence, nor my dignity for a handout. I will never cower before any master, nor bend to any threat. It is my heritage to stand erect, proud and unafraid; to think and act for myself, enjoy the benefit of my

creations and to face the world boldly and to say, this I have done.
All this is what it means to be an American.

— *My Creed*, DEAN ALFANGE

128.   *U. S. A.*

Time there was when we had the right
To argue, differ, even fight
Among ourselves. And as freeborn men
We pray that time may return again.

Right now, every American,
Great or small, is a Union man.
And "Union," spelled with capital U,
Means forty-eight stars in a field of blue.

Now's the time that Americans
Must know we are all republicans
Serving our flag with loyal hands,
"And the Republic for which it stands."

Down with the isms and petty spats!
We're at war! We're all democrats,
Sons and daughters of liberty,
Fighting for life and democracy.

"Empty words," as the cynics said.
"Empty symbols. Their meaning's dead."
Cynics lied! Ask the Wake Marines.
Ask those boys in the Philippines!

Now our national alphabet
Has three letters so let's forget
All the rest 'till some future day.
Keep "United" in U. S. A.

— GENE LINDBERG

129. Americans don't spend millions for amusement. They spend
it in search of amusement.

130. Rome endured as long as there were Romans. America will
endure as long as we remain American in spirit and thought.

— DAVID STARR JORDAN

anger

131. <center>TO GET ANGRY —</center>

When someone calls you a fool is to prove their assertion.

When a competitor succeeds is to admit that he deserves to succeed.

When things cannot be helped is to make them worse.

When people do not agree with you is to discredit the worth of your opinion.

When they slander you is the poorest kind of answer to make.

When you can't have your own way is to prove you cannot be trusted.

When your conscience tells you you are wrong is to fight a losing battle.

132. "When I am angry at myself," says Ed Howe, "I criticize others."

133. He who can suppress a moment's anger may prevent a day of sorrow.

— T<small>RYON</small> E<small>DWARDS</small>

antagonism

134. Mike was about to die and the priest bent over him to give him the last rites of the Church. Bending over Mike, the priest said, "Repeat after me, 'I renounce the devil and all his evil deeds.' " But there was no response from Mike. The priest repeated "Repeat after me, "I renounce the devil and all his evil deeds,' " and still no response from Mike. After the third try, the priest shook Mike and he opened his eyes. "Didn't you hear me?" asked the priest. "Yes," replied Mike, "But you told me I was going to die, and this is a hell of a time to antagonize anybody."

antiques

135. Antique — an object that has made a round trip to the attic.

136. Antique — something no one would be seen with if there were more of them.

anti-semitism — See *Discrimination*

apology

137. Apologizing is a very desperate habit — one that is rarely cured. Nine times out of ten, the first thing a man's companion knows of his shortcoming is from his apology. It is mighty presumptuous on your part to suppose your small failures of so much consequence that you must talk about them.

— OLIVER WENDELL HOLMES, *The Professor at the Breakfast Table*

138. It's wise to apologize to a man if you're wrong — and to a woman if you're right.

appeasement

139. In his dealings with the Fuhrer, Mr. Chamberlain seemed to think that the saving of a million lives was well worth the surrender of England's honor. His conferences with Hitler at Berchtesgaden and Godesberg read like the diary of a young lady crossing the Atlantic for the first time.

> Monday — I feel highly honored at being placed at the Captain's table.

> Tuesday — I spent the morning on the bridge with the Captain. He seemed to like me.

> Wednesday — The Captain made proposals to me unbecoming an officer and a gentleman.

> Thursday — The Captain threatened to sink the ship unless I agreed to his proposals.

> Friday — I saved six hundred lives!

— WILLIS H. KINGSLAND

attire — See *Dress*

auction

140. I am very lucky at auctions. The last one I went to I made bids on 16 different things — and didn't get caught once.

autographs

141. The little old lady was having lunch with her granddaughter in the diner of a crack extra-fare express. Hearing the waiter address by name a distinguished-looking man across the aisle, she grew greatly excited, seized a menu, and murmured to her granddaughter, "I'm going to get his autograph." After a few words with the celebrity, the little old lady came triumphantly back, whispered, "I got it," and settled to her soup.

Presently, with a courtly bow towards grandmother, the man left the car and granddaughter inquired, "What did you say to him to get his autograph?"

"Oh," beamed grandmother, "I just told him how much our Chrysler car means to us and how pleased I was to make his acquaintance and he gave me his autograph right away."

Granddaughter had the grace to be silent, for the name written on grandmother's menu was "Fritz Kreisler."

— ORVILLE E. REED, *Readers Digest*

142. To Madame Curie, discoverer of radium, autograph collectors were life's greatest vexation. During her last years she refused to give her much-sought-after signature to anyone. Knowing this, a zealous autograph hound once sent Madame Curie his personal check for $25, asking that she donate the money to any charity she might choose. He hoped, of course, that the unsuspecting Madame would endorse the check, which would then come back to him with her signature.

The collector's feelings can be imagined when a few days later he received from Madame's private secretary the following note:

"Madame Curie has asked me to thank you most kindly for your check, which, however, she is not going to cash. It so happens that she is an autograph collector and therefore, will add your signature to her collection."

— CECIL DE VADA, *Swing*

automobile – See also *Traffic*

143. Old-timer: one who remembers when it cost more to run a car than to park it.

144. Jeep: man's most nearly successful effort to produce a mechanical mule.

—Minneapolis Star-Journal

145. Bus: a vehicle that has empty seats when going in the opposite direction.

146. After dinner car: V-8

147. Autos are now regarded as necessities, and children as luxuries.

bachelor — bachelorhood

148. Bachelor: a man who does not want to play troth or consequences.

149. Bachelor: a man who hasn't made the same mistake once.

150. Bachelor: a man who, when he accomplishes something, gets all the credit himself.

151. Bachelor: a man who tries to avoid the issue.

152. Bachelor: a man who can have a girl on his knees without having her on his hands.

153. Bachelor: a man who wouldn't take yes for an answer.

— Family Circle

154. Confirmed bachelor: one who thinks that the only thoroughly justified marriage was the one that produced him.

— HARLAN MILLER, Readers Digest

155. What every girl should know: a millionaire bachelor.

156. Bachelors know more about women than married men; if they didn't, they'd be married too.

— H. L. MENCKEN

157. A bachelor never quite gets over the idea that he is a thing of beauty and a boy forever.

— HELEN ROWLAND

baldness

158. When friends josh me about my bald-headedness, I remind them that when I was but a little boy my mother always told me that when I grew up I would come out on top — and she was right about it.

159. When reference is made to the fact that one is bald:
Answer: "I really don't mind at all. I think hair is so unsanitary."

banks — banking

160. A new bank clerk, while dictating, was in doubt as to the use of a certain phrase, so he said to the stenographer: "Do you retire a loan?" And the wistful-eyed one interrupted rather sleepily: "No, I sleep with mama."

161. Banker: a man who offers you an umbrella, then wants it back when it starts to rain.

barber — barber shop

162. The barber looked at the young man's sleek hair and asked if he wanted it cut, or just the oil changed.

— WALTER WINCHELL

bargain

163. A Scotchman went to a dentist to have a tooth pulled. As the dentist began to extract the offending tooth, the Scotchman stopped him in the middle and asked: "If it will cost $2.00 to *pull* the tooth, how much will it cost to *loosen* it?"

bathing

164. "Speaking of bathing in famous springs," said the tramp, "I bathed in the spring of '98."

beauty

165. Never lose an opportunity of seeing anything beautiful. Beauty is God's handwriting.
— CHARLES KINGSLEY

166. When, at 16, I was vain because someone praised me, my father said: "They are only praising your youth. You can take no credit for beauty at 16. But if you are beautiful at 60, it will be your own soul's doing. Then you may be proud of it and be loved for it."
— MARIE STOPES, *Change of Life in Men and Women* (Putnam)

167. Two men who hadn't seen each other for fifteen years met and began reminiscing.
"Is your wife as pretty as she used to be?" asked one.
"Oh, yes," replied the other, "but it takes her quite a bit longer."
— *Quote*

168. Anatomy: something that everyone has but it looks better on a girl.

169. Tell a girl she is pretty and she will like it, but will not be sure you are in earnest; tell her she is prettier than some person she knows is pretty and you have got her.

behavior

170. We often do good in order that we may do evil with impunity.
— LA ROCHEFOUCAULD

171. A hog ought not to be blamed for being a hog, but a man ought.

172. Act the way you'd like to be and soon you'll be the way you act.
— DR. GEORGE W. CRANE, *Psychology Applied.*

173.   Be interested — don't try to be interesting.
Be pleasing — don't expect to be pleased.
Be entertaining — don't wait to be entertained.
Be lovable — don't wait to be loved.
Be helpful — don't ask to be helped.

174.   Always put off until tomorrow the things you should not do today.

175.   Behavior is a mirror, in which everyone shows his image.

— GOETHE

176.   Night Club: a place where the tables are reserved and the guests are not.

177.   Sir Edward Grey was once asked by a young inquirer whether he found it difficult as Foreign Secretary to reconcile his private morality with his public functions. "Well, you see," he said, after a long pause, "I have discovered that to do the right thing is generally the right thing to do."

— HAROLD NICOLSON, Men and Circumstances,
Foreign Affairs.

178.   No one can be caught in places he doesn't frequent.

179.   This is a gay life if your "don'ts" weaken.

bequest

180.   "TO MY SON"

I have no wealth to leave you, and no fame,
This must be your inheritance: My name.
It has not been my fate, in life's sharp struggles,
To win the honors other men have won.
Mine has not been a life of great achievements;
I have not done the deeds some men have done.
But I have kept unsullied and untarnished
That thing — a name — entrusted to my care;
I have not let dishonor dim its luster,
Nor have I let shame leave its black mark there.
I have not let my name be classed with malice,

Nor fear, nor moral cowardice, nor greed,
Nor bigoted intolerance toward others,
Nor lack of charity for those in need,
But I have made instead, my name synonymous
 In all men's minds, with things — the things worthwhile!
With strength to do the right, though none might see me;
With grit to meet disaster with a smile;
With loyalty to those with claims upon me;
With justice equally toward foe and friend;
With honor, truth, integrity, square dealing —
"My word my bond."

— A. G. M. CAMPBELL

bible

181. The Bible is Not a Book. The Bible is to be regarded not as a single volume but as an anthology. Its writings represent more than a thousand years of effort by excellent and mostly anonymous story-tellers, poets, historians, artists, and moral pioneers. Laboriously hand-inscribed on skins or papyrus, the writings we have are not in their original form. As they did their recopying, scribes frequently made additions which were later incorporated into the text, so that a single section may record the views of widely differing authors who lived in totally different eras. Indeed, some Scriptural passages, far from being a unity, are almost like a debate and vividly demonstrate a legitimate diversity of opinion.

182. "Now, children," said the Sunday School teacher, "I have told you the story of Jonah and the whale. Willie, you may tell me what this story teaches."

"Yes'm," said Willie, the brightest son of the pastor, "it teaches that you can't keep a good man down."

183. A customer entered a liquor store, put a Bible on the counter, told the clerk to place his hand on it, and said: "Now swear you haven't any whisky."

P.S. He got a quart.

184. A collector of etchings who had one of the Leaning Tower of Pisa over his desk, was disturbed because, though he straightened it every morning, the next day he found it hanging crooked.

bible

A maid explained: "I have to hang it crooked to make the tower hang straight."

Similarily, some find it necessary to twist the Scriptures in order to justify their own actions and try to make their lives appear right.

— Tarbell's *Teacher's Guide*

185. *The Order in Which the Bible Is Printed Is Not the Order in Which It Was Composed.* Many verses in the opening pages of various Biblical books were written long after some sections now in the middle and at the end. The Talmud itself tells us that there is no relationship between the order in which the books appear and the order in which they were originally created.

186. *The Ideas in the Bible Reflect a Historic Process.* Because the Bible records a long period of time, the ideas in it reflect development and diversity. The concepts of God range from the primitive to the most sublime.

187. *There Are No Saints in the Bible.* The personalities in the Bible are not depicted as flawless individuals, but are painted complete with frailties. Unworthy episodes in the lives of patriarchs and heroes are retained not to throw discredit upon them but to show how they grew in character after sloughing off their immaturities. They are our heroes not because they were endowed with perfection or because in a flash, they were transformed from extreme depravity to saintliness, but because they used God's wisdom to refine their conduct. This is designed to teach the reader that he, too, no matter how unworthy now, may overcome his faults by applying wisdom to his behavior, as did Abraham and Moses, Jacob and Joseph, David and Solomon.

bigotry – See *Discrimination*

blindness

188. An English writer tells of a blind man who always carried a lantern. People were wont to ask of what use the lantern could be to his sightless eyes. "I do not carry it to prevent my stumbling over

others," he replied, "but to keep them from stumbling over me." . . .
Let your light shine so that somebody else will not stumble because
of you.
— Rev. Peter Pleune, *A Shining
Light* — Christian Observer.

189. The myopic, cheese-loving old lady without glasses approached a clerk in a grocery store. She pointed hesitatingly to a
round object which seemed to repose on a distant counter.

"Is that the head cheese?" she asked.

"No, lady," replied the clerk politely, "that's his assistant."

books — See also *Reading*

190. You can read some people like a book, but you can't shut
them up as easily.

191. The oldest books are only just out to those who have not
read them.
— Samuel Butler

192. Rare volume: a borrowed book that comes back.

193. Borrowers of books — those mutilators of collections, spoilers
of the symmetry of shelves, and creators of odd volumes.
— Charles Lamb

194. Never lend books, for no one ever returns them; the only
books I have in my library are books that other folk have lent me.
— Anatole France

boredom

195. A minister, during the course of his sermon, suggested that
there would be a meeting of the Board at the foot of the dais at the
close of the sermon. When it was over, a group collected at the foot
of the platform, but one man looked like a stranger. "You're not a
member of the Board of Directors" said the minister to him. "Oh,
I'm sorry," was the reply, "I misunderstood you. I thought you said
a meeting of those who were bored."

boredom

196. A loud and objectionable bore had been talking for hours about himself and his achievements.

"I'm a self-made man, that's what I am — a self-made man!" he said.

"You knocked off work too soon," came a quiet voice from the corner.

197. Work is the easiest way man has ever invented to escape boredom.

198. Social success is the infinite capacity for being bored.

199. A bore is a guy who keeps the conversation ho-humming.

200. A bore is a fellow who opens his mouth and put his feats in it.

201. Bore: a guy who is here today and here tomorrow.

202. Bore: one whose shortcoming is his long staying.

bragging

203. Great talkers are little doers.

— FRANKLIN

brevity

204. Brevity: words that cover more ground than they occupy.

205. I have made this a rather long letter because I haven't had time to make it shorter.

— BLAISE PASCAL

206. Margot Asquith's unforgettable picture of a portentous lady of the British aristocracy: Rectitude, platitude, high-hatitude.

— *Readers Digest*

brotherhood

207. Abou Ben Adhem — may his tribe increase —
Awoke one night from a deep dream of peace,

42

And saw within the moonlight in his room,
Making it rich and like a lily in bloom,
An angel writing in a book of gold.
Exceeding peace had made Ben Adhem bold,
And to the presence in the room he said;
"What writest thou?" The vision raised its head,
And with a look made all of sweet accord,
Answered: "The names of those who love the Lord."
"And is mine one?" asked Abou. "Nay, not so,"
Replied the angel. Abou spoke more low.
But cheerily still; and said: "I pray thee, then
Write me as one that loves his fellow-men."
The angel wrote, and vanished. The next night
It came again with a great wakening light,
And showed the names whom love of God had blessed,
And lo! Ben Adhem's name led all the rest.

— LEIGH HUNT

208. At the narrow passage there is no brother and no friend.

— Arabian Proverb

business — See also *Enterprise*

209. George Eastman, captain of Kodaks, had always had a genius for detail. After looking over the architect's plan some years ago for a theatre with 6,000 seats which he was planning to give the city of Rochester, Mr. Eastman indicated general approval, but thought there was room for two more seats in the orchestra.

"Why raise the issue about two seats when there are to be 6,000 in the theatre?" queried the architect.

And Mr. Eastman is reported to have replied: "Each extra seat, for which there is ample room would bring in an additional revenue of 30 cents a show, making sixty cents for the day, or $3.60 a week, figuring six performances. At the end of the year, the revenue would amount to $187.20, which, incidentally, is the interest on $3,120 for a year."

— Nation's Business

210. "Every successful business man ought to give his business all he's got in business hours, then slam his desk lid and enter another world, a world of art, music, science, even bridge or billiards. Anything to lose himself."

That is the advice of a prominent department store head as he closes his own desk and starts for Europe.

It is advice that a good many business men need, whether successful or the opposite. Unsuccessful ones might get nearer to success if they followed it, and the successful ones might make themselves happier and their lives more useful by following it.

211. A corporation may spread itself over the whole world, and may employ a hundred thousand men; but the average person will usually form his judgment of it through his contact with one individual. If this person is rude or inefficient, it will take a lot of kindness and efficiency to overcome the bad impression. Every member of an organization who in any capacity comes in contact with the public is a salesman, and the impression he makes is an advertisement, good or bad.

212. Men who complain that the boss is dumb would be out of a job if he were any smarter.

213. Any business man: one who could have made more money with less trouble in an easier line.

214. Racketeer: a capitalist who invests himself with other people's money.

215. We all have our eyes on the *amount* of our profits — but one good way to increase them is to watch the *percentage* of profit. The relation of profits to the selling price — and to your investment — is the real index of business success. — LESTER WITTE

216. A scissors grinder is the only person whose business is good when things are dull.

217. Two Italian businessmen met in a street in Milan.
"How's business?" asked one.
"Very much better," said the other.
"Better?" cried the first in surprise.
"Yes, very much better than next year," the other explained.

218. We are all manufacturers — some make good, others make trouble and still others make excuses.

219. "I see you have a notice, 'We Aim to Please,' " remarked the irritated customer to the chain store manager.

"Yes," replied the manager, "that is our motto."

"Well," said the customer, "you ought to take a little time off for target practice."

220. Good will is the one and only asset that competition cannot undersell or destroy.
— Marshall Field

221. Anybody can cut prices, but it takes brains to make a better article.
— Philip D. Armour

222. Many persons have an idea that one cannot be in business and lead an upright life, whereas the truth is that no one succeeds in business to any great extent, who misleads or misrepresents.
— John Wanamaker

223. One afternoon Mark Twain, who lost more than one hard-earned fortune by investing it in harebrained schemes described to him in glittering terms, observed a tall, spare man, with kindly blue eyes and eager face, coming up the path with a strange contraption under his arm. Yes, it was an invention, and the man explained it to the humorist, who listened politely but said he had been burned too often.

"But I'm not asking you to invest a fortune," explained the man. "You can have as large a share as you want for $500." Mark Twain shook his head; the invention didn't make sense. The tall, stooped figure started away.

"What did you say your name was?" the author called after him.

"Bell," replied the inventor a little sadly, "Alexander Graham Bell."
— Vansant Coryell,
The Christian Science Monitor

224. A jeweler had to go downtown to see about additional Christmas goods, and left his store in charge of his son, Joey.

"You understand the price marks, Joey?" he said. "Five dots for $25, six dots for $30, etc."

"Sure father, I understand," replied the boy.

When the jeweler returned his son met him at the door. "I had good luck, father. I sold two $5 bracelets and three $30 watches."
"Yes, yes, Joey, but we have no $30 watches. The highest we have is $25."

"Then the marks are wrong, father."

The jeweler lifted his eyes and hands heavenward. "Joey," he said, "God bless the flies."

225. Three timid boys entered the village hardware store. The gruff proprietor said to the oldest, "What do you want, Zeke?"

"A dime's worth of BB shot, please."

The old man climbed a ladder, brought down the shelf box that contained the air-rifle shot, made up the packet and returned the box to the shelf above. Then he asked the second boy, "What do you want, Tim?"

"A dime's worth of BB's please," was the meek answer.

"Why didn't you say so before?" said the old man, irritably, as he went for the ladder again. He made up the packet as before, and then turned to the third.

"And do you want a dime's worth of BB's too?" he demanded.

"No," replied Joe hesitatingly.

The old man climbed laboriously to the shelf again and deposited the box of shot. Then he returned to the counter.

"Well, my boy, what do you want?" he demanded of Joe.

"A nickel's worth of BB shot," said Joe.

226. Recession: a period in which you tighten your belt.
Depression: a period in which you have no belt to tighten.

227. Department Store Detective: counter spy.

228. It is stated that in general production there is a preventable wastage of at least 50 per cent, and in distribution of about 75 per cent. The figures seem colossal and are probably exaggerated, but there is too much truth in the allegation that haphazard ways are the undoing of many a firm, and in the interests of the community as a whole, both employer and employee should ensure that every ounce of material used shall fill its purpose and that all human factors shall unitedly and heartily pull their weight.

229.   Man's boldness and woman's caution make an excellent business arrangement.
— ELBERT HUBBARD

230.   "What position did you hold in your last place?" asked the merchant.

"I was a doer, sir."

"A doer! What's that?"

"Well, sir, you see, when my employer wanted anything done, he would tell the cashier, the cashier would tell the bookkeeper, the bookkeeper would tell the clerk, and the clerk would tell me."

"And what would happen then?"

"Well, sir, as I hadn't anyone to tell it to, I'd do it."

231.   "My motto," said the very assertive man, "is: 'Buy dirt cheap and sell in the highest market.' What do you think of it?"

"Well," replied the quiet little man, "I don't really know. You see, I've never bought dirt."

232.
A little bit of *quality*
Will always make 'em smile;
A little bit of *courtesy*
Will bring 'em in a mile;
A little bit of *friendliness*
Will tickle 'em 'tis plain —
And a little bit of *service*
Will bring 'em back again.

233.   Boss: the man who is early when you are late, and late when you are early.

234.   Shoemaker, stick to your last.
— PLINY

235.   The price is what you pay; the value is what you receive.

236.   The man who attends strictly to his own business usually has plenty of business to attend to.

237.   The real boss in any business is the ultimate consumer. This is a good thing for presidents and directors to remember.

camouflage

238. A powdered nose is no guarantee of a clean neck.

capacity

239. Consider well what your strength is equal to, and what exceeds your ability.

— HORACE

240. There is no man living who isn't capable of doing more than he thinks he can do.

— HENRY FORD

cause and effect

241. A teacher while conducting a class said to her pupils: "Now, we have fifteen minutes within which to do nothing else, so let's work some riddles and conundrums. I will ask the first. Let's see who can guess the answer: 'If Washington crossed the Delaware, how old am I?' "

There was a blank stare on everyone's face, but for one little youngster in the back of the room who was busily engaged scribbling on a piece of paper. Finally, he raised his hand and said:

"Teacher, I have the answer."

"What is it, Johnny," said she.

"Forty-eight," came back the answer.

"That's right, but how did you guess it?"

"Oh," said Johnny, "I didn't guess it, I worked it out by arithmetic; you see, we have a brother at home, his name is Tommy, he's twenty-four, and he's half nuts. Two times twenty-four is forty-eight."

242. There is no gathering the rose without being pricked by the thorns.

— PILPAY, *The Two Travellers*

243. New York's Museum of Natural History has boasted of the countless nature-lovers who came to see its wonders. But when a comfort station was erected on a nearby corner, museum attendance fell off 100,000.

244. — for if there be fuel prepared, it is hard to tell whence the spark shall come that shall set it on fire.

— BACON, *Essays*

caution

245. Quincy S. Treagre, manager of a peanut store in Grand Rapids, Michigan, reported to police that a gunman had robbed his place of $75. That figure appeared in newspaper accounts, and soon afterward the police chief received the following letter:

"That Treagre guy said he lost $75 Saturday, but I say he lost only $20.20. My boys are asking for a full split and I can't give them $20 each because I'll lose money on the job. Now I want you to see he puts a retraction in the papers. If he don't, he can't say he wasn't warned."

246. A Minneapolis teacher gave $500 to a charming gyp for a half interest in a mythical training school — and then the man skipped out and couldn't be found.

When she came to the Better Business Bureau with her tale of woe, the Bureau man asked: "Why didn't you investigate first? Didn't you know about our service?"

"Oh, yes, I've known about the Bureau for years," she answered. "But I was afraid you'd tell me not to do it!"

— FRANK W. BROCK, *Coronet*

247. To a quick question, give a slow answer.

— *Italian Proverb*

248. Message written by Noel Coward on a postcard showing a picture of the Venus de Milo: "You see what will happen to you if you keep on biting your nails."

249. There is no way to catch a snake that is as safe as not catching him.

censure

250. Censure is often useful, praise often deceitful.

— WINSTON CHURCHILL

251. Few persons have sufficient wisdom to prefer censure which is useful to them to praise which deceives them.

— LA ROCHEFOUCAULD

252. He that accuses all mankind of corruption ought to remember that he is sure to convict only one. — EDMUND BURKE

253. It is harder to avoid censure than to gain applause; for this may be done by one great or wise action in an age. But to escape censure a man must pass his whole life without saying or doing one ill or foolish thing. — DAVID HUME

chairman — See also *Public Speaking*

254. The Curate (after a song by the village soprano):
"Before Miss Dash started to sing she told me her voice was not in condition and asked me to apologize. I neglected to do so, but I apologize now."

255. If you ever happen to be toastmaster or chairman of some happy meeting, don't make the mistake that this one did who whispered to the main speaker of the evening. "Shall we let them enjoy themselves a little longer, or do you think you'd better begin your speech now?"

256. Irvin S. Cobb, the noted journalist, set out one year to give a course of Chautauqua lectures. He found that at the first meeting, the chairman took up so much time in introducing him that there was very little time left him for his talk. He determined that this would never do, and on the second occasion took along his own chairman, but when he found that the time left for him to deliver his lecture after the chairman's introductory words was still insufficient, he determined from that point on to write the introductory speeches for all his future chairmen.

257. In introducing a pianist or violinist, etc. — "she is the product of a very expensive musical education — her father was sued by three different neighbors at the same time."

258. Lucian Cary tells us that the secretary of the Ladies' Luncheon Club arose after coffee to present the speaker of the day, "the noted author, Mr. Lucian Cary." "Normally," she said with her brightest smile, "this honor would fall to our president, who has never missed hearing any of our speakers. But today she is in Atlantic City — and how we all envy her!"
— *Readers Digest*

259. *Toastmaster's Introduction:* Gentlemen, you have been giving your attention to a turkey stuffed with sage. Now you will hear from a sage stuffed with turkey.

260. *Introduction of a Speaker:* "There are two types of speakers — one needs no introduction; the other deserves none."

261. Two cities claim the birth of our distinguished speaker — Chicago and Detroit. Chicago claims he was born in Detroit, and Detroit claims he was born in Chicago.

262. "Once in Virginia," said a speaker who had received an introduction that promised more than he felt he could deliver, "I passed a small church displaying a large sign. It read: 'Annual Strawberry Festival' and below in small letters, 'On account of the depression, prunes will be served.' "
— *Boston Transcript*

263. At a dinner party recently, a lady seated next to the chairman of a large corporation, asked him just what the functions of a chairman were.

He replied, "My dear madam, that is not too difficult; the functions of a chairman are the same as the piece of parsley that is placed on top of a fish."
— *The Wall Street Journal*

264. It was the first lecture season after Admiral Byrd had retired from his polar exploration. Of course his services were in great demand, and his lecture fees naturally reflected this condition.

Cornelia Otis Skinner was filling an evening engagement in a small mid-western city. Madam Chairman arose for the usual introduction, and began with a delightfully frank explanation: "Since we cannot afford Admiral Byrd on this occasion," she said, "we are having Cornelia Otis Skinner!"

265. The chairman replied in a few appropriated words.
— CECIL HUNT, *This Week*

character

266. Character is a conquest not a bequest.

267. Character is money; and according as the man earns or spends the money, money in turn becomes character.
— EDWARD BULWER-LYTTON

268. It is easier and better to build boys than to repair men.

269. Character is what a man is in the dark.

270. The measure of a man's real character is what he would do if he knew he never would be found out.
— THOMAS B. MACAULAY

271. You can no more blame your circumstances for your character than you can the mirror for your looks.

272. The difference between personality and character: Personality is what you are when lots of people are around; character is what you are when everybody goes home.

273. Character is the result of two things — mental attitude and the way we spend our time.
— ELBERT HUBBARD

274. Two brothers convicted of stealing sheep, were branded on the forehead with the letters ST, for "sheep thief."

One brother, unable to bear the stigma, tried to bury himself in a foreign land. But men asked him about the strange letters. He wandered restlessly, and at length, full of bitterness, died and was buried in a forgotten grave.

The other brother said, "I can't run away from the fact that I stole sheep. I will stay here and win back the respect of my neighbors and myself."

As the years passed he built a reputation for integrity. One day, a stranger saw the old man with the letters branded on his forehead. He asked a native what they signified. "It happened a great while ago," said the villager. "I've forgotten the particulars; but I think the letters are an abbreviation of Saint."
— *Macartny's Illustrations,*
(Abingdon-Cokesbury)

275. Character is made by what you stand for; reputation, by what you fall for.
— ROBERT QUILLEN

276. We have committed the Golden Rule to memory; now let us commit it to life.
— EDWIN MARKHAM

277. The advice of the Mogul emperor to young people was:
"I have lived a long time, but I have yet to see a man lost on the straight road."

278. Humdrum isn't where you live but what you are.
— HAROLD McGRATH

279. So live that you wouldn't be ashamed to sell the family parrot to the town gossip.
— *Quote*

280. Eccentricity has always abounded when and where the strength of character has abounded; and the amount of eccentricity in a society has been proportional to the amount of genius, mental vigor, and moral courage it contained. That so few now dare to be eccentric, marks the chief danger of the times.
— JOHN STUART MILL

charity

281. The great Maimonides once enumerated the various stages of charity, of which the last and most meritorious is to help a man to help himself, to enable him to become self-supporting so that he will no longer have to rely upon the beneficence of others.

282. George Bernard Shaw, doing his duty at a benefit affair, asked a dowager to dance. As they waltzed, she simpered, "Oh, Mr. Shaw, whatever made you ask poor little me to dance?" Replied the gallant G. B. S., "This is a charity ball, isn't it?"
— *Readers Digest*

283. A small boy was sent to church by his father with a nickel and a dollar bill in his pocket.
"You are to put what you please in the offering box, my boy. Listen to the sermon and make your offering in accordance with the impression made upon you."

The boy had returned. "Well, what did you put in the box?" his father asked.

"The nickel. I was going to put in the other when I remembered what the clergyman said in his sermon."

"What was that?"

"The Lord loveth a *cheerful* giver."

284. The lady was out in her motor-car in the snow. As she stepped out to enter a shop she shivered.

"Jackson," she said to her chauffeur, "remind me when we get home to send some coals and blankets for the poor."

She returned to her luxurious home. There was a blazing fire and a hot cup of tea was ready for her.

Presently there was a knock at the door. It was the chauffeur.

"You asked me to remind you, madam, to send some coals and blankets to the poor."

"Ah, yes, I remember, but it is nice and warm now." (This story was quoted by the late Sir Joseph Lyons when presiding once at the opening of the session of a Soup Kitchen in London. Our sympathies are often stirred at suffering. But too soon we forget.)

285.   THE MEASURE OF A MAN
                Not — "how did he die?"
                But — "how did he live?"
                Not — "what did he gain?"
                But — "what did he give?"
                These are the units
                    To measure the worth
                Of a man, as a man,
                    Regardless of birth.

286. "I think you'll pull through," said the doctor to his patient, "but you're a pretty sick man."

"Please, doctor," begged the patient, "do everything you can for me. And if I get well, I'll donate $50,000 to the fund for your new hospital."

Months later the doctor met his former patient on the street.

"How are you?" he asked.

"I'm feeling marvelous!" replied the man.

"I've been meaning to speak to you," continued the doctor, "about that money for the new hospital."

"What are you talking about?"

"You said that if you got well," the doctor reminded him, "you would contribute $50,000."

"I said that?" the former patient exclaimed. "Now you can see how sick I was!"
— *Readers Digest*

287. If you are trying to secure subscriptions to some philanthropic cause and bump into a gent who says, "I have no money for charity now, but I'll remember your organization in my will," you might try telling the prospect the fable about the cow and the pig. The pig said, "I don't understand why men sneer when they use the word 'pig.' They use every part of me. Every part of my flesh is edible and even my bristles are usable." The cow replied, "I also give everything I have — but I give while I am still alive."

288. There was the man who complained because he had no shoes, until he met a man who had no feet.

289. Unless a man is a recipient of charity, he should be a contributor to it.

290. Dean Swift, preaching a charity sermon, promised, "I shall be brief. My text: 'He that giveth unto the poor lendeth unto the Lord.' Brethren, you have heard the terms of the loan. If you are satisfied with the security, put down your cash."

There was a record collection.
— *Quote*

291.   Not what we give, but what we share,
          For the gift without the giver is bare;
          Who gives himself with alms feeds three,
          Himself, his hungering neighbor and Me.
— JAMES RUSSELL LOWELL

292. If the poor man cannot always get meat, the rich man cannot always digest it.
— HENRY GILES

293.   Some folks give their mite,
          Others give with their might,
          And some don't give who might.

294. A long-time friend of the National Probation Association, a woman approaching the century mark, was accused of being on the "sucker list" because of her generosity. "I don't mind that at all," she replied, "if you spell it 'Succor.' "

295. The collectors were pressing down on old man Jones during a drive for church funds. "I can't give nothin'" pleaded the old parishoner. "I owe nearly everybody in this town already."

"But," said one of the collectors, "don't you think you owe the Lord somethin' too?"

"I do, indeed," said the old man, "but He ain't pushing me like my other creditors are." — *Public Service Magazine*

296. A poor, blind woman in Paris put 27 francs into a plate at a missionary meeting. "You cannot afford so much," said one.

"Yes, sir, I can," she answered.

On being pressed to explain, she said, "I am blind and I said to my fellow straw-workers, 'How much money do you spend in a year for oil in your lamps when it is too dark to work nights?' They replied, 'Twenty-seven francs.'

"So," said the poor woman, "I found that I save so much in the year because I am blind and do not need a lamp, and I give it to shed light to the dark, heathen lands."

— *Christian Endeavor World*

297. A famous philanthropist was once asked: "How are you able to give so much, and still have so much?"

"Well," replied the generous man, "as I shovel out, He shovels in; and the Lord has a bigger shovel than I have."

— *Christian Science Monitor*

298.   The stuff which charity bestows
            Is very small, the poor man knows.
            Daily the toiler's board reveals
            A job provides much better meals.

— EDGAR A. GUEST

299. The gentleman's attitude was polite but firm. "I'm sorry," he told the young woman who was selling tickets for the charity concert, "but I won't be able to attend the concert. "It's for a most worthy cause, however, and I assure you I shall be with you in spirit."

"Fine," exclaimed the young woman. "Now where would you like to have your spirit sit? The tickets are $5.00 and $10.00."

The gentleman meekly replied: "I'll take a $10.00 one, please."

— *Readers Digest*

300. A backward land is one where employers pay small wages so they can make enough money to provide charity for needy workmen.

301. Charitable works for the idle rich are something to worry about, too. A bejeweled matron waddled out of Claridges' Hotel in London where she had been cavorting — and eating — all evening at a deluxe charity ball. As she stepped into her Rolls a beggar sidled up to her and whined, "Spare me a six-pence, lady, for charity. I ain't 'ad a bit for three days." The lady recoiled. "How much do you expect from me, you ungrateful fellow?" she demanded. "Don't you realize I've just been dancing for you all night?"

302. He who has conferred a kindness should be silent, he who has received one should speak of it. — SENECA

303. According to William Allen White, there are three kicks in every dollar. The first, is when you make it, the second is when you have it, the third is when you give it away.

304. About a block ahead of a Sacramento cop, who was looking for parking meter violations, a young woman scurried along inserting a coin in every meter that showed a red flag. On the seat of each reprieved car she left an envelope and this note: "Dear Car Owner: You have over-parked and there is a policeman only a few cars away. I have put a penny in your meter, giving you an additional 12 minutes. You have been saved the $2.50 for a parking ticket. Will you put a portion of that money into the attached envelope?"

The envelopes, stamped and addressed to the County Home for Children, brought in a really substantial sum.

— *Readers Digest*

305. It is better to give than to lend, and it costs about the same.

— SIR PHILIP GIBBS

306. For $100, you, all alone, can support the American Red Cross all over the world — for 16 seconds. . . . For $6.00, you, all alone, support the American Red Cross all over the world for one second. — From an advertisement of L. Strauss & Co., men's furnishings store.

307. Speaker (desirous of raising money) — "All who will give $10 stand up."

(Aside to musician) — "Quick! Play the 'Star-Spangled Banner.' "

308. At a benefit performance the hall was crowded and the performers were generously applauded. But the offering amounted to less than $4.00. "Well," said the promoter, addressing the group, "this offering, as you understand, is for the benefit of the poor — and they all seem to be here." — *Church Management*

309. The preacher, after talking to his congregation about free salvation, asked Brother Smith to take up the collection. A parishioner got to his feet and protested: "Parson, I thought you said salvation was free — free as the water we drink."

"Salvation is free, Brother," replied the minister. "It's free and the water is free, but when we pipe it to you, you have to pay for the piping." — *The Wall Street Journal*

310. Who remembers when charity was a personally exercised virtue springing from the heart, and not a systematized business operating from a card index?

311. A member once went out to raise funds for a new church. In one home which he visited, a member of the church refused to give because he felt the church was costing too much. In reply to the objection, the canvasser told the following story:

"About twenty-five years ago a son was born to me. From the moment he came into this world he was an expense. First, it was hospital care, toys, food. Then it was music lessons, books and shoes. Later it was allowance for movies, dances and dates. Finally, he went to college and my expenses mounted. Sometimes I thought the boy was costing me more than was necessary. At about the time he was ready to graduate from college, my son was infected with a grievous disease and died."

The speaker paused to clear his throat, then he continued quietly: "You know, Bill, that boy has not cost me a cent since. Not one cent."

312. They (the majority of people) try to solve the problem of poverty by keeping the poor alive; or in the case of a very advanced school by amusing the poor. But this is not a solution; it is an aggravation of the difficulty. The proper aim is to try and reconstruct society on such a basis that poverty will be impossible. . . . The people who do most harm are the people who try to do most good. . . . charity degrades and demoralizes . . . charity creates a multitude of sins. . . . It is immoral to use private property in order to alleviate the horrible evils that result from the institution of private property. It is both immoral and unfair.

— OSCAR WILDE

313. What is called generosity is generally only the vanity of giving, which we like better than what we give. — LA ROCHEFOUCAULD

314. Lincoln and his law-partner, Herndon, jogging along a muddy road in an old buggy through pouring rain, were discussing a point of philosophy — whether there is such a thing as a disinterested, unselfish act. Lincoln said there was not. Herndon argued that there are such acts.

They passed a pig caught in a crack of an old rail fence, squealing for dear life. A little farther on, Lincoln, who was driving stopped the buggy, got out and let the pig loose. When he climbed back in, his feet were muddy, his clothes wet, his hat dripping.

"There now," said Herndon. "In spite of your fine logic, you have proved my point. Why get out in the mud and let that silly pig out when he would have wiggled his way out anyhow?"

"It was a purely selfish act," said Lincoln. "If I hadn't I would not have slept a wink tonight; his squeal would have echoed in my dreams. He might have wiggled his way out, but I wouldn't have known it. I win the case."

— JOSEPH FORT NEWTON,
Living Every Day (Harper)

315. Benefactor: one who makes two smiles grow where one grew before. — CHAUNCEY DEPEW

316. There are two classes of philanthropists: one alleviates and the other cures. There is one class of philanthropists that undertakes when a man commits an evil to help him out of it. There is another class that endeavors to abolish the temptation. The first is sentiment, the latter is Christianity.

— WENDELL PHILLIPS,
Christianity is a Battle

317. A man whose inordinate love of money was ruining his life once called upon a rabbi to argue a point in the minister's sermon.

Perceiving the man's difficulty, the rabbi opened the Bible, pointed to the word "God," and asked, "Can you see that?"

"Certainly," the man replied.

The rabbi then placed a coin over the word, and said, "Can you see it now?"

The man did not answer, but presently he said,

"I understand."

318. David Starr Jordan, while president of Leland Stanford University, and the greatest ichthyologist (fish expert) of his day, spent a great deal of his time raising funds for the University at the expense of his scholarship and continued study. Once, asked the name of a certain fish, which he could not recall, he commented: "Every time I find a new benefactor, I forget the name of an old fish."

319. Charity is the sterilized milk of human kindness.

— OLIVER HERFORD

320. It is not enough to help the feeble up, but to support him after. — SHAKESPEARE

321. Giving until it hurts is not a true measure of charity. Some are more easily hurt than others.

322. Frequently a philanthropist is one who gives it away when he should be giving it back.

323. A bowl stood on a secluded hall table at the home of Sarah Bernhardt, and one day I noticed that a few of her guests, in leaving, after looking around to make sure they were unnoticed, slipped something from it into their pockets. I asked about it, and Sarah explained that, as many of her friends were in need, she kept the bowl filled with coins. "They know it is there, and for what purpose," she said. "In this way, I can help them without putting them to the necessity of asking for it. — ELSIE DE WOLFE, *Ladies Home Journal*

324. In this world it is not what we *take* up, but what we *give* up, that makes us rich. — HENRY WARD BEECHER, *Life Thoughts*

325. He gives by halves who hesitates to give.

— WILLIAM BROOME

charm

326. Charm: the ability to make someone else think that both of you are pretty wonderful.

cheerfulness

327.

Joke with him who jostles you,
Smile on him who hurries you,
Laugh at him who pushes you,
 It doesn't cost a cent!
Don't be carrying around that chip
Wink your eye and curve your lip,
And from life's sunshine take a sip
 It doesn't cost a cent!
Don't be always first to rile
Your neighbor — give him just a smile,
It will cheer the dullest, while
 It doesn't cost a cent!

child — children — child care

328. Perhaps parents would enjoy their children more if they stopped to realize that the film of childhood can never be run through for a second showing.
— EVELYN NOWN

329. Father of obstreperous youngster to wife reading child-psychology book: "Does it say where we're to apply this free hand we're supposed to give him?"
— CURRIER, *King Features*

330. Children have more need of models than of critics.

— JOSEPH JOUBERT

331. It is easy, like the child, to be spoiled by too much indulgence; it is easy, like the bluebells, to be spoiled by ceaseless sunshine.
— D. F. BOREHAM, A Spoiled
Child, *Christian Herald*

332. Raising children is like baking bread; it has to be a slow process or you end up with an overdone crust and an underdone interior.
— MARCELENE COX, Ask Any
Woman, *Ladies Home Journal*

333. Parents are often so busy with the physical rearing of children that they miss the glory of parenthood, just as the grandeur of the trees is lost when raking leaves.
— MARCELENE COX, *Ladies
Home Journal*

334. If, in instructing a child, you are vexed with it for want of adroitness, try, if you have never tried before, to write with your left hand, and then remember that a child is all left hand.
— J. F. BOYSE, *Tales from Hoffman*

335. The training of children is a profession, where we must know how to waste time in order to save it.
JEAN JACQUES ROUSSEAU

336. Two women sat one day on a wind-swept ocean pier. The first woman had three beautiful children, the other was childless. The latter gazing wistfully out over the tumbling water, said, "I'd give ten years of my life to have three such children as yours!"

"Well," the other woman answered gravely, "three children cost about that."
— THOMAS L. MASSON, *Best Stories
in the World*. (Doubleday)

337. Vital as defense work is, somewhere there is another woman who can do it just as well. . . . But nobody can do a parent's job as well as a parent.
— MARY S. BATCHELOR, *Health Bulletin*

338. A mother of thirteen children was asked, "How in the world do you have time to care for thirteen?"

"Well," she replied, "when I had only one child it took all my time; what more can thirteen do?"
— *Quote*

339. Last summer the personnel manager of a prominent women's dress shop hired a girl whom she met casually at a dinner. When asked why she was so sure the girl would work out well, the woman answered, "I have met her parents. I know that their child could not be too far from the type of girl I want in my store."

— EMILY SEABER PARCHER,
"By Their Parents You Shall
Know Them," *American Home*
(Reprinted by permission)

340. Any man who is content with seeing children of his own district safe and well, not considering the millions of under-privileged ones throughout the country, is a domestic isolationist.

— KATHERINE LENROOT, Chief
U.S. Children's Bureau

341. After a lecture by the late Francis Wayland Parker, great Chicago educator, a woman asked:

"How early can I begin the education of my child?"

"When will your child be born?"

"Born?" she gasped. "Why, he is already five years old!"

"My goodness woman," he cried, "don't stand here talking to me — hurry home; already you have lost the best five years."

— *Survey Graphic*

342. The best inheritance a parent can give his children is a few minutes of his time each day.

— O. A. BATTISTA

343. A child's education should begin at least one hundred years before he is born.

— OLIVER WENDELL HOLMES

344. Don't take up a man's time talking about the smartness of *your* children; he wants to talk to you about the smartness of *his* children.

— EDGAR W. HOWE

345. I have often thought what a melancholy world this would be without children, and what an inhuman world without the aged.

— SAMUEL T. COLERIDGE

346. Boy: a noise with some dirt on it.

347. By the time the youngest children have learned to keep the place tidy, the oldest grandchildren are on hand to tear it to pieces again.

— CHRISTOPHER MORLEY

348. A small boy, mischievous to the imp degree.

— REA MURTHA

63

349. Four-year-old's definition of nursery school: a place where they try to teach children who hit, not to hit, and children who don't hit, to hit back. — Mrs. M. S. N., *Parents' Magazine*

350. Jones has eleven children — he must have gone stork mad.

351. Summer: the season when children slam the doors they left open all winter.

352. Babies: little rivets in the bonds of matrimony.
— Arthur Gordon, *Readers Digest*

353. Baby sitter: one who accepts hush money.

354. Baby: alimentary canal with a loud voice at one end and no responsibility at the other.

chivalry

355. The chivalry of the ante-bellum South is not dead, according to Kay Kyser. He defines a typical old-fashioned Southern gentleman as a man who hadn't embraced his wife for six months, but shot another man who did. — Bennett Cerf, *Laughter, Inc.*
(Garden City Books)

356. Chivalry: a man's inclination to defend a woman against every man but himself.

choice

357. No poet sings because he must sing. At least no great poet does. A great poet sings because he chooses to sing.

358. This is a universe of moral law, no more to be outwitted than is physical law. Look at our world and see. When we choose evil, we get what we want at once and then pay for it afterward; but when we choose good we have to pay for it first before we get it. The young man in college who chooses an idle, lazy life can have that at once; today he can start that; he will pay for it afterward. But the young man who wants a degree with honor cannot get that today. He must pay for it before he gets it, in hard work and self-discipline. If a man wants a life of sensual excess he can have that tonight, with all the wild thrill and mad sense of exhilaration that he seeks. He can seize his passionate desire at once, and pay for it, it may be, long afterward. But a man who wants a noble character that, like a well-rooted tree, holds its own against the storms of life and in the autumn bears fruit for his generation's help, cannot get that at once; he must pay for it first and then get it.

— HARRY EMERSON FOSDICK

359.   The Lord gave us two ends to use,
        One to think with; one to sit on
      It all depends on which you choose:
        Heads you win, tails you lose.

360. *Famous last words:*
"So I leave it with all of you: Which came out of the opened door — the lady or the tiger?"

— FRANK R. STOCKTON,
The Lady or the Tiger

citizenship — See *Government*

civilization

361. Civilization is a slow process of adopting the ideas of minorities.

362. To be civilized is to be incapable of giving unnecessary offense, to have some quality of consideration for all who cross our path. An Englishwoman once said to the artist, James McNeill Whistler, that the politeness of the French was "All on the surface," to which he replied: "And a very good place for it to be." It is this sweet surface politeness, costing so little, counting for so much, which smooths the roughness out of life.

— AGNES REPPLIER, *Americans &*
Others (Houghton, Mifflin & Co.)

363. The end of the human race will be that it will eventually die of civilization.

— RALPH WALDO EMERSON

climax – climactic

364. In everything worth having, even in every pleasure, there is a point of pain or tedium that must be survived, so that the pleasure may revive and endure. The joy of battle comes after the first fear of death; the glow of the seabather comes after the icy shock of the sea bath; and the success of the marriage comes after the failure of the honeymoon. All human vows, laws and contracts are so many ways of surviving with success this breaking point, this instant of potential surrender.

> — G. K. CHESTERTON, *What's Wrong*
> *with the World* (Dodd, Mead & Co.)

clothes – See *Dress*

college

365. During a discussion in my high school English class, the question of choosing colleges was brought up. One bright girl contributed her bit: "Well," she said, "first you've got to decide whether you want to go to a co-educational school or an educational one!"

> — B. HODGES, *Readers Digest*

366. A woman owned a horse which she thought was very smart. Her friends thought the horse very dumb. To prove to them that she was right, she wrote to a certain University (the folks from Yale will tell you it was Princeton; Princeton graduates, however, insist it was Yale) asking that institution to confer a degree upon the horse.

She realized this was a rather unusual request but when she informed the President of the University that it was her intention to will her entire fortune ($250,000) to the University, he acceded to her wish. Came graduation day and the horse was provided with a suitable cap and gown and lined up in the commencement procession along with all the other candidates for degrees.

In conferring a degree upon the horse, the President of the University directed the attention of the audience to the fact this was the first time in the history of the University that a degree was being conferred on a whole horse.

367. Colleges don't make fools; they only develop them.

— HORACE LORIMER

368. All that stands between the graduate and the top of the ladder is the ladder.

369. A Harvard graduate went to a midwestern city to live and applied for a job with a department store. The personnel manager wrote to one of his references in Boston for information, and shortly received a letter outlining in detail the young man's fine social connections and his family tree, which dated back to Pilgrim stock.

The personnel manager wrote back: "Dear Sir: You have perhaps misinterpreted our request for information. We want the young man for working purposes, not breeding purposes."

370. "Isn't there some fable about the ass disguising himself with a lion skin?"

"Yes, but now the colleges do the trick with a sheepskin."

371. The first big shock to the graduate is the discovery that all the jobs are handed out by old fogies like his dad.

372. A University student when sitting for an examination was asked to compose one verse of poetry including the words "analyze" and "anatomy." This is what he wrote:

My Analyze over the ocean
My Analyze over the sea
Oh, who will go over the ocean
And bring back my Anatomy.

373. They're telling this one about a salesman passing through a small town who had several hours to while away. Seeing one of the townspeople, he asked:

"Any picture show in town, my friend?"

"Nope, not a one, stranger."

"Well, is there a pool room or bowling alley?"

"Nope."

"What form of amusement do you have here?"

"Well, come on down to the drug store," the man said. "There's a freshman home from the university."

374. A student who had been loafing for most of the semester, approached his professor. "Do you think," he asked anxiously, "that if I 'bone up' for the next two weeks I can pass the exam?"

"Sir," replied the professor, "you make me think of a thermometer in a cold room. You can make it register higher by holding your hand over it, but you won't be warming the room."

— Magazine Digest

375. By the time the average college boy of today succeeds in accumulating the horsehide, the pigskin, the coonskin, and finally the sheepskin, poor father hasn't much hide left either.

— Pathfinder

376. *Friend:* "So your son is in college? What is he preparing for?"

Father: "I don't know; but from the way he works me, I kind of think he's going to be a diplomat."

377. The two college juniors yawned, and one said, "What shall we do tonight?"

"Let's toss up a coin to decide," replied the other. "If it's heads we'll go to the movies; if it's tails we'll call on Rosie and Susie; and if it stands on the edge, we'll study."

378. Somebody asked a college professor how science helped business, and he replied, "What would the suspender amount to without the law of gravitation?"

— Quote

379. A college education seldom hurts a man if he is willing to learn a little something after he graduates.

380. College-bred refers to something which requires a fearful amount of dough, is seldom self-raising, and usually proves to be nothing more or less than a four-year loaf.

—H. C. WITWER

381. "Are you laughing at me?" demanded the irate professor of his class.

"No," came the answer in chorus.

"Well," insisted the professor, "what else is there in the room to laugh at?"

— College of the Pacific Weekly

382. Nostalgia is the most prevalent ailment on college campuses and one of the chief contributors to low school marks.

— Dr. George W. Crane, *Psychology Applied*

383. Professor: a textbook wired for sound.

384. Professor: one who talks in someone else's sleep.

385. A professor is a man whose job it is to tell students how to solve the problems of life which he himself has tried to avoid by becoming a professor.

386. Parent: (Collegiate definition) the kin you love to touch.

— *Oral Hygiene*

387. A college education is a four-year plan for confusing a young mind methodically.

— *Banking*

388. Coed: a moron with less on.

389. It is not so important to be serious as it is to be serious about the important things. The monkey wears an expression of seriousness which would do credit to any college student, but the monkey is serious because he itches.

— Robert Maynard Hutchins

390. The young graduate is discovering that among the necessaries of life, the most important is living.

comment — commentator

391. A distinguished commentator is one whose predictions are forgotten by the time circumstances prove them wrong.

committee

392. Committee: a body that keeps minutes and wastes hours.

communism

393. A communist is a guy who borrows your pot to cook your goose.

companionship

394.   A company is known by the man it keeps.

395.   Great men taken up in any way are profitable company.

— THOMAS CARLYLE

396.   Stand with anybody that stands right and part with him when he goes wrong.

— ABRAHAM LINCOLN

397.   One day a young man came in great perplexity to the clergy-man, Dwight L. Moody, and said, "Mr. Moody, I want to reform and lead a better life. But I don't know how I can give up my undesirable companions."

"That's not difficult, young man," replied the revivalist. "Just live a good life and the undesirable companions will give you up."

compensation

398.   A child was asked why she talked so much.

"I don't know any big words," she explained, "so I use lots and lots of little ones to make up."

competition

399.   "The world," Dwight Morrow once wrote to his son, "is divided into people who do things and people who get the credit. Try, if you can, to belong to the first class. There's far less competition."

— From *Dwight Morrow*, copyright, 1935, by HAROLD NICOLSON. Reprinted by permission of Harcourt, Brace and Company, Inc.

complexity

400.   Network: a pattern, reticulated and decussated at equal intervals with interstices between the intersections.

— SAMUEL JOHNSON

complimentary — See also *Flattery*

401. In their early and less opulent days, George Burns wanted to send some flowers to Gracie Allen, who was in the hospital. Having exactly enough money to buy eleven roses, he wrote, "Dear Gracie, here's eleven roses. The twelfth one is you."

— George Burns, *True Story*

402. Once when Henry Clay failed to recognize a young lady, she said reproachfully, "Why, Mr. Clay, you don't remember my name!"

"No," answered the statesman in his most gallant manner, "for when we last met I was sure your beauty and accomplishments would soon compel you to change it."

— *The Christian Science Monitor*

403. Speaking of professors, a man after our own heart is the University of Chicago savant who politely turned down an invitation to address the commencement at a fashionable girls' school in Michigan. "I'm much too busy these days," he wrote, "and besides, I find it a lot more interesting to talk to one girl a thousand times than to talk to a thousand girls one time.

404. Every day you look lovelier and lovelier — and today you look like tomorrow.

405. It was an Englishman, met in a train somewhere in Europe, who startled Mark Twain by saying abruptly, "Mr. Clemens, I would give ten pounds not to have read your 'Huckleberry Finn!'" And when Mark looked up, awaiting an explanation of this extraordinary remark, the Englishman smiled and added: "So that I could have again the great pleasure of reading it for the first time."

— Reprinted from *The Tocsin of Revolt* by Brander Matthews by permission of the publishers Charles Scribner's Sons.

406. A friend in conversation with Voltaire said: "It is good of you to say such pleasant things of Monsieur X when he always says such nasty things of you."

To which Voltaire replied: "Perhaps we are both mistaken."

— Edna B. Smith, *The Best I Know* (Waverly)

407. A disconcerted pastor re-read the note that accompanied a box of goodies he and his wife had received from an old lady parishioner: "Dear pastor — knowing that you do not eat sweets, I am sending candy to your wife — and nuts to you."

408. We expected much — and got much more.

compromise

409. Compromise: what two people arrive at to their mutual satisfaction.

410. The middle way is frequently taken by those who do not know where they are going, and so find comfort in having company on both sides.
— PROF. F. A. HARPER,
American Affairs

conceit

411. The bigger a man's head gets, the easier it is to fill his shoes.

condescension

412. We cannot expect other nations to see eye to eye with us if we look down on them.

conduct — See also *Behavior*

413. The main trouble with the "straight and narrow" is that there's no place to park.

414. It is more to one's credit to go straight than to move in the "best circles."

415. When men speak ill of thee, so live that nobody will believe them.
— PLATO

conference

416. A conference is a group of men who individually can do nothing, but as a group can meet and decide that nothing can be done.

417. Conference: the confusion of the loudest talking character multiplied by the number present.

confession

418. There is no refuge from confession but suicide; and suicide is confession.
— DANIEL WEBSTER, *Argument on the Murder of Captain White*

419. Fault confessed is half redressed.

confidence

420. The man who trusts men will make fewer mistakes than the man who distrusts them.
— COUNT CAVOUR

421. Confidence: the feeling you have before you know better.

422. Trust everybody, but cut the cards.
—FINLEY PETER DUNNE

423. It is better to suffer wrong than to do it, and happier to be sometimes cheated than not to trust.
— SAMUEL JOHNSON, *The Rambler*

424. It takes a truly good man to have confidence in the goodness of others.

425. Trust that man in nothing who has not a conscience in everything.
— LAURENCE STERNE

426. Fifteen nations signed the peace treaty, and one thing all have in common is the conviction that fourteen aren't to be trusted.

427.   THE MAN YOU CAN TRUST

The man you can trust is the man who is simple, direct and sincere. When he undertakes a responsible task, he is fully and deeply conscious of his responsibility. He is intent upon fairness and justice to all, even to those who oppose him. To him, the insincerity of the demagogue is as dishonest as the trickery of the con man or the embezzler. To him, honor is dearer than power, and a clear conscience more precious than wealth or fame. He is suspicious of mere brilliance and he is not easily fascinated by the plausibility of quacks, or misled by the enthusiasm of cranks, for good judgment, good character and ripe experience are what he most respects. He does not waver like a leaf in the winds of popular approval or disapproval. When he makes a pledge he can be relied upon to keep it, at whatever cost to himself, for he acts on principles of right and wrong, not on the convenience or expediency of the moment. He is not all things to all men. When he says yes, he means yes, and when he says no, means no. In short, the man you can trust, in the long run, is not necessarily the clever man or the charming man, but the man who keeps his word.

428.   The dog that licks ashes is not to be trusted with flour.

— Italian Proverb

confusion

429.   A Co-ordinator is a man who brings organized chaos out of regimented confusion.

430.   *How confused can you get?*

Think of the man standing in a pasture holding a rope in his hands and saying to himself: "I don't know if I lost a horse or found a rope."

431.   *Young husband to nurse:* "Quick! am I a father or a mother?"

conscience

432.   As long as your conscience is your friend, never mind about your enemies.

74

433. Sometimes a man with a clear conscience only has a poor memory.

> *— A Country Editor,*
> quoted by NEAL O'HARA

434. Quite often when a man thinks his mind is getting broader it is only his conscience stretching.

> *— Quote*

435. Conscience gets a lot of credit that belongs to cold feet.
> *— The Link*

436. How sweet are the slumbers of him who can lie down on his pillow and review the transactions of every day, without condemning himself!

437. Reformer: one who insists upon his conscience being your guide.

438. Conscience: an inner voice that warns us somebody is looking.

> *— H. L. MENCKEN*

439. Conscience is what makes you tell your wife before someone else does.

> *— KENNETH STEIER*

440. There is a difference between him who does no misdeeds because of his own conscience and him who is kept from wrongdoing because of the presence of others.

> *— The Talmud*

441. If I were to try to read, much less answer, all the attacks made on me, this shop might as well be closed for any other business. I do the very best I know how — the very best I can; and I mean to keep doing so until the end. If the end brings me out all right, what is said against me won't amount to anything. If the end brings me out wrong, ten angels swearing I was right would make no difference.

> *— ABRAHAM LINCOLN*

conservative

442. A conservative is one who does not think that anything should be done for the first time.

consistency

443. Calvin Coolidge was once making a speech in a small town in Massachusetts. A small boy in the audience asked his father if he might speak to the President. The father expressed doubt telling his son that he didn't think the President would talk to him. The boy insisted. There was nothing for the father to do but to agree, but in doing so he said he would wager a dollar that the President wouldn't speak three words to him.

The boy took the bet and approached the President saying, "Sir, my father bet me a dollar that you wouldn't speak three words to me."

Mr. Coolidge folded his arms across his chest, and looking down gravely at the lad, slowly replied, "You lose."

consolation

444. It is a consolation to realize that others have troubles just as perplexing and maddening as our own.

445. Mark Twain is reported to have comforted a group of prisoners in a certain jail by saying to them: "If you weren't in this jail, you might be in some other."

contentment

446. O give us the man who sings at his work!

— Thomas Carlyle

447. My God give me neither poverty nor riches; but whatsoever it may be thy will to give, give me with it a heart which knows humbly to acquiesce in what is thy will.

— Gotthold

448. Let us be content in work
To do the thing we can, and not presume
To fret because it's little.

— E. B. Browning

449. Contentment is natural wealth; luxury, artificial poverty.

— Socrates

450. It is right to be contented with what we have, but never with what we are.

— Sir James McIntosh

451. If you do not desire much, little will seem much to you; for small wants give poverty the power of wealth.

— Democritus

452. Discontent is want of self-reliance.

453. The man who has learned to take things as they come, and to let go as they depart, has mastered one of the arts of cheerful and contented living.

454. He is a man of sense who does not grieve for what he has not, but rejoices in what he has.

— Epictetus

455. When we do not find peace of mind in ourselves it is useless to seek it elsewhere.

La Rochefoucauld

456. If things do not turn out as we wish, we should wish for them as they turn out.

— Aristotle

457. The greatest wealth is contentment with a little.

458. Not what we have, but what we enjoy, constitutes our abundance.

— J. Petit-Senn

459. I have observed a number of superficially contented men and women, and I maintain they are dangerous. Personally, I am glad to say there are a lot of things today with which I am not contented. I am not contented with myself, with the development of my character, and with my literary career. And there seems to me very little ground for general contentment. I must repeat — I fear the contented man. I fear him because there is no progress unless there is discontent. Without it today, I even believe, there can be no inner peace of mind.

— John P. Marquand, *Time*

contortionist

460. Contortionist: a guy who can still make both ends meet these days.

control

461. You can't control the length of your life, but
    you can control its width and depth.
You can't control the contour of your
    countenance, but you can control its expression.
You can't control the other fellow's opportunities,
    but you can grasp your own.
You can't control the weather, but you can control
    the moral atmosphere which surrounds you.
You can't control hard times or rainy days,
    but you can bank money now to boost you through both.
Why worry about things you can't control?
    Get busy controlling things that depend on you.

conversation

462. The art of conversation is to be prompt without being stubborn, to refute without argument, and to clothe great matters in motley garb.

— BENJAMIN DISRAELI

463. The man who had learned to share taxis in Washington, D. C. went to Boston. He jumped into a cab with another passenger at the station, sat back with a cheery smile, and, turning to the other passenger, said pleasantly, "My name's Jennings." "Mine," said the Bostonian, coldly, "is not."

464. Many a man gets hot from an over-heated conversation.

465. The true spirit of conversation consists in building on another man's observation, not overturning it. — EDWARD BULWER-LYTTON

466. The art of conversation consists as much in listening as in talking agreeably.

— ATWELL

conviction

467. "I would rather be right than be President."
— HENRY CLAY, Speech,
Missouri Compromise

468. Some people fall for everything and stand for nothing.

cooperation

469. If one man is an expert fisherman, and another an expert at handling a boat, the two working together will catch more than twice as many fish as either working alone. This principle of specializing is important for anyone to understand when he seeks to earn his living.
— JOHN F. WHARTON, *The Theory and Practice of Earning a Living* (Simon & Schuster)

470. A man who keeps his shoulder to the wheel is rarely seen giving others trouble. He's like a mule in the respect that when he's pulling, he can't kick, and when he's kicking, he can't pull.
— REV. ARCHER E. ANDERSON, *It Can Be Done*. Reprinted from *Moody Monthly*. Used by permission.

471. Bees accomplish nothing save as they work together, and neither do men.
— ELBERT HUBBARD

472.   Now this is the law of the jungle,
         As old and as true as the sky;
         And the wolf that shall keep it may prosper,
         And the wolf that shall break it must die.
         As the creeper that circles the tree-trunk,
         So the law runneth forward and back;
         For the strength of the pack is the wolf,
         And the strength of the wolf is the pack.
                              — KIPLING

473. You can employ men and hire hands to work *for* you, but you must win their hearts to have them work *with* you.
— TIORIO

cooperation

474. Help thy brother's boat across, and Lo! thine own has reached the shore.

— Hindu Proverb

475. When one dog barks he soon finds other dogs to bark with him.

— SHEMOTH RABBAH 31:9

476. Freckles: a nice sun tan — if they'd only get together.

477. How extraordinary is the situation of us mortals! Each of us is here for a brief sojourn; for what purpose he knows not, though he sometimes thinks he senses it. But without going deeper than our daily life, it is plain that we exist for our fellow men, in the first place for those upon whose smiles and welfare our happiness depends, and next for all those unknown to us personally but to whose destinies we are bound by the tie of sympathy. A hundred times every day I remind myself that my inner and outer life depend on the labors of other men, living and dead, and that I must exert myself in order to give in the measure as I have received and am still receiving.

— ALBERT EINSTEIN

courage — See also *Fear — Hope — Faith*

478.
They are slaves who fear to speak
for the fallen and the weak;
They are slaves who will not choose
hatred, scoffing and abuse
Rather than in silence shrink
from the truth they needs must think.
They are slaves who dare not be
in the right with two or three.

— JAMES RUSSELL LOWELL

479. There are no hopeless situations; there are only men who have grown hopeless about them.

— CLARE BOOTHE, *Europe in the Spring* (Knopf)

480. Because you have occasional spells of despondency, don't despair. The sun has a sinking spell every night but it rises again all right the next morning.

481. A little boy playing on the deck of a ship in a mighty storm was asked by a passenger if he wasn't afraid. "No, I'm not afraid. My father is the captain of the ship."

> — RUFUS M. JONES, *The Radiant Life* (Macmillan). Used by permission.

482. I reckon among the blessings of my life the preservation of a simple faith. Had I been endowed with greater intellectual powers . . . or if for action I had substituted a habit of speculation, I might have been tossed hither and thither in the winds of strange doctrine. I should have lost the faith of my childhood and gained nothing in exchange. There is something tragic in the spectacle of a man of intellect who has no fixed religious beliefs and wistfully confesses his longing for them.

> — GEORGE WHARTON PEPPER, *A Philadelphia Lawyer* (Lippincott)

483. WHATEVER IS — IS BEST

I know as my life grows older
    And mine eyes have clearer sight —
That under each rank wrong, somewhere
    There lies the root of Right;
That each sorrow has a purpose,
    By the sorrowing oft unguessed,
But as sure as the sun brings morning,
    Whatever is — is best.

I know that each sinful action,
    As sure as the night brings shade,
Is somewhere, sometime punished,
    Tho' the hour be long delayed.
I know that the soul is aided
    Sometimes by the heart's unrest,
And to grow means often to suffer —
    But whatever is — is best.

I know there are no errors
    In the great Eternal plan,
And all things work together
    For the final good of man;
And I know as my soul speeds onward
    In its grand Eternal Quest,
I shall say as I look back earthward,
    Whatever is — is best. — ELLA WHEELER WILCOX

484. LINES FOR A DULL DAY

When the day is dark and gloomy
And the fog obscures your view,
And you feel there is no challenge
Waiting anywhere for you;
When it's routine you must follow
Through a dreary weather chart,
And you feel the hand of duty
Like a millstone on your heart;
Face the skies however darkened,
When you ache to turn away
Do the job that lies before you,
Keep your courage one more day.
You can never guess how often
You affect another's life
By the fact you are a doer
Not a quitter in the strife.

— VINEY WILDER

485. Courage: fear that has said its prayers.

486. One on God's side is a majority.

— WENDELL PHILLIPS

487. COURAGE

Courage! What if the snows are deep,
And what if the hills are long and steep
And the days are short and the nights are long
And the good are weak and the bad are strong.
Courage! The snow is a field of play,
And the longest hill has a well-worn way,
There are songs that shorten the longest night,
There's a day when wrong shall be ruled by right,
So Courage! Courage! 'Tis never so far
From a plodded path to a shining star.

488. After all, there is a time when it is quite fitting and proper to quit a paying job, and it is to the credit of a man if he has the judgment and courage to follow the summons of that inner urge in the face of the world's prejudice. The world would have been the poorer had Robert Louis Stevenson continued his profession of engineer, or Abraham Lincoln stuck to rail splitting, which meant a sure dollar a day.

489. It does not take a very brave dog to bark at the bones of a lion.

490. All problems become smaller if you don't dodge them but confront them. Touch a thistle timidly, and it pricks you; grasp it boldly, and its spines crumble.

— WILLIAM S. HALSEY

491. A disordered life can and should be rearranged and made harmonious. Therefore, do not repress your spirits or lose your courage. All things work according to law, and all things can be made to manifest this law.

courtesy

492. It is said that no one would dare to slap George Washington on the back and address him as "George." Yet he doffed his hat and bowed to an old slave who had first tipped his hat and addressed him, "Good mo'nin', Gen'l Washin'ton." Gen'l Lafayette, who accompanied Washington, asked him why he would bow to a slave. The answer was, "I would not permit him to be a better gentleman than I am."

— CONNOR D. ROSS, "The Ingredients of Good Citizenship," *Outdoor Indiana.*

courts — See *Law*

creative

493. "The whole difference between construction and creation is exactly this: that a thing constructed can only be loved after it is constructed; but a thing created is loved before it exists."

— G. K. CHESTERTON, *Introduction to Dickens*

credit – creditors – debts – debtors

494. "I am sorry I can't pay my instalments this week."
"But you said that last week and the week before."
"Yes, and didn't I keep my word?"

495. A merchant being told he had only a month to live called in a lawyer and said: "Fix it so that my over-draft at the bank goes to my wife — she can explain it. My equity in my car goes to my son. He will then have to work to keep up the payments. Give my good will to the supply houses. They took some awful chances on me and are entitled to something. My equipment you can give to the junkman; he has had his eye on it for several years — and I want six of my creditors for pallbearers. They have carried me so long, they might as well finish the job."

496. The young medico coughed rather gravely.

"I am sorry to tell you," he said slowly, looking down at the very sick man in the bed, "that there is no doubt you are suffering from scarlet fever, and, as you know, it is extremely contagious."

The patient slowly turned his head upon the pillow and looked toward his wife.

"Dearie," he said, in a faint but distinct voice. "If any of my creditors call, you can tell them that at last I am in a position to give them something."

497. The only reason a great many American families don't own an elephant is that they have never been offered an elephant for a dollar down and easy weekly payments.

498. The time to collect a bill is before it gets so large that the debtor never has enough money at one time to pay it.

499. The Chamber of Commerce of the United States some time ago issued a summary of the credit situation under the heading "What Do Bad Debts Cost?" It said:

"Personal credit, or the credit extended by a merchant to his customers, may affect the entire structure of distribution. If a retailer extends credit in a careless manner, he is apt to suffer a great loss and consequently, cannot settle with his jobber. If several retailers dealing with one jobber find themselves in the same predicament, the jobber may go 'on the rocks'; and if many jobbers become insolvent, it spells ruin for some manufacturer. Even the consumer is affected, since he pays higher prices because of these failures."

The trade body pointed out that few retailers investigate why they sustain losses due to bad accounts and said: "In his scramble to outdo his competitors in quantity of business, the retailer often forgets all about quality."

500. George, it seems, was in difficulties. He had loaned a friend $500. He had nothing in writing confirming the loan. The friend proved to be merely friendly. George stood to lose the five hundred. In desperation he consulted his father.

"That's not so hard, George," consoled the father, "write him and say you need the thousand dollars at once."

"You mean the five hundred dollars," George interposed.

"No! I don't. Say a thousand dollars and he will write back he only owes you five hundred. Then you have it in writing."

501. A man struck a match to see whether the gasoline
           tank of his auto was empty. It wasn't.
         A man speeded up to see whether he could beat
           the train to the crossing. He couldn't.
         A man refused credit interchange service, thinking
           he could save money. He didn't.

502. Whenever the first check is received from a new account, a Western credit manager makes a record of the person who signed it; for later, if checks are slow in coming in, he is the person to whom to write; the letter will reach the man with authority to remit. Moreover, collection letters will not be directed to the executive who does the buying.

503. Credit is applied faith. It is the power house of prosperity — the dynamo of business. Credit buys farms and machinery to till them; it builds factories, railroads, business buildings and school houses. By its use men, corporations and nations rise; without it they fall. The measure of credit now used by mankind is the measure of his advance in civilization. Without credit, man would return to the age of barter.

504. It is a strange fact that if you give a man reasonable credit you increase his business with you. But if you give him too much you eventually lose his business altogether to someone else who won't give him any credit at all.

505. A delinquent customer had just wired for another large order to be shipped immediately. The assistant rushed to the credit manager and asked him what he should do.

"Wire him that we can't ship him another order until the last is paid for," said the manager.

The wire was sent and in a few hours this reply came thru. "Cancel the order. I can't wait that long."

506. *Teacher:* "Give an instance of a soul without a body."
Pupil: "An angel."
Teacher: "Now, give an instance of a body without a soul."
Pupil: "A credit man."

507. Mail-Order magnate and philanthropist Julius Rosenwald never had any great trouble with debtors. Whenever a bill was overdue, he would write to the debtor in this wise:

"Your bill is overdue. If not met, we shall be obliged to notify your other creditors that you paid us."

With but few exceptions, a check in full was usually forthcoming posthaste.
— Ray Freedman

508. Credit: a person who can't pay, gets another person who can't pay, to guarantee that he can pay. — Charles Dickens

509. Credit: a commodity that becomes better the less it is used.
— *Coal Dealer*

510. Worried with an accumulation of accounts past due from people who had apparently ceased buying, a credit man sent all of them a bill for more than double the amount owed. The plan proved unusually successful. People who paid no attention to the correct bills wrote, telephoned, or called in person to demand an explanation, giving the credit department an opportunity to apologize for the "mistake," and at the same time to remind the debtor it was high time he paid something on the account. — *American Business*

511. If you say to a debtor, "You will have nothing for yourself but work for me, and pay me all you earn, and earn more and more each year," you will have nothing but a blank. But if you say, "Pay me one half of what you earn, you can have the other half," you leave hope; and hope for the debtor is the main asset in the interest of the creditor.

86

512. A young husband who had agreed to the purchase of a vacuum cleaner protested when he found that his wife had ordered the de luxe model instead of the standard. "But, dear," his wife explained, "it won't cost more. All we have to do is to pay a little longer."

— Readers Digest

credo

513. SOCIAL WORKER'S CREED

1. I respect the dignity of the individual human personality as the basis for all social relationships.
2. I have faith in the ultimate capacity of the common man to advance toward higher goals.
3. I shall base my relations with others on their qualities as individual human beings, without distinction as to race or creed or color or economic or social status.
4. I stand ready to sacrifice my own immediate interests when they conflict with the ultimate good of all.
5. I recognize that my greatest gift to another person may be an opportunity for him to develop and exercise his own capacities.
6. I shall not invade the personal affairs of another individual without his consent, except when in an emergency I must act to prevent injury to him or to others.
7. I believe that an individual's greatest pride as well as his greatest contribution to society, may lie in the ways in which he is different from me and from others, rather than in the ways in which he conforms to the crowd. I shall therefore accept these differences and endeavor to build a useful relationship upon them.
8. I shall always base my opinion of another person on a genuine attempt to understand him — to understand not merely his words, but the man himself and his whole situation and what it means to him.
9. As a first essential to the understanding of others, I shall constantly seek a deeper understanding and control of myself and of my own attitudes and prejudices which may affect my relationships.

— LINTON B. SWIFT, General Director of Family Service Association of America

514. THE ROCKEFELLER CREDO

The ten articles of Mr. Rockefeller's faith are:

I believe in the supreme worth of the individual and in his right to life, liberty and the pursuit of happiness.

I believe that every right implies a responsibility; every opportunity, an obligation; every possession, a duty.

I believe that the law was made for man and not man for the law; that government is the servant of the people and not their master.

I believe in the dignity of labor, whether with head or hand; that the world owes no man a living but that it owes every man an opportunity to make a living.

I believe that thrift is essential to well-ordered living and that economy is a prime requisite of a sound financial structure, whether in government, business or personal affairs.

I believe that truth and justice are fundamental to an enduring social order.

I believe in the sacredness of a promise, that a man's word should be as good as his bond; that character — not wealth or power or position — is of supreme worth.

I believe that the rendering of useful service is the common duty of mankind and that only in the purifying fire of sacrifice is the dross of selfishness consumed and the greatness of the human soul set free.

I believe in an all-wise and all-loving God, named by whatever name, and that the individual's highest fulfillment, greatest happiness and widest usefulness are to be found in living in harmony with His will.

I believe that love is the greatest thing in the world; that it alone can overcome hate; that right can and will triumph over might.

515. THE BUSY MAN'S CREED

I believe in the stuff I am handing out, in the firm I am working for; and in my ability to get results. I believe that honest stuff can be passed out to honest men by honest methods. I believe in working, not weeping; in boosting, not knocking; and in the pleasure of my job. I believe that a man gets what he goes after, that one deed done today is worth two deeds tomorrow, and that no man is down and out until he has lost faith in himself. I believe in today and the work I am doing, in tomorrow and the work I hope to do, and in the sure reward which the future holds.

I believe in courtesy, in kindness, in generosity, in good cheer, in friendship and in honest competition. I believe there is something doing somewhere, for every man ready to do it. I believe I'm ready — *right now!*

— ELBERT HUBBARD

516. "Share your bread with little children, see that no one goes about you with naked feet, look kindly upon mothers nursing their children on the doorstep of humble cottages, walk through the world without malevolence, do not knowingly crush the humblest flower, respect the nests of birds, bow to the purple from afar and to the poor at close range.

"Rise to labor, go to rest with prayer, go to sleep in the unknown, having for your pillow the infinite; love, believe, hope, live, be like him who has a watering pot in his hand, only let your watering pot be filled with good deeds and good words; never be discouraged, be Magus and be father, and if you have lands cultivate them, if you have sons rear them and if you have enemies bless them — all with that sweet and unobtrusive authority that comes to the soul in patient expectation of the eternal dawn."

— *Source Unknown*

crime – delinquency

517. Start them right in high chairs and there will be no criminals for the electric chair.

— *The Adolescent Court and Crime Prevention,* BRILL & PAYNE (Pitman)

518. A career of crime, sociologically conceived, is the culmination of a complex series of inevitable forces at work in the physical and social environment of the individual.

— *The Adolescent Court and Crime Prevention,* BRILL & PAYNE (Pitman)

519. In so far as a definition of delinquency is concerned, it is convenient to accept the interpretation prepared by the Committee on Standard Juvenile Court Laws of the National Probation Association, revised in 1933. This holds that the words "delinquent child" include:

(a) A child who has violated any law of the state or any ordinance or regulation of a subdivision of the state.

(b) A child who by reason of being wayward or habitually disobedient is uncontrolled by his parent, guardian, or custodian.

(c) A child who is habitually truant from school or home.

(d) A child who habitually so deports himself as to injure or endanger the morals or health of himself or others.

> — J. E. JOHNSTONE, Superintendent
> of the State Colony, Woodbine,
> N. J.

520. Juvenile delinquency is nothing more than the fruit which has grown from the seeds of parent delinquency, religious delinquency, educational delinquency, judiciary delinquency and municipal delinquency.

> — DR. VINCENT P. MAZZOLA

521.   DELINQUENCY — CAUSES

1. Breakdown of parental and community control.
2. Poverty.
3. Slum conditions.
4. Mental abnormalties.
5. Emotional instability.
6. Low standard of home and community morals.

522. A girl answered the knock of a young social worker who was making a family survey in the hillbilly country.

"Where are your parents?" asked the agent.

"Mom is in the County Home," the girl replied, "and Pop is in the 'pen.' "

"Have you any brothers or sisters?" the social worker inquired.

"Sis is in the Home for Delinquent Girls; Jo-Jo is in the Reform School, and Spike is at Harvard."

This is a very sad and unusual situation, mused the young man. "Your mother in the county home, your father in the penitentiary, your sister in the home for delinquent girls, one brother in the reform school, and another studying at Harvard?"

"Studying at Harvard," gasped the girl. "He's not studying at Harvard; — they're studying him!"

523. Youths who break under the social and economic pressure of society, lacking the proper moral and ethical training which would have bolstered up their resistance are not to be blamed any more as individuals than is the society which fails to provide the proper training, the proper wholesome conditions for development and a reasonable opportunity for employment and security when the time arrives.

— The Adolescent Court and Crime Prevention, BRILL & PAYNE (Pitman)

524. The finest prison stands as a monument to neglected youth.

525. The unimpassioned judicial attitude of science does not label conduct by opprobrious names but undertakes to understand it and if possible to guide it into useful and successful channels.

526. There is no surer symptom of delinquency in a child than truancy from school.

527. A miniature courtroom installed in one of Brooklyn's public schools — complete with bar, jury box, witness chair and press box — has proved successful in teaching children to appreciate the services of their neighborhood policemen. Children serve on juries to try playmates who have been fighting, climbing fences, or otherwise committing breaches of playground peace. Those found guilty are sent to jail — a rope and wood enclosure — for sentences of from 5 to 45 minutes.

Coming from neighborhoods where the policeman is considered an enemy, these children have learned from their own court that the police are really public servants. They have even formed a make-believe police force, from which it is a disgrace to be dropped for misbehavior.

— N. Y. Herald Tribune

528. Do you remember "Way Back When," before the days of radio, gangster and cowboy stories, we kids got a thrill reading Anderson's Fairy Tales and Gulliver's Travels?

529. One often wonders where mothers learned all about the things they tell their daughters not to do.

530. A small city in North Carolina has a novel plan to combat juvenile delinquency — a "knee pants baseball league." Boys from 10 to 15 years old are eligible and their batting and pitching averages are posted each week so that everyone in town may see what they are doing on the diamond. The youngsters sign contracts providing for regular attendance at Sunday School, requiring them to be home in bed by 10 o'clock and to protect and respect others' personal property.

— Quote

531. Delinquent children are those who have reached the age where they want to do what mama and papa are doing.

— Quote

532. The many studies of exterior conditions or physical states or personal habits which have been or are being made of delinquents are not to the point if they are not interpreted in relation to actual causation of the delinquent's misbehavior. Nothing is any more striking to the careful student than the fact that reactions between personality and living conditions are not fixed and are not a priori predictable. Poverty, in one case a stimulus to formation of fine character tendencies, in another instance is the motivation of even major crimes. Bad neighborhood conditions in some cases result in disgust rather than in acceptance of local standards of morality. Adolescent strivings and aggressiveness may lead in the direction of ambition and fine accomplishment, or may find outlets largely in delinquent trends.

— WILLIAM HEALY, The Practical Value of Scientific Study of Juvenile Delinquents

533. A community is infinitely more brutalized by the habitual employment of punishment than it is by the occasional occurrence of crime . . . the more punishment is inflicted the more crime is produced . . . the less punishment, the less crime. Where there is no punishment at all, crime will either cease to exist, or, if it occurs, will be treated by physicians as a very distressing form of dementia, to be cured by care and kindness. For what are called criminals nowadays are not criminals at all. Starvation, and not sin, is the parent of modern crime.

— OSCAR WILDE

534. The late Dr. George Washington Carver, internationally known Negro scientist, believed there was no such thing as a bad boy, and no such thing as a weed — meaning by weed, any useless vegetation. To him, a weed was something good whose usefulness we humans had not been smart enough to discover. The potato was once thought of as a useless weed, and the tomato was looked upon as something poisonous.

— Quote

535.   Poverty will not alone incite to crime; it depends on who it is who is poor. Of two boys brought up in the same tenement room, one may become a gangster while the other turns into a college professor.

— *Is Germany Incurable?* BRICKNER

536.   He who has never tested jail,
          Lives well within the legal pale,
        While he who's served a heavy sentence,
          Renews the racket, not repentance.

— OGDEN NASH

537.   Because more than nine tenths of the crimes in this country are committed by men, must we conclude that women are better than men — or only cleverer in not getting caught? The explanation is probably that the majority of crimes have to do with getting money — traditionally the masculine function. This theory is further borne out by the fact that more than half of women's crimes are murder or other "crimes of passion." Men are more prone to cold-blooded acts; women have to get good and mad before they break loose.

538.   In men whom men condemn as ill
          I find so much of goodness still;
          In men whom men pronounce divine,
          I find so much of sin and blot
          I do not dare to draw a line
          Between the two, where God has not.

— JOAQUIN MILLER (Written of Byron)

539.   Crime must no longer be defined as an act which is punishable, but as something which demonstrates that the criminal is socially dangerous. "Shall be punished by imprisonment in the penitentiary" must be translated into "Shall be treated in a manner designed to prevent further injurious activity."

— JOHN BARKER WAITE, "Revenge Costs
Too Much." *Harper's Magazine*

540.   JUVENILE COURT
        One wonders what is crime, what ignorance?
        Which lie is truth, which truth a lie, and whether
        Error or doom or accident or chance
        Assembles judge and culprit here together
        In mutual hostility? One wonders

If Age, not Youth, be really here on trial,
And our indifferent generation's blunders
Accomplices, indicted past denial?
Ah well, who cares? Each case is lost or won;
Each earned desert doled out. The clock-hand travels,
And traveling, metes out the verdict years.
Court stands adjourned at last, and, justice done,
His Honor, as the traffic's urge unravels,
Resumes his ride toward home, too tired for tears.
— LISTER ALWOOD

541. Stone walls do not a prison make nor iron bars a cage.
— RICHARD LOVELACE

542. In these days of world chaos we are thinking and talking more and more about democracy and that priceless thing which is part and parcel of it — the freedom of the individual. But acceptance of the rights and importance of the individual as the basic principle of a democratic government carries with it responsibility as well as privilege. We must work to correct — ultimately to prevent — those inequalities in our social system which result in crime. In probation, which is one aspect of the treatment of crime, we concentrate on the personal problems of the unhardened offender in an effort to restore him to good citizenship by skilled and friendly supervision, tapping the resources of the community in his behalf. Such a conservation of human values, such a concept even, is unthinkable in a state dominated by a dictator. Probation is consistent only with the process of a democratic society.
— MARJORIE BELL, *Forum Magazine*

543. Years ago someone said that there was less crime among writers, actors and musicians than in any other profession. It was explained that they were more expressed people — that any number of the facets of human nature came into play in their lives. The routine worker who uses but a part of his mind and none of his emotions is the potential criminal — because he is more apt to explode under pressure.
— MARGERY WILSON, "Are You Too Emotional?" *Woman's Life*

544. In one year (1942) there were eight percent more inmates of prisons, jails, mental institutions, and alms houses than there were students in colleges and universities — 1,777,000 inmates compared with 1,096,000 students.

545. Don't you feel sorry for the rascal who spent years becoming a skilled second-story man — when along came ranch-type houses and put him out of business?

This story is similar to the one about the forger who worked on a victim's signature for months only to have the bank return the check stamped "insufficient funds."

546. FROM A LETTER TO THE EDITOR

"You seem surprised that 'All across the country there is a wave of malicious destruction. Parties are crashed, homes wrecked, people hurt and ruined.' The criminals are kids who operate under the protection of family and friends. They have affluent parents. They are *over*-privileged, not under-privileged."

547. Predisposing factors towards crime and delinquency cited by the author of this volume in an article in The Atlantic Monthly, November 1939, under caption, "I Like Bad Boys" —

1. Lack of proper discipline in home and school.
2. Destructive toys and games.
3. Improper literature.
4. Movies, radio, newspaper comic strips, (now, add television).
5. Alcoholic liquor.
6. Unsupervised groups such as basement or cellar clubs.
7. The automobile.
8. Idleness and unemployment.
9. Improper home conditions.

548. Even toy soldiers should be abolished. We must disarm the nursery!

— DR. PAULINA LUISI

549. Juvenile delinquents: other people's children.

550. A just chastisement may benefit a man, though it seldom does; but an unjust one changes all his blood to gall.

— OUIDA

551. Care should be taken that the punishment does not exceed the guilt; and also that some men do not suffer for offenses for which others are not even indicted.

— CICERO

552. The chief constable of a small English town was also an expert veterinary surgeon. One night his telephone bell rang. "Is Mr. Blank there?" said an agitated voice. Mrs. Blank answered, yes, and inquired: "Do you want my husband in his capacity of veterinary surgeon, or as chief constable?" "Both, madam," came the reply. "We can't get our new bulldog to open his mouth, and — there's a burglar in it."

553. It is safer that a bad man should not be accused, than that he should be acquitted.

— Livy

554. They were taking the prisoner's history on his arrival at the penitentiary. He said he got his first degree at Illinois; he then went to Harvard where he got his second degree, and the Hammond Police gave him the third degree. Asked what was the third degree, he replied: "Professor Quiz with a rubber hose."

555. Corporal punishment falls far more heavily than the most weighty pecuniary penalty.

— Seneca

criticism

556. Criticism is something you can avoid by saying nothing, doing nothing and being nothing.

557. Mr. - - - - writes his plays for the ages — the ages between five and twelve.

— George Jean Nathan

558. A critic is a legless man who teaches running.

— Channing Pollock

559. Criticism takes the cumbersome mass of creative work, and distills it into a finer essence.

— Oscar Wilde

560. Note from an art critic's column: "They couldn't find the artist, so they hung his picture.

—Froth

561. Last night our high-school band played Beethoven. Beethoven lost.

562. Criticism is a study by which men grow important and formidable at very small expense.

— Samuel Johnson

culture

563. That person is cultured who is able to put himself in the place of the greatest number of other persons.

— JANE ADDAMS

564. Culture is the sum of all the forms of art, of love and of thought which, in the course of centuries, have enabled man to be less enslaved.

— ANDRE MALRAUX

curiosity

565. "They say that bright eyes indicate curiosity."
"Yes, so do black eyes."

566. A small boy came hurriedly down the street, and halted breathlessly in front of a stranger who was walking in the same direction.
"Have you lost half a dollar?" he asked.
"Yes, yes, I believe I have!" said the stranger, feeling in his pockets. "Have you found one?"
"Oh, no," said the boy. "I just want to find out how many have been lost today. Yours makes fifty-five."

567. A woman visitor to the London Zoo asked a keeper whether the hippopotamus was a male or a female.
"Madam," replied the keeper sternly, "that is a question that should be of interest only to another hippopotamus."

— JULIAN HUXLEY, Secretary,
Zoological Society of London

568. The encouragement of intellectual curiosity is not like pouring water into a vessel. It's like watering and feeding a plant. The plant takes in nourishment and grows according to its own nature. So does the mind.

— FRANK N. FREEMAN

cynicism

569. Cynic: one who looks down on those above him.

customs

570. Of all the good-byes I have heard, the Japanese sayonara — "Since it must be so" — is the most beautiful. Unlike "Auf Wiedersehen" and "Au Revoir," it does not try to cheat itself by having any bravado "Till we meet again," any sedative to postpone the pain of separation. It does not evade the issue like "Farewell," which is a father's good-bye — "go out into the world and do well, my son." It is encouragement and admonition, but it passes over the significance of the moment; of parting it says nothing. "Good-bye" and "Adios" say too much; they try to bridge distance, almost to deny it. Good-bye is a prayer: "You must not go — I cannot bear to have you go! But you shall not go alone, unwatched. God will be with you." But sayonara says neither too little nor too much; it is a simple acceptance of fact. All understanding of life lies in its limits; all emotion, smoldering, is banked up behind it. It is the unspoken good-bye, the pressure of a hand, "sayonara."

> — Adapted from *North to the Orient,* copyright 1935, by ANNE MORROW LINDBERGH. Reprinted by permission of the author and Harcourt, Brace and Company, Inc.

571. The position of the geisha girl in Japanese society has baffled the minds of many westerners.

Geisha means "accomplished one." Her calling is ancient and honorable. Girls between 15 and 21 are paid — and paid well — to be entertaining and amusing at parties. To sing, to dance the oriental posture dances, to converse, to make tea gracefully and serve sake is her vocation. For the Japanese she takes the place of chorus girls and night club hostesses, but she is superior to them in education, training, and culture.

572. While Thanksgiving Day in its present form is a distinctively American holiday, it did not spring minerva-like from the brain of Governor Bradford in 1621, as some imagine.

On the contrary, we may trace its origin back through the ages and nations to the land of the Canaanites from whom the children of Israel copied many of their customs.

The vintage or harvest celebration appeared later among Hebrews as an act of worship to Jehovah and was called the Feast of Tabernacles, because everyone lived in booths or tents during the festival in memory of the years when the nation had no settled home.

The Romans worshipped this harvest diety under the name of Ceres. Her festival which occurred yearly on October 4th was called the Cerelia. It began with a fast among the common people who offered her a sow and the first cuttings of the harvest.

There were processions in the fields with music and rustic sports and the ceremonies ended with the inevitable feast of Thanksgiving.

In England the autumnal festival was called the Harvest Home which may be traced back to the Saxons of the time of Egbert.

And in so being in the blood of America's first settlers, the custom reappeared early in our land.

— Source Unknown

573. Japanese musical show programs usually contain the name, address and telephone number of every girl in the chorus.

— Readers Digest

574. A white youth in Hawaii, seeking the advice of an older Japanese man as to his courtship of a Japanese woman, asked: "Will she object to my color?"

"Not to your color," was the reply, "but perhaps to your ancestry."

"Why, what's wrong with my ancestry?"

"Well, according to your traditions, you are descended from a monkey; while according to her traditions, she is descended from the sun goddess."

— CLIFFORD GESSLER, Hawaii: Isles of Enchantment, copyright, 1937, D. Appleton-Century Co., Inc.

575. A Chinese visitor says: "Funny people, you Americans. You take a glass, put in sugar to make it sweet, and lemon to make it sour. You put in gin to warm you up, and ice to keep you cool. You say, "Here's to you!" and then you drink it yourself."

— Quote

576. In 1830 an American on his way to Constantinople from Berlin rode through territory in which hundreds of acres of roses were grown, the rose blossoms to be made later into "attar of roses," the Turk's favorite perfume.

Hundreds of Turkish women were at work in those rose fields gathering the blossoms. Their entire costume was one skirt, hanging from the waist down, nothing else whatever. As the man on horseback, the "Giaour," which is the Turkish name for Christian, came in sight, each modest Mohammedan lady stopped picking her roses, reached down with both hands, and lifted her petticoat up over her head, that the face might not be seen.

dancing

577. Those who perform the modern dances exercise about everything except discretion.

578. Hula Dancer: a shake in the grass.
— *Wall Street Journal*

579. Rhumba: a fox trot with the backfield in motion.

death — See also *Life*

580. Grant but memory to us, and we lose nothing by death.
— WHITTIER, *My Summer with Dr. Singleton*

581. It has always seemed to me a major tragedy that so many people go through life haunted by the fear of death — only to find when it comes that it's as natural as life itself. For very few are afraid to die when they get to the very end. In all my experience only one seemed to feel any terror — a woman who had done her sister a wrong which it was too late to right.

Something strange and beautiful happens to men and women when they come to the end of the road. All fear, all horror disappears. I have often watched a look of happy wonder dawn in their eyes when they realized this was true. It is all part of the goodness of nature and, I believe, of the illimitable goodness of God.
— A Veteran Nurse, *The American Magazine*

debt – debtor — See also *Credit — Creditor*

582. Vacation: a trip to put you in the pink — and leave you in the red!

583. Debts: the certain outcome of an uncertain income.

584. The only thing that doesn't become smaller when it is contracted is a debt.

585. Take from the bad debtor, even if it is only a stone.
— *Arabian Proverb*

586. One day Jo Davidson, the sculptor, handed me a check, saying, "I thought you might need it." I did need it badly, and having some prospects of repaying it, I accepted. Jo went on, "In my struggling days in Paris, a rich friend financed me for a year. A long time afterward, when I had plenty of money, I invited him to lunch and he brought up the question of the debt. I said, 'No sir, I have no intention of paying you. I have passed on many times that amount to struggling youngsters. Loans to young artists should not be repaid — they should be passed on'." Jo paused and looked at me. "Orrick, you can do the same with this money!"
— ORRICK JOHNS, *Time of our Lives*

587. By the time father gets the vacation bills paid it will be time to think about the Christmas presents.

588. He who wants Lent to seem short should contract a debt to be repaid at Easter.
— *Italian Proverb*

deceit

589. We are inclined to believe those whom we do not know, because they have never deceived us.
— SAMUEL JOHNSON, *The Idler*

decisions

590. When War Mobilizer James F. Byrnes submitted his resignation to President Roosevelt, he told the press this story to illustrate how he felt:

"A South Carolina farmer hired a man to dig post-holes. The fellow cleaned up the job in jig time, came back next day and cleared stumps in record order.

The third day the farmer rewarded him with an easy job — sorting good and bad potatoes. After about three hours the chap fainted. Revived, he exclaimed:

"Oh, the job was easy enough — but those damn decisions just mowed me down!"

delay

591.   Dare to be wise; begin! He who postpones the hour of living rightly is like the rustic who waits for the river to run out before he crosses.

— HORACE

592.   There is an imaginary person who seeks a permanent home in your ledger. He is Mr. Procrastination.

He goes through your books each month, ruthlessly striking out your profit here and there. He puts his mark on a page and it withers.

He whispers, "Don't turn that account over — he's all right — try one more letter — wait!" and by these tactics piles up a loss at the end of the year that eats a tremendous hole in your dividends.

deletion

593.   Editor's Choice: On one occasion the delicate Boston Transcript's standing injunction against any reference to anatomy in its columns was ignored by a reporter who used the word "navel" in an article. The edition was already running before the managing editor spotted it. He stopped the presses with a stern order to chisel out the offensive word. Unhappily he had not had time to read the full context. The Transcript appeared on the streets that evening with the sinister information that a concert musician had been "in a state of repose as complete as that of a Buddhist regarding his   ."

— CLEVELAND AMORY, *The Proper Bostonians* (Dutton)

delinquency — See *Crime*

democracy

593a.   Let us show ourselves Americans by showing that we do do not want to go off in separate camps or grounds by ourselves, but that we want to co-operate with all other classes and all other groups in a common enterprise which is to release the spirits of the world from bondage — That is the meaning of democracy.

— WOODROW WILSON

594. Let us remember that it takes both the white and black keys of the piano to play the Star-Spangled-Banner.

> — DR. FRANK P. GRAHAM, addressing Southern Conference for Human Welfare.

595. Democracy is a small hard core of common agreement, surrounded by a rich variety of individual difference.

596. Democracy is based upon the conviction that there are extraordinary possibilities in ordinary people.

> — HARRY EMERSON FOSDICK

597. Theodore Roosevelt, in advocating physical training for young men, said of military training camps: "Next to the public school, the military tent, where boys sleep side by side, will go down in our history as the greatest agent of health and democracy."

598.   THE HIGHEST DEMOCRACY

> For they have finished to begin
>   And greater things they do —
> Who came so far to die so young
>   And live again in you.

> — DR. DANIEL A. POLING

599. Somewhere in this plot of ground there may lie the man who could have discovered the cure for cancer. Under one of these Christian crosses, or beneath a Jewish Star of David, there may rest now a man who was destined to be a great prophet . . . Now they lie here silently in this sacred soil, and we gather to consecrate this earth to their memory . . . Here lie officers and men, Negroes and whites, rich men and poor . . . Here are Protestants, Catholics and Jews . . . Here no man prefers another because of his faith, or despises him because of his color. Here there are no quotas of how many from each group are admitted or allowed. Theirs is the highest and purest democracy. Any man among us, the living, who . . . lifts his hand to hate against a brother, or thinks himself superior to those who happen to be in the minority, makes of this ceremony and of the bloody sacrifice it commemorates, an empty, hollow mockery.

> — CHAPLAIN ROLAND B. GITTELSOHN, dedicating 5th Marine Division Cemetery on Iwo Jima

600. The fundamental truth of democracy is that the real pleasures of life are increased by sharing them. — HENRY DWIGHT

601. Democracy becomes a government of bullies tempered by editors. — RALPH WALDO EMERSON

602. Democracy is that form of society, no matter what its political classification, in which every man has a chance and knows that he has it.

603. Democracy: a state of mind in which every man is as good as every other man, provided he really is.

despair

604. There is no despair so absolute as that which comes with the first moments of our first great sorrow, when we have not yet known what it is to have suffered and be healed, to have despaired and to have recovered hope. — GEORGE ELIOT

destiny

605. Go straight ahead, you can't dodge destiny.

determination

606.   IT CAN BE DONE

Somebody said that it couldn't be done,
    But he with a chuckle replied,
That "maybe it couldn't" but he would be one
    Who wouldn't say so till he'd tried.
So he buckled right in with the trace of a grin
    On his face. If he worried, he hid it.
He started to sing as he tackled the thing
    That couldn't be done. And he did it.

Somebody scoffed: "Oh, you'll never do that,
    At least no one ever has done it."
But he took off his coat and took off his hat
    And the first thing he knew he'd begun it.

With the lift of his chin and a bit of a grin,
    If any doubt rose he forbid it;
He started to sing as he tackled the thing
That couldn't be done, and he did it.

There are thousands to tell you it cannot be done,
    There are thousands to prophesy failure;
There are thousands to point out to you, one by one,
    The dangers that wait to assail you,
But just buckle right in with a bit of a grin,
    Then take off your coat and go to it.
Just start in to sing as you tackle the thing
    That cannot be done, and you'll do it.

— Source Unknown

607.   Consider the postage stamp my son: Its usefulness consists in its ability to stick to one thing until it gets there.

— Josh Billings

608.   Emulate the pin. Its head keeps it from going too far.

609.   They can conquer who believe they can.

— John Dryden

610.   Holding a strong position often arouses strong opposition.

611.   The world makes way for a resolute soul; obstacles get out of the path of a determined man who believes in himself.

dictatorship

612.   Dictatorship: a place where public opinion can't even be expressed privately.

— Walter Winchell

613.   Dictatorship: a system of government where everything that isn't forbidden is obligatory.

614.   Many of the greatest tyrants on the records of history have begun their reigns in the fairest manner. But this unnatural power corrupts both the heart and the understanding.

— Edmund Burke

diet — See also *Food*

615. Adversity: the only diet that will reduce a fat head.

616. An adult is one who has stopped growing except in the middle.

dilemma

617. *Shear Nonsense:* A New York merchant came into his office looking haggard and wan from persistent insomnia. "Count sheep, advised his partner. "It's the best known cure."

The next morning the merchant looked more bleary-eyed than ever. "I counted up to 50,000," he told his partner. "Then I sheared the sheep and made up 50,000 overcoats. Then came the problem that kept me awake all the rest of night: Where could I get 50,000 linings?"

diplomacy

618. Diplomat: a man who has learned that you can't bend a nail by hitting it squarely on the head.

619. Diplomacy: lying in state.

620. Diplomacy: the art of letting someone else have your own way.

621. Diplomat: a gent who thinks twice before he says nothing.

622. A diplomat is a man who remembers a woman's birthday but forgets her age.

623. I have discovered the art of fooling diplomats; I speak the truth and they never believe me.

— BENSO DI CAVOUR

direction

624. One ship drives east and another drives west
With selfsame winds that blow;

It's the set of the sails and not the gales
   That tells them where to go.

Like the winds of the sea are the winds of fate,
   As we voyage along through life;
It's the set of the soul that decides its goal,
   And not the calm or the strife.

disagreement

625.   One should learn to disagree without becoming disagreeable.

disappointment

626.   DISAPPOINTMENT

I'll not send little girls to school,
Blue ribbons on their hair;
I'll not warn little boys to watch
For fear their pants will tear.

I'll never fill a cookie jar
With spicy, fragrant things
And know a whispered secret,
Or a round, red mouth that clings.

Or hum a snatch of lullabies
When heads begin to nod,
And figure how to buy new shoes —
I wanted to, though, God!

                    — HELEN WELSHIMER

627.   When we do not succeed our friends are disappointed in us; but when we do they are annoyed.   — STEPHEN HUGUENOT

628.   Cheesecake: a magazine with a beautiful girl on the cover — and no cover on the girl.

629.   "Johnny," said his mother, "change your clothes, and be sure your face and hands are clean this afternoon. I'm expecting your auntie to tea."

"But," complained the astute Johnny, not moving, "What if she doesn't come?"

630. The wife of the poet Louis Untermeyer delights in telling this about her talented spouse: "We went to a costume party one night. Louis was looking his silliest in a paper hat, tooting a horn for nobody's particular benefit, when a young college girl walked up to him, looked him up and down and turned on her heel with: "Huh! And you're Required Reading!"

— NEAL O'HARA, *N. Y. Post*

discipline

631. When the archaeologists were digging in the ruins of Nineveh they came upon a library of plaques containing the laws of the realm. One of the laws reads, in effect, that anyone guilty of neglect would be held responsible for the result of his neglect. . . . If you fail to teach your child to obey, if you fail to teach him to respect the property rights of others, *you and not he* are responsible for the result of your neglect.

— WILLIAM TAIT, *Is It Juvenile or Adult Delinquency?*

632. I can still give my child the discipline of hard work. True, there are no longer rails to split or woodboxes to keep full. But the regular responsibility of watering the flowers, weeding the garden, mowing the lawn, feeding the pup or shining family shoes is a fair substitute. Shoveling a path thru a tall snowdrift can teach modern young fry all the virtues of pioneering which strengthened our forefathers and helped mold their firm character.

— CONSTANCE J. FOSTER, *Things I Can Give My Child*

633. Small boy on being disciplined: "Don't say must, mother, It makes me feel *won't* all over."

discouragement

634. It is a healthy symptom when a man is dissatisfied without being discouraged.

— ROY L. SMITH

635. Do not lay things too much to heart. No one is really beaten unless he is discouraged.

— LORD AVEBURY

636. Don't get discouraged — it's often the last key in the bunch that opens the lock.

discovery

637. And what is a weed? A plant whose virtues have not been discovered.

— RALPH WALDO EMERSON

discretion

638. Never get into a squirting match with a skunk! ! !

discrimination – bigotry – intolerance – prejudice and tolerance

639. The most lovable quality any human being can possess is *tolerance*. It is the vision that enables one to see things from another's viewpoint. It is the generosity that concedes to others the right to their own opinions and peculiarities. It is the bigness that enables us to let people be happy in their own way instead of our way.

640. One of her boys . . . came running home shouting "I saw a big negro and I threw a stone at him." Mama took him to the window and asked, "Do you remember the snow you saw when it was winter? How white it was and how it covered everything? It came from heaven and it lay over all things, and you said, 'The world is white: there's nothing but snow.' And, then as you looked thru this same window when spring began to creep in, you saw patches of brown earth like small hands reaching up to God also, and the ground was no longer white. Did God make only the white snow? Did he not make the brown earth also, son?"

> — RAYMOND FORER, "Little Girl,"
> in *Common Ground*, Morris S.
> Lazaron (Liveright)

641. Equality is a thing which should not be demanded, because it cannot be granted; it has to be earned. No Utopian dreamer can achieve it for another man. You can't drink from the spring high on the mountain unless you climb for the water. If the Negro wants equality, except for opportunity, he must pay for it, and the unalterable price is character and achievement.

> — C. C. SPAULDING, Pres., North Carolina Mutual Insurance Co., most successful Negro insurance company in the U. S.

642. A distinguished social psychologist once told of a class he polled in a western university, about the time of the Armenian trouble, to determine among other things the title for "the worst race." The Turks won handily. Then he asked how many had ever known a Turk. No one had.

> — LYLE OWEN, "An Ozarker and the Jews," *Common Ground*, by Morris S. Lazaron (Liveright)

643. The University of Alabama was on the War Department's list of approved schools giving correspondence courses to men in the armed forces. A Negro soldier in the Pacific applied for enrollment in a course that was not offered by any other school on the list. But the university refused to accept a Negro student even by mail.

> — *The Nation*

644. In the closing days of the war in Europe, 175 Yank prisoners — Catholic and Protestant — gave Nazi captors a lesson in Americanism.

The word got around that Jewish soldiers in the group of American prisoners were to be separated from others and assigned to a special, back-breaking labor detail. The boys talked it over; the Jewish soldiers, about 75 in number, urged their buddies not to stick their necks out. But the following morning the Kommandant rasped: "Achtung! All prisoners of Jewish blood advance one pace forward." And 250 Americans stepped out!

> — *New York Daily Mirror*

645. The history of persecution is a history of endeavors to cheat nature, to make water run up hill, to twist a rope of sand. It makes no difference whether the actors be many or one, a tyrant or a mob.

> — EMERSON, *Essay on Compensation*

646. One American political campaign after another has been marred by low appeals to racial and religious prejudice. Many religious conservatives opposed Taft in 1908 because he was a Uni-

tarian. The rumor was circulated in 1920 that Harding was part
Negro. The 1928 political campaign let loose a tidal wave of anti-
Catholic prejudice and charges that Washington was already "packed"
with Catholic appointees. In 1936 and 1940 American fascists tried
to sell the country the idea that the New Deal was "packed" with
Jews. Base appeals to bigotry have been all too common in lesser
political campaigns over the years.

647.   "Shall I ask the brave soldier, who fights by
      my side
    In the cause of mankind, if our creeds agree?
      Shall I give up the friend I have valued and
      tried,
    If he kneel not before the same altar with me?
      From the heretic girl of my soul should I fly,
    To seek somewhere else a more orthodox kiss?
      No, perish the hearts, and the laws that try
    Truth, valor, or love by a standard like this!"

648.   The John C. Winston Publishing Co. of Philadelphia some
years ago, decided to eliminate from its dictionaries all words that
are used as uncomplimentary epithets in referring to different races
and nationalities. Among such words are nigger, coon, dago, wop,
etc. That decision sounds very good and we commend the spirit
of it. But the dictionary does not create words or build a vocabulary.
Words get into the dictionary because they have come into the
language. To get rid of them we must begin at the beginning, not
with the words themselves, but with the ideas that the words are
intended to express. If a man has an ugly idea he will eventually
find a word to express it.   — Editorial, *Religious Telescope*

649.   The test of courage comes when we are in the minority;
the test of tolerance comes when we are in the majority.
        — REV. RALPH W. SOCKMAN

650.   This is the truth which you shall find;
    Good flourishes in all mankind,
    And soon or late some evil man
    Disgraces every sect and clan.
    Be not deceived by form or creed.
    Some bad appears in every breed;

discrimination, bigotry, intolerance, etc.

> But Gentile, Jew, nor brown, nor white
> By birth alone are wholly right.
> My son, despise not race or clan;
> Pass judgment only on the man.
> Make friends or enemies by deeds,
> Never by boundaries or creeds.
> — EDGAR A. GUEST

651. The civil and religious rights of all American groups are assured only by the fact that every group enjoys them in equal measure. The rights of all are endangered when the rights of any one are circumscribed or taken away. Hatred and deprivation of human rights spread like a forest fire. After one group is destroyed, another becomes the next victim. Every group jealous of its rights and prerogatives should join with the others to restore the rights of any group receiving unjust treatment. In so doing, justice is being served and all groups are safe-guarding themselves from tyranny at a future date. — *Source Unknown*

652. The dominant political, social or economic group in a country sometimes proves so selfish and unreasonable in its attitude toward the poverty of the common people that revolt threatens. This danger can be averted in one of two ways; either by granting the desired social and economic reforms, or by turning the wrath of the people against some small minority group in the nation. The dominant classes may be unwilling to adopt the first solution for fear that their position of privilege will be jeopardized. Therefore, they adopt the second. They initiate, by means of their wealth and control of the channels of public opinion, a savage campaign of vilification against some small out-group. This out-group must be partially successful economically. It must be small in numbers. It must be unpopular because of its differences in matters of religion, dress, or custom. A striking example of this was the pogroms against the Jews under the Czars in the late 19th and early 20th centuries.
— *Source Unknown*

653. When a minority becomes a majority, and seizes authority, it hates a minority.

654. A small group is often persecuted for its virtues rather than its weaknesses. Through hard work, imagination and application

112

of sound methods, members of minority groups often render important social and economic service to society. And usually they profit accordingly. Less capable and diligent individuals within the majority group justify their own failures by ascribing the success of their competitors to chicanery, unethical business practice and bad faith. Sometimes they carry this propaganda to the explosive point, and the successful among the minority group are ham-strung by discriminative legislation, or are eliminated by violent means. This, of course, is a policy of nihilism which retards the progress and achievement of the entire nation.

— *Source Unknown*

655. In times of prosperity or economic expansion minority groups are seldom disturbed. They are even invited in to help develop an expanding economy, as in the case of Holland in the 16th century, Poland in the 17th, American frontiers in the 19th century, American industrial centers in the 20th. With the coming of depression, however, the minority groups begin to suffer. Their economic success is resented, especially by those who are on the brink of bankruptcy. Attempts are made to eliminate them from the business, professional, or labor fields, to insure the position or the jobs of those who eliminate them.

— *Source Unknown*

656. Every group is self-conscious and preserves its own tradition and history. It recalls most vividly its heroism in the past, its achievements and its unjust sufferings. On the other hand, it tends to gloss over or completely forget its cruelties against others and the blood it has shed. Group memory is a powerful force. Inasmuch as oceans of blood have been spilled in the past by Protestants, Catholics and Jews in their relations one with another, and inasmuch as each group retains in its memory the injustices it has suffered without always tempering that memory with the recognition of the injustices it has inflicted, present day Protestant-Catholic-Jewish relations are made more difficult. There can be no question that events of the past create social distance and distrust in the present. For instance, Franco-German relations have been beclouded in the twentieth century by the memory of what each nation has inflicted on the other in past centuries.

— *Source Unknown*

657. There is a legend that came out of Germany in the dark days of Jewish persecution. A pastor, acting on Nazi orders, said to his congregation, "All of you who had Jewish fathers will leave and not return." A few worshippers rose and slipped out.

The pastor said, "Now all of you who had Jewish mothers must go and not return." Again a few of the worshippers left. Then all those who remained turned pale, for the Figure on the crucifix above the altar loosed itself and left the sanctuary.

— *Southern Churchman*

658. If we were to select the most intelligent, imaginative, energetic, and emotionally stable third of mankind, all races would be represented.

— Franz Boas, *Anthropology & Modern Life*

659. "Race" is the cheap explanation tyros offer for any collective trait that they are too stupid or too lazy to trace to its origin in the physical environment, the social environment, or the historical environment.

— E. A. Ross, *Social Psychology*

660. Of all the possible modes for interpreting history (climate, geographical resources, economics, cultural diffusion and the like) that of race has the greatest popular appeal. If the leading civilizations of the past are believed to have decayed through infusions of "inferior" blood, it is comforting to be under the delusion that the civilization of our own race may be automatically maintained by the simple expedient of group inbreeding.

661. EFFECTS OF PREJUDICE ON ITS VICTIMS

1. Disastrous psychological consequences. Consciousness of being universally judged to be inferior leads to loss of self-respect, which in turn often brings about loss of a sense of responsibility to society.
2. Makes life hard, bitter, devoid of opportunity and emptied of the joy of living.
3. In some it incites to violence.
4. Others are sorely tempted to skate close to the edge of the law, or actually commit crime to find their livelihood.
5. Destroys initiative and impairs the creative and inventive aptitudes.

662. Every group is extremely jealous of its ego. Therefore it refuses to accept responsibility for failure no matter how overwhelming the evidence. Someone else must bear the blame. In our day

of grossly exaggerated nationalism, minority groups within strongly nationalistic states are in an extremely precarious position, for without fail they are blamed for everything that goes wrong. The majority group does not have to be convinced by plausible evidence of the responsibility of the minority group. Rather, it wants to be convinced, and will reward the demagogue who supplies "evidence," no matter how ludicrous.
— JAMES G. MCDONALD

663. Minority groups impeded by discriminations usually apply themselves more diligently than the more secure dominant group. They must be "twice as good to get half as far."

664. The persecuted people of today will yet stand at the grave of their persecutors.
— *Source Unknown*

665. The last decade has written large what we Christians have long known, that anti-Semitism is anti-Christianity. This anti-Semitic appeal is a long studied insult to Christ who taught love for all men, Jew and Gentile alike. This un-American racism would place our Christian creed below the level of our nation's constitutional creed. The Christianity that gave birth to America must not now become a scandal to Americanism. Christians dare not repeat the mistake of German Christians who failed to speak forth their condemnation clearly and unequivocally when this evil first raised its head in that unhappy land.
— *Statement signed by 700 Protestant clergymen and educators.* (Published in *The Protestant Digest.*)

666. Bismark once remarked to Disraeli: "The Germans have just bought a new country in Africa where Jews and pigs will be tolerated."

Disraeli, without hesitation replied: "Fortunately we are both here."

667. Whenever someone with prejudices speaks up against a group attacking Jews, Italians, or Negroes, there is usually someone else who comes up with a classic line of defense. "Look at Einstein!" "Look at Toscanini!"

They mean well, these defenders. But their approach is wrong — What a minority group wants is not the right to have geniuses among them but the rights to have fools and scoundrels — without being condemned as a group. Every group has about the same proportion

115

of wrongdoers. But when wrongdoers belong to a minority their number is magnified in the minds of other people. Minorities would gladly give up the reflected glory of their great men, if only the world didn't burden them with the ignominy of their scoundrels.

> — LIBBY BENEDICT, "The Right to Have Scoundrels," *Saturday Review of Literature*

668. A friend in London once confided in me that he had never spent a holiday on the Continent because "they drive on the wrong side of the street." Not "on the right side, while we drive on the left," mind you, but "on the *wrong* side." I've often related this as an illustration of instinctive intolerance, but it's even more an instance of how firmly our habits become fixed, and how much we are troubled by the need of setting them aside.

> — CHANNING POLLOCK, "Is All This Really Necessary," *The Rotarian*

669. When a group or nation falls on evil days, it seeks an over-simplified explanation of its difficulties. Moreover, it refuses to blame itself, but casts about for some small out-group on which to heap all the blame. Thus, the early Christians were blamed for the burning of Rome in Nero's day; the English Catholics were blamed for the fire of London in 1666; the German Jews were said to have stabbed the army in the back and caused Germany's loss of the World War. Today the French Masons and liberals are blamed for France's swift and terrible defeat in 1940.

670. Where a community or nation has a dominant majority, this larger group is often tempted to force similarity of habit and conduct on smaller groups which follow other practices. Only a democratic society has reasonably succeeded in keeping a majority group urge in check.

671. There is no Breton race, but a Breton people.
There is no French race, but a French nation.
There is no Aryan race, but Aryan languages.
There is no Latin race, but a Latin civilization.

> — MARCEL BOULE, quoted by John LaFarge, S. J., *Interracial Justice*

672. Hegel once said, "We learn from history that we learn nothing from history." Present attempts to achieve a radical solution of cultural diversity only repeat the errors of the past. No group of any size can be eliminated in toto by violence. No minority can be driven from a country without irretrievable loss to that country's social, economic, scientific and political life. When attempts are made to assimilate a group by force, the more fiercely self-conscious of its own identity the group becomes. History teaches us that the problems of human relations are not solved but only aggravated by the use of violent methods. It is up to us to act upon the lessons of history.

673. The blindest prejudice of all the pre-judgments that have driven men to brutality is the prejudice with respect to race. When men are prejudiced, they are not just. When there is no justice, there can be no enduring peace.

674. When you hear a man say, "I hate," adding the name of some race, nation, religion, or social class, you are dealing with a belated mind. That man may dress like a modern, ride in an automobile, listen over the radio, but his mind is properly dated about 1000 B.C.
— HARRY EMERSON FOSDICK

675. In 1790, George Washington, then recently elected as first President of the United States, visited the Jewish synagogue in Newport, and in response to the official reception of the Jewish community, later wrote: "For happily the government of the United States which gives to bigotry no sanction, to persecution no assistance, requires only that they who live under its protection shall demean themselves as good citizens."

676. Prejudice: being down on something you're not up on.

677. Civilization is just a slow process of getting rid of our prejudices.

678. What cannot be cured must be endured.
— FRANCOIS RABELAIS

679. The unpardonable sin in a person of a different race or religion from ours is to be smarter than we are.

dissatisfaction

680. Nearly every man in the city wants a farm until he gets it.

681. *Father:* "What do you want now — haven't I just set your husband up in business?"
Married Daughter: "Yes, but George wants you to buy him out!"

682. What a fool he must be who thinks that his El Dorado is anywhere but where he lives.

— H. D. THOREAU

divorce — See *Marriage*

doctors — medicine

683. An old time practising physician whose son had just graduated from medical school was anxious to be helpful in starting him off in practice. His first bit of advice was to the effect that while it was all right to make use of "those new-fangled methods" in making diagnoses, it was still best to rely upon careful bedside observation in order to arrive at accurate conclusions.

He suggested that his son accompany him while he was making his hospital "rounds." The first patient they called on was advised by the father to cut down on his smoking. Bewildered, the son asked the father how he managed to come to that conclusion after so limited an examination.

"Just look around the room and observe the large number of cigarette ashes and cigarette "butts' " was his answer.

In like manner the second patient was directed to stop eating so much candy, and again the new practitioner was bewildered. "How come?" he asked. "You didn't look," observed the father, "for if you had, you would have noticed all the candy boxes all over the room." "I think I've got the idea," said the son, "Let me try this technique on the next patient."

The third room held a woman patient. Following the procedure he had observed, the son came up with the suggestion that the patient cut down on her interest in things involving the Church. It was now the senior's turn to express amazement. On leaving the room he asked his son what it was that led him to his conclusion, since the Church had not been mentioned in his conversation with the patient, and careful scrutiny of things around the room had given him no clue which might justify the diagnosis made by the son. "Well, Dad, I'll tell you, it was like this," said the son. "Didn't you observe that I dropped the thermometer? When I bent down to pick it up, I couldn't help noticing the preacher under the bed."

684. A doctor examining an attractive new patient carefully, beamed, "Mrs. Atherton, I've got good news for you."

The patient said, "Pardon me, it's Miss Atherton."

"Oh," said the doctor. "Well, Miss Atherton, I've got bad news for you."

685. A doctor, picking up his car at a garage, was highly indignant at the size of the repair bill. "All this for a few hours' work!" he yelped. "Why, you charge more for your work than we of the medical profession do!"

"Well now," drawled the mechanic, "the way I look at it, we got it coming to us. You guys have been working on the same old model since time began, but we gotta learn a brand-new model every year."

— Readers Digest

686. *Socialized medicine:* A man went for treatment and found himself in a room with two doors; one marked Chronic, the other, Acute. He knew his condition was acute so he went through that door and found himself in a room with two doors: One marked: Above the Waist, the other: Below the Waist. He entered the former and found himself in a room with two doors. One was marked Republican; the other, Democrat. He went through the one marked Republican and found himself out on the street.

687. *Patient:* "Doctor, isn't it somewhat out of your way to visit me here?"

Doctor: "Not too bad. I have another patient nearby so I'll kill two birds with one stone."

688. *Doctor:* "Above all, you must not worry. When a worry comes along just throw it aside."

Patient: "Right. I'll remember that when your bill comes along."

689. A doctor's telephone rang one night, awakening him from fitful slumber. It was one of his regular patients, a young man in a wild state of alarm. "My wife, Doctor!" he shouted. "It's her appendix. You'd better come around quick!"

The doctor sighed and told the young man to go back to bed. "Give her some bicarbonate or ginger ale, and I'll look in tomorrow," he said. "She doesn't have appendicitis."

The husband became even wilder, insisting that she did too have appendicitis. "Well, she can't have!" the doctor shouted. "I took her appendix out three years ago, and I never heard of anyone having two appendixes."

"Ever hear of anybody having two wives?" the young man asked bitterly.

The doctor went around right away and it was a good thing he did, because the second wife did have appendicitis.

— By permission. Copyright, 1939.
The New Yorker Magazine, Inc.

690. "Where's the undertaker's office?" asked a Nebraska farmer, as he halted his flivver at the curb.

"What's the matter, Bill, somebody dead?" asked a bystander.

"No, but my wife's awful sick," replied the farmer.

"Man, you want a doctor, not an undertaker."

"I know what I want," said the farmer, "I belong to the Nebraska Farmers' Union, and we're cutting out the middle man."

691. "Did your husband die a natural death?" Mrs. Donwiggle was asked.

"Oh, no," she replied. "He had a doctor."

692. An Irishman coming out of ether in the ward after an operation exclaimed audibly:

"Thank God! That's over!"

"Don't be too sure," the man in the next bed said. "They left a sponge in me and had to cut me open again." And the patient on the other side said, "Why, they had to open me, too, to find one of their instruments."

Just then the surgeon who had operated on the Irishman stuck his head in the door and yelled, "Has anybody seen my hat?"

Pat fainted.

693. A man of seventy-five won $20,000.00 in a sweepstakes. His family was afraid to tell him because he had a weak heart, and they were afraid of what the shock might do to him. So they consulted the family physician who said that he would take care of the situation and that they should leave the matter in his hands. The doctor approached the old man and very casually asked him what he would do if he were lucky enough to win $20,000.00 in a sweepstakes, and the old gent replied: "I'd give you half." With that the old Doc, himself, keeled over and died.

694. Jones was worried. His wife was undergoing an operation.
"With me, it's like this," he told a friend. "I don't mind the forty dollars so much. It's the terrible danger."
"Don't be silly," smiled his friend. "What kind of dangerous operation could it be when it costs only forty dollars?"

695. Patient: "Here I am again, doctor."
(The reason for that is that the patient just heard that the doctor charged ten dollars for the first visit and two dollars for the second.)

696. A young doctor and a young dentist shared the services of a receptionist and both fell in love with her.
The dentist was called away on business, so he sent for the receptionist and said: "I am going to be away for ten days. You will find a little present in your room."
She went in, and found ten apples.

— Financial Post (Toronto)

697. A man of sixty who had been a grumbler all of his life, had long made a practice of changing his physician at the slightest provocation. One day he called in a young doctor who had gained a considerable reputation.
He was telling the doctor what he thought was the matter with him, when the young M.D. ventured to disagree with him.
"I beg your pardon," said the patient, "it isn't for a young man like you to disagree with an old, experienced invalid like me!"

698. Mrs. Van Twiller (who mistakes Dr. Jovial for a physician) — "And what do you practice, Doctor?"
The Reverend Dr. Jovial — "Ah, madam, I do not practice; I only preach."

121

699. Young mother, in maternity ward: He's a wonderful doctor — only this morning, he said we look more like sisters than mother and daughter.
— Cartoon by Lichty,
N. Y. World Telegram

700. "Have you been to any other doctor before you came to me?" asked the grouchy doctor.

"No, sir," replied the meek patient, "I went to a druggist."

"You went to a druggist?" exclaimed the doctor. "That shows how much sense some people have! And what idiotic advice did the druggist give you?"

"He told me to come and see you," replied the patient.

701. Dr. William Osler, having been invited to inspect a famous London hospital, was proudly shown about by several physicians and surgeons. Finally the charts were reached, and he looked them over carefully, observing the system of abbreviations: SF for Scarlet Fever, TB for Tuberculosis, D for Diphtheria, and so on. All diseases seemed to be pretty well under control except one indicated by the symbol GOK.

"I observe," said the famous doctor, "that you have a sweeping epidemic of GOK on your hands. This is a symbol not in common use in American medical circles; just what is GOK?"

"Oh!" one of his hosts lightly replied, "when we can't diagnose, God Only Knows."
— WALTER NEALE, *Life of Ambrose Bierce*

702. A young doctor returned to the village of his birth and called upon the old family physician.

"I suppose that you intend to specialize," remarked the elder.

"Oh, yes," replied the youth, "in the diseases of the nose; the ears and throat are too complicated to be combined with the nose for purposes of study and treatment."

Thereupon the family physician inquired: "Which nostril are you concentrating on?"

703. God heals, the doctor takes the fee.
— BENJAMIN FRANKLIN,
Poor Richard's Almanac

704. Maybe the old time doctor didn't know, but he didn't soak you ten dollars for sending you to somebody who did.

705. There's another advantage in being poor — a doctor will cure you faster.

— ELBERT HUBBARD

706. A doctor in a clinic was interviewing a new patient. "If I find an operation necessary," he asked, "would you have the money to pay for it?"

"Listen, Doc," replied the man, "if I didn't have the money, would you find the operation necessary?"

— HARRY HERSHFIELD,
New York Daily Mirror

707. No man is a good physician who has never been sick.

—Arabian Proverb

708. Sign in Dentist's Office:
"Never select a set of plates from a Window Display. It is impolite to pick your teeth in Public."

709. Specialist: a doctor whose patients are expected to confine their ailments to office hours.

710. A cold is both positive and negative; sometimes the *eyes* have it and sometimes the *nose*.

— WILLIAM LYONS PHELPS

711. *Doctor:* "Are you bothered with things dancing before your eyes?"

Tired Business Man (ardent musical comedy first-nighter): "No, in fact, I rather like it."

712. Dyspeptic: one who can eat his cake and have it too.

713. *Patient:* "Five dollars is an awful lot of money for pulling a tooth — two second's work."
Dentist: "Well, if you wish, I can pull it slowly."

double entendre

714. In a swank photography studio a society matron was look·ing at a new picture she'd had taken. "Why, that picture's an outrage!" she stormed. "Now I ask you, does it look like me?"

The suave photographer was flustered for a moment, but quickly regained his composure. "Madam," he said, bowing slightly, "the answer is in the negative."

715. Stork: a bird with many things charged against it which should have been blamed on the lark.

716. A lot of live wires would be dead if it weren't for their connections.

717. It's easy enough to "do a fellow up brown" if he's already "half-baked."

dreams

718. You have to stay awake to make your dreams come true.

dress – style – attire

719. I hold that gentleman to be best dressed whose dress no one observes.

— WILLIAM MAKEPEACE THACKERAY

720. When the Bishop of Texas was in London sometime ago, he was taken to a swanky ball at which the ladies' dresses were cut very low, and he was asked if he had ever beheld such a sight.

"Not," said the Bishop, "since I was weaned."

721. *Rube:* "Been to New York City, Hank, I heered."
Hank: "Yep. Had a fine time. Seen everythin'."
Rube: "Did yer see any of them ladies in new clothes?"
Hank: "Sure did. The ladies' clothes down there put me in mind of the bob-wire fence around our farm."
Rube: "By ginger, how in old Sam's hill could ladies' clothes put you in mind of a bob-wire fence?"
Hank: "Well, you see, Rube, it's this way, — they appear to protect the property without obstructin' the view."

722. Her clothes are so designed that she is always seen in the best places.

723. A lady is one who never shows her underwear unintentionally.

724. Only men who are not interested in women are interested in women's clothes; men who like women are not interested in what they wear.

— ANATOLE FRANCE

725. All women's dresses are merely variations on the eternal struggle between the admitted desire to dress and the unadmitted desire to undress.

— LIN YUTANG

726. Strapless gown: a compromise between the law of decency and the law of gravity.

727. Strapless gown: when a woman won't shoulder the responsibility.

728. Hat: something the average man covers his head with, the beggar passes around, the statesman throws into the ring, and the politician talks thru.

— *Viking*

729. Eat whatever thou likest, but dress as others do.

— *Abrabian Proverb*

730. As soon as Eve ate the apple of wisdom, she reached for the fig leaf; when a woman begins to think, her first thought is of a new dress.

— HEINRICH HEINE

drug store – druggist

731. Sign in a New York Drug Store: "We dispense with accuracy."

732. A young bride walked into a drug store and approached a clerk timidly.

"That baby tonic you advertise —" she began — "does it really make babies bigger and stronger?"

"We sell lots of it," replied the druggist, "And we've never had a complaint."

"Well, I'll take a bottle," said the bride after a moment, and went out. In five minutes she was back. She got the druggist into a corner and whispered into his ear:

"I forgot to ask about this baby tonic," she said under her breath. "Who takes it — me or my husband?"

education

733. Students have been working their way through college for years. This is a good time for the colleges to try to work their way through some of the students.

734.
A builder builded a temple,
He wrought it with care and skill,
Pillars and groins and arches,
Were fashioned to meet his will
And men said when they saw its beauty:
"It shall never know decay,
Great is thy skill, O, builder,
Thy fame shall endure for aye."

A teacher builded a temple,
She wrought with skill and care,
Forming each pillar with patience,
Laying each stone with care.
None saw the unceasing effort
None knew of the marvelous plan,
For the temple the teacher builded
Was unseen by the eyes of man.

Gone is the builder's temple,
Crumbled into dust,
Pillars and groins and arches,
Food for consuming rust.
But the temple the teacher builded
Shall endure while the ages roll,
For the beautiful unseen temple
Was the child's immortal soul.

—Author Unknown

735. "Well, son," asked the father, "how are your marks at school?"

"Under water," was the cryptic response.

"And what do you mean by that?" persisted the parent.

"Well," said the son reluctantly, "they're all below 'C' level."

736. Education does not mean teaching people to know what they do not know; it means teaching them to behave as they do not behave.

— JOHN RUSKIN

737. Benjamin Franklin once sagely said: "If a man empties his purse into his head, no man can take it from him."

738. For some years we have heard the revolutionary slogan in public and secondary schools — "We don't teach subjects, we teach pupils" — and the child-centered school has now arrived. This idea is safe, only so long as the pupil is not nourished on the idea that he is the center of all things and that subject matter is rather incidental after all. Colleges cannot yield to this temptation. The dignity and majesty of the great fields of subject matter — for they are fields of commanding truth — take precedence over the particular wishes, notions and vagaries of individual students. Those disciplines open up great avenues of stern duty and service to those who wish to enter. There is danger that in American institutions we may produce self-centered individualists who may some day through their own lack of inner iron discipline self-imposed furnish easy victims for that outside discipline which dictators are always glad to supply.

— DR. BESSIE C. RANDOLPH,
President, Hollins College

739. What sculpture is to a block of marble, education is to a human soul.

— JOSEPH ADDISON, *The Spectator*

740. We speak of educating our children. Do we know that our children educate us?

— LYDIA SIGOURNEY

741. Charles W. Eliot, famous president of Harvard University, while being honored one night by a group of educators, made use of the following "reverse process."

"Permit me to congratulate you on the miracles you have performed at the university," remarked one educator. "Since you became president, Harvard has become a storehouse of knowledge."

"That is true," laughed Eliot, "but I scarcely deserve the credit for that. It is simply that the freshmen bring so much knowledge in, and the seniors take so little out."

742. The difference between intelligence and education is this — that intelligence will make you a good living.
— CHARLES F. KETTERING

743. One pound of learning requires ten pounds of common sense to apply it.

744. If we moderns had more curiosity we could get along with considerably less formal education. Progress depends upon curiosity. Curiosity is the only intelligence test which tells what one may become as well as what one is.
— Editorial, *Saturday Review of Literature*

745. Learning is like rowing upstream; not to advance is to drop back.
— *Chinese Proverb*

746. Nothing is easier in America than to attend college and nothing is harder than to get educated.
— DOUGLAS WOODRUFF, *Nectar in a Nutshell*

747. A Ph.D. thesis consists of transferring bones from one graveyard to another.
— J. FRANK DOBIE

748. After encountering numerous failures in business and politics Abraham Lincoln kept right on reading books. "What good is all that education?" a critic scoffed. "It has never earned you a decent living yet!" Lincoln smiled. "Education is not given for the purpose of earning a living; it's learning what to do with a living after you earn it that counts."
— *Coronet Magazine*

749. Accumulations on grocery shelves are not really food, for dietary elements become food only when they are digested and brought to the body tissues in the blood stream. The same can be said for knowledge. A million well-chosen books on the shelves of a library are not in and of themselves knowledge. They are just educational groceries. They can reach the blood stream of a nation's intelligence thru the action of many distributors.

— JOHN WILCOX, "The Place of
Excellence," *School & Society*

750. Stephen Leacock, the Canadian professor and humorist, once wrote an anecdote about the elective system at its extreme. He had, he reported, met an American student during the summer vacation. He asked him what he was going to take in the way of courses that autumn. "Turkish, music and architecture," the student promptly replied. "Do you expect to be choirmaster in a Turkish cathedral?" Mr. Leacock asked. "No," said the student, "those courses come at 9, 10, and 11 o'clock."

— IRWIN EDMAN, "To Teach Men
to Know How to be Free," *N. Y.
Times Magazine*

751. We need more appreciation of the fact that the youngsters in our classrooms are infinitely more significant than the subject matter scheduled for teaching.

752. A teacher is one who, in his youth, admired teachers.

— H. L. MENCKEN

753. "Johnny," said the teacher, "if coal is selling at $20 a ton and you pay your dealer $80, how many tons will he bring you?"

"A little over three tons, ma'am," said Johnny promptly.

"Why, Johnny, that isn't right," said the teacher.

"No ma'am, I know it ain't," said Johnny, but they all do it."

754. A teacher was conducting a lesson in history.

"Tommy Jones," she said, "what was there about George Washington which distinguished him from all other famous Americans?"

"He didn't lie," was the prompt answer.

755. Education is an ornament to the fortunate, a haven of refuge to the unfortunate.

— DEMOCRITUS, *Ethica*

756.   THE GARDENER OF SOULS
                by Joseph Auslander

Who is the master teacher? He
Who from despair and fear sets free
The restless, sullen soul of youth

129

To range the harsh terrain of truth,
And from the blind abyss of folly,
The blackest pits of melancholy
To climb, to fall, to cling, to grope
Up the grim Everest of hope
Until above himself he stands,
A new strength in his bleeding hands,
And knows that by his faith he won
The shining summits of the sun.

Who is the master teacher? He
Who shows that to be truly free
No pain can be too much, no price
In discipline and sacrifice
Too great; that freedom is a pledge,
A promise and a privilege,
A glory earned, a grace to cherish,
Or lightly held, as lightly perish.

He is the teacher who gives vision,
And courage to outface derision;
Who in an angry time can teach
A tolerance in thought and speech
Which stones may strike, but never reach.
He is the plowman who plows deep
The stubborn soil where passions sleep,
Each one for good or ill a seed,
And plucks the nettle and the weed,
Laboring hour upon hour
To bring the best in men to flower,
And finds in labor for the Lord
His recompense and his reward,
Toiling as his great Teacher toils,
Who is the Gardener of Souls.

— Reprinted by Special Permission
of *The Saturday Evening Post,*
copyrighted 1944 by The Curtis
Publishing Co.

757. *"Teacher!"* — Hers is the most familiar of America's faces.
. . . You've adored and despised her, brought her apples and pep-
pered her with spitballs. But you wouldn't be what you are today
without her. She's the fount of all knowledge, the funnel for the

wisdom and experience of the ages — history, spelling, philosophy, grammar, chemistry, the mathematics of Archimedes, the Latin of Virgil. She's tired and tireless, plain and beautiful with the true beauty of the giver. Yet what of her when she leaves her classroom world? Where does she board? Who are her friends? What fun does she have — if any? You don't know, do you? You ought to know because you are her children and she lives and has her reward in your lives. You should not let her become the forgotten woman.

> — DALE EUNSON, *Cosmopolitan*

758. When someone asked Aristippus what should be the content of the education of youth, he replied: "Those things which they will use when men." Amplified to fit the requirements of modern times, the statement of the Greek philosopher might say: "The purpose of education is to prepare men and women to live, to think, to see, to be happier and better citizens of the state."

> — LEWIS H. BROWN, "Free Enterprise or State-Planned Economy?" *Dun's Review*

759. The businessman is coming to realize that education is to business what fertilizer is to farming.

> — W. H. PILLSBURY, Supt. of Schools, Schenectady, N. Y. *Quote*

760. Yes, teachers belong to a great company — the company of the Nazarene, Socrates, Plato and Aristotle; of Abelard and St. Thomas; of Rousseau, Pestalozzi and Froebel; of Horace Mann and William James. Ours is a vital work for into our keeping is placed the destiny of nations.

> — Condensed from a report to the Representative Assembly of the N.E.A., July 6, 1944.

761. Education today, more than ever before, must see clearly the dual objectives: Educating for living and educating for making a living.

> — JAMES MASON WOOD

762. "Teacher, can any one be punished for something he didn't do?"

"Why, no, of course not."

"Well, I haven't done my arithmetic."

"You bad boy. I wish I was your mother for about twenty-four hours."

"All right, teacher, I'll speak to Dad and maybe I can fix it up."

763.   'Tis education forms the common mind;
Just as the twig is bent, the tree's inclined.
> — Pope, *Moral Essays,*
> Epis. i, Line 149

764.   Mildred McAfee once defined an educated person as one who voluntarily does more thinking than is necessary for his own survival. Such a person is not only educated; he is psychologically young. For he has not permitted himself to slip into either the self-centeredness or the apathy of old age.
> — Bonaro W. Overstreet, "How to
> Stay Alive as Long as You Live,"
> *National Parent-Teacher*

765.   Those who can do; those who can't, teach; and those who can't do anything at all, teach the teachers.

766.   To say that those who can, do, and that those who can't, teach is far from fair.
> — George Bernard Shaw

767.   Learning is not picked up only within four walls. The ability to read books is not in itself of a higher order than the ability to read nature: to detect, for instance, a bird by its song, or to name a tree by its leaf. In times of threatened famine, would it still be a greater achievement for a boy or man to be able to write his name and address on straight and successive lines than to plough a field in straight and parallel ones? It would certainly not be so practically useful.
> — C. J. Woolen, "Some Aspects of
> Modern Education," *Homiletic
> & Pastoral Review*

768.   Men in teaching others, learn themselves.
> — Seneca, *Epistles No. 7*

769.   Television can be very educational. Everytime somebody turns on the set I go into the other room and read a book.

770.   Don't fail to get a good education while you're young. It will come in handy when you have to help with your children's home work.

771.   First grade teacher: one who knows how to make little things count.

772.   Education: a debt due from present to future generations.
> — George Peabody

773. The teacher is like the candle which lights others while consuming itself.

774. An educational system isn't worth a great deal if it teaches young people how to make a living and doesn't teach them how to live.

775. If ever I am an instructress, it will be to learn more than to teach.
— MADAME DELUZY

776. You cannot teach a man anything; you can only help him to find it within himself.
— GALILEO

777. You cannot by all the lecturing in the world enable a man to make a shoe.
— SAMUEL JOHNSON

778. The education of a man is never completed until he dies.
— ROBERT E. LEE

779. An educated person is one who voluntarily does more thinking than is necessary for his own survival.

780. It is what we learn after we think we know it all, that counts.

781. If he is a man of learning, good; if he is a man of learning and of noble birth, very good; if he is of noble birth but not a man of learning, the fire may consume him.

782. I had, out of my sixty teachers, a scant half dozen who couldn't have been supplanted by phonographs. — DON HEROLD

783. The more we study the more we discover our ignorance.
— PERCY BYSSHE SHELLEY

effectiveness

784. It is possible to make a sound argument without making a lot of noise.

efficiency

785. The efficient man is the man who thinks for himself, and is capable of thinking hard and long. — Charles W. Eliot

effort

786. "Here, young man, you shouldn't hit a boy when he's down." "G'wan! Wat d'yer tink I tuk all dat trouble ter git 'm down fer?"

787. Chop your own wood and it will warm you twice.

788. It is one thing to itch for something and another to scratch for it.

789. Spend little effort and you will have little else to spend.

790. Your ship won't come in till you row out to meet it.

791. Rest is for the dead. — Thomas Carlyle

792. Everything comes to him who hustles while he waits. — Thomas A. Edison

793. Foundations are important. Often I have passed by a piece of excavation going many feet into the ground and upon inquiry been told this was to be the site of a skyscraper. To the uninitiated it looked as if they were going in the wrong direction, but they were going down in order to go up. — John L. Hill, *The Defender*

794. No man ever worked his way anywhere in a dead calm; kites rise against, not with the wind. — John Neal

ego – egotism

795. Ego: some spark within us which leads us to believe that we are better than we are, and which is often instrumental in proving it.

796. Egotist: a man who is always me-deep in conversation.

797. Egotism: an anesthetic that nature gives to man to deaden the pain of being a darn fool.

798. Egotism: self-confidence looking for trouble.

— Redbook

799. Utterly egoless men are rare and perhaps without value; need for self-expression has as often served the social weal as the social woe.

— From *They Also Ran*, by IRVING STONE. (Copyright 1943 by Irving Stone, reprinted by permission of Doubleday & Company, Inc.)

800. When two egotists meet it is a case of an I for an I.

embarrassment

801. A young lady, with a touch of hay fever, took with her to a dinner party two handkerchiefs, one of which she stuck in her bosom. At dinner she began rummaging to right and left in her bosom for the fresh handkerchief. Engrossed in her search, she suddenly realized that conversation had ceased and people were watching her, fascinated. In confusion she murmured, "I know I had two when I came."

—Contributed by JOHN ERSKINE, *Readers Digest*

802. To my embarrassment I was born in bed with a lady.

—WILSON MIZNER

803. At a large party in New York, Mrs. Joseph Schildkraut said good-bye to the British consul, then shook many other hands, and finally found herself shaking his hand again. "But you've already said good-bye to me once," he remonstrated.

"Oh, yes, Mr. Campbell," she replied archly, "but it's always a pleasure to say good-bye to you."

— Contributed by TOM POWERS, *Readers Digest*

employer – employment

804. The clerk wanted to get the afternoon off to take his wife to a matinee. His employer flatly refused to grant the request, and soon thereafter left the office, saying he was going to see a ball game. The other clerks assured their fellow-worker that the boss would not be back that afternoon, and after much hesitation he hurriedly departed. Reaching his home, and happening to glance through the window, he saw his fond wife comfortably seated on the boss's knee. He grew pale and a cold sweat gathered on his brow. Noiselessly retreating from the window, he flew back to the store and sank in a chair, exhausted. When asked the reason for his excitement, he pantingly replied: "Such a narrow escape! I was nearly caught!"

805. Manager: "We want a man for our information bureau. He must be wide awake and accustomed to complaints."
Applicant: "That's me. I'm the father of twins."

806. Most recommendations are good because you secure them when the firm is in fine humor over getting rid of you.

encouragement

807. When you reach the mountain top, wig-wag courage to the fellow in the foothills.

808. There are high spots in all of our lives and most of them have come about through encouragement from someone else. I don't care how great, how famous or successful a man or woman may be, each hungers for applause.

Encouragement is oxygen to the soul. Good work can never be expected from a worker without encouragement. No one ever climbed spiritual heights without it. No one ever lived without it.

Note how good you feel after you have encouraged someone else. No other argument is necessary to suggest that you never miss the opportunity to give encouragement. — GEORGE MATTHEW ADAMS,
Readers Digest

809. If you must strike a man from behind, slap him on the back.

810. I don't set up to be no judge of right and wrong
in men,
I've lost the trail sometimes myself an' may get
lost again;
An' when I see a chap who looks as though he'd
gone astray,
I want to shove my hand in his an' help him find
the way. — J. A. FOLEY

energy

811. The same water which drives a mill also decays it.

812. The speed of a runaway horse counts for nothing.
— JEAN COCTEAU

enterprise — See also *Business*

813. Why not go out on a limb? Isn't that where the fruit is?
— FRANK SCULLY

entertainment

814. I am a great friend to public amusements, for they keep people from vice.
— SAMUEL JOHNSON

enthusiasm

815. Enthusiasm is very good lubrication for the mind.

816. Enthusiasm is that kindling spark which marks the difference between the leaders in every activity and the laggards who put in just enough to "get by."

817. Opposition always enflames the enthusiast, never converts him.
— JOHANN FRIEDRICH SCHILLER

envy

818. The praise of the envious is far less creditable than their censure; they praise only that which they can surpass, but that which surpasses them they censure.
— C. C. COLTON

819. Envy among other ingredients, has a mixture of the love of justice in it. We are more angry at undeserved than at deserved good fortune.
— WILLIAM HAZLITT

820. Stones and sticks are thrown only at fruit-bearing trees.
— SAADI

821. When men are full of envy they disparage everything, whether it be good or bad. — PUBLIUS TACITUS

822. The truest mark of being born with great qualities is being born without envy. — LA ROCHEFOUCAULD

823. Envy provides the mud that failure throws at success. — *N. Y. Globe*

824. Envy, like flame, blackens that which is above it, and which it cannot reach. — *Petit-Senn*

equality

825. All men are equal; it is not birth but virtue alone, that makes the difference. — VOLTAIRE

826. Men are made by nature unequal. It is vain, therefore, to treat them as if they were equal. — JAMES ANTHONY FROUDE

827. When gravity pulls an apple to the earth, it pulls the earth to the apple in exactly the same degree — with respect to their relative sizes.

828. The presence of large private fortunes — the inequality in the distribution of wealth — is to certain persons a sign that there is something wrong with the world. Perhaps there is. That is another question. What I am pointing out is that ignorant efforts to promote equality through ill-considered attacks upon interest and profits and upon those who receive them may result in destroying the motive for saving capital and employing it in industry. We may indeed thus reduce inequality, but only at the cost of reducing the efficiency of national industry, whose products sustain the comforts and necessities, indeed the very lives of us all. The notion that anything that hurts the rich thereby helps the poor is, like the companion notion that an injury to capital is a gain to labor, one of those popular fallacies which is today checking the flow of capital into industry and blocking the path of economic recovery.
— PROF. FRED R. FAIRCHILD, *The Sun*, N.Y.

esteem

829. Of two heroes, he is the greater who esteems his rivals most. — BEUMELLE

eternal

830. CLEANLINESS — OF HEART

A Tibetan lama was performing his rites when two travelers came along. He was unkempt in appearance, not because of negligence but because of his environment. The travelers criticized the old priest scornfully, unaware that he understood their language. When he had finished his ritual, he turned to the two and said quickly, "But my heart is clean —."

> — Ruth Ann Leadbeater, "A Doctor in the House," *Christian Advocate,* 8-23-'45.

831. *Mr. Meyerson, (a writer):* "I want to write something that will live forever."

Mr. Nathan: "All right; write your name on a mortgage."

etiquette — See *Manners.*

evolution

832. Great occasions do not make heroes or cowards; they simply unveil them to the eyes of men. Silently and imperceptibly, as we wake or sleep, we grow strong or weak; and at last some crisis shows us what we have become.

> — Cannon Westcott, *Readers Digest*

exaggeration

833. One swallow maketh not a summer.

> — John Heywood, *Proverbs*

834. *Johnny (looking out of the window):* "Oh, mother, a car as big as a barn has just gone by."

Mother: "Johnny, why do you exaggerate so terribly? I've told you 40 million times about that habit of yours and it doesn't do a bit of good."

example

835. An old man gives good advice in order to console himself for no longer being in condition to set a bad example.

> — La Rochefoucauld

example

836.   THE PRINCESS AND RABBI JOSHUA

Rabbi Joshua, the son of Hananiah, was one of those men whose minds are far more beautiful than their bodies. He was so dark that people often took him for a blacksmith, and so plain as almost to frighten children. Yet his great learning, wit, and wisdom had procured him not only the love and respect of the people, but even the favor of Emperor Trajan. Being often at court, one of the Princesses rallied him on his want of beauty. "How comes it," she said, "that such glorious wisdom is enclosed in so mean a vessel?" The Rabbi, no ways dismayed, requested her to tell him in what sort of vessels her father kept his wine. "Why, in earthen vessels, to be sure," replied the Princess. "Oh!" exclaimed the witty Rabbi, "this is the way that ordinary people do; an Emperor's wine ought to be kept in more precious vessels." The Princess, thinking him in earnest, ordered a quantity of wine to be emptied out of the earthen jars into gold and silver vessels; but to her great surprise, found it, in a very short time, sour, and unfit to drink. "Very fine advice, indeed, Joshua, hast thou given me!" said the Princess the next time she saw him; "do you know the wine is sour and spoiled?" "Thou art then convinced," said the Rabbi, "that wine keeps best in plain and mean vessels? It is even so with wisdom." "But," continued the Princess, "I know many persons who are both wise and handsome." "True," replied the sage, "but they would, most probably, be still wiser were they less handsome."   *— The Talmud*

837.   A man profits more by the sight of an idiot than by the orations of the learned.   *— Arabian Proverb*

excess

838.   Samuel Goldwyn, who was seeking a film story for Bob Hope, received a phone call from a Hollywood writer. "I have a wonderful comedy," the writer told him excitedly. "It's ideal for Hope." "Fine, fine," Goldwyn said. "Not only is it a great comedy," the writer went on, "but it also has a message."

"A message?" repeated Goldwyn. "Just write me a comedy. Messages are for Western Union." *— LEONARD LYONS, Readers Digest*

839.   All sunshine makes the desert.   *— Arabian Proverb*

exile

840. Exile is terrible to those who have, as it were, a circumscribed habitation; but not to those who look upon the whole globe but as one city.
— CICERO

existence

841. If God did not exist, it would be necessary to invent Him.
— VOLTAIRE

expediency

842. You will never get me to support a measure which I believe to be wrong, even although by doing so I may accomplish that which I believe to be right.
— ABRAHAM LINCOLN

experience

843. Experience is a wonderful thing. It enables you to recognize a mistake when you make it again.

844. A gem is not polished without rubbing, nor a man made perfect without trials.
— *Chinese Proverb*

845. The educational value of experience is recognized in proverbs in all homes. We say, "Experience is the best teacher." The Arabs say, "No man is a good physician who has never been sick." Dozens of similar maxims, all making the same point, could be given. All suggest the indirectly great benefit which can accrue from happenings at the moment most trying and unpleasant — and, from a dollar and cents standpoint, most unprofitable.

As preparation for successful business life, no one can gainsay the value of a childhood not too easy. Innumerable instances of outstanding business success can be traced to a boyhood which, full of deprivation and hardship, developed ability and character that magnificently equipped the youngster for business life.

846. A little experience upsets a lot of theory.
— S. PARKES CADMAN

847. A financier of our acquaintance says that the suckers haven't permanently deserted the stock market. They are merely waiting until the prices get too high again.

848. We should be careful to get out of an experience only the wisdom that is in it — and stop there; lest we be like the cat that sits down on the hot stove-lid. She will never sit down on a hot stove lid again — and that is well; but also she will never sit down on a cold one any more. — MARK TWAIN, *Following the Equator* (Harper)

849. The late Simon Bolivar Buckner used to tell a story of an old resident in his Kentucky home who was celebrated for his wisdom.

"Uncle Zeke," a young man once asked, "How does it come you're so wise?"

"Because," said the old man, "I've got good judgment. Good judgment comes from experience, and experience — well, that comes from poor judgment!" — *Quote*

850. The sheepskin conferred on a student by a college, hardly compensates for the human hide that will be knocked off him later in the school of experience. — *Charley Jones' Laugh Book*

851. If money is your only hope for independence, you will never have it. The only real security that a man can have in this world is a reserve of knowledge, experience and ability.
— HENRY FORD

852. Men are wise in proportion not to their experience, but to their capacity for experience. — GEORGE BERNARD SHAW

853. An employer, interviewing an applicant remarked: "You ask high wages for a man with no experience."

"Well," the prospect replied, "It's so much harder to work when you don't know anything about it." — *Readers Digest*

854. A prudent man profits from personal experience, a wise one from the experience of others. — DR. JOSEPH COLLINS

855. Never throw away hastily any old faith, tradition or convention. They may require modification, but they are the result of the experience of many generations. — OLIVER LODGE

856. Past experience should be a guide post, not a hitching post.
— D. W. WILLIAMS, Vice Chancellor,
Texas A. & M. College

857. Experience is not what happens to man. It is what a man does with what happens to him. — ALDOUS HUXLEY

858. Experience is the name an older man gives to his mistakes.

859. A colored man in the south was about to be electrocuted for having murdered a man. He entered the death chamber slowly, made his way to the fatal chair, and sat down.

The warden spoke: "Now Charlie," he said, "before the current is turned on, is there anything you'd like to say?"

"Yes sir," answered the condemned man reflectively, "I'se moved to remark that this 'lectrocution is shure gwine to teach me a lesson."

860. To regret one's own experiences is to arrest one's own development. To deny one's own experiences is to put a lie into the lips of one's own life. It is no less than a denial of the soul.
— OSCAR WILDE

861. Those who have known grief seldom seem sad.
— DISRAELI, *Endymion*

862. One doesn't want men of experience working for him. The experienced man is always telling one why something can't be done. He is smart; he is intelligent; he thinks he knows the answers. The fellow who has not had any experience is so dumb he doesn't know a thing can't be done — and he goes ahead and does it.

experiment

863. *Farmer (as he met another farmer on the road):* "Si, I've got a mule with distemper. What'd ye give that one of yours when he had it?"

Si: "Turpentine. Giddap."

A week later they met again.

"Si, I gave my mule turpentine and it killed him."

Si: "Killed mine, too. Giddap."

864. A man was trying to teach his dog to live without eating. One day he was approached by a friend and asked "How are you getting on with your experiment?" To which he replied: "I was getting on real well, but just as the dog was learning to live without eating, he died."

865. We often discover what will do by finding out what will not do; and probably he who never made a mistake never made a discovery. — SAMUEL SMILES

expert

866. Expert: a person who can take something you already knew and make it sound confusing.

867. An expert is a man from another city, and the farther away that city is, the greater the expert.

868. An expert is an ordinary man away from home.

869. An efficiency expert is a man who knows less about your business than you do and gets paid more for telling you how to run it than you could possibly make out of it even if you ran it right instead of the way he told you to.

explanation

870. It takes less time to do a thing right than to explain why you did it wrong. — HENRY WADSWORTH LONGFELLOW

871. Asked by his hostess to tell her about relativity "in a few simple words," Einstein said: "Madam, I was once walking in the country on a hot day with a blind friend, and said I could do with a drink of milk.
"Milk?" said my friend. "Drink I know; but what is milk?"
" 'A white liquid,' I replied.
" 'Liquid I know,' said the blind man; but what is wite?'
" 'Oh, the color of a swan's feathers.'
" 'Feathers I know. What is a swan?'
" 'Swan? A bird with a crooked neck.'
" 'Neck I know — but what is this crooked?'

"Thereupon I lost patience. I seized his arm and straightened it. 'That's straight,' I said. Then I bent it at the elbow. 'And that's crooked.'

" 'Ah,' cried the blind man, 'now I know what you mean by milk!' "
— ROBERT GRAVES and ALAN HODGE,
The Long Week-End (Ryerson)

872. "Lillian," said the mother severely, "there were two pieces of cake in the pantry this morning, and now there is only one. How does this happen?"

"I don't know," replied Lillian regretfully. "It musta been so dark I didn't see the other piece."

extravagance

873. All progress is based upon a universal innate desire on the part of every organism to live beyond its income.
— SAMUEL BUTLER

facts

874. Facts do not cease to exist just because they are ignored.
— ALDOUS HUXLEY

875. The next best thing to knowing a fact is knowing where to find it.

failure — See also *Success*

876. If you keep in the rut too long it will get so deep that it becomes your grave.

877. It is an infamy to die and not be missed.
— CARLOS WILCOX

878. *Mother:* "I've tried so hard to make you a good child, Margaret, and yet in spite of all my efforts you are still rude and naughty."
Margaret (deeply moved): "What a failure you are, mother."

879. The probability that we may fail in the struggle ought not to deter us from the support of a cause we believe to be just.
— ABRAHAM LINCOLN

880. This is about the untalented actress who gave two performances simultaneously recently — her first and her last.

faith — See *Courage, Confidence*

fame

881. Distinction is the consequence, never the object, of a great mind.
— Washington Allston

882. Sometimes, when a man is in the public eye, he is just a cinder.

883. Every man who has become famous for something, ought to pray for strength not to be interviewed on other things.

family

884. A Minneapolis family brought their teen-age son into the living room for a conference the other night on the girl he was going with. His reply to their objections to her was this: "She's the best I can get with the car we've got."

885. Where there's a will, there are relatives.

886. "I wish you could make the kind of bread my mother used to make."
"Well, dear, I wish you could make the kind of dough father used to make."

887. "Every one in our family is some kind of animal," said Jimmie to the amazed preacher.
"Why, you shouldn't say that," the good man exclaimed.
"Well," said Jimmie, "mother's a dear, the baby is mother's little lamb, I'm the kid, and dad's the goat."

888. The pastor of a thriving congregation in Jacksonville was speaking to one of his flock.
"Brother," he said, "I hears very bad reports of your youngest son. That boy doesn't seem to do you much credit."
"Credit?" replied this parishioner, "Huh, you puts it mild. Tha's the worst child ever I seen in my 'hole life. In fact, Elder, strick'ly between ourse'fs, we regards him ez de w'ite sheep of the family."

889. The family was seated at the table with a guest who was a business acquaintance of dad's, all ready to enjoy the meal, when the young son blurted out, "Why mother, this is roast beef!"

"Yes," answered the mother, "what of it?"

"Well, daddy said this morning that he was going to bring a big fish home for dinner tonight."

890. Blood is thicker than water—and it boils quicker.

fanaticism

891. A fanatic is a person who is highly enthusiastic about something in which you are not even remotely interested.

— Successful Farming

farm – farming

892. "We have a red cow that eats green grass and gives white milk."

"That's nothing, we have a red cow that eats green grass and gives no milk."

"Aw, go on — that's the bull!"

893. Farm: what a city man dreams of at 5 p.m., never at 5 a.m.

fate

894. You can't blame nudists for being the way they are, they were born that way.

faults

895. The greatest of faults is to be conscious of none.

— Thomas Carlyle

896. Nothing is easier than fault-finding; no talent, no self-denial, no brains, no character are required to set up in the grumbling business.

— Robert West

147

897. If you see a fault in others, think of two of your own, and do not add a third one by your hasty judgment. — FLAMMER

fear — See also *Courage*

898. We often pretend to fear what we really despise, and more often to despise what we really fear. — C. C. COLTON

flattery

899. Flattery: a commodity that makes everybody sick except those who swallow it. — *Quote*

900. Flattery: telling the next fellow exactly what he thinks of himself.

901. As the Greeks said, many men know how to flatter; few know how to praise. — AMBROSE PHILLIPS

902. Imitation is the sincerest form of flattery.

903. When I was a little boy, my mother used to tell me that flattery like perfume should be inhaled and not swallowed.

904. For envy, to small minds, is flattery. — EDWARD YOUNG

905. The human body is remarkably sensitive. Pat a man on the back and his head swells. — *Banking*

flirtation

906. Flirtation: the art of gaining attention without intention. — *Magazine Digest*

907. Flirt: a girl who got the boy you wanted.

food — See also *Diet*

908. Travels of a French Fried Potato: In your mouth a few minutes, in your stomach a few hours, on your hips the rest of your life. — *Health News*

909. Violent exercise after 40 is especially harmful if you do it with a knife and fork.
— *N.E.A. Journal*

910. In the window of a reducing salon: "What have you got to lose?"

911. The poor always eat more relishable food than the rich; hunger makes the dishes sweet, and this occurs almost never with rich people.

912. If thou woulds't preserve a sound body, use fasting and walking; if a healthful soul, fasting and praying; walking exercises the body, praying exercises the soul, fasting cleanses both.
— Francis Quarles

913. Reducing: wishful shrinking.

914. *Diner:* "Waiter, I can't find a single clam in this chowder."
Waiter: "That's nothing! You might just as well try to locate a set of wicker furniture in our cottage pudding."

915. Balanced diet: what you eat at buffet suppers.

916. Mealtime: when youngsters sit down to continue eating.
— *The Office Economist*

917. Salmon: a fish that lurks in a can and only comes out when unexpected company arrives.

folly

918. We spend half our lives unlearning the follies transmitted to us by our parents, and the other half transmitting our own follies to our offspring.
— Isaac Goldberg

919. Fools make feasts, and wise men eat them.
— Benjamin Franklin

920. When you are arguing with a fool, two fools are arguing.

921. Sometimes when we argue with a fool, he is doing the same thing.

922. When you argue with a fool be sure he isn't similarly engaged.

923. How is it possible for a man to have his ear to the ground, his head in the clouds, and still have his foot in his mouth?

924. For one word a man is often deemed to be wise, and for one word he is often deemed to be foolish. We ought to be careful indeed what we say. — CONFUCIUS, *Analects*

925. A woman, collecting a pile of bills from a bookie, exclaimed: "When I think of what I might have lost if that horse hadn't won, I could shoot myself for being such a fool as to back him." — MAURICE HALL, *Punch*

926. The fence around a cemetery is foolish, for those inside can't come out and those outside don't want to come in. — ARTHUR BRISBANE

927. If fifty million people say a foolish thing, it is still a foolish thing. — ANATOLE FRANCE

928. Few of the many wise apothegms which have been uttered have prevented a single foolish action. — THOMAS B. MACAULEY

929. To discuss an opinion with a fool is like carrying a lantern before a blind man. — DEGASTON

930. What is the difference between the wise man and the fool? The fool says what he knows — The wise man knows what he says.

931. The fool who eats till he is sick must fast till he is well. — GEORGE WALTER THORNBURY

932. It is a man's inalienable right to make a fool of himself but he should not use up all his privilege at one time.

forgiveness

933. Forgiveness is the fragrance the violet sheds on the heel that has crushed it.

934.   Doing an injury puts you below your enemy; revenging one, makes you even with him; forgiving it sets you above him.
— *Nylic Review*

935.   The noblest revenge is to forgive.   — THOMAS FULLER

936.   Courage is always greatest when blended with meekness; intellectual ability is most admired when it sparkles in the setting of a modest self-distrust; and never does the human soul appear so strong as when it forgoes revenge and dares to forgive any injury.

937.   A countryman with a local reputation as a vocalist attended a dinner, and was asked to sing. Altho he had no music with him, and was as hoarse as a frog, he consented to try, but broke down.

"Never thee mind, lad," said an elderly guest, trying to cheer him up; "never mind the breakdown. For thee's done thy best; but th' fellow as asked thee t' sing ought to be shot."

938.   When anyone has offended me, I try to raise my soul so high that the offense cannot reach it.   — RENÉ DESCARTES

939.   If any man cease to attack me, I never remember his past against me.   — ABRAHAM LINCOLN

frankness

940.   To admit error candidly, to begin over again courageously, to accept advice thankfully, to act only after careful thinking, to make mistakes pay, to apologize when found wrong — these are painful duties we owe ourselves — duties that pay when put into practice.
— *Source Unknown*

freedom

941.   ONLY OUR DEAD WILL BE FREE

If we lose in our struggle for freedom;
If we fail at the task we must do;
If we shrink from the turmoil of conflict,
Or quit — ere the battle is through . . .
If we heed not the plight of the vanquished;
If we turn from the brunt of the clash;
If we barter our souls, in our folly,
For the yoke — and the goad — and the lash.

It is we, who will envy the fallen
Should we bow to the tyrant's decree:
— Only our dead will find solace;
And only our dead will be Free!

In bondage, our loved ones will cower;
Abject and despised and depraved:
Our faith and our tenets, "Verboten" —
Our hopes and our children enslaved!
"Old Glory" will be but a mem'ry
As we mourn by Liberty's bier;
A once proud and resolute Nation,
Degraded and cringing in fear:

Our Shrines will be crumbled and broken,
And the slaver will scoff at our plea . . .
— Only our dead will be Victors;
And only our dead will be Free!

       — ADAM N. REITER

942.   The history of liberty is the history of the limitations on the power of the government.   — WOODROW WILSON

943.   Freedom is not worth having if it does not include the freedom to make mistakes.   — GANDHI

944.   Not like the brazen giant of Greek fame,
With conquering limbs astride from land to land;
Here at our sea-washed sunset gates shall stand
A mighty woman with a torch, whose flame
Is the imprisoned lightning, and her name
Mother of Exiles; From her beacon-hand
Glows world-wide welcome; her mild eyes command
The air-bridged harbour that twin cities frame.

"Keep, ancient lands, your storied pomp!"
  cries she
With silent lips. "Give me your tired, your
  poor,
Your huddled masses yearning to breathe free,
The wretched refuse of your teeming shore.
Send these, the homeless, tempest-tost to me,
I lift my lamp beside the golden door!"

      — EMMA LAZARUS, *Sonnet inscribed*
       upon the Statue of Liberty

945. To liberate a canary from its cage is to give him a freedom that is death. To liberate is not freedom if the peoples of the world's devastated areas find themselves in a vortex of national and international insecurity, bewilderment, and fear.

— RAYMOND H. CRAWFORD, *Quote*

946. Creating all men free and equal isn't enough. Some means must be devised to keep them free and equal.

947. Men fight for freedom; then they begin to accumulate laws to take it away from themselves.

948. No man is free who is not master of himself. — EPICTETUS

949. I may disapprove of what you say, but will defend to the death your right to say it.

— VOLTAIRE

950. Liberty is being free from the things we don't like in order to be slaves of the things we do like.

951. Let's not fight for more liberty until we learn to handle what we've got.

952. Eternal vigilance is the price of liberty.

— Ascribed to Thomas Jefferson (Quoted by Wendell Phillips in his speech, "Public Opinion," Jan. 28, 1852)

953. My children, France comes to make us slaves. God gave us liberty; France has no right to take it away.

— L'OUVERTURE, in the time of Napoleon

friendship – friends

954. Silences make the real conversations between friends. Not the saying but the never needing to say is what counts.

955.   You have no enemies, you say?
        Alas! my friend, the boast is poor —
    He who has mingled in the fray
        Of duty, that the brave endure,

Must have made foes! If you have none,
    Small is the work that you have done;
You've hit no traitor on the hip;
    You've never turned the wrong to right —
You've been a coward in the fight!
                     — CHARLES MACKAY

956.   Despite the bitterness engendered by the Civil War, Lincoln never missed an opportunity to speak kindly of the South. An ardent Union supporter once took him to task for this attitude. "Why try to make friends with your enemies?" he protested. "You should destroy them."

"Am I not destroying my enemies," gently replied Lincoln, "when I make friends of them?"

957.   Be slow in choosing a friend, slower in changing.
              — BENJAMIN FRANKLIN, *Poor
              Richard's Almanac*

958.   Do good to thy friend to keep him — to thine enemy to gain him.   — BENJAMIN FRANKLIN

959.   At a recent meeting of Dale Carnegie fans, one man testified how he had applied the prophet's teachings to an encounter with a business prospect. "I did everything in the rule book. I started off by greeting him warmly, then I smiled at him and asked him about himself. I paid very close attention while he told me. I went out of my way to agree with his views on how wonderful he was. He talked for nearly an hour and when we finally parted company, I knew I'd make a friend for life." The man paused for breath. "But, boy!" he concluded: "What an enemy *he* made!"   — *Maclean's*

960.   Just as tall trees are known by their shadows, so are good men known by their enemies.   — *Old Chinese Proverb*

961.   The better part of one's life consists of his friendships.
                          — ABRAHAM LINCOLN

962.   Every man is said to have his pet ambition. Whether it be true or not, I can say for one that I have no other so great as that of being truly esteemed by my fellow-men by rendering myself worthy of their esteem.   — ABRAHAM LINCOLN

963. Instead of loving your enemies, treat your friends a little better.
— ED HOWE

964. The time to make friends is before you need them.

965. Friendship is to be purchased only by friendship. A man may have authority over others, but he can never have their heart but by giving his own.
— THOMAS WILSON

966.
"You have your money and your friend,
You loan your money to your friend,
You ask your money from your friend,
You lose your money and your friend."

967.
Make new friends,
But keep the old;
The first are silver
The latter, gold.

968.
When a man ain't got a cent, and he's feeling
kind o' blue,
An' the clouds hang dark and heavy, an' won't
let the sunshine through;
It's a great thing, O my brethren, for a
feller just to lay
His hand upon your shoulder in a friendly
sort of way!
— JAMES WHITCOMB RILEY

969. The holy passion of Friendship is of so sweet and steady and loyal and enduring a nature that it will last through a whole life-time, if not asked to lend money.
— MARK TWAIN, *Pudd'nhead Wilson* (Harper)

970. Never explain — your friends do not need it, and your enemies will not believe it anyway.

971. A visitor to the White House once asked President Lincoln, "What is your definition of a friend?"

"My definition of a friend?" the Great Emancipator repeated slowly. "One who has the same enemies you have."
— LOUIS HIRSCH, *Readers Digest*

972.   The only reward of virtue is virtue; the only way to have a true friend is to be a true friend.   — RALPH WALDO EMERSON

973.   A friendship founded on business is a good deal better than a business founded on friendship.   — JOHN D. ROCKEFELLER

974.   What a great blessing is a friend with a heart so trusty you may safely bury all your secrets in it, whose conscience you may fear less than your own, who can relieve your cares by his conversation, your doubts by his counsels, your sadness by his good humor, and whose very looks give you comfort.   — SENECA

975.   Sharing a bit of friendliness with others does not impoverish a man.

976.   Life has no pleasure nobler than that of friendship.

977.   A man should keep his friendship in constant repair.
   — SAMUEL JOHNSON

978.   He that hath many friends, has no friends.

979.   It is well, when one is judging a friend, to remember that he is judging you with the same godlike and superior impartiality.
   — ARNOLD BENNETT

980.   With money you can buy all the friends you want, but they never are worth the price.

981.   So long as we love, we serve. So long as we are loved by others we are indispensable; and no man is useless while he has a friend.   — ROBERT LOUIS STEVENSON

982.   Trouble is a great sieve through which we sift our acquaintances; those who are too big to pass through are friends.
   — *North Carolina Churchman*

983.   Some people have no enemies, but all their friends hate them.

984.   Friendship consists in forgetting what one gives and remembering what one receives.   — *Dumas, the Younger*

985. At a party in Hollywood, Helen Deutsch, the screen writer, noticed a new arrival antagonizing every person to whom he was introduced. "Young man," she told him, "you have the knack of making strangers immediately." — LEONARD LYONS, *Readers Digest*

986. Inflict not on an enemy every injury in your power, for he may afterwards become your friend. — SAADI, *The Gulistan*

987. Treat your friend as if he might become an enemy.
— PUBLIUS SYRUS, *Maxims*

988. The silence of a friend commonly amounts to treachery. His not daring to say anything in our behalf implies a tacit censure.
— HAZLITT, *Characteristics*

989. Always forgive your enemies; nothing annoys them so much.
— OSCAR WILDE

990. We make more enemies by what we say than friends by what we do. — JOHN C. COLLINS

991. A book issued by the Army gives all manner of advice to noncommissioned officers. It even tells how to make men who have quarreled friends again. The men are put to washing the same window, one outside, the other inside. Looking at each other, they soon have to laugh and all is forgotten. It works; I have tried it.
— From *My War with the United States*,
LUDWIG BEMELMANS (Viking)

992. Reprove a friend in secret, but praise him before others.

993. A real friend is one who will tell you of your faults and follies in prosperity, and assist you with his hand and heart in adversity.

994. Thousands of appeals for pardon came to Lincoln from soldiers involved in military discipline. Each appeal was as a rule supported by letters from influential people. One day a single sheet came before him, an appeal from a soldier without any supporting documents.

"What!" exclaimed the President. "Has this man no friends?"
"No, sir, not one," said the adjutant.
"Then," said Lincoln, "I will be his friend."

995. Friendship improves happiness, and abates misery, by doubling our joy, and dividing our grief. — JOSEPH ADDISON

996. "Go often to the house of thy friend for weeds choke up the unused path."

997. Friend: one before whom one may think aloud.

998. Friend: one who knows all about you and loves you just the same.

998a. True friendship is like sound health, the value of it is seldom known until it is lost.
— C. C. COLTON

999. A man cannot be too careful in the choice of his enemies.
— OSCAR WILDE

1000. Man has three friends on whose company he relies. First, wealth; which goes with him only while good fortune lasts. Second, his relatives; they go only as far as the grave, leave him there. The third friend, his good deeds, go with him beyond the grave.
— *The Talmud*

furniture

1001. Desk: wastebasket with drawers.

1002. A rummage sale is where you buy stuff from somebody else's attic to store in your own.

futility

1003. The idea of daylight saving comes from an old Indian who cut off one end of his blanket and sewed it on the other to make it longer.

future, the

1004. I do not believe today everything I believed yesterday; I wonder will I believe tomorrow everything I believe today.
— ISAAC GOLDBERG

1005. We can pay our debt to the past by putting the future in debt to ourselves.
— JOHN BUCHAN

1006. Patrick Henry said, "I have no means of judging the future but by the past."

1007. "The best verse hasn't been rhymed yet,
    The best house hasn't been planned,
  The highest peak hasn't been climbed yet,
    The mightiest rivers aren't spanned;
  Don't worry and fret, faint-hearted,
    The chances have just begun
  For the best jobs haven't been started,
    The best work hasn't been done."

gambling

1008. Gambling is the child of avarice, the brother of iniquity, and the father of mischief.
  — GEORGE WASHINGTON, Letter, Newburgh, Jan. 15, 1783

1009. There are two times in a man's life when he should not speculate; when he can't afford it, and when he can. — MARK TWAIN

1010. Money can be lost in more ways than won.

1011. No horse can go as fast as the money you bet on him.
  — NATE COLLIER

garden

1012. Grass: the green stuff that wilts in the yard and flourishes in the garden.

1013. Garden: something that dies if you don't water it and rots if you do.

1014. Vacation time: that period when the flowers in the home garden are at their best and only the neighbors are around to enjoy them.

generalization

1015. All generalizations are dangerous, even this one.
  — ALEXANDRE DUMAS

1016. Nothing is more dangerous than to make generalizations about the social and economic conditions of a country through which one has traveled more or less hastily. I often recall the story of an American who made a grand tour of Europe on a plan which allowed 48 hours at the most for each of the great capitals. When he returned to "God's country," a neighbor asked him if he had seen Venice.

"Yes," he replied; "but when we got there they were in the midst of a terrible flood. All the streets were under water and all the people were traveling around in boats, so we didn't stay."

— LAWRENCE F. ABBOTT

generosity

1017. A true test of generosity is to give the hat check girl a quarter without wondering if a dime would have been enough.

1018. Speak encouragingly to those whom you meet, be generous and credit a man's good points.

genius

1019. Genius is one per cent inspiration and ninety-nine percent perspiration.

— THOMAS A. EDISON

gentility

1020. It is only people who possess firmness who can possess true gentleness. In those who appear gentle, it is generally only weakness, which is readily converted into harshness.

— LA ROCHEFOUCAULD, *Reflections*

gentleman

1021. A gentleman is a man who doesn't pretend to be anything that he isn't.

1022. Gentleman: a man who is always as nice as he sometimes is.

1023. Gentleman: a man who remembers a girl's birthday but forgets her age.

1024. When two men quarrel, he who is first silent, is the greater gentleman. — *The Talmud*

1025. A man that's clean inside and outside; who neither looks up to the rich nor down on the poor; who can lose without squealing; who can win without bragging; considerate to women, children and old people; who is too brave to lie, too generous to cheat, and too sensible to loaf; who takes his share of the world's goods and lets other people have theirs — this is the ideal conception of the true gentleman.

1026. This is the final test of a gentleman: His respect for those who can be of no possible service to him. — WILLIAM LYON PHELPS

gift

1027. The late John M. Scribner, a prominent member of the New York bar, was as bald as a bat and then some. He was speaking to Mr. Joseph H. Choate about the approaching marriage of one of the Vanderbilts to a foreign nobleman.

"It would be absurd to give a Vanderbilt a costly gift," he said. "I should like to find something not intrinsically valuable, but interesting because it is rare."

"Nothing easier, John," Mr. Choate said. "Just send her a lock of your hair."

1028. Housewarming: the last call for wedding presents.

1029. Gift shop: a place where you can see all the things you hope your friends won't send you for Christmas.

glamor

1030. When the value of the package exceeds that of the contents. — *Woman's Home Companion*

glory

1031. The greater the difficulty, the greater the glory. — CICERO

goal

1032. The story is told of Dwight Morrow. He was travelling on a train. The conductor came along and asked him for his ticket. He searched all of his pockets in vain. Finally, the conductor spoke up and said: "It's all right, send it in to the company when you find it." Answered Morrow, "That part's all right, but what bothers me is, where in the hell am I going?"

gold digger

1033. Gold digger: a young woman who likes to go buy buy.

1034. Gold digger: a girl who will date any man that can pass the asset test.   — *Louisville Courier-Journal*

1035. Gold digger: a girl who breaks dates by going out with them.

1036. A gold digger is a girl with a gift for grab.

1037. Gold digger: a human gimme pig.

golf

1038. It happened in a sporting-goods store: A woman asked to see a "low handicap," explaining that her husband wanted one so much that she thought it would be nice to surprise him on his birthday.   — *Detroit News*

1039. George Gershwin, the famous composer, spent weeks trying to learn the game of golf, but with very little success. In an effort not to appear ridiculous before his friends, he hired a caddy and went off to practice in a remote corner of the country club. After badly slicing several shots he turned grimly to the little lad. "Son, can you tell me what's wrong with my form?" he pleaded.

The kid pondered the matter a moment. "Mister," he proclaimed, "you just ain't got rhythm!"   — *Christian Science Monitor*

1040. "That efficiency expert makes it a rule to search five ninutes — no more and no less — when he loses a golf ball."

"It's a good rule too. I played with him once when he lost a ball, and we found three in five minutes."   — *American Legion Weekly*

1041. Golf is a good walk spoiled. — MARK TWAIN

1042. The proper score for a business-man golfer is 90. If he shoots below that he is neglecting his business; if he shoots above that he is neglecting his golf.

1043. A golfer has one advantage over a fisherman. He doesn't have to show anything to prove it.

1044. *Caddie Master (to new recruit):* "Now then, young feller, hop to it, and don't just stand aroun' lookin' dumb like as if you was a member of the club!"

1045. *Golfer:* "Doctor, you remember you recommended golf to take my mind off my work?"
Doctor: "Yes."
Golfer: "Well, can you prescribe something now to get it back again?"

1046. *Golfer (to members ahead):* "Pardon me, but would you mind if I played through? I've just heard that my wife has been taken seriously ill."

1047. The golfer stepped up to the tee and swung one of those carelessly careful drives.
The ball sailed straight down the fairway, leaped gaily across the green, and dived into the hole like a rabbit.
"What have you suddenly gone crazy about?" inquired the golfer's wife, who was trying to learn something about the game.
"Why, I just made a hole in one!" yelled the golfer, as he essayed a double handspring with a wild gleam of delight in his eyes.
"Did you?" said his wife. "Please do it again, dear, I didn't see you."

1048.   "Who's that stranger, Mother dear?
        Look, he knows us — ain't he queer?
    Hush, my own, don't talk so wild,
        He's your father, dearest child.
    He's my father? No such thing;
        Father died away last Spring.

Father didn't die — you dub;
　Father joined a golfing club,
But they closed the club, so he
　Has no other place to go, you see —
No place left for him to roam —
　That's why he's coming home.
Kiss him — he won't bite you, child;
　All them golfing guys look wild.　　— *Author Unknown*

1049.　The man in the rainbow stockings was trying to play golf. The difficulty was, of course, to hit the ball. It was so much easier to hit the ground. He hit that every time. The turf flew in all directions. Swish! Swosh! More excavations. Something was wrong somewhere. It couldn't be his stockings. It must be the links. He turned hopelessly to his opponent.

"What do you think of these links?" he exclaimed.

"What do I think of 'em?" gasped his opponent, wiping a bit of soil from his lips. "Pouf! Best I ever tasted."　　— *The Argonaut*

1050.　*Golfer:* "My lad, do you know what becomes of little boys who use bad language while they are playing marbles?"

Small boy: "Yes, sir: they grow up and play golf."

1051.　Golf: a game where the ball usually lies poorly and the player well.

1052.　On the Athens, Texas, golf course, a shapely miss, attired in the briefest of shorts, stepped up to the number one tee and prepared to address the ball. Three caddies and five male golfers stepped aside and watched. She swung prettily, hooked the ball and lost sight of it. "Could you tell me where my ball went?" she asked the onlookers. Sheepish grins passed over eight faces. Not one of them had had his eye on the ball.　　— *Morning Telegraph* of Tyler, Texas

1053.　You can judge a man by the golf score he keeps.

1054.　　Last night I had a funny pain
　　　And to the Doc I flew
　　Said he, "That comes from overwork,
　　　There's nothing I can do."

> "You need a month of quiet rest,"
> He added with a smile.
> "You'd better drop your golf and try
> The office for a while."
> — *Source Unknown*

1055. "I am sorry," said the dentist, "but I can give you no appointment this afternoon. I have eighteen cavities to fill." And with that he picked up his golf bag and out of the office he went.

goodness

1056.
> If good men were only better,
> Would the wicked be so bad?
> — JOHN WHITE CHADWICK

gossip

1057. The more you are talked about, the less powerful you are.
— DISRAELI, *Endymion*

1058. He who openly tells his friends all that he thinks of them, must expect that they will secretly tell his enemies much that they do *not* think of him.
—C. C. COLTON

1059. Gossip: a newscaster without a sponsor.

1060. Gossip: the art of saying nothing in a way which leaves nothing unsaid.

1061. Gossip: something negative that is developed and then enlarged.

1062. Restricted: a piece of inside news you get from a civilian.

1063. Scandalmonger: a prattlesnake.

1064. Gossip columnists are the spies of life.

1065. Rest satisfied with doing well, and leave others to talk of you as they will.
— PYTHAGORAS

1066. Listen carefully, because I can tell it only once — I promised never to repeat it.

1067.   If wisdom's ways you wisely seek,
Five things observe with care —
Of whom you speak — to whom you speak,
And how — and when — and where.

1068.   No one would talk much in society if he only knew how often he misunderstands others.   — GOETHE, *Elective Affinities*

1069.   There is so much that is bad in the best
of us,
And so much that is good in the worst of
us,
That it doesn't behoove any of us,
To talk about the rest of us.
— *Source Unknown*

1070.   To live so that you would not be ashamed to sell the family parrot to the town gossip, is to have lived well.

1071.   The secret of being tiresome is to tell everything.
— VOLTAIRE

government — See also *Politics*

1072.   Many people consider the things which government does for them to be social progress, but they consider the things government does for others as socialism.   — EARL WARREN

1073.   He serves his party best who serves the country best.
— RUTHERFORD B. HAYES,
Inaugural Address

1074.   Patriotism is the last refuge of a scoundrel.
— SAMUEL JOHNSON

1075.   Self-government assumes, not that every man can safely govern himself, but that it is safer to leave every man to govern himself than to put any man under the government of another man; or any class of men under the government of another class.
— Reprinted by permission of Dodd,
Mead & Company from *Problems
of Life* by LYMAN ABBOTT

1076.   All of us are working for the government. The trick is to get paid for it.

1077. There is one fixed rule about government — the less it's worth the more it costs.

1078. Honesty is also the best foreign policy.

1079. Who was it said that if the average American found himself on an airliner about to crash he would take time to appoint a Landing Committee?

1080. "You are charged," said the judge, "with beating up this government inspector. What have you to say?"

"Nothing," replied the grocer. "I am guilty. I lost my head. All morning I held my temper while government agents inspected my scales, tasted my butter, smelled my meat, graded my kerosene. In addition, your honor, I had just answered three federal questionnaires. Then this bird came along and wanted to take moving pictures of my cheese and I pasted him in the eye."

1081. The way things are being done in Washington now days reminds one of the fellow who sawed off a board three times and it was still too short.

1082. Society is well governed when the people obey the magistrates, and the magistrates obey the law. — Solon

1083. "Congress is so strange," reported Boris Marshalov, the Russian actor and dramatic coach, after a visit to the spectators' gallery of the House of Representatives. "A man gets up to speak and says nothing. Nobody listens — and then everybody disagrees."
— Leonard Lyons, *N. Y. Post*

1084. Republics end through luxury; monarchies through poverty.
— Montesquieu

1085. PRESIDENTIAL PROFILES

John Quincy Adams, undoubtedly the worst dressed Chief Executive wore the same hat for ten years. Chester A. Arthur had 80 pairs of trousers and other clothes in proportion. He loved night clubs, his dinner parties were Lucullan, and as an authority on etiquette he surpassed Emily Post.

1086. Grover Cleveland had an artificial upper jaw of vulcanized rubber. George Washington wore a set of false teeth made from rhinoceros ivory. The reason he looks tight-lipped in his portraits is because he had difficulty keeping the teeth in place. Theodore Roosevelt lost the sight of one eye while boxing with a young naval officer in the White House.

1087. Fillmore and Harding were considered the handsomest presidents; Van Buren and Arthur the most polished.

1088. For 72 years no president wore a beard or mustache. After the Civil War there came the bearded succession of Grant, Hayes, Garfield and Benjamin Harrison. Cleveland and Theodore Roosevelt and Taft wore mustaches. Then followed the present smooth-shaven era. John Quincy Adams was the only bald-headed president.

1089. Washington and Jefferson each were 6 feet 2 inches tall, and Lincoln was 6 feet 4. James Madison was 5 feet 4 inches in height, and weighed less than 100 pounds.

1090. Taft, who weighed 332 pounds, was once stuck in the White House bathtub. John Quincy Adams also had bath trouble. It was his custom to go swimming in the Potomac in the early morning. One day a tramp stole his clothes and the president had to stay immersed until a small boy came fishing and was sent on an emergency errand to the White House.   — CHESTER HOPE and DON SMITH

1091.   LOUISIANA PURCHASE

The Post Office Department at Washington searching the titles to post-office sites in Louisiana, was dissatisfied with one because it went back no farther than 1803. To the Department's request for earlier information, the attorney for the owners replied as follows:

Please be advised that the Government of the United States acquired the Territory of Louisiana, including the tract to which your inquiry applies, by purchase from the Government of France, in the year 1803.

The Government of France acquired title by conquest from the Government of Spain.

The Government of Spain acquired title by discovery of Christopher Columbus, explorer, a resident of Genoa, Italy, who, by agreement concerning the acquisition of title to any land he discovered, traveled under the sponsorship and patronage of Her Majesty, the Queen of Spain.

The Queen of Spain had received sanction of her title by consent of the Pope, a resident of Rome, Italy, and ex-officio representative and vice-regent of Jesus Christ.

Jesus Christ was the son and heir apparent of God.

God made Louisiana.

I trust this complies with your request.

> — Contributed by WALTER F. DILLINGHAM,
> *Readers Digest*

1092. A small boy in the visitor's gallery was watching the proceedings of the Senate chamber.

"Father, who is that gentleman?" he asked, pointing to the chaplain.

"That, my son, is the chaplain," replied his father.

"Does he pray for the Senators?" asked the boy.

"No, my son; when he goes in he looks around and sees the Senators sitting there, and then he prays for the country."

1093. Can one generation bind another, and all others, in succession forever? I think not. The Creator has made the earth for the living, not the dead. . . . A generation may bind itself as long as its majority continues in life; when that has disappeared, another majority is in place, holds all the rights and powers their predecessors once held, and may change their laws and institutions to suit themselves. Nothing, then, is unchangeable but the inherent and inalienable rights of man. — THOMAS JEFFERSON in a letter to John Cartright in 1824. *The Jeffersonian Cyclopedia*, vii, 378

1094. Fiddler: It is an old maxim and a very sound one that he that dances should always pay the fiddler. Now, sir, if any gentlemen, whose money is a burden to them, choose to lead off a dance, I am decidedly opposed to the people's money being used to pay the fiddler. — ABRAHAM LINCOLN

1095. BOLSHEVISM DEFINED

One Irishman asked another for the definition of Bolshevism.

"Well, you see," he said, "if you have two automobiles, under Bolshevism you keep one yourself, and give up the other to the State."

"Well, that's fine," spoke up the other.

"And if you have two pianos, you keep one and give the other to the State."

"That's ideal," the other chimed in.

The first continued: "Should you have two cows, likewise, you keep one and give the other to the State."

"Well, I don't like that so well."

"Why not?"

"You see, I have only one automobile and one piano, but I have two cows."

1096. Posterity: what the founding fathers wouldn't have talked about so glowingly if they had known we were going to be it.

1097. Wherever there is a man who exercises authority, there is a man who resists authority.
— OSCAR WILDE

1098. The consciousness of the world is awaking today to the realization that the welfare of the individual is inseparable from the welfare of society at large, and not inimical to it; that success cannot be wrested from society by the individual intent upon selfish aggrandizement at the expense of his fellow men, but is bestowed by society upon the individual who serves it well. For every individual and every institution, the measure of success is the measure of service. If you would be a master of men, you must become a servant of men.
— LORD BEACONSFIELD

gratitude

1099. There is as much greatness of mind in acknowledging a good turn, as in doing it.
— SENECA

1100. *Daughter (after getting a new mink coat as a birthday gift from father):* "I don't see how such a wonderful fur can come from such a low, sneaking little beast."

Father: "I don't ask for thanks, dear, but I do insist on respect."

greatness

1101. There is no such thing as a little country. The greatness of a people is no more determined by their number than the greatness of a man is determined by his height.
— *Wesleyan Christian Advocate*

1102. If living conditions don't stop improving in this country, we're going to run out of humble beginnings for our great men.

— RUSSELL P. ASKUE, *Ladies Home Journal*

1103. Only a little man is troubled because someone should fail to appreciate his greatness.

1104. One of the marks of greatness is a sense of proportion, for only those can have a feeling for gradations to whom the main issue is no longer in doubt. In every age, courtesy has been the complement of strength, just as rudeness is usually the mark of the man who is not sure of being able to maintain his ground. This is true even of such diverse types as humorists and social reformers. The horse-laugh comes from the man who is not sure that his joke will be appreciated, and the damning of all society is usually the speech of the reformer who is not quite sure how he would administer the world if he had it.

Those who have the touch of mastery see many tints and shades between white and black. Dickens accomplished social changes that the modern propagandist would hardly dream of reaching. So did Thackeray. But neither one ever painted a villain without some redeeming human touch. Cervantes made delicious fun of the Don Quixote of his own creation, but he loved the luckless knight even in his misfortunes. Dear old James Weber Linn once pointed out that "to know people, you have to love them, and to love them is a liberal education."

Power to be used effectively in any line, should be held the way a fencing master tells his pupils to hold a foil — as though you held a live bird in your hand and wished to control without crushing it.

— ROYAL F. MUNGER

1105. To be great is to be misunderstood.

— RALPH WALDO EMERSON

1106. Great men are rarely isolated mountain peaks; they are the summits of ranges.

— THOMAS W. HIGGINSON

1107. No horse gets anywhere until he is harnessed. No steam or gas ever drives anything until it is confined. No Niagara is ever turned into light and power until it is tunneled. No life ever grows great until it is focused, dedicated, disciplined.

— HARRY EMERSON FOSDICK, *Living Under Tension* (Harper)

171

1108. It is not the square miles but the square people who make a nation great.

1109. Censure is the tax a man pays to the public for being eminent.
— JONATHAN SWIFT

1110. It takes a great man to make a good listener.
— SIR ARTHUR HELPS, *Brevia*

1111. Mountains never shake hands. Their roots may touch; they may keep together some way up; but at length they part company, and rise into individual, insulated peaks.
— J. C. and A. W. HARE, *Guesses at Truth*

1112. Greatness is not mortal. The qualities which the great have to give, they give perpetually. Their gifts are taken into the pattern of life, and they appear thereafter in the fabric of the lives of nations, renewing themselves as the leaves of the trees are renewed by the seasons.
— ROBERT TROUT, in a radio tribute to Franklin D. Roosevelt

greed

1113. An Indian Princess who had fasted for a week, was led to a row of ripe, golden corn and told, "You may have as many ears for yourself as you can hold in your arms." There was only one reservation: she could not retrace her footsteps.

She began moving slowly down the row, fingering many ears, but leaving all of them on the stalks. "The ones ahead," she told herself, "will even be better."

Suddenly, however, she found herself at the end of the row — and she had gathered not a single ear of corn! All of which, of course, is another way of stating that old adage about a bird in the hand.

1114. We rarely think about the other fellow until we become the other fellow.

1115. The ass went seeking for horns and lost his ears.
— *Arabian Proverb*

1116. Another of the inexhaustible supply of stories about Abraham Lincoln has come to light. This one concerns the time a Springfield neighbor saw Lincoln striding past her house with two of his boys, both wailing loudly. "Why, Mr. Lincoln," asked the neighbor, "Whatever is the matter with the boys?" "Just what's the matter with the whole world," Lincoln replied. "I've got three walnuts and each wants two."

1117. You must learn not to overwork a dollar any more than you would a horse. Three percent is a small load for it to draw, six, a safe one; when it pulls in ten for you, it's likely working out West and you've got to watch to see that it doesn't buck; when it makes twenty, you own a blame good critter or a mighty foolish one, and you want to make dead sure which; but if it draws a hundred it's playing the races or something just as hard on horses and dollars; and the first thing you know you won't even have a carcass to haul to the glue factory. — GEORGE HORACE LORIMER

guilt complex

1118. Sir Arthur Conan Doyle used to tell how he sent a telegram to each of twelve friends, all men of great virtue and reputation and of considerable position in society. The message was worded, "Fly at once, all is discovered." Within twenty-four hours, the story goes, all twelve had left the country.
— FRANCIS L. WELLMAN, *Success in Court*

habit

1119. Habits are cobwebs at first; cables at last.
— *Chinese Proverb*

1120. The best way to stop a bad habit is never to begin it.
— J. C. PENNEY

1121. "When I was a little boy," remarked an old man, "somebody gave me a cucumber in a bottle. The neck of the bottle was small, the cucumber large. I wondered how it got in there. Then, out in the garden one day, I came upon a bottle slipped over a little green fellow. Then I understood. The cucumber had grown in the bottle."

"Often I see men with habits, I wonder how any strong, sensible man could form. Then I reflect that likely they grew into them when young, and cannot now slip out of them. They are like the cucumber in the bottle!"
— *Christian Herald*

happiness – joy – grief

1122. John Mason Brown, the noted critic, writes:
"What happiness is, no person can say for another. But no one, I am convinced, can be happy who lives only for himself. The joy of living comes from immersion in something that we know to be bigger, better, more enduring and worthier than we are. People, ideas, causes — these offer the one possible escape not merely from selfishness but from the hungers of solitude and the sorrows of aimlessness. No person is as uninteresting as a person without interests."
— *Words to Live By,* edited by William Nichols

1123. The best cure for worry, depression, melancholy, brooding, is to go deliberatively forth and try to lift with one's sympathy the gloom of somebody else. — ARNOLD BENNETT

1124. One thing I know; the only ones among you who will be really happy are those who will have sought and found how to serve.
— DR. ALBERT SCHWEITZER

1125. Happiness is a perfume you cannot pour on others without getting a few drops on yourself.

1126. The happiest people are those who think the most interesting thoughts. Those who decide to use leisure as a means of mental development, who love good music, good books, good pictures, good company, good conversation, are the happiest people in the world. And they are not only happy in themselves, they are the cause of happiness in others. — WILLIAM LYON PHELPS

1127. If you observe a really happy man you will find him building a boat, writing a symphony, educating his son, growing double dahlias in his garden, or looking for dinosaur eggs in the Gobi desert. He will not be striving for it as a goal in itself. He will have become aware that he is happy in the course of living life twenty-four crowded hours of the day.
— From *How to Be Happy Though Human,* copyright 1931, by W. BERAN WOLFE. Reprinted by permission of Rinehart & Co., Inc., Publishers.

1128. Happiness is like a kiss — in order to get any good out of it you have to give it to somebody else.

1129. Happiness comes more from loving than being loved; and often when our affection seems wounded it is only our vanity bleeding. To love, and to be hurt often, and to love again — this is the brave and happy life.
— J. E. BUCKROSE, "What I have Gathered," *Readers Digest*

1130. The secret of happiness and prosperity in this world, as in the world to come, lies in thinking of the welfare of others first, and not taking one's self too seriously.
— J. KINDLEBERGER

1131. The secret of happiness is in getting what you want — not what you want others to think you want.

1132. A statesman once remarked that the greatest of all rules for human happiness is to talk things over. Half of the troubles in life come from not understanding each other, and the other half from not trying to understand. Once hatch your grievance into words and you will be surprised to find how much smaller it is than you thought it was when you sat brooding on it. "In conversation," said Bacon, "doubts are resolved." Charles Lamb used to say that he could never hate a man if he knew him.

1133. The city of happiness is in the state of mind.

1134. I have found that most people are about as happy as they make up their minds to be.
— ABRAHAM LINCOLN

1135. The man who radiates good cheer, who makes life happier wherever he meets it, is always a man of vision and faith.
— ELLA WHEELER WILCOX

1136. Grief can take care of itself; but to get the full value of joy you must have somebody to divide it with.
— MARK TWAIN

1137. To be without some of the things you want is an indispensable part of happiness.
— BERTRAND RUSSELL

1138. For every minute you are angry you lose sixty seconds of happiness.
— RALPH WALDO EMERSON

1139. This is the true joy of life, the being used for a purpose recognized by yourself as a mighty one.
— GEORGE BERNARD SHAW, in the preface to *Man and Superman*

1140.   If I thought that a word of mine
      Perhaps unkind and untrue,
Would leave its trace on a loved one's face,
      I'd never speak it —
          Would you?
If I thought that a smile of mine
      Might linger the whole day through
And lighten some heart with a heavier part,
      I'd not withhold it —
          Would you?   *— Author Unknown*

1141.   So long as we contribute to the development, happiness or comfort of any human being, we are of importance in the world — and no longer. Not our personal enjoyment, nor yet our seeming success in life, but our part in God's plan for others is the measure of our importance in this world.   *— Source Unknown*

1142.   Action may not always bring happiness; but there is no happiness without action.   *— Benjamin Disraeli*

1143.   It isn't your position that makes you happy or unhappy, it's your disposition.

1144.   It is good always to remember that it is the pursuit of happiness to which the Declaration of Independence refers as an inalienable right, not happiness itself.

1145.   Happiness consists in being perfectly satisfied with what we have got as well as with what we haven't got.

1146.   Happiness is a way station between too little and too much.
          — Channing Pollock

1147.   Happiness is a delicate balance between what one is and what one has.

1148.   One should seek virtue for its own sake and not from hope or fear, or any external motive. It is in virtue that happiness consists, for virtue is the state of mind which tends to make the whole of life harmonious.

haste

1149. When Samuel Goldwyn finished reading a fresh script from a newly optioned scenarist one morning, he called the anxious writer to him and said, "This is a perfect script. It's the only scenario I ever saw that there's nothing wrong with. I want you to have 100 copies made, and send one to every member of my staff. I want everybody at this studio to see a perfect script." The writer was delirious with pleasure. "And hurry," added Goldwyn, "before I start rewriting it."

— Stage

1150. The hasty and the tardy meet at the ferry.

— Arabian Proverb

hate — See *Love*

health

1151. Health is the thing that makes you feel that now is the best time of the year.

1152. In spite of the emphasis being put on bodily fitness for military service, it is not the thing America needs most. To develop military and naval geniuses is more important for the national security. There is no formula for this, but physical fitness is not necessarily the key. Many of the world's greatest military figures would have been rejected by the draft boards for these reasons:

George Washington, false teeth; Bismarck, overweight; Napoleon, ulcers of the stomach; U. S. Grant, alcoholism; Julius Caesar, epilepsy; Horatio Nelson, one eye, one arm; Kaiser Wilhelm, withered arm; Duke of Wellington, underweight.

— Dr. Logan Glendening,
Nation's Business

1153. The fate of a nation has often depended on the good or bad digestion of a prime minister.

— Voltaire

1154. We who have no time for our health today, may have no health for our time tomorrow.

heart

1155. The human heart is like a millstone in a mill: When you put wheat under it, it turns and grinds and bruises the wheat to flour; if you put no wheat in, it still grinds on, but then 'tis itself it grinds and wears away. — MARTIN LUTHER

heredity

1156. If your folks didn't have any children, there's a good chance that you won't have any.

1157. Heredity is something every man believes in until his children begin to act like fools.

1158. No man believes genius is hereditary until he has a son.

1159. Somebody asked Texas Guinan if genius was hereditary. "I don't know," she replied. "I've never had any children."

1160. Two friends who had not seen each other for some time met in the street one day. "You're looking rather down in the mouth, old man," said one to the other. "Are you feeling sick?"

"Not exactly," replied his friend, "but I'll admit that I've been worried of late. You remember, that I hired a man to trace my pedigree?"

"Yes," said the other. "What's the trouble? Hasn't he been successful?" "Successful! I should say he has!" came the reply in despairing tones. "I'm having to pay him hush money."

1161. The bad traits a child gets from the other side of the family.

1162. Genealogy: tracing yourself back to people better than you are. — JOHN GARLAND POLLARD

1163. I don't know who my grandfather was; I am much more concerned to know what his grandson will be. — ABRAHAM LINCOLN

1164. Family tree: the only tree whose branches seek the shelter of its roots.

1165. The worst misfortune that can happen to an ordinary man is to have an extraordinary father. — AUSTIN O'MALLEY

1166. Gypsy Rose Lee's succint biography of another girl: "She is descended from a long line that her mother listened to."

1167. Two negroes were discussing family trees.

"Yes," said Ambrose, "I can trace my relatives back to a family tree."

"Chase 'em back to a family tree," said Mose.

"No — trace 'em, trace 'em."

"Well, there ain't but two kinds of things dat lives in trees — birds and monkeys — and you shu' ain't got no feathers on you."

1168. An Irishman was seated in a train beside a pompous individual who was accompanied by a dog.

"Foine dog ye have," said the Irishman. "Phwat kind is it?"

"A cross between an Irishman and an ape," replied the man.

"Sure an' it's related to both of us," the Irishman rejoined.

history

1169. Charles A. Beard, the historian, was asked: "What lessons have you learned from all the history you have known?" He replied:

"1. When it gets darkest, the stars come out.

"2. When a bee steals from a flower it also fertilizes it.

"3. Whom the gods would destroy, they first make mad with power.

"4. Though the mills of God grind slowly, yet they grind exceedingly small."

1170. We learn from history that we learn nothing from history. — GEORGE WILHELM FRIEDRICH HEGEL

1171. Human beings, not anonymous forces, determine the course of history. — FRITZ REDLICH

1172. It is much more difficult to talk about a thing than to do it. — Anybody can make history. Only a great man can write it. — OSCAR WILDE

1173. A youngster whose love of history was not any too intense expressed his opinion on the inside cover of his history book as follows: "In case of fire, please throw this in."

1174. Who among Americans has not heard of the Midnight Ride of Paul Revere? But how many have heard of William Dawes? Very few, if school histories had anything to do with it; they follow Longfellow's poetic version, giving full credence to lines he penned in the imaginative recesses of his own study.

Yet William Dawes was the official messenger chosen to ride to Lexington and warn Sam Adams and John Hancock that the British were coming, as Paul Revere himself testifies. Revere was sent out after Dawes had already started, in case Dawes should be captured on the way; the two messengers met at Lexington, roused the countryside and then traveled on together toward Concord. But on the road Revere was captured. Dawes put spurs to his horse, made his escape, and thereupon dropped out of history; while to the discomfited Revere, decades later, a poet's whim dealt out immortality.

— NATHAN SCHACHNER, *American Mercury*

hobbies

1175. As a practicing lawyer, Supreme Court Justice Louis D. Brandeis made plenty of money. When he had acquired a sufficient fortune to support his family on a comfortable scale, he began a long series of unpaid public services — work on Interstate Commerce Commission rate cases and other intricate legal projects which intimately concerned public welfare. This work became his hobby; in discussing it he stated: "Some men buy works of art, others delight in yachts. My luxury is to invest my surplus effort in the pleasure of taking up a problem and helping solve it for the people without any compensation. Your yachtsman would lose much of his enjoyment if he were obliged to do for pay what he is doing for the love of the thing itself. So I should lose much of my satisfaction if I were paid for public services of this kind." — EDWARD G. LOWRY, *Today*

1176. The reason a hobby is so useful in overcoming tension is that it puts to work those unused talents which might otherwise become restless, and it provides us with a form of activity in which there is no need whatever to strive for success. There is no compulsion, no fear of failure. . . . We find it becomes easy to achieve, even though in other activities we have been barred from success by inadequacies or by fears in various forms, fears and their defeatist tensions. In this way, hobbies show us how to live and act without fear — an exhilarating experience which, through habit, becomes a habit of success in other activities. — HAL FALVEY, *Ten Seconds That Will Change Your Life* (Wilcox & Follett)

1177. Hobbies should be wives, not mistresses. It will not do to have more than one at a time. One hobby leads you out of extravagance; a team of hobbies you cannot drive until you are rich enough to find corn for them all. Few men are rich enough for that.

— EDWARD BULWER-LYTTON

1178. Hobby: hard work you wouldn't do for a living.

home

1179. Nostalgia: longing for the place you wouldn't move back to.

1180. What seems to be most needed in the modern home is the family.

1181. Ash tray: something for a cigarette butt when there is no floor.

1182. Home: where part of the family waits until the rest of them bring back the car. — *Bank Notes*

1183. A recent writer has told a story of a modern girl who said to a real estate agent when he wanted to sell her a house, "A home? Why do I need a home? I was born in a hospital, educated in a college, courted in an automobile, and married in a church; I live out of the delicatessen and paper bags; I spend my mornings on the golf course, my afternoons at the bridge table, and my evenings at the movies, and when I die, I am going to be buried at the undertaker's. All I need is a garage." — EVELYN A. CUMMINS

honesty — See also *Integrity*

1184. Lock your door and keep your neighbor honest.

— *Chinese Proverb*

1185. There are very honest people who do not think that they have had a bargain unless they have cheated a merchant.

— ANATOLE FRANCE

1186. Those who stay on the level rise higher in the end.

1187. While it pays to be honest you are often a long time collecting.

1188. A rich man is an honest man, no thanks to him, for he would be a double knave to cheat mankind when he had no need of it. — DANIEL DEFOE, *Serious Reflections*

1189. The teacher asked Johnny if the world was round. He answered, "No."
   "Is it flat?"
   "No."
   "If it isn't round and it isn't flat, what is it?"
   "Daddy says it's crooked!"

1190. Every man cheats in his way, and only he is honest who is not discovered. — *Susannah Centlivre*

1191. Make yourself an honest man, and then you may be sure that there is one rascal less in the world. — THOMAS CARLYLE

1192. It is paradoxical that many climb to considerable heights by remaining on the level.

honor

1193. One of the greatest sources of suffering is to have an inborn sense of honor. — BENJAMIN DeCASSERES

1194. Dignity does not consist in possessing honors, but in deserving them. — ARISTOTLE *hope* — See also *Courage*

1195. There are no hopeless situations; there are only men who have grown hopeless about them.   — Quoted by Clare Boothe,
Europe in the Spring

1196. There is more hope for a self-convicted sinner than there is for a self-conceited saint.

hotels

1197. A hotel guest was awakened early one morning by a knock on his door.

"What is it?" he called, drowsily.

"A telegram, boss," came the response.

"Well, can't you shove it under the door without waking me up so early?" the man asked irately.

"No, suh," the boy answered; "it's on a tray."

1198 *Guest:* "Do you operate a bus between the hotel and the railroad station?"

Manager of Ritzy Hotel: "No, sir."

Guest: "That's strange. All my friends said you would get me coming and going."

1199. *Patron:* "May I have some stationery?"

Hotel Clerk (haughtily): "Are you a guest of the house?"

Patron: "Heck, no. I am paying twenty dollars a day."

1200. *Chemistry Professor:* "What can you tell me about nitrates?"

Freshie: "Well — er — they're a lot cheaper than day rates."

1201. "Have you left anything?" is a sign placed in many American hotels. There are hotels in London where a more appropriate question to the departing guest would be, "Have you anything left?"

1202. Sign outside a small hotel:

"Have your next affair here."

1203. A colored porter in a hotel was asked why rich men usually gave him small tips, while poor men were liberal.

"Well, suh, boss, I don't know, 'cept the rich man don' want nobody t' know he's rich, an the po' man don' want nobody t' know he's po'."

1204. *Hotel Guest (to manager):* "These flowers are for the phone girls."

Manager: "Thank you, sir. You compliment our service."

Hotel Guest: "Compliment, nothing — I thought they were all dead."

1205. Hotel: a place where you give up good dollars for bad quarters.

humiliation

1206. Humiliation: an emotion caused by suddenly shrinking to one's normal proportions.

humility

1207. The doctrine of human equality reposes on this: That there is no man really clever who has not found that he is stupid. There is no big man who has not felt small. Some men never feel small; but these are the few men who are.

— Reprinted by permission of Dodd,
Mead & Company from *A Miscellany of Men* by G. K. CHESTERTON

1208. The mark of the man of the world is absence of pretension. He does not make a speech, he takes a low business tone, avoids all brag, promises not at all, performs much. He calls his employment by its lowest names, and so takes from evil tongues their sharpest weapon.

— RALPH WALDO EMERSON

1209. I have three precious things which I hold fast and prize. The first is gentleness; the second is frugality; the third is humility, which keeps me from putting myself before others. Be gentle and you can be bold; be frugal and you can be liberal; avoid putting yourself before others and you can become a leader among men.

— LAO TZU

1210. Humility, like darkness reveals the heavenly lights.
— Henry David Thoreau

1211. Do not practise excessive humility.   — Dr. John Todd

1212. Blessed are the meek, for they shall inherit the earth.
— *The Bible*

husband and wife — See *Marriage*

hypocrisy

1213. A bad man is worse when he pretends to be a saint.
— Bacon, *Moral and Historical Works*

1214. Accordionist: one who can successfully play both ends against the middle.

1215. Newspapers are writing columns of editorials denouncing the sweepstakes and printing full-page photographs of the winners.

1216. HYPOCRISY

It is all in vain to preach the truth,
To the eager ears of a trusting youth,
If, whenever the lad is standing by,
He sees you cheat and he hears you lie:
Fine words may grace the advice you give,
But youth will learn from the way you live.
Honor's a word that a thief may use,
High-sounding language the base may choose.
Speech is empty and preaching vain,
Though the truth shines clear and the lesson's plain;
If you play false, he will turn away,
For your life must square with the things you say.
He won't tread the path of your righteous talk,
But will follow the path which you daily walk.
"Not as I do, but do as I say,"
Won't win him to follow the better way;
Through the thin veneer of your speech he'll see
Unless you're the man you would have him be.
The longer you live you will find this true:

> As you would teach, you must also do.
> Rounded sentences, smooth and fair,
> Were better not said if your deeds aren't square,
> If you'd teach him to live to his very best
> You must live your life by the self-same test.
>
> — EDGAR A. GUEST, (Published by The
> Reilly & Lee Co., Chicago and re-
> printed by permission.)

ideal

1217. Utopia: conditions that will prevail when Americans enjoy 1955 wages, 1926 dividends, 1932 prices, and 1910 taxes.

idealism

1218. Ideals are like stars; you will not succeed in touching them with your hands. But, like the seafaring men on the desert of waters, you choose them as your guides, and following them reach your destiny. — CARL SCHURZ

ideas

1219. It is useless to send armies against ideas.
— GEORG BRANDES

1220. Put a man in prison for his ideas and you have a Martyr; execute him and you'll have a Saint; laugh at him and you've made a Fool.

1221. Two Chinese coolies were arguing heatedly in the midst of a crowd. When an onlooker expressed surprise that no blows were struck, his Chinese friend said: "The man who strikes first admits that his ideas have given out."

identification

1222. The door of the postoffice opened and a man whom the postmistress did not recognize as one of the people living in the district walked in.

"I am expecting a registered letter to be left here for me," he announced, as he approached the counter.

"What name, please?" asked the postmistress.

The man gave his name and the letter was produced, but the woman had some doubts as to whether she ought to give it up, as she had no means of identifying the caller.

Upon hearing this the stranger took a photograph from his pocket and handed it to the postmistress, remarking:

"I think that ought to satisfy you as to who I am."

She looked long and earnestly at the portrait and then said:

"Yes, that's you, right enough, here's your letter."

idleness

1223. He is not only idle who does nothing, but he is idle who might be better employed. — SOCRATES

ignorance

1224. Behind every argument is someone's ignorance. — LOUIS D. BRANDEIS

1225. Beware of an over-pious ignoramus.

1226. Nothing is more terrible than to see ignorance in action. — GOETHE

imagination

1227. Michelangelo's famous statue of David, was fashioned from a block of marble that had been spoiled in the quarrying and cast away as of no value. The great creative artist used his imagination; first he built up in his mind's eye a vision of what could be done with that spoiled block of marble. Working patiently over a long period of time he brought into existence the beauty and wonder that he had built up in his mind.

1228. Imagination: something that sits up with a woman when her husband comes home late.

imitation

1229.   They copied all they could follow
But they couldn't copy my mind,
And I left 'em sweating and stealing,
A year and a half behind.   — KIPLING, *Mary Gloster*

1230.   Imitation is the sincerest form of flattery.
— C. C. COLTON

1231.   To do exactly the opposite is also a form of imitation.

1232.   Next to the originator of a good sentence is the first quoter of it.
— RALPH WALDO EMERSON, *Letters and Social Aims*

1233.   Every human being is born as an original and dies as a copy.

1234.   It is by imitation far more than by precept that we learn everything; and what we learn thus we acquire not only more effectually, but more pleasantly.   — EDMUND BURKE

1235.   A good imitation is the most perfect originality.
— VOLTAIRE

1236.   There is much difference between imitating a good man and counterfeiting him.   — BENJAMIN FRANKLIN

impatience

1237.   Impatience (a child's definition): Waiting in a hurry.

index

1238.   I certainly think that the best book in the world would owe the most to a good index, and the worst book, if it had but a good single thought in it, might be kept alive by it.
— HORACE BINNEY

1239. So essential did I consider an index to be to every book, that I proposed to bring a bill into Parliament to deprive an author who publishes a book without an index of the privilege of copyright, and, moreover, to subject him for his offense to a pecuniary penalty.
— LORD CAMPBELL, *Lives of the Chief Justices*

indispensability

1240. The graveyards are full of people the world could not do without.
— ELBERT HUBBARD

individuality

1241. Where all think alike, no one thinks very much.
— WALTER LIPPMANN

industrious

1242. Thank God — every morning when you get up, that you have something to do which must be done, whether you like it or not.
Being forced to work, and forced to do your best, will breed in you a hundred virtues which the idle will never know.
— CHARLES KINGSLEY

inevitable

1243. It seems to me, when it cannot be helped, that defeat is great.
— WALT WHITMAN

inferiority

1244. No one can make you feel inferior without your consent.
— ELEANOR ROOSEVELT

inflation

1245. Inflation: a fate worse than debt.

1246. Inflation: a period when two can live as steep as one.
— *Des Moines Register*

ingenuity

1247. Two engineers recently were faced with the problem of locating the points at which nitrogen gas was leaking from some buried cables. Scientific gadgets failed miserably. But these were ingenious fellows. They pumped into the cables a gas concoction which bore a cat odor. Then they hired a small dog and walked him over the cable route. Every time they hit a leak, the dog began to dig like mad. Mission accomplished.

1248. At a state banquet given by Frederick the Great of Prussia to his courtiers and noblemen, the monarch asked those present to explain why his revenues continued to diminish despite incoming taxes. An old general of the Hussars remarked dryly, "I will show Your Majesty what happens to the money." Procuring a piece of ice, he lifted it high for inspection; then he handed it to his neighbor and requested it be passed on from hand to hand to the King. By the time it reached Frederick, it was about the size of a pea.

— Christian Science Monitor

1248a. A man once owned a very fine horse which was the envy of all his acquaintances, one of whom, a shrewd trader, often asked to buy the animal. The owner always refused, but when the horse died, he had it sent to the trader. Some time later the two men met and the practical joker asked the other how he had liked the gift. The trader replied, "I made $3600 off him."

"How did you manage to make that off a dead horse?"

"Oh," said the trader, "I sold raffle tickets."

"My dear fellow, didn't anyone object?"

"Oh, yes," the trader answered calmly, "but the only one who objected was the man who won the horse, and I gave him back his money." *— Readers Digest*

1248b. Paul Wruger, President of the Transvaal, once decided a dispute between two brothers about an inheritance of land in South Africa thus: "Let one brother divide the land, and let the other have first choice." — The quotation from *Cecil Rhodes* is given by permission of MRS. SARAH GERTRUDE MILLIN and Messrs. Chatto and Windus, her English publishers.

1249. A shop was giving away toy balloons to children. One little fellow asked if he might have two. "Sorry," said the clerk, "but we only give one balloon to each boy. Have you a brother at home?"

The youngster was truthful, but he did want another balloon.

"No," he replied regretfully, then added hopefully, "but my sister has, and I want one for him."

1250. One much sought-after bachelor claims that what contributes most to his peace of mind when week-ending is the knowledge that he's going to receive a telegram. He never ventures to the country without having it thoroughly understood with his valet that a telegram will be sent to him. If he's enjoying himself, he reads the telegram without comment. If he is bored and can't bear the idea of staying out the week-end, after reading the wire, he announces that Aunt Jessie has just died or that a friend from England has been suddenly taken ill in New York. At any rate the telegram is a way out. — WILLIAM B. POWELL, *Arts and Decoration*

1251. Having tried in vain to prevent youngsters smearing their shop windows on Halloween, the merchants of Itasca, Illinois, some years ago offered prizes for the best pictures drawn on the windows with soap. The plan not only curbed mischief, but uncovered talent. Crowds viewed the windows as if it were an art exhibition. One year the townspeople were so impressed with the beauty of two of the soap paintings that they sent the young artists to art school.

1252. Each Sunday afternoon a certain automobile full of youngsters came to a filling station in Georgia to buy two gallons of gasoline. They invariably had the attendant put the gas in two one-gallon jugs instead of in the gasoline tank.

One day the station operator's curiosity got the best of him and he asked them why. The driver explained:

"Well, suh, we puts one gallon in de tank jes before we leave town and rides until de car stops going. Den we knows it's time to come home. And so we puts in de other gallon. We ain't never got stranded out on de road yet!" — CONSTANCE MARTIN, *Readers Digest*

1253. A hospital in Reading, Pennsylvania, has found a way to divert the flowers, candy and magazines that often flow into sick-rooms in an overwhelming flood, into a more useful channel. Sympathetic friends of a sick person may pay for one day of the patient's hospital bill and a card is delivered stating: "This indicates

ingenuity

that you are my guest in the Reading Hospital for the day. I wish you a speedy recovery."

— Hospital Topics

1254. An old Italian decided to open a shoeshine parlor near the gates of Camp Upton. His friends pointed out that there were already six shoeshine emporia on that self same street.

"I fix," said the little Italian. Within two weeks five times as many soldiers were patronizing his stand as all his competitors together.

Directly over his stand was a sign with big letters:

"One shoe shined free."

— The Pocket Book of War Humor
(Pocket Books)

1255. A British tar, home on leave and celebrating the occasion, had got himself into a dilemma. He had hired a taxi, only to discover when approaching his destination that he was penniless. He had dined and wined, not wisely, but too well. But the British navy is a training-school of resourcefulness. He caught up the speaking tube, shouted, "Stop!" and jumped out. "I just want to pop into this tobacconist's and get some matches," he explained to the driver. "I've dropped a pound note somewhere in the cab and can't find it in the dark." He entered the tobacconist's and as he had anticipated, the cab and its driver vanished into the night.

— The Argonaut

1256. A gentleman went into a Paris barbershop with a small boy one day and explained that since he had an appointment in the neighborhood he would like his own hair cut first. This accomplished, he handed the small boy up into a chair, urged patience upon him, and departed. When the boy's haircut was finished, the gentleman had not returned, and the barber sat him in a chair. A half hour passed. "Don't worry," said the barber reassuringly. "I'm sure your father will be back soon." The boy looked startled. "He isn't my father," he said. "He just came up to me in the street and said, 'Come along, let's both get a haircut.'"

— Foreign Travel

1257. Two women in a train argued concerning the window and at last one of them called the conductor.

"If this window is open," she declared, "I shall catch cold and will probably die."

"If the window is shut," the other announced, "I shall suffocate."

192

The two glared at each other.

The conductor was at a loss, but he welcomed the words of a man who sat near. These were: "First open the window. That will kill one. Next, shut it. That will kill the other. Then we can have peace."

1258. This story of an imaginative criminal concerns a young married couple in London who got a pleasant surprise in the mail one morning — two tickets to the best musical show in town: The donor neglected to send his name, and all day the couple's question was "Wonder who it is?"

They enjoyed the show; when they reached home they found that all their wedding presents had been taken. There was a note from the burglar, propped on the pillow in the bedroom, saying: "Now you know."

1259. At eighteen, Mary began to stay out at parties later than her parents thought advisable. They would sit up until she came in, and when they remonstrated over the lateness of the hour, she complained that they treated her like a baby.

Her parents hit upon a solution. Ahead of time, they all agreed upon the homecoming hour, usually a compromise between Mary's ideas and theirs, and set an alarm clock for that time. It was up to Mary to be home in time to "unset" the alarm. Her parents can now retire when they feel like it, and need not worry about her unless the bell wakes them.

1260. "How in the world do you make a go of things at all?" a traveling salesman inquired of a shopkeeper.

"You see that fellow there?" replied the merchant, pointing to the clerk at the far end of the counter. "Well, he works for me, and I can't pay him; so in two years he gets the store. Then I work for him till I get it back." — *Montreal Gazette*

1261. During the depression of the '30's, my father and I took a load of sweet corn into Janesville, Wis., and tried to sell it house to house at ten cents a dozen ears. We covered all one side of a street without a sale. Deciding that the housewives were balking at the implied obligation to buy by the dozen, we switched our price to one cent an ear, and canvassed the other side of the same street. The new strategy worked. We sold at nearly every house.

And, strangely enough, nearly every housewife took a dozen ears or more — at a price of two cents more a dozen!

— JENNINGS CHRISTENSEN of
Broadhead, Wis., *Readers Digest*

1262. Traveling a deserted road in Montana, a salesman ran out of gas 40 miles from the nearest gas station. He was dismayed until he noticed the phone lines along the road, and remembered an A.T. & T. ad which stated that, if a break occurred anywhere in their wires, "trouble shooters" were rushed out instantly to make repairs. The salesman drew his revolver, shot two wires apart and sat down to wait. A repair truck arrived within an hour. The salesman got his gas.

1263. The Air Corps has a new system for finding female companions. You look in the phone book for any name with a "Miss" in front of it, then phone thus:

"This is Private Joe Smith (or whatever *her* last name is). My father who lives in California wrote me that a cousin of mine by the name of Smith lives here."

"Well, I don't know whether I have any relatives in California, but ours is a pretty large family."

"May I ask how old you are, Miss Smith?"

"Twenty-two."

"My father said my cousin would be in her early 20's. May I see you and discuss this further?"

If she is nice, who knows what may happen? If she isn't, there is always another number. — *Readers Digest*

1264. "I know how to settle this unemployment problem," said the club wag. "If we put all the men of the world on one island, and all the women on another, we'd have everybody busy in no time."

"Well, what would they be doing?"

"Why, boat-building."

1265. To get fast service, try to sit two at a table for four. The waiter will rush your order to get rid of you.

— JIMMY CANNON, *New York Post*

1266. The customer with a puzzled expression contemplated a display of half a dozen dressed chickens.

"You see," she confided to the butcher, "I keep boarders. I wish you would pick out the three toughest hens in this lot."

The butcher gladly complied.

"Now," said the customer, "that's fine, I'll take the other three!"

— *Magazine Digest*

1267. In his latest volume of reminiscences, Sir Henry Luey relates the following story: One of Queen Victoria's grandsons wrote to her for a "tip." She replied, "warning the youth against the consequences of forming extravagant habits in early youth," whereupon he replied: "Dearest Grandma — I received your letter and hope you do not think that I was disappointed because you could not send me the money. It was very kind of you to give me the good advice, and I sold your letter for forty pounds, ten shillings."

1268. The English tell a story about a reluctant conscript asked by the army oculist to read a chart. "What chart?" asked the draftee. "Just sit down in that chair and I'll show you." "What chair?" asked the man. Deferred because of bad eyesight, the draftee went to a nearby movie. When the lights came on, he was horrified to discover the oculist in the next seat. "Excuse me," said the conscript as calmly as he could, "does this bus go to Shipley?" — *News Week*

1269. The mother of three teen-agers solved her problem of getting her teen-age children home and in bed early by ruling that the last one in on Saturday night had to get Sunday morning breakfast for the entire family.

1270. A man finding a hearing aid on the deck of a ferry, picked it up and shouted, "Hey, there!" Every head turned but one and the aid was returned to the rightful owner.

1271. Have you heard the story about the man in the market for a new car who saw an ad in a Long Island paper offering a 1952 Cadillac for sale for $50. The first day he passed it up as a joke, but when it appeared for the third time he went to look at the car. The address given turned out to be a beautiful estate. The owner, an attractive middle-aged woman, showed him the car and let him drive it. It was in perfect condition, and he promptly clinched the deal. After the bill of sale was in his hand, he couldn't suppress his curiosity any longer. "Would you mind," he asked the woman, "telling me why you're selling such a beautiful car for $50 when you could have gotten at least $4,000?"

"Not at all," she replied. "In my husband's will he left instructions to deliver the proceeds from the sale of his Cadillac to his secretary, who had been so kind to him." — *Readers Digest*

1272. An Oxford medical student dug up an ancient University regulation that said he was entitled to a pint of beer as refreshment while cramming for final exams. He was so persistent that the authorities finally gave in and provided him with his pint.

They also searched the regulations, and slapped on him a fine of £5 ($14) for not wearing a sword. — *Readers Digest*

1273. The way to drive a baby buggy is to tickle its feet.

1274. Alvin Eggling, when Recreation Director for Austin, Texas said that he'd learned how to really make Committee members work; he certainly must have for he got wonderful results from them. He used the "Blinder" system, whatever that is, but he explained it by telling the story of a friend of his, a Texan farmer who was plowing a field with only one horse. The farmer yelled at the horse, "Giddap Jack, giddap Casey, giddap Jerry, giddap Cromwell." Alvin once asked his farmer friend why he called his single horse all those different names. "Oh," said the farmer, "his name is Jack and he doesn't know his own strength. So I put blinders on him and yell those other names. Then he works and pulls fine 'cause he thinks he's got three other horses helping him."

1275. When Voltaire visited England in the year 1727, feeling ran high against the French, and the great author felt this dislike keenly. Once he was accosted by an angry crowd of people as he went for a walk. "Kill him! Hang the Frenchman!" cried threatening voices around him. Voltaire stood on the curbstone and cried out: "Englishmen! You want to kill me because I am a Frenchman! Am I not already punished enough in not being an Englishman?"

The crowd applauded this speech and escorted him home in safety. — *The Toastmaster*

1276. A man moved to a new city. He was chilled by the cool reception tendered him at the church which he attended. Determined to compel the pastor or some of the members to call on him, he cut a bank note in two pieces, and having written across one half, in red ink, this message, he dropped it in the contribution box: "If

196

the pastor, or any of the members of this church will be kind enough to call on John Smith, 192 Hope St., who is a regular attendant upon the services of this church, he will be pleased to deliver up the other half of this bill, and be thankful for the privilege of a little Christian fellowship in a strange city." A visit and apologies quickly followed.
— *Church Management*

1277. I was walking with Sir Herbert Tree one day when my hat blew off. I was about to hurl myself into the thick of traffic in pursuit when Tree restrained me: "My brother Max says," he told me gravely, "Never run after your hat. Someone is sure to bring it to you!"

True enough, a moment later a passer-by dashed up breathlessly and restored my hat to me. — VALENTINE WILLIAMS, *World of Action* (Houghton Mifflin)

1278. A father annoyed by his young son who was creating a rumpus around the house, in order to quiet him took a page from the newspaper he was reading, and on which was a map of the world. He tore it in fifty bits and gave these to the youngster telling him to "try to put the world together." The father figured this would take a very long time and that in the meantime the youngster would be quiet. In three or four minutes the boy was back with the whole thing put together and the pieces held in place by strips of scotch tape. The father wondered how this was done so quickly and the son showed him that on the back was a picture of a man. The boy said he had tried to put the "world" together but found it difficult until he noticed on the back side of the strips of newspaper were the features of a man. He then turned all the pieces of paper on the reverse side and first put together the "man." When he had finished this he discovered that he had also put together the "world." And so it is, if we would succeed in "putting the *world* together," we must first "put *man* together."

1279. In a Winnipeg restaurant a frustrated would-be diner took a sign reading WAITRESS WANTED out of the window, put it on his table. He got service — pronto. — *Winnipeg Tribune*, quoted by Thomas Richard Henry, *Toronto Telegram*

1280. In a crowded hall a little Irishman arose to his feet and asked in stentorian tones: "Is there a Christian Scientist in the hall?"

Receiving no answer he repeated his question, and over in the opposite corner a little poetical looking fellow stood up and said: "I am a Christian Scientist."

"Then would ye mind changin' seats with me, there's a draft here on my back." — MORRIS FISHBEIN, *Doctors and Specialists* (Bobbs-Merrill)

1281. Two men were hunting when the game warden suddenly appeared on the scene, and demanded to see their licenses. One of the two took to his heels and pursued by the warden he ran for fifteen minutes but was finally overtaken. He surprised the warden by pulling out his license as soon as he recovered his breath.

"But why did you run when you had a license?"

"Well, you see, sir, the other fellow doesn't have one."

1282. *Ticket Taker:* Here, you two boys can't get in on one ticket!

Youngster: I'd like to know why not. We're half brothers.

1283. *Confessor:* "I have stolen a fat goose from the poultry yard!"

Priest: "That is very wrong."

Confessor: "Would you like to accept it, father?"

Priest: "Certainly I will not receive stolen goods — return it to the man from whom you stole it."

Confessor: "But I have offered it to him and he won't have it."

Priest: "In that case you may keep it yourself."

Confessor: "Thank you, father."

The priest arrived home to find one of his own geese stolen.

1284. *Newsboy:* "Extra! Extra! Read all about it. Two men swindled."

Passerby: "I'll take one . . . Say, there isn't anything in here about two men being swindled."

Newsboy: "Extra! Extra! Three men swindled."

1285. Visiting her son at a U. S. Army Reception Center in Michigan, a mother was amazed at the spotless condition of the rest room adjoining the visitors' lounge. Then she saw the large sign: KEEP THIS PLACE LOOKING NEAT. YOUR SON MAY HAVE TO CLEAN IT. — Contributed by ALICE BALESKY, *Readers Digest*

1286. Some people use one half their ingenuity to get into debt, and the other half to avoid paying it. — GEO. D. PRENTICE

1287. *First Wallflower:* "Did you see Odette purposely stumble so that that young millionaire could catch her?"
Second Wallflower: "Yes, that sure was a business trip."

1288. A street car inspector was watching the work of the green Irish conductor. "Here, Foley, how is this?" he said. "You have ten passengers and only nine fares are rung up."

"Is that so?" said Foley. Then turning to the passengers he shouted, "There's wan too many av yez on this car. Git out o' here, wan av yez!"

initiative

1289. When you have saved a boy from the possibility of making a mistake, you have also prevented him from developing initiative.

1290. There's pay for the man who can follow a plan
    And carry the details through;
But the man whose pay is the most per day
    Is the man who can plan and do.
When a man has to ask you to point out his task,
    There's very small pay attached to it;
For the man gets the pay who is able each day
To discover his task and then do it. — FRANK H. PHILLIPS

innocence

1291. It was a fruit all right that caused all the trouble in the Garden of Eden, but was it an apple or a green pear?

innovation

1292. As the births of living creatures at first are ill-shapen, so are all innovations, which are the births of time.
— BACON, *Essays*

installment buying — See also *Credit*

1293. To get a proper idea of Eternity, try paying for a $2,000 automobile on the installment plan.

institution

1294. An institution is the lengthened shadow of one man; as, the Reformation of Luther; Quakerism, of Fox; Methodism, of Wesley; Abolition, of Clarkson. — EMERSON, *Essays*

insult

1295. There are two insults which no human will endure: the assertion that he hasn't a sense of humor, and the doubly impertinent assertion that he has never known trouble. — SINCLAIR LEWIS

integrity — See also *Honesty*

1296. Integrity: the thing which keeps you from looking ahead to see how the story ends.

1297. Knowledge without integrity is dangerous and dreadful. — SAMUEL JOHNSON

intelligence

1298. A highbrow is one whose learning has outstripped his intelligence. — VINCENT MASSEY

1299. An intelligent girl is one who knows how to refuse a kiss without being deprived of it.

1300. An intelligent girl is one who knows less than the man with whom she happens to be talking at the moment.

interference

1301. Snuff maker: a man who puts his business in someone else's nose.

intrinsic

1302. Rotten wood cannot be carved. — *Chinese Proverb*

intuition

1303. Intuition — the strange instinct that tells a woman she is right whether she is or not.

invention

1304. Window screen: a device to prevent the escape of insects.

jealousy

1305. "Why did the foreman sack you yesterday?"
"Well," was the reply, "a foreman is one who stands around and watches his gang work."
"I know; but what's that got to do with it?"
"Why, he got jealous of me! People thought I was the foreman."

1306. HOW TO OVERCOME JEALOUSY
You are jealous of the other person because you think you are not as good as he is. If, instead, you recognize his superiority and enjoy it with him, you have increased your own value. The enjoyment of another's greater ability or good looks makes it not only his possession but yours as well. Jealousy builds a wall between you and your friends. Acceptance and enjoyment of another's gifts can bring you much closer to that person. — WILLARD M. RUTZEN

1307. Moral Indignation: jealousy with a halo.
— H. G. WELLS

1308. Jealousy: the friendship one woman has for another.

judges — See *Law Courts*

judgment

1309. "We shoot the shadows on the screen instead of turning around and shooting at the operator of the machine."
Story of some wild westerners watching the Perils of Pauline. They see the villain attack Pauline; become incensed and begin to shoot

the attacker on the screen, little realizing that there will be another of the series of the serial the following week and all they succeed in accomplishing is putting some nicks in the wall, whereas if they had turned around and shot the operator of the projecting machine, they might have accomplished something of a lasting nature.

1310. Always keep in mind the part that mood can play in affecting one's judgment of a piece of work; be cautious of enthusiasm when the sun shines bright, and slow to dismissal when the clouds hang low.
— J. DONALD ADAMS,
The N. Y. Times Book Review

1311. Don't call the world dirty because you have forgotten to clean your glasses.

1312.
If I was as bad as they say I am,
And you were as good as you look,
I wonder which one would feel the worse
If each for the other was took?
— GEORGE B. BAKER

jury — See *Law*

justice

1313. Justice is truth in action. — JOSEPH JOUBERT

1314. Justice Brewer once said:
"For it is written by the finger of the Almighty on the ever-lasting tablets of the Universe that no nation can endure and prosper into and through whose life does not run the golden thread of equal, exact and universal Justice."

1315. There is only one thing worse than Injustice, and that is Justice without her sword in her hand. When Right is not Might, it is Evil. — OSCAR WILDE

1316.
I know not whether Laws be right,
Or whether Laws be wrong;
All that we know who lie in gaol
Is that the wall is strong;
And that each day is like a year,
A year whose days are long.
— OSCAR WILDE, *excerpt from*
The Ballad of Reading Gaol

1317. Justice is always violent to the offending, for every man is innocent in his own eyes. — DANIEL DE FOE, *Shortest Way With Dissenters*

1318. The test, after all, is not whether a certain law is popular, but whether the law is based upon fundamental justice, fundamental decency and righteousness, fundamental morality and goodness. What we need is not law enforcement, but law observance. In a modern society there is no real freedom from law. There is only freedom in law. — PETER MARSHALL

1319. Justice delayed, is justice denied. — WILLIAM E. GLADSTONE

1320. If judges would make their decisions just, they should behold neither plaintiff, defendant, nor pleader, but only the cause itself. — LIVINGSTON

1321. The Law's Delays: About 560 years before Christ, Solon made reference to the slowness of justice; Horace in the year 24 B.C. announced that justice was still "moving slowly"; Shakespeare in 1601 had Hamlet include "the law's delay" among those things that justified suicide; a third of a century later George Herbert complained that "lawsuits consume time." A century passed during which no changes were rung on this ancient complaint until Bishop Burnet, in his "History of His Own Times," in 1723, set it down that "the law of England is the greatest grievance of the nation, very expensive and dilatory." Dickens devoted a volume to the subject, and Walter Savage Landor, in his "Imaginary Conversations," gave us the since overworked-phrase "delay of justice is injustice."

We are at death grips in America with the age-old problem of government. Progress, gratifying progress, has been made. Let us tighten our hold and go on until the history of our time will record as its greatest achievement justice, sure and speedy, for all. — FRANK J. HOGAN, Former President of the American Bar Assn.

1322. It is just as well that justice is blind: she might not like some of the things done in her name if she could see them.

1323. Justice: what we get when the decision is in our favor. — JOHN W. RAPER, *What This World Needs*

1324. He reminds me of the man who murdered both his parents, and then, when sentence was about to be pronounced, pleaded for mercy on the ground that he was an orphan. — ABRAHAM LINCOLN

1325. He hurts the good who spares the bad.

— PUBLIUS SYRUS

1326. Who shall put his finger on the work of justice, and say, "It is there"? Justice is like the kingdom of God: it is not without us as a fact; it is within us as a great yearning. — GEORGE ELIOT

1327. Justice is the insurance which we have on our lives and property; to which may be added, and obedience is the premium which we pay for it.

1328. Justice, being destroyed, will destroy; being preserved, will preserve. — GLAVILL

1329. No obligation to justice does force a man to be cruel, or to use the sharpest sentence. — JEREMY TAYLOR

1330. Above all other things is justice: success is a good thing; wealth is good also; honor is better; but justice excels them all.

— DAVID DUDLEY FIELD

1331. It is impossible to be just if one is not generous.

— JOSEPH ROUX

1332. Justice discards party, friendship, kindred, and is always, therefore, represented as blind. — JOSEPH ADDISON

1333. He who is only just is cruel. — LORD BYRON

1334. Goodness lies in abstaining not merely from injustice, but from the desire for injustice. — DEMOCRITUS, *Ethica*

1335. Use the memory of thy predecessor fairly and tenderly; for if thou dost not, it is a debt will surely be paid when thou art gone.

— FRANCIS BACON, *Essays*

1336. A stranger and I had been waiting some time for Sir Herbert Beerbohm Tree at His Majesty's Theater. Finally he came in and flung himself into a chair between us. "Consider yourselves introduced," said he, looking at the ceiling, "because I only remember one of your names, and that wouldn't be fair to the other."

— HESKETH PEARSON, *Thinking It Over* (Harper)

1337. But what boots it that rights are guaranteed in a dozen constitutions, and that there are courts with power to enforce them, if these rights are as a matter of fact, denied to litigants too ignorant or too poor to give bonds and perfect appeals from justice courts that render unconstitutional and illegal judgments and demand oppressive bonds?

— FRANCIS E. WINSLOW

1338. The surest test of a square deal is that both parties are dissatisfied.

1339. When one divides, the other should have the right of first choice.

— LEGAL MAXIM

1340. Justice is better when it prevents rather than punishes with severity.

— LEGAL MAXIM

1341. Where the law is most strictly administered, it sometimes causes the greatest wrong.

— LEGAL MAXIM

1342. My concern is not whether God is on our side; my great concern is to be on God's side.

— ABRAHAM LINCOLN

juvenile delinquency — See *Crime*

kindness

1343. I shall pass thru this world but once. If, therefore, there be any kindness I can show, or any good thing I can do, let me do it now; let me not defer it or neglect it, for I shall not pass this way again.

— ETIENNE DE GRELLET

1344.   "What is real good?"
        I asked in a musing mood:
        "Order," said the law court;
        "Knowledge," said the school;
        "Truth," said the wise man;
        "Pleasure," said the fool,
        "Love," said the maiden,
        "Beauty," said the page,

> "Freedom," said the dreamer,
> "Home," said the sage,
> "Fame," said the soldier,
> "Equity," the seer ——
> Spake my heart full sadly: "The answer is
> not here;" Then, within my bosom, softly,
> this I heard:
> "Each heart holds the secret —
> Kindness is the word." — JOHN BOYLE O'REILLY

kiss

1345. Stealing a kiss may be petty larceny but sometimes it's also grand.

1346. A kiss that speaks volumes is seldom a first edition.
— *Ohio State Sun Dial*

1347. High heels according to a friend of ours, were invented by a woman who had been kissed on the forehead.

1348. It was a balmy evening in the park, clouds drifted across the face of the moon. The leaves whispered dreamily. They occupied one-eighth of a park bench together. They were all in all to each; there was no room in their blissful unconsciousness for the shadow of a policeman, approaching nearer and nearer. It was quite a shock to have a kiss sundered by a surly voice.

"This here's public property," growled the arm of the law. "And it ain't run for no private pleasure."

So arm in arm, they went to the railroad station, and stood at the gate, and every time a train pulled in or a train pulled out they mingled with the incoming and outgoing travelers, and kissed.

Thus they maintained their average without interference.

Finally an observant porter discovered the ruse and grinned broadly, showing two rows of teeth.

"Say," he whispered to the young man, "Why don't you go downstairs? There's a local leaves every minute."

1349. "Very interesting conversation in here?" asked papa, suddenly thrusting his head through the conservatory window, where Ethel, Mr. Thomkins and little Eva sat very quietly. "Yes, indeed," said Ethel, ready on the instant with a reply. "Mr. Thomkins and I were discussing our kith and kin weren't we Eva?" "Yeth, they wath," replied little Eva. "Mr. Thomkins said, 'May I have a kith?' and Ethel said, 'You kin.'"

1350. When women kiss, it always reminds me of prize fighters shaking hands.

— H. L. MENCKEN

1351. A pretty young woman stepped into a music shop in the city the other day. She tripped up to the counter where a new clerk was assorting music and in her sweetest tones asked: "Have you 'Kissed Me in the Moonlight'? "

The clerk turned, looked, and said: "It must have been Ira Jones at the other counter. I've only been here a week."

1352. *Boss:* "Who told you that just because I kissed you a couple of times you could neglect your work around here?"

Secretary: "My attorney."

knowledge

1353. Knowledge is power, if you know it about the right person.

— ETHEL WATTS MUMFORD

1354. The wisest men have the best reference libraries.

1355. When one begins to know that he doesn't know, then he first begins to know a great deal.

— ROBERT MARK WENLEY

1356.   He who knows and knows that he knows is a master.
     He who knows and does not know that he knows, needs
       a teacher.
     He who does not know and knows that he does not know,
       needs love.
     He who does not know and does not know that he does
       not know, is lost.   — *Ancient Proverb*

labor

1357. Andrew Carnegie, asked which he considered the most important factor in industry: labor, capital or brains, replied, "Which is the most important leg of a three-legged stool?"

1358. When labor quarrels with capital, or capital neglects the interests of labor, it is like the hand thinking it does not need the eye, the ear or the brain.   — JAMES FREEMAN CLARKE, *Self-Culture*

1359. The money the other fellow has is capital. Getting it away from him is labor.

1360. When a worker, frozen in his railroad job by law, was offered a better-paying position, his only way out was to get fired. He tried reporting late, lying down on the job, refusing to obey orders. Nothing worked.

Then he got the big idea, walked into the boss's office, carefully took the glasses off the superintendent's nose, and slugged him right where the glasses used to be.

Result: he was arrested for assault and battery, released under $250 bond. His name was not removed from the payroll — it would set a bad precedent, the railroad's attorney said, if a worker could get fired merely by socking his boss in the nose.

1361. No man needs sympathy because he has to work, because he has a burden to carry. Far and away the best prize that life offers is the chance to work hard at work worth doing.
— THEODORE ROOSEVELT, Labor
Day address at Syracuse, 1903

1362. It is to labor and to labor only, that men owe everything possessed of exchangeable value. Labor is the talisman that has raised him from the condition of the savage; that has changed the desert and the forest into cultivated fields; that has covered the earth with cities, and the ocean with ships; that has given us plenty, comfort, and elegance, instead of want, misery, and barbarism.
— M'CULLOCH

1363. It is not work that kills men, it is worry. Work is healthy, you can hardly put more upon a man than he can bear. Worry is rust upon the blade. It is not the revolution that destroys the machinery, but the friction. Fear secretes acids, but love and trust are sweet juices.   — BEECHER

1364. Workingmen are at the foundation of society. Show me that product of human endeavor in the making of which the workingman has had no share and I will show you something that society can well dispense with. — SAMUEL GOMPERS

1365. The distance between capital and labor is not a great gulf over which is swung a Niagara suspension bridge; it is only a step, and the laborers here will cross over and become capitalists and the capitalists will cross over and become laborers. Would to God they would shake hands while they are crossing, these from one side, and those from the other side. — REV. T. DEWITT TALMAGE

laughter

1366. A man isn't poor if he can still laugh.
— RAYMOND HITCHCOCK

1367. No error is so common as to suppose that a smile is a necessary ingredient of the pleasing. There are few faces that can afford to smile. A smile is sometimes bewitching, in general vapid, often a contortion. But the bewitching smile usually beams from the grave face. It is then irresistible. — BENJAMIN DISRAELI

1368.
　　　　　Laugh a little now and then
　　　　　　It brightens life a lot;
　　　　　You can see the brighter side
　　　　　　Just as well as not.
　　　　　Don't go mournfully around,
　　　　　　Gloomy and forlorn;
　　　　　Try to make your fellow men
　　　　　　Glad that you were born. — *Author Unknown*

1369. The world looks brighter from behind a smile.

law – legal – courts – judges – jury

1370. Trial by jury has come into wide use only in modern times. During the Middle Ages, it was customary to test an accused person by making him go through some dreadful ordeal. This was done with the idea that God would protect the innocent, but permit the guilty to suffer physical harm.

A common form of such trial was the ordeal by fire. Red-hot plowshares were sometimes placed in a row. More often, a bed of hot coals was prepared. While it still glowed, the accused was forced to walk barefoot across the inferno. If he stumbled and burned to death, he was pronounced guilty. But if he succeeded in crossing the coals, he was acquitted.

It meant extreme danger and fearful pain to be hauled over the coals. Even if a man survived, he never forgot his fearful ordeal. Hence, this phrase, "raked over the coals," for a severe testing remains in the language centuries after barbarous ordeal by fire was abandoned. — WEBB B. GARRISON

1371. The first thing we do, let's kill all the lawyers.
— SHAKESPEARE, *Henry VI., Act iv, Sc. 2*

1372. Where law ends, tyranny begins.
— WILLIAM PITT, Speech Jan. 9, 1770

1373. No law can possibly meet the convenience of everyone: we must be satisfied if it be beneficial on the whole and to the majority. — LIVY, *Histories,* xxxiv, 3

1374. There is no doubt that if there were a super-Supreme Court (of the United States) a substantial proportion of our reversals of state courts would also be reversed. We are not final because we are infallible, but we are infallible only because we are final. — JUSTICE ROBERT H. JACKSON,
Brown v. Allen, 344 U.S. 443, 540

1375. Every man believes in trial by jury until he is called for jury duty.

1376. A lawyer was drawing up papers of partnership for two manufacturers. He went over the papers before the final signing, but he found them incomplete.

"There is no mention here," he said, "of fire or bankruptcy. These must go in."

"Quite right," said the partners, speaking together; "put them in, but the profits are to be divided equally in both cases."

1377. A man was charged with stealing a case of canned goods from the storeroom of a grocery store.

"Now," said his lawyer, "if I take your case you must tell me honestly. Did you or did you not steal those canned peaches?"

"Well, yes sir, I did," the man admitted.

"That's all right," replied the lawyer. "You give me half of them."

When the case came into court the lawyer addressed the jury thus: "This man did not get any more of those peaches than I did."

The verdict was "not guilty."

1378. A Swede consulted a lawyer. He wanted to buy a piece of property but wanted a mortgage. The lawyer told him he needed a deed. The Swede insisted on a mortgage because his friend Olsen had had a deed and the fellow with the mortgage came along and took his property away from him. So he wanted a mortgage!

1379. *Lawyer —* "What made you wait so long before suing this man Smith for calling you a hippopotamus?"

Mr. Dumb — "Well, it was because I never saw a hippopotamus till yesterday at the zoo."

1380. *Judge:* "Can't this case be settled out of court?"

Kelly: "Sure. That's what we were trying to do, your honor, when the police interfered."

1381. Recently a young man was brought up in court on a charge of robbery. The case against him had been closed, and no testimony was forthcoming from the defendant. The judge turned to him impatiently. "Where are your witnesses? Haven't you any witnesses to produce in this case?" The prisoner somewhat bewildered replied, "Witnesses? Not me. I never take along any witnesses when I commit robbery."

1382. *Judge:* "What possible excuse did you fellows have for acquitting that murderer?"

Juryman: "Insanity."

Judge: "Really? All twelve of you?"

1383. *Woman juror to eleven exasperated men jurors:* "If you men weren't so stubborn we could all go home!"

1384. A boy was being tried in a Texas court for the theft of an automobile. When the testimony had all been given, the judge in his instructions to the jury asked for a not-guilty verdict.

211

Rising, the foreman of the jury announced dutifully: "Your Honor, we find the boy that stole that car not guilty."

MARION L. COONSE

1385. In a New England murder trial years ago, a defense witness testified that the accused had been out of sight of anyone and able to have committed homicide for a matter "of only two or three minutes." Whereupon the district attorney turned to the jury and said, "Gentlemen, here is my watch which I hold before you. We shall all pause, not for three minutes, but for only two minutes, and you may judge what could have been done by the defendant in that space of time."

It seemed interminable as the jury waited for 120 seconds to be ticked off. And they later returned a verdict of guilty.

— NEAL O'HARA, *Readers Digest,*
(McNaught Syndicate)

1386. The famous Rufus Choate, than whom there was never a shrewder cross examiner, was questioning a witness in an assault case in which his client was the accused. He maneuvered the fellow into admitting that he hadn't actually seen the offense committed.

"So," purred the famous attorney, "you say you didn't actually see the defendant bite off this man's ear?"

"Naw," growled the witness, "I didn't see him bite it off. I just seen him spit it out on the ground!"

The jury roared — and Choate knew full well he had lost his case on that one break. — PAUL W. KEARNEY, "When You Take
the Witness Stand," *Redbook*

1387. *Courtroom Strategy:* A. S. Trude, the famed trial lawyer, and the distinguished Dr. Frank Billings lived next door to each other in Chicago. One day Billings testified as a medical expert against Trude. Trude's cross examination of his eminent neighbor was brief. "Was Marshall Field one of your patients?" he began.

"Yes."

Trude asked, "Where is Mr. Field now?" and the doctor said, "Dead." Trude named other patients of Billings — Mr. Armour, Mr. Pullman, Mr. Cudahy, all of whom had died natural deaths. Each time Trude asked: "Where is he now?" and each time Dr. Billings had to answer: "Dead."

"That's all, thank you," the lawyer concluded, and won his case.

— LEONARD LYONS, *Readers Digest*

1388. When President Franklin D. Roosevelt was a young lawyer just getting started in New York, he was retained to handle a difficult civil case. The opposing lawyer was a very effective jury pleader and completely outshone his youthful rival in the argument to the jury. However, he made one fatal mistake: he orated for several hours. As he thundered on, Roosevelt noticed that the jury wasn't paying much attention. So playing a hunch when his turn came, he rose and said:

"Gentlemen, you have heard the evidence. You also have listened to my distinguished colleague, a brilliant orator. If you believe him and disbelieve the evidence, you will have to decide in his favor. That's all I have to say."

The jury was out only five minutes and brought in a verdict for Roosevelt's client.
— DREW PEARSON and ROBERT S. ALLEN, *Washington Merry-Go-Round*

1389.
Here lies a Lawyer,
　Laugh, if you will,
In mercy, kind Providence
　Let him lie still.
He lied for his living,
　He lived while he lied.
When he couldn't lie longer
　He lied down and died.　　*— Anonymous*

1390. *Judge:* "Your wife says you keep her continually terrorized."

Prisoner: "But, honestly, your honor —"

Judge (whispering): "Now, not in my official capacity, but as man to man, what is your system?"

1391. You will search history in vain for any instance where tyranny or despotism has been established by a court; and on the other hand, one of the first steps in the establishment of a despotism is to limit the power of the judiciary. — JUDGE JOHN J. PARKER, JR.

1392. A person may have acquired all the knowledge of music and be able to execute the most difficult composition with skill, yet if he does not have a passionate love of music in his soul he can never become a really great musician. So, however learned, however wise, however well-intentioned a judge may be, unless his heart is

on fire with love for his fellow men, with sympathy of the humblest of that innumerable host called the common people, he never can be a great judge.
— M. K. Harris

1393. Lawyer: the only man in whom ignorance of the law is not punished.
— Elbert Hubbard

1394. Judge: a law student who marks his own examination papers.
— H. L. Mencken

1395. Judges ought to be more learned than witty, more reverent than plausible, and more advised than confident. Above all things, integrity is their portion and proper virtue.
— Sir Francis Bacon

1396. *Prison Warden (to released convict):* "I'm sorry. I find we have kept you here a week too long."
Convict: "That's all right, sir. Knock it off next time."

1397. "One of the finest examples of the value of precedent that I have ever seen," President James Burrill Angell, of the University of Michigan, used to say to his class in International Law, "is one of the paths which you fellows make across the grass of the campus. We take that as clear proof that a walk should be there, and set about building one."

1398. "A little bird told me what kind of a lawyer your father was."
"What did the bird say?"
"Cheep, cheep."
"Well, a duck told me what kind of a doctor your old man was."

1399. If nothing else, the old codger was an experienced juryman who had sat in on many trials. Seeking to glean some useful information, an attorney asked, "Who influences you the most — the lawyers, the judge or the witnesses?"
The old man pondered for a moment before replying. At last he drawled: "Well, I'll tell ye. I'm a plain and reasoning man, and I ain't influenced by anything the lawyers say, nor by what the witnesses say — no, nor by what the judge says. I just look at the man in the dock and I asks myself, 'If he ain't done nothing wrong, why's he here?' So I brings 'em all in guilty."
— *The Highway Traveler*

1400. A man charged with murder consulted a famous attorney, but balked at the proposed fee, saying that another lawyer had offered to defend him for much less.

"I would suggest," said the famous attorney, "that you retain this other fellow. He will charge you half the fee and you won't even have to pay it. Your heirs will!"

1401. Counsel, upon receiving an adverse decision, rose and said:

"If your Honor please, the late Justice Bailey of our Supreme Court, used to tell the classes, when he was a preceptor in the Chicago College of Law, that there were only two things which a beaten lawyer could do. One was to take an appeal, and the other was to take his client to the Court House steps and damn the Court; and in this case," continued the lawyer, "I intend to insist upon all my prerogatives — and I do not intend to take an appeal."

1402. A minister, a doctor and a lawyer, adrift on a raft, sighted a distant island. There were signs of human habitation, but no persons in view.

Since the drift was away from the island, the lawyer volunteered to swim ashore and bring help. Just as he was about to dive into the sea, the minister urged a word of parting prayer, and a brief religious service was held.

Eagerly the two remaining voyagers watched their companion. Presently they were horrified to see a huge shark making directly for the lawyer. At the last moment, however, the shark ducked and the swimmer was saved. Later, another shark came into view and he, too, ducked as he approached the struggling man.

"There!" said the minister triumphantly. "Observe an answer to our prayers. Because of that service we held, the Lord has preserved our friend from the hungry sharks."

"Well, that may be," said the Doctor dubiously, "but personally I'm inclined to think it was professional courtesy." — *Quote*

1402a. "Prisoner, have you anything to offer in your own behalf?"

"No, your Honor, I've turned every cent I own over to my lawyer and a couple of jurymen." — *The American Legion Weekly*

1403. An English lady, self-appointed supervisor of village morals, accused a workman of having reverted to drink because "with her own eyes" she had seen his wheelbarrow standing outside a public house.

The accused man made no verbal defense, but the same evening, he placed his wheelbarrow outside her door and left it there all night.
— *The Country Man* (England)

1404. Cross-examining lawyers think that most of us are as useless and as aggravating as Ole, in this story that comes from the wilds of Pittsburgh.

The attorney for the defense was cross-examining the prosecution's star witness, a Norwegian lumberjack.

"You mean to tell me, Ole, that you saw this murder with your own eyes?"

"Yes."

"At half past nine in the evening?"

"Yes."

"And at the same time, as you have admitted, you were a quarter of a mile away?"

"O val," replied Ole, stretching his arms and legs and suppressing a yawn, "Ay tank Ay don't gif a dem about dis trial anyhow."

1405. If your little boy wants to become a lawyer, don't be discouraged. Think of the money he will save not having to hire one.
— *N. Y. World Telegram*

1406. A well-known lawyer was accosted on the street by a business man who discussed with him some financial rather than strictly legal question.

On the following day the business man received a bill from the lawyer for a sizeable sum.

Shortly thereafter the business man again happened to meet the attorney on the street.

"It's nice weather we're having," said the business man. "Remember, Mr. Attorney, I am telling it to you, not asking."

1407. "Well," said the lawyer, "I must tell you before the case comes up that it would have been better had you acted more on defensive lines. If you had not struck first you would have had the law on your side."

The man who was suing his neighbor for what he termed a murderous attack shook his head disgustedly.

"P'haps I would 'ave 'ad the law on my side," he muttered doubtfully; "but, at the same time, I should 'ave 'ad his blinkin' boot in me jaw."

1408. The awakened moral conscience of the country can find no better object for its influence than in making lawyers understand that their obligation to their clients is only to see that their clients' legal rights are protected, and that they ought not to lose their identity as officers of the law in the cause of their clients and recklessly resort to every expedient to win the case.

— WILLIAM HOWARD TAFT

1409. It was during the impaneling of a jury that the following colloquy occurred:

"You are a property-holder?"

"Yes, your honor."

"Married or single?"

"I have been married for five years, your honor."

"Have you formed or expressed any opinion?"

"Not for five years, your honor."

1410. *Juryman:* "You can tell that man is guilty by his looks."
Foreman: "Sh-h-h. That's the District Attorney."

1411. The courts are the tribunals prescribed by the Constitution and created by the authority of the people to determine, expound, and enforce the law. Hence, whoever resists the final decision of the highest judicial tribunal aims a deadly blow at our whole republican system of government — a blow which, if successful, would place all our rights and liberties at the mercy of passion, anarchy, and violence. — ABRAHAM LINCOLN

1412. Returning from a visit to his birthplace, Clarence Darrow, the noted criminal lawyer, met a doctor friend.

"If you had listened to me," said the friend, "you, too, would be a doctor."

"Why, what's the matter with being a lawyer?"

"I don't say that all lawyers are crooks," said the doctor, "but even you will have to admit that your profession doesn't exactly make angels of men."

"No," replied Darrow, "you doctors have the better of us there."

— *Capper's Weekly*

1413. A forger is a fellow who gives a check a bad name.

1414. Some girls were arrested recently at a New York smoker because of a certain dance. When they were in court the magistrate asked to see the costumes worn in the dance. He had to discharge the girls for lack of evidence.

1415. While examining a witness who was notorious for the ease with which he perjured himself, the well-known lawyer, Ralph Lockwood, purred, "I want to ask you just one question. Would you believe yourself under oath?"　　　— MIRIAM ALLEN DE FORD

1416. The late commissioner of baseball, Kenesaw Mountain Landis, once sat on the Federal bench. One day an old offender came before him. After a severe reprimand, the judge sentenced him to five years in prison.

"But, your Honor," the felon protested, "I'll be dead long before that. I'm a sick man — I can't do five years!"

Landis glared at him. "You can try, can't you?"
— JOSEF S. CHEVALIER, *Readers Digest*

1417. An aged criminal lawyer explains how he was always able to cheat the gallows for his clients: "I never say 'my client' or 'the defendant'; I always say 'Tom Jones' or 'Henry Brown.' Juries will hang clients and defendants, but they haven't the heart to hang Tom Jones or Henry Brown."

1418. Jury: twelve men who are chosen to decide which of the parties before the bar has the better attorney.

1419. A young lawyer pleading his first case had been retained by a farmer to prosecute a railway company for killing twenty-four hogs. He wanted to impress the jury with the magnitude of the loss.

"Twenty-four hogs, gentlemen — twice the number there are in this jury-box."

1420. *Judge:* "You are accused of stealing a chicken. Anything to say?"

Prisoner: "Just took it for a lark, sir."

Judge: "No resemblance whatever. Ten days."

1421. Said the law professor, "If you have the facts on your side, hammer them into the jury, and if you have the law on your side, hammer it into the judge."

"But if you have neither the facts nor the law?" asked a student.

"Then hammer on the table," answered the professor.

218

1422. A boy was a witness in court, and the lawyer said: "Did anyone tell you what to say in court?"

"Yes, sir."

"I thought so. Who was it?"

"My father, sir."

"And what did he tell you?"

"He said the lawyers would try to get me all tangled up, but if I stuck to the truth, I would be all right."   *— Quote*

1423. Lawyer: a person who helps you get what's coming to him.

1424. *Visitor in county jail:* "What terrible crime has this man committed?"

Warden: "He didn't commit any crime at all. He was going down the street a few days ago and saw one man shoot another, and he is held as a material witness."

Visitor: "And where is the man who committed the murder?"

Warden: "Oh, he's out on bail."

1425. A criminal lawyer whose clients, especially when tried for murder, were almost invariably convicted, boasted in the hearing of Montague Williams, "I have been forty years at the Bar, and I have never had a complaint about the way I have looked after my clients' interests." "That is because dead men tell no tales," retorted Williams.

1426. "Moses," said Uncle Eben, "was a great lawgiver. But de way he was satisfied to keep de ten commandments short an' to de point shows he wasn't no regular lawyer."

— Washington Evening Star

1427. Legal education was previously negligible both as to quality and quantity. "My rule," said an examiner of the old school, "is to pass any man whose examination I can mark 50%. Well, I asked the applicant two questions. The first was 'What is the rule in Shelley's case?' He answered that it had something to do with poetry. Of course that was wrong. Then I asked him 'What is a contingent remainder?' He answered that he was sure he didn't know. Well, that was right. So I passed him. He was 50% right!"

1248. *Lawyer (handing check for $100 to client who had been awarded $500):* "There's the balance after deducting my fee. What are you thinking of? Aren't you satisfied?"

Client: "I was just wondering who got hit by the car, you or I."

1429. There is but one law for all; namely the law which governs all law, — the law of our Creator, the law of humanity, justice, equity; the law of nature and of nations.

— EDMUND BURKE

1430. The burglar's wife was in the witness box and prosecuting counsel was conducting a vigorous cross-examination:

"Madam, you are the wife of this man?"

"Yes."

"You knew he was a burglar when you married him?"

"Yes."

"How did you come to contract a matrimonial alliance with such a man?"

"Well," said the witness sarcastically, "I was getting old and had to choose between a lawyer and a burglar."

The cross examination ended there.

1431. After an arduous session of the Supreme Court, the Justices at once decided on a three-day boat trip for relaxation. On the second day out the late Justice Cardozo, somewhat the worse for mal-de-mer, was leaning over the rail of the boat which was rocking badly, when Chief Justice Hughes sauntered along. "Can I do anything for you?" said the Chief Justice. "Yes," answered Judge Cardozo, "overrule the motion."

— MRS. B. GREENSBURG, *Readers Digest*

1432. Four things belong to a judge: to hear courteously, to answer wisely, to consider soberly and to decide impartially.

— SOCRATES

1433. As a student in law school, they called him "Necessity" because he knew no law.

1434. What a judge may on occasion do with a jury's decision is illustrated by the following story.

"Prisoner at the Bar, you yourself think that you are innocent; your lawyer thinks you are innocent; the prosecuting attorney seems to think that you are innocent; the judge on the bench feels that you are innocent. And yet the jury, with their superior knowledge of men and things, have found you guilty. It is therefore my bounden duty to sentence you. I therefore sentence you to one day, and, as that day was yesterday, you are free to take your hat and coat and leave the courtroom."

1435.   IF I WERE A JUDGE

If I were a Judge, I'd remember, too,
　　That when life is over, my labors through,
I, too, must stand at the Judgment seat,
　　And the 'God of Justice' be forced to meet;
And I'd want to feel on that great day
　　That none of us know, is so far away,
That the Lord of Heaven could say to me:
　　'Your work was done in sincerity;
Tho' you've made mistakes, yet I know you've tried
　　To be always and ever on Justice side;
And because of that, all else is forgiven,
　　And we welcome you to the Court of Heaven!'

If I were a Judge, it seems to me,
　　I would strive my level best to be
Humane, but upright — just, but kind,
　　Meeting all problems with open mind;
Hearing with patience from day to day,
　　Trials of humans, who passed my way.
I would grant no favors to rich or great,
　　That were not the due of their just estate;
Nor would I withhold from the humblest slave
　　The fullest justice — that I might save
Or keep, or hold my place of power,
　　For a single day, or a single hour.

If I were a Judge, I would keep in mind,
　　That the purest justice is always blind,
And that no distinctions 'twixt high or low,
　　Does the 'Goddess of Justice' note or know
No mortal man be he serf or king,
　　Would cause me to swerve, nor to grant a thing
That I should withhold — If I knew I should
　　Because I thought they were bad or good,

> For no man is so bad, and none is so pure,
> That we can be always and ever, sure,
> That there isn't some virtue, or taint of sin
> Mixed up with the other side of him.
> — HUGH R. PORTER

1436. Don't take the will for the deed; get the deed.
— ETHEL WATTS MUMFORD

1437. Before the bar of justice a wife brought charges of desertion and nonsupport. Mose Brown meekly admitted his guilt and offered nothing in extentuation except that the lady talked too much.

"That's no excuse for desertion, Mose," the court said. "Don't you know that the Constitution guarantees every woman the right to talk all she wants to?"

"Yas suh, Jedge. I knows it do. Only Lucy she never stop talkin'. She keep it up stiddy mo'nin, noon and night, day in, day out, till it git so I jess can't stand it no mo', Jedge."

His mournful earnestness impressed the court. "She does? What does she talk about?"

Mose wagged his head sorrowfully.

"Jedge, Suh," he said, "she don't say."

1438. The late Judge Francis Adams, well known to the older members of the Bar, was frequently direct and forceful in giving oral opinions. A demurrer to a declaration came up for argument, and the Court asked counsel his ground for demurring. Counsel replied that he had not read the declaration, but that it was two hundred pages long.

"Is this true?" asked the Judge of the reputed father of the declaration.

"It is," replied the latter.

"The demurrer will be sustained," said the judge, "there cannot be a declaration two hundred pages long without errors in it."

1439. The law, in its majestic equality, forbids the rich as well as the poor to sleep under bridges, to beg in the streets, and to steal bread.
— ANATOLE FRANCE

1440. A Union Pacific shopman, drawn for jury service, asked the judge to excuse him. "We are very busy at the shops," said he, "and I ought to be there."

"So you are one of those men who think the Union Pacific couldn't get along without him," remarked the judge.

"No, your Honor," replied the shopman, "I know it could get along without me, but I don't want it to find out."

"Excused," said the judge.

1441. The judge had just charged the jury; then asked: "Are there any questions any jurymen would like to ask before considering the evidence?"

"There's a couple of us jurymen, your honor," began one of the jurors, "who would like to know if the defendant boiled the malt one or two hours, and how does he keep the yeast out?"

— Capper's Weekly

1442. He who is his own lawyer has a fool for a client.

— Old Maxim

1443. A unique formula is followed by the United States Supreme Court in order to insure secrecy of its opinions. No official of the court other than the reporter is allowed to see a decision before it is sent to the printer. At the print shop, the decision is cut into different sections and handed to different linotype operators, so that none of them sees more than small unrelated sections. These sections are assembled under careful safeguards, proofs are pulled and sent back to the justices who are concurring in that particular decision. They write "I agree" on the margin, or sometimes suggest slight changes in the text. This is rare, however, since the case has been discussed very thoroughly before it is printed.

1444. My husband, a lawyer, often refuses to accompany me to parties because so many people spoil his evening by asking him for advice. I asked a doctor if this happened to him. "All the time!" he said.

"Then how do you get rid of these people?"

"I have a wonderful remedy," the doctor grinned. "When someone begins telling me his ailments, I stop him with one word, 'Undress!' "

— Readers Digest

1445. I sometimes wish that people would put a little more emphasis upon the observance of the law than they do upon its enforcement.

— Calvin Coolidge

1446. He is no lawyer who cannot take two sides.

— CHARLES LAMB

1447. "So you fought with this man because he said your wife was the ugliest woman in town?" asked the judge of the man brought before him on a charge of disturbing the peace. "Why, you haven't even got a wife."

"Yes, sir, Judge, I know that," pleaded the culprit, "but I was just fighting for the principle of the thing."

1448. Laws are not made like nets — to catch, but like sea-marks — to guide.

— SIR PHILIP SIDNEY

1449. Laws are not masters, but servants, and he rules them who obeys them.

— HENRY WARD BEECHER

1450.
A youthful lawyer who had just
　　Hung out his sign and name,
Was trying his first case before
　　A judge of local fame.
Said he, "I never use a book
　　To earn my legal bread,
For all the law I ever need
　　Is stacked within my head."
Whereat, the judge replied at once,
　　Without a smile or laugh,
"The law that's stacked within your head,
　　Is bound of course in — calf!"

1451. *Judge:* (looking at defendant who is unscathed after serious automobile accident): "It must feel pretty good to be alive."

Defendant: "I don't know, judge, I've never been dead."

1452. Law and equity are two things which God hath joined together, but which man hath put asunder.

— C. C. COLTON

1453. No man can make another a debtor against his will.

— *Legal Maxim*

1454. No man can give what he has not.

— *Legal Maxim*

1455. He who does not blame, approves.

— *Legal Maxim*

1456. Let every man remember that to violate the law is to trample on the blood of his father, and to tear the charter of his own and his children's liberty. Let reverence for the laws be breathed by every American mother to the lisping babe that prattles on her lap; let it be written in primers, spelling books, and almanacs; let it be preached from the pulpit, proclaimed in the legislative halls, and enforced in courts of justice. In short, let it become the political religion of the nation. — ABRAHAM LINCOLN

1457. A prominent citizen received a letter from an attorney charging him with alienating the affections of his client's wife. The communication set forth, "That unless you call at my office at 10 o'clock next Thursday forenoon, I will commence suit for $25,000 damages." The recipient replied promptly as follows: Dear Sir: — I have received your circular letter, and will attend the meeting.

1458. A bad agreement is better than a good law suit.
— *Italian Proverb*

laziness

1459. Nothing can cure a man of laziness; but a second wife will sometimes help.

1460. When a man feels that the world owes him a living, he is usually too lazy to collect it.

1461.
The hours we waste are golden hours
  And stand for money lost,
For every idle minute spent
  We have to meet the cost.
The man who wastes two hours a day
  Has hindered his career,
And shortened up his working time
  Six hundred hours per year.

1462. More men get crooked by dodging hard work than become bent by honest toil.

1463. I have often been struck by the fact that the symptoms of laziness and fatigue are practically identical.
— FREDERICK LEWIS ALLEN

leadership

1464. When you are getting kicked from the rear it means you're in front.
— Bishop Fulton J. Sheen

1465. Discipline is then not the end, but a means to an end — the end that each man shall be imbued with a spirit of loyalty to leader and to organization, which will result in unity and promptness of action in instant response to the will of the leader.
— Captain L. C. Andrews, U.S.A.

1466. A man who cannot lead and will not follow invariably obstructs.

1467. One great, strong, unselfish soul in every community would actually redeem the world.
— Elbert Hubbard

1468. What we want are the unpractical people who are beyond the moment, and think beyond the day. Those who try to lead the people can only do so by following the mob. It is through the voice of one crying in the wilderness that the ways of the gods must be prepared.
— Oscar Wilde

1469. To be a leader of men one must turn one's back on men.
— Havelock Ellis

leisure

1470. Every person in the world may not become a personage. But every person may become a personality. The happiest people are those who think the most interesting thoughts. Interesting thoughts can live only in cultivated minds. Those who decide to use leisure as a means of mental development, who love good music, good books, good pictures, good plays at the theater, good company, good conversation — what are they? They are the happiest people in the world; and they are not only happy in themselves, they are the cause of happiness in others.
— William Lyon Phelps, *Readers Digest*

1471. You will soon break the bow if you keep it always stretched.
— Phaedrus

letters

1472. Letters that should never have been written and ought immediately to be destroyed are the only ones worth keeping.
— SYDNEY TREMAYNE

liberalism

1473. A liberal: a man with his mind open at both ends.

liberty — See *Freedom*

life

1474. Life is easier to take than you'd think; all that is necessary is to accept the impossible, do without the indispensable, and bear the intolerable.
— KATHLEEN NORRIS

1475. The measure of a man's life is the well-spending of it, and not the length.
— PLUTARCH

1476. The book of life begins with a man and woman in a garden. It ends with Revelations.
— OSCAR WILDE

1477. A life spent worthily should be measured by deeds, not by years.
— RICHARD B. SHERIDAN

1478. Most of the shadows of this life are caused by standing in our own sunshine.
— RALPH WALDO EMERSON

1479. Life is a campaign, not a battle, and has its defeats as well as its victories.
— DON PIATT, *The Lone Grave of the Shenandoah and Other Tales*

1480. He who saves one life is considered as if he had preserved the whole world.
— *Talmud*

1481. I wept when I was born and every day explains why.
— *Spanish Proverb*

1482. That man lives twice who lives the first life well.

— HERRICK

1483. A useless life is only an early death. — GOETHE

1484. Life admits not of delays; when pleasure can be had, it is fit to catch it. Every hour takes away part of the things that please us, and perhaps part of our disposition to be pleased.

— SAMUEL JOHNSON

1485. Life can only be understood backwards, but it must be lived forwards. — SOREN AABYE KIERKEGAARD

1486. Life's greatest achievement is the continual remaking of yourself so that at last you know how to live.

— SMILEY BLANTON and NORMAN VINCENT PEALE, *Faith Is the Answer* (Prentice-Hall)

1487. Is life worth while? . . . That is a question for an embryo, not for a man. — SAMUEL BUTLER

1488. The secret of life is not to do what you like, but to like what you do. — *A World Treasury of Proverbs,* edited by Davidoff (Random)

1489. Life is too serious to take too seriously.

1490. Begin at once to live, and count each day as a separate life.

— SENECA

1491. We are always getting ready to live, but never living.

— RALPH WALDO EMERSON

1492. There are two things to aim at in life: first to get what you want; and after that, to enjoy it. Only the wisest achieve the second. — LOGAN PEARSALL SMITH

1493. For he that lives more lives than one
More deaths than one must die.

— OSCAR WILDE, *The Ballad of Reading Gaol*

1494. A long life may not be good enough, but a good life is long enough. — BENJAMIN FRANKLIN, *Poor Richard's Almanac*

logic

1495. Abraham Lincoln won many arguments through sheer force of logic. On one occasion, having failed to make a stubborn opponent see the error of his reasoning, Lincoln said, "Well, let's see. How many legs has a cow?"

"Four, of course," came the ready answer.

"That's right," said Lincoln. "Now suppose we call the cow's tail a leg, how many legs would the cow have?"

"Why, five, of course."

"Now that's where you're wrong," said Lincoln. "Simply calling a cow's tail a leg doesn't make it a leg."

— JOSEPH TAUSEK, "The True Story of the
Gettysburg Address," *Readers Digest*

love – hate

1496. Love is like a well; all right to taste of but bad to fall into.

1497. Hatred is self-punishment. — HOSEA BALLOU

1498. Men hate those to whom they have to lie.
— VICTOR HUGO, *The Toilers of the Sea*

1499. Love for the same thing never makes allies. It's always hate for the same thing. — From *My Son, My Son,* copyright 1938
by Howard Spring

1500. Three Men Are My Friends:
He that loves me, he that hates me, he that is indifferent to me. Who loves me, teaches me tenderness. Who hates me, teaches me caution. Who is indifferent to me, teaches me self-reliance.
— PANIN

1501. When a man falls in love with himself, it's usually the beginning of a life-long romance.

1502.   HEART SONG
Unless you can feel when left by one
That all men else go with him;
Unless you can muse in a crowd all day
On the absent face that fixed you;
Unless you can love as the Angels may
With the breath of Heaven betwixt you;

229

Unless you can dream that his faith is fast,
Unless you can die when the dream is past,
Oh, never call it loving.
— ELIZABETH BARRETT BROWNING

1503.   IF THIS BE ALL
How goodly are the ways we walked, Beloved,
Together and how firm, how true your hand;
But our glad hours of golden morning pass;
Our sun climbs high and higher and the sand
For all our love, runs swiftly in the glass.
If this be all (though I have other faith)
If we can journey in this camaraderie
But once, yet, at the end, I'll seek my rest;
Content that it was you who came to me,
Content that the short way could be so blessed.
— *Author Unknown*

1504. No one loves the man whom he fears.
— ARISTOTLE

1505. On his tour an inspector of city high schools came before a class of girls. He wrote on the blackboard 'LXXX.' Then, peering over his spectacles at a good looking girl in the first row, he asked:
"Young lady, I'd like to have you tell me what that means."
The girl replied, "Love and kisses." — *Washington Labor*

1506.   I love you,
Not only for what you are,
But for what I am
When I am with you.
I love you,
Not only for what
You have made of yourself
But for what you are making of me.
— ROY CROFT

1507. Love is like a mushroom. You never know whether it's the real thing until it's too late.

1508. Love is not blind — it sees more, not less. But because it sees more, it is willing to see less. — RABBI JULIUS GORDON

1509. The love you liberate in your work is the only love you keep.
— ELBERT HUBBARD

1510. In love, as in politics, it is always a "third party" that stirs up all the trouble — and throws the machinery out of order.

1511.
If you don't feel just right,
If you can't sleep at night,
If you moan and you sigh,
If your throat feels dry,
If you don't care to smoke,
If your food makes you choke,
If your heart doesn't beat,
If you're getting cold feet,
If your head's in a whirl —
Why not marry the girl?
— BAGOLO

1512. Love is like a rubber band. The longer it is drawn out, the thinner it gets, until finally it breaks.

1513. The ability to make love frivolously is the chief characteristic which distinguishes human beings from beasts.
— HEYWOOD BROUN, *Readers Digest*

1514.
Hate is that evil
State of mind
Which feeds the worst
In human kind.
— EDGAR A. GUEST

1515.
Love has the patience
To endure
The fault it sees
But cannot cure.
— EDGAR A. GUEST

1516. Love is like quicksilver in the hand. Leave the fingers open and it stays in the palm; clutch it and it darts away.
— DOROTHY PARKER, *Readers Digest*

1517.   WALK SLOWLY
If you should go before me, dear, walk slowly
Down the ways of death, well worn and wide,
For I should want to overtake you quickly
And seek the journey's ending by your side.

> I should be so forlorn not to descry you
>> Down some radiant road and take the same;
> Walk slowly dear, and often look behind you
>> And pause to hear if someone calls your name.
>>>> — *Author Unknown*

1518. Hating people is like burning down your own house to get rid of a rat. — HARRY EMERSON FOSDICK

1519. Success in love consists not so much in marrying the one person who can make you happy as in escaping the many who could make you miserable.

1520. The quickest way to go broke is to start loving beyond your means.

1521. True love is like ghosts, which everybody talks about and few have seen. — LA ROUCHEFOUCAULD, *Maxims*

1522. There is a wealth of unexpressed love in the world. It is one of the chief causes of sorrow evoked by death; what might have been said or might have been done that never can be said or done. — ARTHUR HOPKINS, *Ladies Home Journal*

1523. To love and win is the best thing; to love and lose the next best. — WILLIAM M. THACKERAY

1524. Most of these love triangles are wrecktangles.

1525. All the world loves a lover except when he is driving a motor car in crowded traffic.

1526. Love is a gross exaggeration of the difference between one person and everybody else. — GEORGE BERNARD SHAW

1527. Platonic love: all of the pleasures with none of the responsibilities.

1528. Platonic love: the gun you didn't know was loaded.

1529. Puppy love: the beginning of a dog's life.

1530. Despise not any man, and do not spurn anything; for there is no man who has not his hour; nor is there anything that has not its place.
— BEN AZAI, *Mishna*

1531. If you go through the proper motions, you'll soon begin to feel the corresponding emotions. (This is for jilted young people who think they can never fall in love again.)
— DR. GEORGE W. CRANE,
Psychology Applied

1532. "Should a man propose to a girl on his knees?"
"Either that or she should get off."

loyalty

1533. Great souls are always loyally submissive, reverent to what is over them: only small mean souls are otherwise.
— THOMAS CARLYLE, *Heroes and Hero Worship*

1534. To thine own self be true, and it must follow, as the night the day, thou canst not then be false to any man.
— WILLIAM SHAKESPEARE

1535. Our country! In her intercourse with foreign nations, may she always be in the right; but our country, right or wrong.
— STEPHEN DECATUR

luck – good luck – bad luck

1536. A traveler strolled up to a fisherman.
"Having any luck?"
"Pretty good," replied the angler. "I haven't had a bite in three hours."
"What's so good about that?" asked the amazed traveler.
"You see that guy over there Well, he hasn't had a bite in six hours."
— *Victorian Magazine*

1537. I never knew an early rising, hard-working, prudent man, careful of his earnings and strictly honest, who complained of hard luck. A good character, good habits, and iron industry are impregnable to the assaults of all ill-luck that fools ever dreamed of.
— JOSEPH ADDISON

1538.   THE FOUR LEAF CLOVER

What we call luck
Is simply pluck
    And doing things over and over;
Courage and will,
Perserverance and skill,
    Are the four leaves of luck's clover

1539.   Shallow men believe in luck.   — RALPH WALDO EMERSON

1540.   Good luck is the lazy man's estimate of a fighter's success.

1541.   Charles Schwab once said that luck is first of all hard work and then an indomitable, unshakable conviction that you deserve to be lucky and that you-are-going-to-be-lucky.

1542.   THE LAGGARD'S EXCUSE

He worked by day
    And toiled by night,
He gave up play
    And some delight.

Dry books he read
    New things to learn
And forged ahead,
    Success to earn.

He plodded on
    With faith and pluck,
And when he won
    Men called it luck.

1543.   The man who was born luckiest is the man who doesn't believe in luck.

1544.   Someone asked the French writer Jean Cocteau if he believed in luck. "Certainly," he said, "how else do you explain the success of those you don't like?"

1545.   Luck means the hardships nad privations which you have not hesitated to endure; the long nights you have devoted to work; the appointments you have never failed to keep and the trains that you have never failed to catch.

234

1546. Luck is ever waiting for something to turn up. Labor, with keen eyes and strong will, will turn up something. Luck lies in bed, and wishes the postman would bring him the news of a legacy. Labor turns out at 6 o'clock, and with busy pen or ringing hammer lays the foundation of a competence. Luck whines. Labor whistles.

malice

1547. With malice toward none, with charity for all, with firmness in the right as God gives us to see the right, let us strive on to finish the work we are in. — ABRAHAM LINCOLN

man – men

1548. The true perfection of man lies, not in what man has, but in what man is. . . . Nothing should be able to harm a man but himself. Nothing should be able to rob a man at all. What a man really has is what is in him. What is outside of him should be a matter of no importance. — OSCAR WILDE

1549. We fly in the air like *birds;* swim in the sea like *fish.* Wouldn't it be wonderful if we could walk on the earth like *men?*
— *Weslyan Christian Advocate*

1550. Men are born with two eyes, but with one tongue, in order that they should see twice as much as they say. — C. C. COLTON

1551. Man is that foolish creature who tries to get even with his enemies — and ahead of his friends.

1552. The desire to take medicine is perhaps the greatest feature which distinguishes man from animals.
— HARVEY CUSHING, *Readers Digest*

1553. When I speak of men, I speak of them as embracing women.

1554. Man is like a lamp wick — trimmed lots of times before he gets the right flame. — *Quote*

1555. "Men," mused Miss Meekins, "men are just like eggs — they're fresh, rotten and hard-boiled."

1556. Men are like trains — they are at their best when on the level.

1557. Men are like cellophane — transparent but hard to remove once you get wrapped up in them.

1558. *She:* "Let me take five dollars, will you?"
The Boss: "See here, young lady, I'll have you understand that I make no advances to my stenographers."

1559. No man has an enemy worse than himself.
— CICERO, 50 B.C.

1560. Man is not the creature of circumstance — circumstances are the creatures of men. — BENJAMIN DISRAELI

1561. Let us be men, not males.

1562. It took millions of years to make men out of monkeys, but sometimes it takes only a few minutes to reverse the process.

1563. Men always want to be a woman's first love — women like to be a man's last romance. — OSCAR WILDE

1564. The first Adam-splitting gave us Eve, a force which man in all the ages since has never got under control.
— *Richmond (Va.) Times Dispatch*

1565. It is not so much what a man is descended from that matters as what he will descend to. — H. PATTINSON-KNIGHT

1566. Man: a creature who buys football tickets three months in advance and waits until Christmas Eve to do his gift shopping.

1567. Before man made us citizens, great nature made us men.
— JAMES RUSSELL LOWELL

1568. Some men think they have an inferiority complex, when, as a matter of fact, they are just inferior.

1569. No man can serve two masters; yes-men can serve hundreds.

1570. The good man who goes wrong is usually the bad man found out.

1571. Man is born with his hands clenched, but his hands are open in death, because on entering the world he desires to grasp everything, but on leaving, he takes nothing away.
— *The Talmud*

1572. Average man: one who thinks he isn't.

1573. Think like a man of action and act like a man of thought.
— HENRI BERGSON

1574. Man comes into this world without his consent, and leaves it against his will. In his infancy he is an angel; in his boyhood he is a devil; in his manhood he is everything from a lizard up; in his duties he is a darn fool; if he raises a family he is a chump; if he raises a small check he is a thief; if he is a poor man he is a poor manager and has no sense; if he is rich he is dishonest; if he goes to church he is a hypocrite; if he stays away from church he is a sinner; if he donates to foreign missions he does it for show; if he doesn't he is stingy and a tight wad. When he first comes into the world, everybody wants to kiss him, before he goes out they all want to kick him.

1575. Fox: a wolf that sends flowers.

1576. Wolf: a guy who strikes while the eyein' is hot.
— MARTIN RAGAWAY, *Hollywood Reporter*

1577. Sugar daddy: a form of crystallized sap.

1578. Those who see any difference between soul and body have neither.
— OSCAR WILDE

1579. It is a man's job to solve the problems and overcome the difficulties which his own legitimate activities have created.

1580. A smart man is one who hasn't let a woman pin anything on him since he was a baby.

manners – good manners – bad manners

— See also *Etiquette*

1581. A southern lady once observed to me that gaiety is one of the surest marks of the aristocrat: and it is one of the unwritten laws of French politeness that a long face is a breach of manners.

— RICHARD LE GALLIENNE

1582. Another explanation of the modern child's manners is that too many woodsheds have been converted into garages.

1583. Good manners are made up of small sacrifices.

— RALPH WALDO EMERSON

1584. A bird in the hand is very bad taste.

1585. *First Stranger (at the party):* "Very dull, isn't it?"
Second: "Yes, very."
"Let's go home."
"I can't. I'm the host."

1586. Civil service: a commodity formerly obtainable in restaurants.

1587. Which kind of person are you: a crumber or a brusher? Between courses, do you automatically brush them away? Or surreptitiously nibble them? Doubtless some professor of psychology can place the crumbers and brushers each in their respective categories. Meantime, look around the table at your next dinner party and see for yourself who are what.　— *House and Garden*

1588. In introductions, present the younger person to the older, and a man, unless he is very much older or extremely distinguished, is presented to the woman. Speak the name first of the party to whom the other party is being introduced.

Thus, "Mrs. Older, Miss Young:" "Mrs. Woman, may I present Mr. Man?"

marriage – married life – husband and wife – divorce

1589. Marriage entitles women to the protection of strong men who steady the stepladder for them while they paint the kitchen ceiling.

1590. Marriage begins when women stop dating and start intimidating.

1591. The secret of happy marriage is simple: Just keep on being as polite to one another as you are to your best friends.
— ROBERT QUILLEN

1592. A man has no business to marry a woman who can't make him miserable; it means that she can't make him happy.

1593. Many a girl who can't stand a man's ways marries him for his means.

1594. *Pop:* "You never kiss me except when you want money."
Mom: "Well, isn't that often enough?"

1595. Hardly any woman reaches the age of thirty without having been asked to marry, at least twice — once by her father; once by her mother.

1596. *First wife:* "How do you get money out of your husband?"
Second Wife: "Oh, I say I'm going back to mother and he immediately hands me railroad fare."

1597. "Does your husband forget anniversaries?"
"Never. I remind him of it in June, and again in January. — And always get two presents!"

1598. It's impossible for a woman to be married to the same man for fifty years. After the first twenty-five — he's not the same man.

1599. People wouldn't get divorced for such trivial reasons, if they didn't get married for such trivial reasons.

239

1600. "Allow me to congratulate you. I'm sure you will always look upon this as the happiest day of your life."

"But I'm not getting married until tomorrow."

"Yes, I know."

1601. A man who gives in when he is wrong is wise. A man who gives in when he is right is married.

1602. The ladies at a sewing circle usually darn more husbands than they do socks.

1603. Men who say they are the boss in their own homes will lie about other things, too.

1604. Marriage is like a tourniquet; it stops your circulation.

1605. A woman was helping her husband pick out a new suit. After much disagreement, she finally said, "Well, go ahead and please yourself. After all, you're the one who will wear the suit."

"Well, dear," said the man meekly, "I figure I'll probably be wearing the coat and vest anyway." — *Louisville Courier-Journal*

1606. When a man decides to get married, it may be the last decision he is allowed to make. — KENNETH L. KRICHBAUM,
The Saturday Evening Post

1607. One tried and sure method of getting your wife home from an out-of-town vacation is to send her a copy of the local paper, with one item clipped out. — *The Welfarer*

1608. Married folk have an advantage at Christmas. Two can give as cheaply as one.

1609. The trouble with marriage is that, while every woman is at heart a mother, every man is at heart a bachelor.
—E. V. LUCAS, *Readers Digest*

1610. The one word above all others that makes marriage successful is "ours." — ROBERT QUILLEN

1611. When I hear people say they have lived together twenty-five years and never had the least difference, I wonder whether they have not had a good deal of indifference. — ROBERT COLLYER

1612. Landed gentry: men who are either married or engaged.

1613. *Henry:* "Ah you all workin' much nowadays, Sam?"
Sam: "Workin'? Man I'se just worked to death. I done wish I hadn't married Sally — she sure keeps me busy gettin' washings for her to do."

1614.　　　　　　Better a bachelor's life
　　　　　　　　　Than a slovenly wife.

1615. "I think that card playing, not the occasional game, but the constant round of bridge clubs, is ruining the American home," said Clarence Darrow, after returning from a trip to Europe. "We used to value fidelity as one of our greatest domestic assets, but it is old fashioned now and infidelity hardly creates a ripple any more.
"A well-known Chicago club woman called on me one day concerning some legal papers and during our conversation remarked that she had just discovered that her husband was leading a double life.
'And what are you going to do about it?' I asked her.
'Oh, I've redoubled,' she replied with a careless laugh."
　　　　　　　　　　　　　　— From Mr. Darrow's Collection

1616. *Husband:* "Every time I argue with my wife, words flail me."

1617. Mrs. Lottie Myrons was granted a divorce when she told the judge that since their marriage her husband had spoken to her but three times. She was awarded the custody of their three children.
　　　　　　　　　　　　　　— Readers Digest

1618. Running into her former suitor at a party, a girl decided to snub him.
"So sorry," she murmured when the hostess introduced him, "but I didn't get the name."
"I know you didn't," said the unabashed ex-suitor, "but you certainly tried hard enough."　　　　　*— The Carpenter*

1619. There is entirely too much worrying about unhappy marriages. All marriages are happy. It's only living together afterward that causes the trouble.　　　　*— Louisville Courier-Journal*

241

1620. Every now and then a fellow loses his best friend by marrying her.

1621. Woman begins by resisting a man's advances and ends by blocking his retreat.   — Oscar Wilde

1622. *GI:* "Let's get married or something."
Girl Friend: "We'll get married or nothing."

1623. When women think of themselves as the creators of their children and put less responsibility on God, we'll probably have a healthier race. And perhaps parents will develop a keener sense of duty.   — Mrs. Walter Ferguson, *NEA Syndicate*

1624. He who marries *might* be sorry. He who does not *will* be sorry.   — *Czechoslovakian Proverb*

1625. By all means marry. If you get a good wife, you will become very happy; if you get a bad one, you will become a philosopher — and that is good for every man.   — Socrates

1626. Marriage is an arrangement like the block booking of motion pictures, in which a number of less desirable features must be accepted in order to obtain one or two of major attraction.
          — Helen P. St. Boulanger, *Readers Digest*

1627. The man who marries to have someone to tell his troubles to soon has plenty to talk about.

1628. Everything was in readiness for the marriage ceremony, and both groom and best man had arrived at the church in plenty of time. The former, however, was uneasy.
   "What's worryin' ye, Tamson?" asked the best man, tiptoeing up the aisle. "Ha'e ye lost the ring?"
   The other gazed at his friend's immaculate attire and general air of gay bachelordom. Then he heaved a woeful sigh.
   "Na," he answered rather despondently; "the ring's safe enough, man, but I've lost my wild enthusiams!"

1629. Wife to husband: *"You* say I'm overdrawn — *I* say you're underdeposited!"

1630. My friend Julius, bartender at the Gramercy Park, discussing his recent marriage at an age when one might have supposed he would remain a bachelor, remarked:

"A married man lives like a dog, but dies like a king. A single man lives like a king, but dies like a dog." — EDWIN A. LAHEY

1631. What is the difference between an old maid and a married woman?

There is no difference. The old maid is always looking for a husband and so is a married woman.

1632. *Squire Perkins:* "Nell, after I die, I wish you would marry Deacon Brown."

Nelly: "Why so, Hiram?"

Squire: "Well, the deacon trimmed me on a horse trade once."

1633. Schoolboy wisdom (from an examination paper): A passive verb is one in which the subject is the sufferer, such as "He was married to her."

1634. "Jack, dear, I'm to be in an amateur theatrical. What would people say if I were to wear tights."

"They'd probably say that I'd married you for your money."

1635. A happy marriage is a long conversation that always seems too short. — ANDRE MAUROIS, *I Remember, I Remember* (Harper)

1636. The man and woman who can laugh at their love, who can kiss with smiles and embrace with chuckles, will outlast in mutual affection all the throat-lumpy, cow-eyed couples of their acquaintance. Nothing lives on so fresh and evergreen as the love with a funnybone. — GEORGE JEAN NATHAN

1637. Woman accepts man for the sake of matrimony and man accepts matrimony for the sake of woman.

— GREGORY MASON, *Esquire*

1638. The test of a happily married — and a wise woman is whether she can say, "I love you" far oftener than she asks, "Do you love me" — DOROTHY DAYTON, *Mademoiselle*, reprinted from Mademoiselle, copyright Street & Smith Publications, Inc.

243

1639. Marriage is a job. Happiness or unhappiness has nothing to do with it. There was never a marriage that could not be made a success, nor a marriage that could not have ended in bitterness and failure.   — KATHLEEN NORRIS

1640. The chain of wedlock is so heavy that it takes two to carry it — sometimes three.   — ALEXANDER DUMAS

1641. The honeymoon has ended when a wife stops making a fuss over her husband, and begins to make a fuss with him.

> — Copyright by *The Progressive Farmer* and used by special permission.

1642. Many a man who is a five-ton truck at the office is nothing but a trailer at home.

1643. Suppose your wife suddenly disappeared and you decided to advertise for someone to do her job. Your classified announcement would read something like this: Woman wanted: To help in house. 18-hour day, 7-day week, Sleep in. Must have knowledge of cooking, sewing, medicine, law, child welfare, elementary electricity, bookkeeping and men. Must be strong and willing. One who can help in garden preferred. No wages, only room and board.

> — *Quote*

1644. *Wife to husband:* "I was just as unreasonable when we were first married, but you thought it was cute."

1645. It takes only one to make an argument — if she's your wife.

1646. The young man who was her ideal before marriage may prove to be her ordeal afterward.

1647. Bonds of matrimony: worthless unless the interest is kept up.

1648. Don't marry for money; you can borrow it cheaper.

> — *Scotch Proverb*

1649. Second marriage: the triumph of hope over experience.

> — SAMUEL JOHNSON

1650. When a couple agree to try marriage and get a divorce if it don't work, it's just doin' wrong with a license.

1651. *Mr. Kootiesitch:* "That new fellow on the third floor boasts that he has kissed every woman in this flat except one."

Mrs. Kootiesitch: "I'll bet that's that stuck-up Mrs. Murphy upstairs."

1652. Marriages are made in heaven, but they are lived on earth.
— NATHAN HOWARD GIST

1653. "The time will come," shouted the speaker, "When women will get men's wages."

"Yes," said the little man in the corner. "Next Saturday night."

1654. *Jackson:* The idea of letting your wife go about telling the neighbors that she made a man of you! You don't hear my wife saying that.

Johnson: No, but I heard her telling my wife that she had done her best.

1655. A prominent man, when asked what other person he would rather be than himself, replied, "My wife's second husband." That was true love and beautiful loyalty. — NATHAN HOWARD GIST

1656. Biggest mystery to a married man is what a bachelor does with his money.

1657. Weaving home after a mellow evening, Colonel Washington Cloud, a noted Southern lawyer, met a neighbor woman who upbraided him about his condition. "If I were your wife," she said angrily, "I would poison you."

With a courtly bow the colonel replied, "Madam, if you were my wife I would gladly take it." — MEANS RAY, *Readers Digest*

1658. The gods gave man fire, and he invented fire-engines; they gave him love and he invented marriage.

1659. What doth it profit a man to have the initiative if his wife has the referendum.

1660. There comes a time in every man's life when his wife remarks complacently, "I can read you like a book, John."

And we've just heard the appropriate reply:

"Why don't you, then? You skip what you don't like in a book, but in me you linger over it."

1661. The fellow who thinks he picked out his wife is a soft touch for any good salesman.

1662. *Mr. Blue:* "Are you positive it was a marriage license you gave me last month"
Registrar: "Why, certainly."
Mr. Blue: "Well, I've certainly led a dog's life ever since."

1663. "Now, Charles," said the teacher, "if your father can do a piece of work in one hour and your mother can do it in one hour, how long would it take both of them to do it together?"
"Three hours," answered Charles, "counting the time they would waste in arguing."

1664. On boarding the Pullman, the bride and groom tipped the porter generously to keep their newly-wedded state a secret. The next morning, conscious of the knowing glances cast his way, the angry groom called the porter to account.
"Goodness, boss," he replied, "I didn't tell anybody. Some people asked me if you two was just married, and I says no, they're just good friends."
— Fort Meyers Flexigun

1665. "There was a time when she could have married anyone she pleased."
"And she never married?"
"Well, she didn't please anyone."

1666. After a few years of marriage, a man can look right at a woman without seeing her — and a woman can see right through a man without looking at him.
— HELEN ROWLAND, Ladies Home Journal

1667. A young ensign, very insistent he must have leave, was asked the reason by his commanding officer.
"My wife is expecting a baby," he replied.
"Listen, young man, remember this — you are only necessary at the laying of the keel. For the launching you are entirely superfluous."
— Readers Digest

1668. Your marriage stands a better than average chance of being successful, according to Dr. L. S. Cottrell of Cornell and

Professor E. W. Burgess of the University of Chicago,
 If:

    Your courtship lasted between four and five years.

    You are not an only child.

    You were married in a church.

    You lived in the country during childhood and adolescence.

    You are fond of your mother and father.

    You don't change your residence often.

    The wife worked before marriage.

    The wife is a year or more older than the husband.

                                — Your Life

1669. Hollywood wedding: one where they take each other for better or worse — but not for long.   — BOB BURNS

1670. Many a matrimonial flare-up has been caused by an old flame.   — OLIN MILLER

1671. At a dinner party in New York, a South American visitor was telling about his country and himself. He concluded, "And I have a most charming and sympathetic wife but, alas, no children." Then, as his companions seemed to expect further enlightenment, he continued haltingly, "You see, my wife is unbearable."

This was greeted with puzzled glances, so he sought to clear the matter up: "I mean, my wife is inconceivable." Seeing that this, too was not understood, and floundering deeper and deeper in the intricacies of English, he finally explained triumphantly: "That is, my wife, she is impregnable!"   — *Readers Digest*

1672. A successful marriage is an edifice that must be rebuilt every day.   — ANDRE MAUROIS

1673.   A Bible entry: "Born, a girl,"
                  A knitted shoe, a golden curl,
                  A wooly lamb, gay colored blocks,
                  Some wee worn garments in a box
                  Some dog-eared books, a pair of skates,
                  Old photographs of all her mates,
                  Boarding-school letters full of jokes
                  And "love to all the dear home-folks,"

> A glove, a program from a dance,
> A rose pressed in an old romance;
> A rain of rice along the hall —
> Tears on my cheeks and that is all!

1674. *Husband:* Now that we are married, perhaps I might venture to point out a few of your little defects.

Wife: Don't bother, dear. I'm quite aware of them. Those little defects prevented me from getting a much better man than you are.

1675. The man who brags, "I run things in my house," usually refers to the lawn mower, washing machine, vacuum cleaner, baby carriage, and the errands.

1676. In Cochin China the parties desiring divorce break a pair of chopsticks in the presence of witnesses and the thing is done.

Among some tribes of American Indians, the sticks given to witnesses of a marriage are broken in case of divorce.

If the wife of a Turkman asks his permission to go out, and he says "Go," without adding "Come back again," they are divorced.

In Siam the first wife may be divorced, but not sold, as the others may be. She may claim the first child. The others belong to the husband.

Among the Moors, if the wife does not become the mother of a boy, she may be divorced and, with the consent of the tribe, can marry again.

In the Arctic regions a man who wants a divorce leaves home in anger and does not return for several days. The wife takes the hint and departs.

In China, divorces are permitted in all cases of criminality, mutual dislike, jealousy, incompatibility of temperament or too much talking on the part of the wife.

Among the Tartars, if the wife is ill treated she complains to the magistrate, who, attended by leading citizens, accompanies her to her house and pronounces a divorce.

— BASIL BANE, *Des Moines Register*

1677. *She:* "Kiss me once more like that and I'm yours for life."

GI: "Thanks for the warning."

— *The Bealiner,* Camp Beale, California

1678. *Child:* "The Lord gives us our daily bread, doesn't he, Mama?"

Mother: "Yes dear."

Child: "And Santa Claus brings the presents?"

Mother: "Yes dear."

Child: "And the stork brings the babies?"

Mother: "Yes dear."

Child: "Then what's the use of having Papa hanging around?"

1679. *Mrs. Bee:* "And how do you audit your budget?"

Mrs. Dee: "Oh, I usually add up the deficits and ask Henry to write out a check."

1680. A woman awakens her sleeping husband saying: "John, you had better get up, there's a burglar going through your pants pockets."

"All right," he says as he turns over, "you two fight it out between yourselves."

1681. *Mrs. Jones:* "How did you stop your husband from staying out late?"

Mrs. Smith: "When he came in too late I called out, 'Is that you, Jack?'"

Mrs. Jones: "How did that stop him?"

Mrs. Smith: "My husband's name is Bill."

1682. If thou wouldst marry wisely marry thine equal.

— Ovid

1683. Rastus after being reprimanded by the judge for deserting his wife: "Jedge, ef you' knowed dat woman like Ah does, you' wouldn't call me no deserter. Ah's a refugee."

1684. After his wedding, Arthur Kober sent the following wire to the other regulars at the weekly session of the Hoyle Club: "Sorry I can't join you tonight as there is no way of bettering the perfect hand I am now holding." — Louis Sobol

1685. Success in marriage is much more than finding the right person; it is a matter of being the right person. — B. R. Brickner

249

1686. *From Broadcast of Marriage License Bureau:*
Just after getting license, prospective bride was asked what she considered the most serious fault of her husband-to-be.

"He snores too loud," was her reply.

1687. The extreme penalty for bigamy? Two mothers-in-law.
— LORD CHIEF JUSTICE RUSSELL

1688. An actor, discussing the previous night's party, asked his wife: "Was that you I kissed out in the patio?"

The little woman thought for a moment, then countered: "About what time, dear?"
— JIMMY FIDLER, *McNaught Syndicate* (Coronet)

1689. *Hubby:* "What does this mean? I opened a banking account for you last week, and now I learn that it is overdrawn."
Wife: "Impossible! I have half of the checks still left!"

1690. "Aren't you going to marry that pretty girl after all?"
"No; unfortunately, she has an impediment in her speech."
"How sad! What is it?"
"She can't say yes."

1691. *Customer:* "I want to get a diamond ring set in platinum."
Salesman: "Certainly, sir. Let me show you our combination sets of three pieces: engagement, wedding and teething rings, at 10 per cent discount."

1692. I met my wife at a travel bureau. She was looking for a vacation and I was the last resort.

1693. Many husbands now take their wives to a night club instead of to a theater. That's about the only place that is still open by the time she is ready.
— *Cape Argus*

1694. The best way you can surprise a woman with an anniversary gift is to give her just what she wanted.
— ARBUTH ARUNDALE, *Readers Digest*

1695. "Can you define matrimony?"
"Sure. It's just like making a call. You go to adore, you ring a belle, you give your name to a maid . . . and then you are taken in."

1696. My wife's always entering magazine contests, but she never won anything. It ain't that she ain't smart. She just can't say anything in twenty-five words.

1697. Fathers are what give daughters away to men who aren't nearly good enough for them so they can have children smarter than anybody's.

1698. "Who introduced you to your wife?"
"We just met. I don't blame nobody."

1699. Wife, to husband inquiring why they never have any money: "It's the neighbors, dear. They're always doing something we can't afford."

1700. The allowances husbands give cannot compare with the allowances wives make. — HOWARD W. NEWTON, *Redbook Magazine*

1701. The wife who drives from the back seat isn't any worse than the husband who cooks from the dining room table.

1702. "The rapidly increasing divorce rate," remarked the wit, "indicates that America is indeed becoming the land of the free."
"Yes," replied his prosaic friend, "but the continued marriage rate suggests that it is still the home of the brave."
— *The American Legion Weekly*

1703. Marriage: a process for finding out what sort of guy your wife would have preferred.

1704. Marriage: a ceremony in which rings are put on the finger of the lady and through the nose of the gentleman.
— HERBERT SPENCER, *Readers Digest*

1705. When the husband of a vacationing wife telephoned her that she had taken the mailbox key with her, she obligingly mailed it back to him. — *Readers Digest*

1706. Mrs. Hicks, a Maine housewife, is so painfully neat that she makes life miserable for her family. One of her rules is that all members of the household must remove their shoes before entering the house.

"Bill," she remonstrated one day with her husband, "I found a grease spot on one of the dining room chairs and I think it came off those pants you wear in the shop."

A brief silence ensued, then a volcanic eruption. "Well, Mirandy, for the last fifteen years I have taken off my shoes every time I come in this house, but I'll be hanged if I'll go further."

— Harper's Magazine

1707. There can be only one end to marriage without love, and that is love without marriage. — JOHN C. COLLINS

1708. One should choose for a wife only such a woman as he would choose for a friend, were she a man. — JOSEPH JOUBERT

1709. Marriage is a great institution — but who wants to live in an institution?

1710. Many a man in love with a dimple, makes the mistake of marrying the whole girl. — STEPHEN LEACOCK

1711. My notion of a wife at forty is that a man should be able to change her, like a bank note, for two twenties.

1712. The honeymoon is over when the dog brings your slippers and your wife barks at you.

1713. There is one thing more exasperating than a wife who can cook and won't, and that's the wife who can't cook and will.

— ROBERT FROST

1714. Waiting for a man to get ready to get married is like waiting for an egg to fry itself.

1715. Matrimony is a bargain, and somebody has to get the worst of the bargain. — HELEN ROWLAND

1716. When you see what some girls marry, you realize how they must hate to work for a living. — HELEN ROWLAND

1717. Desertion: the poor man's method of divorce.

1718. In England there is a law forbidding a man marrying his mother-in-law. A law like that is not needed in America.

1719. Wife: a former sweetheart. — H. L. Mencken

1720. Bigamy is having one husband too many and monogamy is frequently the same thing.

1721. Bigamist: a person who took one too many.

1722. Checkmate: the gal you marry for her money.

1723. Bigamy: two rites that make a wrong.

1724. Alimony: a man's cash surrender value.

1725. A wife is an illogical creature who asks, "Where did you have it last?" and goes there, and there it is.
— H. V. Wade, *Readers Digest*

1726. A shotgun wedding may be defined as troth or consequences. — Pete Simer, *Readers Digest*

1727. Reno: residence of the bitter half.

1728. Delegate-at-large: a man at a convention whose wife didn't accompany him.

1729. Divorce: hash made from domestic scraps.

1730. The man who said "talk is cheap" never had a wife with a charge account in a department store.

1731. The professional beggar was anxious to marry off his daughter and a younger competitor was the best match in view.

"And what will you give me if I marry your daughter?" the prospective husband wanted to know.

"Do you know the towns of Bjernin and Brakov?" the father asked. "I will not beg there any more, and will give you the exclusive rights to both of them."

1732. An insurance company received a claim from a woman and asked for some additional evidence concerning the husband's death.

After a good deal of correspondence the firm received the following letter from the widow:

"I am having such lot of trouble to get my money that sometimes I actually wish my husband were not dead."

1733. Husband: one who lays down the law to his wife, and then accepts all her amendments.

1734. Husband: what's left of a sweetheart after the nerve has been killed.

1735. Many husbands are second story men — their wives seldom believe the first one.
— FRANCES RODMAN

1736. Good husband: one who will wash up when asked and dry up when told.

1737. Honeymoon: the vacation a man takes before starting to work for a new boss.

1738. Keep your eyes wide open before marriage, and half-shut afterwards.
— BENJAMIN FRANKLIN

1739. One way for a husband to get the last word is to apologize.
— PEGGY CAROLINE FEARS, *The Saturday Evening Post*

1740. *Domesticity At Large* — In one of the night clubs a gentleman and a lady were sitting quietly supping when another lady entered, strode up to the man, fixed her eye on him coldly, said: "I may be only your wife, but —" and, picking up the tomato bisque before him, poured it over his shirt-front. We report this rowdy incident only to call the attention of the humanists to the masterful way in which the head waiter met the emergency. With suave reproach he admonished the wife: "Madame, the place for that is in the home."
— *The New Yorker*

1741. It is a characteristic of good wives that they feel and resent an injury to their husbands much more than they themselves do. Women's feelings are only aroused when we have regained the guiding-rope which seemed to slip out of our hands.
— BISMARCK, *collection by von Poschinger*

1742. "Do angels fly, Mother?"

"Yes, dear."

"Then when is nursie going to fly, 'cause Daddy called her an angel last night?"

"Tomorrow, darling."

1743. Engagement: the time a girl takes until she finds out if she can do any better.

1744. "They say that a single oyster will lay from one to eight million eggs a year."

"Gosh! Think of the married ones!"

1745. Alimony: bounty on the mutiny.

1746. Alimony: giving comfort to the enemy.

1747. Alimony: the high cost of leaving.

1748. An old Scotch lady on her death bed was discussing the funeral arrangements with her husband.

"Ye ken, Jock," she said, "Ye haven't spoken to my sister Annie for twenty years, and my dying wish is that ye drive to my funeral in the same carriage with Annie."

"I'll do it," replied Jock, sadly, "but I'm telling ye it will entirely spoil the day for me!"

1749. Alimony: the high cost of loving.

1750. Alimony: man's best proof that you have to pay for your mistakes.

1751. A draftee claimed exemption on the grounds of poor eyesight — and brought his wife along to prove it.

1752. Our tastes change as we mature. Little girls like painted dolls; little boys like soldiers. When they grow up, girls like the soldiers and the boys go for the painted dolls.

1753. Marry your son when you please and your daughter when you can.

married life – See *Marriage*

maxims

1754. Maxims are to the intelligent what laws are to actions; they do not enlighten, but they guide and direct, and, although themselves blind, are protective. — JOUBERT, *Pensées*

medicine – See *Doctors*

memory

1755. He who receives a good turn should never forget it – he who does one should never remember it.

1756. Nothing is as short as the public's memory . . . it is little more than week-minded.

1757. A great man quotes bravely, and will not draw on his invention when his memory serves him with a word as good. — RALPH WALDO EMERSON

1758. Oh, if, in being forgotten, we could only forget! — LEW WALLACE, *Ben Hur*

1759. Scrawled beneath a large likeness of a dollar bill chalked by a sidewalk artist: "Drawn From Memory." — E. A. CHAFFEE, *Readers Digest*

1760. A good storyteller is a person who has a good memory and hopes other people haven't. — IRVIN S. COBB

1761. We commit the golden rule to memory and forget to commit it to life.

1762. When the teacher asked Johnny what George Washington was noted for, he surprised her by replying, "His memory."
"Why do you think his memory was so great?" she inquired.
Replied Johnny:
"Because they erected a monument to it!"

1763. The rememberance of the good done those we have loved is the only consolation left when we have lost them. — DEMOUSTIER

1764. Darling: the popular form of address in speaking to a person of the opposite sex whose name you cannot at the moment recall.
                                                    — OLIVER HERFORD

military

1765. It was during World War I. The company chaplain observed one of "his boys" trembling from head to foot with fear and fright. "There's nothing for you to worry about" he said in an effort to comfort him, "every bullet that comes over here has a name on it. If it's got your name on it, it's going to get you, and nothing is going to save you. If it hasn't your name on it, it's not intended for you and there is no need for you to worry about it."

"Yes, Father, I know that if it has my name on it, it's going to get me, and I'll take your word for it that those that have some other name on them are not intended for me. But what worries me are all those bullets that come over here with nothing on them but "to whom it may concern.""

1766. Chow line: the men behind the men . . . behind the men . . . behind the men.

1767. *Jeep:* "Would you blame me for something I didn't do?"
Sergeant: "Of course not."
Jeep: "Well, I didn't get up for reveille." — *The Communiqué,*
                                                    Camp Livingston, La.

1768. If you've ever wondered why the Army holds back exact details on such things as illnesses, disabilities, minor epidemics in camps, here's the explanation:

For years, life-insurance companies have built up statistical tables which, at a quick glance, show exactly what percentage of people are affected by specific epidemics and illnesses in one period. If the enemy read a report that 150 men at Camp Blank had measles, for example, they would simply turn to their insurance actuary tables, discover the percentage of people affected by a measle epidemic, multiply. Presto! — they would have a closely guarded military secret: the total number of men at that camp.

1769. A corporal is as high as you can go and still have friends.

1770. We like the story that was very popular with the Army in France.

It is the tale of a negro who was beating it for the back areas as fast as he could go, when he was stopped by a white officer.

"Don't delay me, suh," said the negro. "I's gotta be on my way."

"Boy," replied the officer, "do you know who I am? I'm a general."

"Go on, white man, you ain't no general."

"I certainly am," insisted the officer, angrily.

"Lordy!" exclaimed the negro, taking a second look. "You sure is! I musta been travelin' some 'cause I didn't think I'd got back that far yit." — *Ottawa Evening Citizen*

1771. The wife and daughter of Lieutenant Berry of the Great Lakes Naval Training station, approaching a gate to the station, were halted by a sentry on duty who had orders to allow no one to enter by that gate.

"Sorry, but you'll have to go around to the main gate."

"Oh but we're the Berrys."

"Lady, I don't care if you're the cats meeow, you can't go through this gate."

1772. Draft board: where young men are weighed and found wanted.

1773. A paratrooper is a soldier who climbs down trees he never climbed up.

1774. "When I was a little boy," sweetly piped the hardboiled sergeant, "I had a set of wooden soldiers. One day I lost those soldiers, and I cried very much, but my mother said, 'Never mind, Johnny! Some day you will get your wooden soldiers back.' And believe me, you bunch of wooden-headed dumbbells, that day has come."

1775. Paratrooper: the only man who gets up in the world by falling down on the job. — *San Francisco Examiner*

1776. The common soldier's blood makes the general great.
— *Italian Proverb*

mind

1777. Merely having an open mind is nothing. The object of opening the mind, as of opening the mouth, is to shut it again on something solid.
— G. K. CHESTERTON

1778. To change one's mind is rather a sign of prudence than ignorance.
— *Spanish Proverb*

1779. Minds are like parachutes — they only function when open.

1780. Have you filled out that blank yet?
Which blank?
Why, the one between your ears.

1781.
It was just the other day,
In a fortune-telling place,
A pretty maiden read my mind —
And then she slapped my face.

miser

1782. Punishment of the miser: to pay the drafts upon him in his tomb.
— NATHANIEL HAWTHORNE,
American Note-Books

misfortune

1783. Disraeli was once asked to define the difference between a misfortune and a calamity.

"Well," he answered, "if Gladstone fell into the Thames, it would be a misfortune. But if anybody dragged him out, that would be a calamity."

misplaced

1784. Everything has its place, but that doesn't relieve the man with a boil on his nose.

mistake

1785. Show me a man who makes no mistakes and I will show you a man who doesn't do things. — THEODORE ROOSEVELT

1786. Code of conduct: I may be wrong in regard to any or all of them (opinions expressed) but, holding it a sound maxim that it is better only some times to be right than at all times to be wrong, so soon as I discover my opinions to be erroneous, I shall be ready to renounce them. — ABRAHAM LINCOLN, March 9, 1832

1787. In a small New Hampshire town, the Masons met in the same lodge hall with the Grangers, only on different nights. One night, a farmer, thinking it was the meeting night of his Grange went up to the Lodge hall and sounded an alarm on the door. It happened that the Masons were meeting that night. The tyler said from within, "Who comes here?" To which the farmer replied, "I sow, I plow, I reap." The tyler answered, "The hell you do." The granger at once recognized that he was in the wrong place. He started down the stairs and out of the door and began walking hurriedly down the street when he came upon a fellow Granger.

"See here," he said, "I thought our Grange was meeting tonight and I went up to the Lodge hall, but found the Masons were holding their meeting. Well, I didn't get in but I got their pass word."

1788. Jones called an undertaker and told him that his wife had passed away and asked him to come and take charge of the body and to make all the necessary arrangements for the burial. The undertaker registered surprise saying that he recalled having buried the man's wife three years before. "Oh, that was my first wife, you see I got married again," said the caller. "You got married again?" said the undertaker. "Then, congratulations to you."

1789. When a plumber makes a mistake he charges it.
When a lawyer makes a mistake it is just what he wanted, because he has a chance to try the case all over again.
When a carpenter makes a mistake it is just what he expected.
When a doctor makes a mistake he buries it.
When a judge makes a mistake it becomes the law of the land.
But when an editor makes a mistake — Good night!

1790. *He:* "Mabel says she thinks I'm a wit."
She: "Well, she's half right."

1791. Where the motive to do right exists and the majority of one's acts are right, we should avoid referring to past mistakes.

— MARY BAKER EDDY

1792. *Passenger (on board ship):* "I say my clothes are gone!"
Steward: "Where did you put them?"
Passenger: " In that little cupboard with the glass door."
Steward: "Bless me, that's no cupboard — that's a porthole, sir."

1793. Make mistakes, but make only one of a kind.
One mistake simply shows you are careless or inexperienced.
The same mistake made the second or third time will prove you are either incapable or indifferent.

1794. Crowded trolley car. Young lady is vainly groping for her purse to pay the fare.
Young man: "Pardon me miss, but may I not pay your fare?"
Young lady: "Sir? ! !"
(Several seconds of groping.)
Young man: "I beg your pardon again, but won't you let me pay your fare?"
Young lady: "Why, I don't even know you, and anyway, I'll have this purse open in a minute." (Continued groping.)
Young man: "I really must insist on paying your fare. You've unbuttoned my suspenders three times."

1795. Nothing is opened by mistake as often as one's mouth.

1796. Two Irishmen were watching a Shriners' parade.
"Who are those fellows, Mike?"
"They're Shriners."
"And what are Shriners?"
"Why, they're Masons."
"Sure, and what the devil do they want now?" They gettin' $18 a day!"

1797. A clergyman, anxious to introduce some new hymn books, directed the clerk to give out a notice in church in regard to them.

The clerk, however, had a notice of his own. Accordingly, at the close of the sermon he announced, "All those who have infants they wish to have baptized, please send their names at once."

The clergyman, who was somewhat deaf, supposing the clerk was giving the notice requested by him rose, and said: "And for the benefit of those who haven't any, they may be obtained from me any day between three and four o'clock; the ordinary ones at 15¢ and the special ones with red backs at 25¢ each.

1798. A man who has committed a mistake and doesn't correct it is committing another mistake. — Confucius

1799. The best eraser in the world is a good night's sleep.

1800. *Mr. G.:* "Did you know that George made $50,000 in Chicago in a week?"

Mr. C.: "I don't believe it."

Mr. G. (calling over his friend Mr. W.): "Isn't it true that George made $50,000 in Chicago in a week?"

Mr. W.: "Sure it's true, but it's wrong in four places. It wasn't Chicago, it was Toledo. It wasn't a week, it was a year. It wasn't $50,000, it was $5,000, and he didn't make it, he lost it."

misunderstanding

1801. *Referee:* "You say you signed that financial statement? It shows you have $4500.00 in cash in the bank. Is that right?"

Bankrupt: "Sure, I told the man who wrote it up that I had 4 to 5 hundred dollars.

1802. A tramp had been admitted to the casual ward of an English workhouse late one evening and the following morning he duly appeared before the master.

"Have you taken a bath this morning?" was the first question he was asked.

"No, sir," answered the man in astonishment, "is there one missing?"

1803. A haughty lady had just purchased a postage stamp at a substation.

"Must I stick it on, myself?" she asked.

"Positively not, madam," replied the clerk. "It will accomplish more if you stick it on the letter."

1804. A bashful young couple, who were evidently very much in love, entered the crowded street car.

"Do you think we can squeeze in here, Mabel?" he asked, looking doubtfully at her blushing face.

"Don't you think, John, we had better wait until we get home?" was the low, embarrassed reply.

1805. In the pre-World War I days, ex-President Taft had a reception at the White House which was attended by Government officials, members of the Army and Navy, members of the Diplomatic Corps, and leading Washington citizens. As these lined up to shake hands with the President, the President's tailor also fell into line. As he reached the President, the latter grasped his hand remarking, "You look familiar to me, but I can't just place you." "Why, Mr. President," he replied, "I made your pants." "Oh, yes, yes, why how do you do Major Pants," was the president's reply.

1806. The mistakes of the learned man are like a shipwreck which wrecks many others with it.
                                                    — *Arabian Proverb*

1807. Bill Smith, a country shopkeeper, went to the city to buy goods. They were sent immediately and reached home before he did. When the boxes were delivered, Mrs. Smith, who was keeping the shop, uttered a scream, seized a hatchet, and began frantically to open the largest one.

"What's the matter, Sarah?" asked one of the bystanders, who had watched her in amazement. Pale and faint, Mrs. Smith pointed to an inscription on the box.

It read: "Bill inside."

1808. A charming wife of a French diplomat had never quite thoroughly mastered the English language.

She was urging an American officer to attend a dinner, the invitation to which he had already declined. The lady insisted that he must go, but the young officer said he had burned his bridges behind him.

The lady misunderstood the word. "That will be all right," she explained, "I'll lend you a pair of my husband's."

1809. "Your name," said the officer at the station.

"Sam Jones," replied the army trombonist.

"Your rank," said the officer.

"I know it," sighed Sam. — JOE SHONER

1810. Mr. Adams was enjoying the motion picture at the theater until two women in the row behind him began to talk incessantly.

"Excuse me," he said politely, turning around, "but I can't hear a word."

"Listen, mister," answered one of the women, "what we are talking about isn't any of your business."

1811. Pat called on his friend Mike who was not at home. Mike's wife asked Pat to hold the baby while she prepared supper for Mike whom she expected momentarily. While holding the baby, Mike came in and seeing Pat for the first time in a long while asked, "Pat, and how are things with you?" to which Pat replied: "Oh, I'm holding my own," and then and there the excitement started.

modesty

1812. The great man is he who does not lose his child's heart.

— MENCIUS

1813. No padlocks, bolts or bars can secure a maiden so well as her own reserve. — CERVANTES

1814. The modest man has everything to gain, and the arrogant man everything to lose; for modesty has always to deal with generosity, and arrogance with envy. — RIVAROL

1815. Modesty is the lowest of the virtues, and is a confession of the deficiency it indicates. He who undervalues himself is justly undervalued by others. — HAZLITT

1816. Great men never feel great. Small men never feel small.

1817. Don't leave an impression that is bigger than you are. Shadow boxers never score a knockout.

1818. It wasn't until quite late in life that I discovered how easy it is to say, "I don't know." — SOMERSET MAUGHAM

1819. One coin in the money-box makes more noise than when it is full.
— *Arabian Proverb*

1820. It seems I have been climbing the ladder of success wrong by wrong.
— ADLAI E. STEVENSON

money

1821. Movie actor's salary: the haul of fame.

1822. Money and time are the heaviest burdens of life, and the unhappiest of all mortals are those who have more of either than they know how to use.
— SAMUEL JOHNSON

1823. Money may buy the husk of many things, but not the kernel. It brings you food, but not appetite, medicine but not health, acquaintances but not friends, servants but not faithfulness, days of joy but not peace or happiness.
— HENRIK IBSEN

1824. There's a great difference between "winning" money and "making" it; a great difference between getting it out of another man's pocket into ours, or filling both.
— RUSKIN

monument

1825. No monuments are erected for the righteous; their deeds perpetuate their memory.
— *The Talmud*

1826. Monuments and eulogy belong to the dead.
— DANIEL WEBSTER

1827. I agree with you entirely in condemning the mania of giving names to objects of any kind after persons still living. Death alone can seal the title of any man to his honor, by putting it out of his power to forfeit it.
— THOMAS JEFFERSON, Letter to Dr. Benjamin Rush

mother

1828. A mother is she who can take the place of all others, but whose place no one else can take.
— CARDINAL MERMILLOD

265

1829. One good mother is worth a hundred school masters.
— GEORGE HERBERT

1830. The future destiny of the child is always the work of the mother. — NAPOLEON

1831. Most of all the other beautiful things in life come by twos and threes, by dozens and hundreds. Plenty of roses, stars, sunsets, rainbows, brothers and sisters, aunts and cousins, comrades and friends — but only one mother in the whole world.
— KATE DOUGLAS WIGGIN (Buck Bils)

1832. I grew up to be the kind of a kid my mother didn't want me to play with.

1833. Through historical precept and religious injunction Mother's Day has special significance to the Jew. The child is admonished in the Book of Proverbs: "Hear, O my son, the instruction of thy father, and neglect not the teaching of thy mother." The home influence of mothers has been the largest single factor contributing to the continued existence of the Jewish people. Where laws and rules failed, where peremptory command was ignored, the gentleness of mothers has had greatest effect in shaping history. Their influence has never been better stated than in the old Talmudic saying "that God could not be everywhere, and therefore he made Mothers."

1834. Summer camps — those places where little boys go for mother's vacation.

mother-in-law

1835. Mother-in-law sandwich: cold shoulder and tongue.

1836. "Mr. Chairman, may I be excused. My mother-in-law is coming in on the four o'clock broom and I promised to meet her."

1837. Mixed emotions: to see your mother-in-law go over the cliff in your brand new Cadillac.

1838. The mother-in-law frequently forgets that she was a daughter-in-law.

266

music

1839. Two women listening to an out of door band concert could not agree on the tune being played. "I think it is the serenade from Faust," said one. "I am sure it isn't," said the other. "It's from Il Trovatore"— then they caught sight of a sign on the band stand. It was too far for them to read so they sent a little girl to settle the question. "What does it say?" they asked eagerly on her return. "Refrain from spitting," replied the little one.

1840. Violinist: a man who is always up to his chin in music.

1841. If you have the right key, you can sing in any flat.

mystery

1842. A woman sent her little boy to the store for two pounds of plums. Presently she telephoned her grocer to complain that she had weighed the plums and found only a pound and a half.

"I'm sure my scales are correct," insisted the merchant. "Have you weighed your son?"

— DROKE, *Anthology*

names

1843. Nicholas Longworth, better known as "Nick," was a popular speaker of the House of Representatives. It had been said of him while he lived that "If Nick Longworth were to die today, more cheeks would be wet with physical tears than for any other man in public life in Washington." Longworth came from a most distinguished family of Cincinnati. There is a story told of his great-grandfather, who, calling on Longfellow, remarked that his name and the poet's began with the same syllable. Longfellow answered, "You have the better of the argument. Worth makes the man, and want of it the fellow."

1844. She was their maid and they nicknamed her "Sanka" because there was "no active ingredient in the bean."

1845. Why cannot parents be reasonable when it comes to naming their children? Why must they always satisfy their own whims to such matters? It is the child, not the parent, who must carry the name through life. Why load him with the burden of a name which is either ridiculous or sentimental and silly? His parents generally impose sufficient burden upon him when they give him life and the heritage of their own characteristics. There is no need to add to such burdens by making him a potential butt of jokes, abuse, and ridicule. In common decency to their offspring, parents should be reasonable with their names. — *Source Unknown*

1846. On the first day of the second semester in school, the little boys took their seats and waited until the teacher came down among them to get their names. The first one to whom she came replied that his name was Si.

"No," the teacher corrected, "you mustn't say Si, say Silas."

Next she came to one who said his name was Tom.

"No," the teacher said impressively, "it's Thomas."

"And now, little boy," she inquired of a lad in the end row, "what is your name?"

"Jackass," replied the bright lad.

1847. The Chinese give young children a milk name — a first name which they are at liberty to change, later on, for one of their own selection. Surely that custom is more civilized than ours. Many of us go through life detesting the names our parents inflicted upon us. Why not adopt the Chinese custom of the temporary name which children can drop if they want when they grow up?

> — Princess Alexandra Kropotkin,
> *Liberty*

1848. A soldier in the army of the Duke of Marlborough once took the name of that general for his own. The Duke, learning of it, sent for the man and reprimanded him for his effrontery.

"I am not to blame, General," was the soldier's ingenious defense. "I did the best I could. If I could have found a more illustrious name than yours I would have taken that."

naval – See *Military*

neglect

1849. A little neglect may breed great mischief. For want of a nail the shoe was lost; for the want of a shoe the horse was lost; and for want of a horse the driver was lost, being overtaken and slain by the enemy; all for want of a little care about a horse-shoe nail.
— BENJAMIN FRANKLIN, *Poor Richard's Almanac*

neighbor

1850. Good neighbor: a fellow who smiles at you over the back fence, but doesn't climb it. — ARTHUR ("Bugs") BAER, *Ladies' Home Journal*

1851. Were it not for the misfortunes of our neighbors, life would be positively unbearable. — *The Maxims of Marmaduke*

observation

1852. A certain man was asked to talk to a company of business men about the depression. He tacked up a big sheet of white paper. Then he made a black spot on the paper with his pencil and asked a man in the front row what he saw. The man replied promptly, "A black spot."

The speaker asked every man the same question and each replied, "A black spot." With calm and deliberate emphasis the speaker said: "Yes, there is a little black spot, but none of you saw the big sheet of white paper. That's the point of my speech."

1853. A Glasgow professor, in order to emphasize the value of observation, prepared a little cupful of kerosene, mustard, and castor oil, and calling the attention of his class to it, dipped a finger in to the atrocious compound and then sucked his finger. He next passed the mixture around to the students who all did the same. When the cup returned and he observed the faces of his students, he remarked: "Gentlemen, I am afraid that you did not use your powers of observation. The finger that I put into the cup was not the same one that I stuck in my mouth." — SIR WILLIAM GRENFELL, *Forty Years for Labrador* (Houghton, Mifflin)

observation

1854. Do you wish to find out a man's weak points? Note the failings he has the quickest eye for in others.

— J. C. and W. A. HARE,
The Pathfinder

obstacle

1855. An overland traveler who had walked all the way from San Francisco to New York said that the hardest obstacle he had to face was not the Rockies. It wasn't the Alleghenies. The greatest hazard he had to fight was not the swollen Mississippi. It wasn't the Ohio. What had almost defeated him was the sand in his shoes! And that's nothing but the A B C of human experience!

The incidents we call trivial, and the people we call obscure, are really the incidents and the people that make all the difference that's made.

— PAUL SCHERER, *The Place Where
Thou Standest* (Harper)

old-age

1856. When you see an old man amiable, mild, equable, content, and good-humored, be sure that in his youth he has been just, generous, and forbearing. In his end he does not lament the past, nor dread the future; he is like the evening of a fine day.

— *Arabic Proverb*

old maid

1857. An old maid is a debutante who overdid it.

1858. Old maid: slipping beauty.

1859. Old maid: a girl who knows all the answers but is never asked the questions.

opinion

1860. The weakness of public opinion is that so many people express it only privately.

1861. Some men never change their opinion because it's been in the family for generations.

opportunity

1862. Next to knowing when to seize an opportunity, the most important thing in life is to know when to forego an advantage.

— BENJAMIN DISRAELI

1863.　　　　"Four Things Come Not Back —

> The spoken word
> The sped arrow
> The past life
> The neglected opportunity"

So wrote Omar in Persia a long time ago — for us to think about today.

1864. An ostrich with its head in the sand is just as blind to opportunity as to disaster.

1865. "May I ask you the secret of success?" an ambitious young man said to a great merchant.

"There is no easy secret," replied the merchant. "You must jump at your opportunity."

"But how can I tell when my opportunity comes?"

"You can't," snapped the merchant. "You have to keep jumping."

— *Grit*

1866. One of Ripley's famous cartoons pictured a plain bar of iron worth $5. This same bar of iron when made into horseshoes would be worth $10.50. If made into needles, it would be worth $3,285, and if turned into balance springs for watches, its worth becomes $250,000. The same is true of another kind of material — you. Believe it or not!

1867. They wrong opportunity who say she knocks but once.

1868. It is practically a law in life that when one door closes to us another opens. The trouble is that we often look with so much regret and longing upon the closed door that we do not see the one which has opened.

1869. Some people are waiting for opportunity to break the door down and come in.

1870. Great minds must be ready not only to take the opportunities, but to make them.
— C. C. Colton

1871. The Bill of Rights is our freedom of opportunity — our leave to live, by no man's leave, underneath the law.
— Rudyard Kipling

1872. Whatever you have, you must either use or lose.
— Henry Ford

1873. He fasted for a whole year and then broke his fast with an onion.
— *Arabian Proverb*

1874. On the fall of an oak, every man gathers wood.
— Menander

1875. The reason a lot of people do not recognize an opportunity when they meet it is that it usually goes around wearing overalls and looking like hard work.
— *Christian Science Monitor*

1876. Sir Arthur Conan Doyle once related a bantering conversation he had had with a $10-a-week actor who was in the cast of one of his plays. The young chap had laughingly suggested that the two agree to divide their incomes with each other for the rest of their lives, but naturally Sir Arthur had refused such a ridiculous offer. The $10-a-week youngster was Charlie Chaplin.
— *Christian Science Monitor*

1877. When you are an anvil be patient; when a hammer, strike.
— *Arabian Proverb*

optimism

1878. The optimist is as often wrong as the pessimist, but he is far happier.

1879. It's a gay old world when you're gay,
And a glad old world when you're glad.
But whether you play or go toiling away
It's a sad old world when you're sad.

It's a grand old world when you're great
  And a mean old world when you're small,
It's a world full of hate for the foolish who prate
  On the uselessness of it all.

It's a beautiful world to see,
  Or it's dismal in every zone,
The thing it must be in its gloom or its gleam
  Depends on yourself alone.

1880.   Some one started the whole day wrong —
      Was it you?
  Some one robbed the day of its song —
      Was it you?
  Early this morning some one frowned;
  Some one sulked until others scowled;
  And soon harsh words were passed around —
      Was it you?

  Some one started the day aright —
      Was it you?
  Some one made it happy and bright —
      Was it you?
  Early this morning, we are told,
  Some one smiled and all through the day —
  This smile encouraged young and old —
      Was it you?

                                    — *Author Unknown*

1881.   An optimist is the fellow who fell out of the 20th story window of a skyscraper and as he passed the fourth floor said "so far so good."

1882.   An optimist is someone who tells you to cheer up when things are going his way.

1883.   An optimist is a man who is just starting to shovel out a long driveway; a pessimist is one who has been working at it for five minutes.   — RICHARD ATTRIDGE, *Readers Digest*

1884.   *St. Peter (to applicant):* "Where are you from?"
  Applicant: "California."
  St. Peter: "Come on in, but I don't think you'll like it."

273

1885. It never hurts to crack a smile.

1886. Look for the best in the other fellow — you will always find something good.

1887. "Ah done bin down to one o' dese-heah optimists an' got me a new set ob glasses," said Rastus. "I sho' can see good now."

"You mean 'Optometrist,' don't you, Rastus? An optometrist fits you up with glasses; an 'optimist' is a man who thinks everything is going to come out all right."

"Da'ss him," beamed the man of color. "He done trusted me fo' de glasses!"

1888. Don't be sorry if the bottle is half empty. Be glad that it is half full.

order

1889.   ORDER — A Text For Every Executive

"What comfort, what strength, what economy there is in order — material order, intellectual order, moral order. To know where one is going and what one wishes — this is order; to keep one's word and one's engagements — again order; to have everything ready under one's hand, to be able to dispose of all one's forces, and to have all one's means of whatever kind under command — still order; to discipline one's habits, one's effort, one's wishes; to organize one's life, to distribute one's time, to take the measure of one's duties and make one's rights respected; to employ one's capital and resources, one's talent and one's chances profitably — all this belongs to and is included in the word order. Order means light and peace, inward liberty and free command over one's self; order is power. Aesthetic and moral beauty consist, the first in a true perception of order, and the second in submission to it, and in the realization of it, by, in, and around one's self. Order is man's greatest need and his true well-being."

As true today as when Henri Amiel, the great Swiss philosopher, wrote it for his *Journal Intime,* seventy years ago!

Order is the greatest need of business. To establish it in all departments is to set the scene for assured success.

origin – words– phrases

1890. In the late 19th century Evanston, Illinois, nicknamed "Heavenston" by Frances Willard, was a Methodist-minded town, so pious that the town fathers, resenting the dissipating influences of the soda fountain, passed an ordinance forbidding the sale of ice cream sodas on Sunday. Some ingenious confectioners, obeying the law, served ice cream with syrup but without soda. This sodaless soda was the Sunday soda, and became so popular that orders for "Sundays" crossed the counter every day of the week. When objection was raised to christening the dish after the Sabbath, the spelling was changed to Sundae, and so developed one of America's most characteristic dishes. — RICHARD LLOYD JONES, quoted by William Lyon Phelps, *Autobiography* (Oxford University Press)

1891. The phrase "giving him the cold shoulder" dates back to a medieval custom in French chateaux. Honored guests were served hot-meat dishes, but when they overstayed their welcome or became otherwise unpopular, their host literally gave them a "cold shoulder" of beef or mutton.

1892. Daniel Drew got his start after the War of 1812 driving cattle into New York City. He got a brilliant idea of feeding them lots of salt. They drank their heads off and built up their weight right smartly so that Daniel made handsome profits.

Hence the term "watered stock."

1893. How the term "hitch-hiker" originated: When two men, with only one horse between them, went on a journey, one man would mount and ride an allotted distance, dismount and hitch the horse to a tree or fence and proceed on foot. The other man would walk until he came to the horse, then ride on until he caught up with the hiker. — OSCAR AMERINGER, *If You Don't Weaken* (Holt)

1894. Caesarean operation has no relation to the birth of Julius Caesar. The term goes far back into antiquity, and the operation is supposed to have been performed by the early Greeks. The word "Caesarean" derives from the Latin past participle, caesus, from caedere, meaning to cut. — *Liberty*

275

1895. To "the bitter end" has a nautical origin. A ship's anchor chain, at the point where it was fastened to a vertical timber called the bitt, was know as the bitter end. Thus when the chain has been played out to the bitter end, there's nothing more that can be done.
— Ships

1896. "Not worth a rap" does not refer to knocking the knuckles on wood. In the language of a few hundred years ago it meant literally a thing of no value — for the allusion is to an 18th century Irish coin called a "rap," worth about half a farthing, the equivalent of a quarter of an American cent.
— Jean Newton, Capper's Weekly

1897. Among the ancient Greeks there was a class of men who learned how to make themselves welcome at the tables of rich men by providing dinner entertainment of a flattering nature. To such a man was applied the term parasitos made up of the preposition para meaning "beside" and sitos meaning "food." The term was transliterated into the Latin as parasitus and into English as parasite.
— Catholic Digest

1898. The present English word, "jubilee," comes from the Hebrew word, "yobel," which means a rams' horn blown at the beginning of a holy year.
— The American Weekly

1899. That "Roman salute" invented by D'Annunzio, which became also the "German salute," was copied from some statue or fresco. He forgot that in Ancient Rome citizens greeted each other by shaking hands — only slaves made the sign adopted by the subjects of Mussolini and Hitler.
— Count Carlo Sforza, Books Abroad

1900. Many slang expressions now in use can be dated back a century or more:
Lousy: 1690
Mad as a March Hare: 1535, More
Tell it to the marines: 1830, Moncrieff
Needle in a haystack: 1565
Plain as the nose on one's face: 1660
Put one's oar in (to intrude): 1596, Florio
Taken down a peg: 1664, Butler
Pin-money: 1673, Wycherley
Put one's better foot forward: 1596
It never rains, but that it pours: 1749

276

Like a drowned rat: 1508
Two birds with one stone: 1656, Hobbes
Make oneself scarce: 1749, Smollett
So-So (Mediocre): 1530, Palgrave
To call a spade a spade: 1588
Spliced (married): 1751, Smollett
Sponge (a parasite): 1598, Shakespeare
Tan one's hide: 1731, Coffey
Through thick and thin: 1359, Gaytrigg
Three's a crowd: 1430
Steal one's thunder: 1709
Wild goose chase: 1595, Shakespeare

— J. LOUIS KUETHE, *American Speech*
Columbia University Press

1901. The barber's pole began its career in the Middle Ages, when the art of surgery and the trade of barber were combined. Blood-letting was then a great cure-all: a vein in the arm was opened and the patient was given a stick or pole to grasp tightly, thus making the blood flow more freely. When not in use, the stick was hung outside the shop, with a white bandage wound around it in a spiral ready for use — indicating that a surgeon was available. But the sight of the gory pole was discouraging to the squeamish, so in time the barbers displayed a pole painted red and white, instead of that actually used in the operation. — From the book, *Handwrought Ancestors,* by MARION NICHOLL RAWSON, copyright, 1936 by E. P. Dutton & Co., Inc.

1902. The tipping custom originated in England when small sums were dropped into a box marked T.I.P.S. — to insure prompt service.

1903. In the middle ages King Charles I of England was so impressed by an attractive platter of beef that he touched it with his sword and dubbed it "Sir Loin."

That is how the term sirloin for a cut of beef originated.

A T-bone steak, is so named because of its T-shape. The crown roast, as applied to pork, lamb, and veal, refers to a cut which is fashioned into the shape of a crown. Porterhouse steak originated years ago in a New York hotel where a proprietor named Porter built up a big business with quality steaks.

1904. The first northern Memorial day observance was held in 1868, after General John A. Logan of Illinois issued his famous General Orders, No. 11 to the Grand Army of the Republic. They began as follows:

Headquarters
Grand Army of the Republic
Washington, D. C., May 5, 1868. General Orders, No. 11:

1. The 30th day of May, 1868, is designated for the purpose of strewing with flowers, or otherwise decorating the graves of comrades who died in defense of their country during the late rebellion and whose bodies now lie in almost every city, village, hamlet, and churchyard of the land.

Prior to this time, several southern states observed "Decoration day" on May 30. Later, some southern states began to observe June 3, the birthday of Jefferson Davis, as Confederate Memorial day, and elsewhere in the south Memorial day is observed on April 26 or May 10.

originality

1905. He will never worship well the image on the altar who knew it when it was a trunk of wood in the garden.

— *Spanish Proverb*

1906. Originality: undetected imitation.

panacea

1907. For those who have panaceas for world's ills: Remember the student who told his professor: "I have invented a universal solvent. This chemical will dissolve anything and everything." "Fine — but what are you going to keep it in?"

parasite

1908. A parasite is one who goes through a revolving door on another's push.

278

parenthood

1909. THE BOY'S IDEAL

I must be fit for a child to play with,
Fit for a youngster to walk away with,
   Fit for his trust and fit to be
   Ready to take him upon my knee;
Whether I win or lose my fight,
I must be fit for my boy at night.

I must be fit for a child to come to,
Speech there is that I must be dumb to.
   I must be fit for his eyes to see,
   He must find nothing of shame in me,
Whatever I make of myself, I must
Square to my boy's unfaltering trust.

I must be fit for a child's glad greeting,
His are eyes that there is no cheating;
   He must behold me in every test,
   Not at my worst, but my very best;
He must be proud when my life is done,
To have men know that he is my son.

      — ERWIN HIRSCH

1910. Parents represent the last stand of the amateur. Every other trade and profession has developed standards, has required study and practice and licensing before releasing the student into his work. . . . Only one profession remains untutored and untrained — the bearing and rearing of our children.

      — EVELYN MILLS DUVAL, *Marriage and Family Living*

1911. Maternity is a matter of fact; paternity always a matter of opinion.   — Ridpath's *History of the U.S.*

1912.

I gaze with hope and pride and joy
Upon my graduating boy,
And know a sudden mute relief
As deep as love, as sharp as grief:
Sharing his victory today,
I graduate from PTA!

      — ELEANOR GRAHAM VANCE, *Colliers*

parenthood

1913. Parents: people who spend half their time wondering how their children will turn out, and the rest of the time when they will turn in.

1914. Father's Day; just like Mother's Day, only you don't spend as much on the present.

1915. Groucho Marx asked a contestant, who was a member of the parent-teacher association: "How many men would you say there were in the PTA?"

"I'd say about 80 per cent of the parents are women," the contestant innocently replied.

Groucho flicked his cigar and observed: "All I can say is that things have changed since I was a kid."

past, the

1916. Lost, yesterday, somewhere between sunrise and sunset, two golden hours, each set with sixty diamond minutes. No reward is offered, for they are gone forever. — HORACE MANN

patience

1917. Our real blessings often appear to us in the shape of pains, losses and disappointments; but let us have patience, and we soon shall see them in their proper figures. — JOSEPH ADDISON

1918. No school is more necessary to children than patience, because either the will must be broken in childhood or the heart in old age. — JEAN PAUL RICHTER

1919. Patience ornaments the woman and proves the man. — TERTULLIAN

1920. How poor are they that have not patience?
What wound did ever heal, but by degrees? — WILLIAM SHAKESPEARE

1921. He that can have patience can have what he will. — BENJAMIN FRANKLIN

1922. What I have done is due to patient thought.
— Sir Isaac Newton

1923. Patience is the ballast of the soul, that will keep it from rolling and tumbling in the greatest storms; and he that will venture out without this to make him sail even and steady will certainly make shipwreck and drown himself, first in the cares and sorrows of this world, and then in perdition. — Hopkins

1924. Infinite patience is the price that many a man has paid for success. Gibbon worked twenty years on his "Decline and Fall of the Roman Empire." Noah Webster spent thirty-six years on his dictionary. George Bancroft spent twenty-six years on his "History of the United States."

1925.
Not now, but in the coming years
  It may be in the Better Land,
We'll read the meaning of our tears
  And there, sometime, we'll understand.

We'll catch the broken threads again
  And finish what we here began;
Heaven will then the mysteries explain
  And then, ah then, we'll understand.

Then, trust in God through all thy days
  Fear not, for He doth hold thy hand;
Though dark the way, still sing and praise,
  Sometime, sometime we'll understand.
— *Anonymous*

1926. About the only thing that comes to him who waits is whiskers.

1927. Patience and the mulberry leaf become a silk robe.
— *Chinese Proverb*

1928. The secret of patience is doing something else in the meanwhile.

patriotism

1929.   BETWEEN MIDNIGHT AND MORNING

You that have faith to look with fearless eyes
    Upon the tragedy of a world at strife,
And know, that out of night and death shall rise
    The dawn of ample life:

Rejoice! whatever anguish rend your heart,
    That God hath given you this priceless power,
To live in these great times and have your part
    In Freedom's crowning hour;

That you may tell your sons, who see the light
    High in the heavens, their heritage to take: —
"I saw the powers of darkness put to flight!
    I saw the morning break!"   — OWEN SEAMAN

1930.   TO UNCLE SAM

Uncle Sam, I give my son to you,
A tall young lad, whom you'll find loyal, true;
He joins brave men who've come from far and wide
To keep aloft our heritage and pride.
These eighteen years, my boy has laughed and played;
Grew to young manhood eager, unafraid.
A way of life, blessed by the one above,
That he will guard with all his strength and love.
Uncle Sam, my son belongs to you,
Now proudly clad in uniform of blue;
When victory's won, and men again are free,
God willing, you will give him back to me.
                    — BESSIE KINGSBURY

1931.   I know only two tunes; one of them is "Yankee Doodle,"
and the other isn't.   — ULYSSES S. GRANT

1932.   "My country, right or wrong" is like saying, "My mother,
drunk or sober."   — G. K. CHESTERTON

1933.   The greatest honor which this nation can bestow upon the
"unknown hero" would be to live for the things for which he died.

people

1934. History tells of a white-haired shepherd of Sparta, who learned to understand men perfectly from always having lived alone with his sheep.

1935. The only real people are the people who never existed. . . . The justification of a character in a novel is not that other persons are what they are, but that the author is what he is. . . . In point of fact what is interesting about people in good society . . . is the mask that each of them wears, not the reality that lies behind the mask.

— OSCAR WILDE

1936. Some people are like blotters — they soak it all in and get it all backwards.

perfection

1937. A gem is not polished without rubbing, nor a man made perfect without trials.

1938. A rookie complained to his sergeant that he did not like parachute-jumping; that he didn't mind doing anti-aircraft work; that trench fighting was all right but that he just did not like parachute-jumping.

"But, why not," asked the sergeant.

"Well," replied the recruit, "I don't like to practice at anything at which I have to be perfect the first time."

perseverance

1939. Jacob Riis, in his drive against slums, never allowed a chance to pass of telling the people of New York what they were harboring. But it took a lot of telling, and he sometimes grew discouraged. "But," he said, "when nothing seems to help I go and look at a stonecutter hammering away at his rock perhaps one hundred times without as much as a crack showing in it. Yet at the one hundred and first blow it will split in two, and I know that it was not that blow that did it, but all that had gone before."

— JACOB A. RIIS, *The Making of an American* (Macmillan) Used by permission

1940. There's only one method of meetin' life's test:
Jes' keep on a-strivin' an' hope for the best;
Don't give up the ship an' quit in dismay;
'Cause hammers are thrown when you'd like a bouquet.
This world would be tiresome we'd all get the blues
If all the folks in it jest held the same views;
So finish your work, show the best of your skill,
Some folks won't like it, but other folks will.
— *Author Unknown*

1941. Carlyle said, "Every noble work is at first impossible." It matters not how difficult the task or how many reverses may come, if we keep everlastingly at it and our faith never flags, success will crown our efforts in the end. Faith will remove mountains. If headed in the right direction we will reach the goal. — Arthur E. Maysey

1942.   The quitter gives the match away
Past all denying;
I think it better far to stay
And fail by trying.   — Edgar A. Guest

1943. If you want a crop for one year, grow millet. If you want a crop for ten years, grow a tree. If you want a crop for one hundred years, grow men.   — *Chinese Proverb*

1944. Keep on going and the chances are that you will stumble on something, perhaps when you are least expecting it. I have never heard of anyone stumbling on something sitting down.
— Charles F. Kettering

1945. Great works are performed not by strength but by perseverence.   — Samuel Johnson, *Rasselas*

1946. It is often the last key on the ring which opens the door.

1947. The difference between perseverance and obstinacy is that one comes from a strong will and the other from a strong won't.

1948. Every noble work is at first impossible.
— Thomas Carlyle

1949. The great question is not whether you have failed, but whether you are content with failure.

1950. The lowest ebb is the turn of the tide.
— HENRY WADSWORTH LONGFELLOW

1951. The hard part of making good is that you have to do it every day.

1952. In a gun factory, a great bar of steel was suspended vertically by a delicate chain. Nearby, a bottle cork was suspended by a silk thread. Could the cork set the steel bar in motion?

The cork was swung gently against the steel bar: the bar remained motionless. But this was repeated again and again. In ten minutes the bar gave evidence of feeling uncomfortable, a "nervous chill" ran over it. Ten minutes later the chill was followed by vibration. At the end of half an hour the great bar was swinging like a pendulum. Yet there are people who dare assert that they exert no influence in the world! — *Presbyterian Standard*

1953. Sloth, like rust, consumes faster than labor wears, while the used key is always bright. — BENJAMIN FRANKLIN, *Poor Richard's Almanac*

1954. The conscientious plodder is nearly always outdistanced by the fellow who stops occasionally to analyze and plan.
— W. J. CAMERON

personality

1955.
We are all blind until we see
    That in the human plan
Nothing is worth the making, if
    It does not make the man.
Who build these cities glorious
    If man unbuilded goes?
In vain we build the work, unless
    The builder also grows. — EDWIN MARKHAM

pessimism — See also *Optimism*

1956. There are many isms today to perplex us — nazism, communism, fascism and so forth — but most of them will cancel each other out. There is only one ism which kills the soul, and that is pessimism. — LORD TWEEDSMUIR, Governor-General of Canada

285

pessimism

1957. Pessimists of other days:

In 1783, William Pitt, British Prime Minister: "There is scarcely anything around us but ruin and despair."

Archbishop Wilberforce, in the early 1800's: "I dare not marry. The future is so dark and unsettled."

Queen Adelaide of England, in 1837: "I have only one desire: to play the part of Marie Antoinette with bravery in the coming revolution."

Lord Shaftesbury, in 1848: "Nothing can save the British Empire from shipwreck."

Disraeli, in 1849: "In industry, commerce and agriculture there is no hope."

The Duke of Wellington, in 1851, shortly before he died: "I thank God I will be spared from seeing the consummation of ruin that is gathering around."　　　　　　　　　*— Readers Digest*

pettiness

1958. What is your personal grievance costing you?

Aren't you mighty small when you turn down some man for membership in your lodge on account of a personal grievance?

The rules of your order state that a black ball against a man is to be cast for some other reason than a personal grudge.

When you joined the order you said you would be governed by its rules.

Now when you have a chance to get even with a man for reasons of your own you do all you can to keep him out of an order with which he wishes affiliation. Then you would try to make believe that you are not prejudiced.

The ill-feeling you have for this man may cover a period of years.

But what have you gained through harboring it?

It has robbed you of many hours which you might have enjoyed. Thoughts of vengeance have brought you misery and turbulence of spirit.

You are really punishing yourself more than the one to whom you are unfriendly.

You may get a certain satisfaction out of the thought that you kept him out of your lodge, but you did not get wholesome pleasure out of it.　　　　　　　　　*— J. J. Mundy*

philosophy

1959. Philosopher: a person who says he doesn't care which side his bread is buttered on, because he eats both sides anyway.

1960. Philosophers are people who talk about something they don't understand, and make you think it's your fault.

1961. Philosophy: a study which enables man to be unhappy more intelligently.

photography

1962. If you look like your passport photo — you need the trip.

pleasure

1963. Pleasure has three facets:
1. anticipation
2. realization
3. remembrance

poetry

1964. A poet can survive everything but a misprint.
— OSCAR WILDE, *The Children of the Poets*

point of view

1965. A Chinese delegate to the U.N. was besieged by reporters when he arrived in New York. One of the questions flung at him was: "What strikes you as the oddest thing about Americans?"

He thought for a moment, then smiled. "I think," he said, "it is the peculiar slant of their eyes." — *This Week Magazine*

1966. Humphrey Bogart and Lauren Bacall were in the Stork Club when Harry Cohn, president of Columbia Pictures, walked by their table and whispered a few words to Bogart. The actor turned to his wife, and beamed: "The picture's a hit."

287

"What makes you so sure?" asked Miss Bacall.

"Because Mr. Cohn referred to it as 'Our Picture,'" Bogart explained. "If it was a flop, he'd say 'Your Picture.'"

— LEONARD LYONS

1967. He was introduced to a young lady with a whole string of degrees: "She's not a human being, she's a thermometer," was his only comment.

1968.   YOUTH SPEAKS

German . . . for a man!

I swear by God this holy oath, that I will unconditionally obey the Fuehrer of the German Reich and the German people, Adolf Hitler, Commander in Chief of the Army; as a brave soldier I will forever defend this oath at the cost of my own life.

— *The Soldier in the New Reich,*
(an official German handbook)

American . . . for an idea!

I, ... , do solemnly swear (or affirm) that I will bear true faith and allegiance to the United States of America; that I will serve honestly and faithfully against all their enemies whomsoever; and that I will obey the orders of the President of the United States and the orders of officers appointed over me, according to the rules and Articles of War.   — *The Oath of Enlistment in the United States Army*

1969. Alas: early Victorian for oh, hell. — OLIVER HERFORD

1970. When Robert Benchley was a student at Harvard, he took a course in international law. The final examination confronted him with a question something like this: Discuss the arbitration of the international fisheries problem in respect to hatcheries protocol and dragnet and trawl procedure as it affects (A) the point of view of the United States and (B) the point of view of Great Britain.

Benchley was frank, as well as somewhat desperate, and wrote as follows: "I know nothing about the point of view of Great Britain in the arbitration of the international fisheries problem, and nothing about the point of view of the United States. Therefore, I shall discuss the question from the point of view of the fish."

— EDWARD Y. BLEWETT and JOHN HOLMES, *The Saturday Evening Post*

1971. If the price of duck feathers is raised it means that down is up.

1972. In a certain city council of Sweden, the two political parties are about equally divided. At one time, it is related, the peasant member from Upsala made a bitter speech against his adversaries, the Communists, and terminated with this remark:

"Half of the members of this assembly are idiots."

Inevitably, there was an uproar of protests. The farmer was obliged to make a written apology. That same night, he posted the following declaration on the door of the city hall:

"I wish to assert that half of the members of the municipal council are not idiots."

1973. Whether the pitcher strike the stone, or the stone the pitcher, the pitcher suffers. — CERVANTES, *Don Quixote*

1974. The modernist says — "There ain't no such thing as Hell."
The fundamentalist's answer — "The Hell there ain't!"

1975. A floor-walker, tired of his job, gave it up and joined the police force. Several months later a friend asked him how he liked being a policeman. "Well," he replied, "the pay and the hours are good, but what I like best of all is that the customer is always wrong." — *Sales Scrap Book*

1976. A girl recently sent this extraordinary request to the editor of her home paper:

"Do you think it is right for a girl to sit in a man's lap, even if she is engaged?"

The editor answered her question thus: "If it were our girl and our lap, yes; if it were another fellow's girl and our lap, yes; but if it were our girl and another fellow's lap, never! never! never!"

1977. A man, whose father was hanged, when asked how his father met his death, replied that he died at a public function when the platform gave way.

1978. A kind old gentleman seeing a small boy who was carrying a lot of newspapers under his arm said: "Don't all those papers make you tired, my boy?"

"Naw, I don't read 'em," replied the lad.

1979. A fine robust soldier, after serving his country faithfully for some time became greatly reduced in weight owing to exposure and scanty rations until he was so weak he could hardly stand. Consequently he got leave of absence to go home and recuperate. He arrived at his home station looking very bad. Just as he stepped off the train one of his old friends rushed up to him and said, "Well, well, Pat, I am glad to see you're back from the front."

"Begorra, I knew I was getting thin, but I never thought you could see that much," remarked Pat. — *Ladies Home Journal*

1980. "We are both in great trouble," Sam Goldwyn told Darryl Zanuck, his fellow movie producer.

"Trouble?" Zanuck puzzled.

"Because you have an actor that I got to get," explained Goldwyn. — *Newsweek*

1981. Some years ago, we are told by a European traveler, Einstein was asked whether he preferred to be called a Jew or a German. He replied: "There is an expedition now in the south seas which will make observations either verifying or discrediting my reckonings. And if they verify my predictions I will be known as a Jew in England and a German in Germany."

1982. The wealth of colors and shades in our language is a never-ending source of wonder. Speaking of a young man who has lost his position, the old home paper says: "Mr. Jones has resigned his place with Smith Company to take a more lucrative position, which will be announced later." His old boss says: "Mr. Jones was discharged for incompetency." Mr. Jones himself says: "I got the gate 'cause the general manager seen I was a comer and got jealous." — *Kansas City Star*

1983. If you steal from one author, of course that's plagiarism; if you steal from twenty authors, that's research.

1984. When Thomas Mann was visiting America for the first time, one of Hollywood's literati abased himself before the novelist, emphasizing that he was nothing, a mere hack, his work not to be mentioned in the same breath with that of the master. Mann listened

290

with infinite patience and courtesy. But when the party was over, he turned to his host, an old friend, and said: "That man has no right to make himself so small. He is not that big."   *— Life*

1985.   *Motorist to native:* "Where is the main highway to Quincy?"
Farmer: "I don't know."
Motorist: "Well, where is the highway to Hannibal?"
Farmer: "I don't know."
Motorist: "Where does this highway go?"
Farmer: "I don't know."
Motorist: "You don't know much, do you?"
Farmer: "No, but I ain't lost."

1986.   *Irate Customer:* "Here; look what you did!"
Laundryman: "I can't see anything wrong with that lace."
Irate Customer: "Lace? That was a sheet!"

1987.   The pessimist reminds us that the lily belongs to the onion family, while the optimist reminds us that the onion belongs to the lily family.

1988.   A woman stepped off the penny scales and turned to her husband. He eyed her appraisingly and asked, "Well, what's the verdict? A little overweight?"
"Oh, no," said his wife, "I wouldn't say that. But according to that height table on the scale I should be about six inches taller!"
            — New Jersey Bell Telephone News

1989.   "Honest, Claude, I don't see how you make a living on this farm," I once remarked to a Vermont Yankee. "Look at the rocks everywhere!"
"I ain't so poor as y' think I be," retorted the farmer. "I don't own this durn farm!"   *— DONALD WILHELM*

1990.   "Washington," said the idle rich man to his valet, "I dreamed last night that I went to the Negro paradise. It was dirty and full of rubbish and just packed to the heavenly gates with your people in rags."
"That's nothin', sah!" chuckled the colorado-maduro lad, "Ah done dreamt I went to de white folkses' heaven. It shoh was nice dere. Flowers and pretty smells and trees everywhere. But, my gosh, it was empty!"

1991. On a certain ocean liner a great many of the passengers were sick. One young man in particular was very much worse than his shipmates. Among the passengers was an elderly lady who wished to be as sympathetic as possible, so walking up to the young man who was draped over the rail, she asked, "My dear boy, is your stomach weak?"

"Weak stomach, nothing, ain't I getting as much distance as any one?"

1992. You can usually tell when a high school boy is serious about a girl by the way she calls him up every evening.

1993. On his program "Double or Nothing" Bert Parks asked a young couple, "How long have you two been married?"

"Eight years," replied the husband.

"Eight and a half," corrected the wife.

"What difference does half a year make?" Parks teased.

"Well," retorted the wife, "we have a little girl seven and a half."
— MAE McCAFFERY, *Readers Digest*

poise

1994. Always behave like a duck — keep calm and unruffled on the surface but paddle like the devil underneath.

politeness

1995. Politeness in an individual is as necessary as paint on both sides of a fence, for a person, like a fence, faces out as well as in.
— MARCELENE COX, *Ladies Home Journal*

politicians — See *Politics*

politics — See also *Government*

1996. All free governments are party governments.
— EDMUND BURKE

1997. They have such refined and delicate palates
That they can discover no one worthy of their ballots,
And then when someone terrible gets elected
They say, There, that's just what I expected!
— OGDEN NASH

1998. That government is best which governs least.
— THOMAS JEFFERSON

1999. A typical politician, when he comes to the parting of the ways, goes both ways.

2000. The word "politician" has acquired a sinister connotation because it is so often used to describe their opponents.

2001. Political troubles are always multiplied by division.

2002. Politicians are of two classes — the appointed and the dis-appointed.

2003. In politics, as elsewhere, a nut goes with every bolt.

2004. Politics makes berths for strange fellows.

2005. Political difference is wholesome. It is political indifference that hurts.

2006. Nothing is politically right which is morally wrong.
— DANIEL O'CONNELL

2007. There was a politician in Indiana who was really honest. When he was bought, he stayed bought.

2008. Politicians who try to please everybody at once remind one of a pup trying to follow four kids at the same time.

2009. Now, as to young men. You must not wait to be brought forward by the older men. For instance, do you suppose I should have ever gotten into notice if I had waited to be hunted up and pushed forward by older men? — ABRAHAM LINCOLN

2010. The trouble is there are too many Democratic and too many Republican senators and not enough United States Senators.

2011. "Papa, what is a traitor in politics?"

"A traitor is a man who leaves our party and goes over to the other one."

"Well, then, what is a man who leaves his party and comes over to yours?"

"A convert, my boy."

2012. People vote their resentment, not their appreciation. The average man does not vote for anything, but against something.
— H. H. Munro

2013. The famous politician was trying to save both his faces.
— John Gunther

2014. Politicians frequently talk themselves red, white and blue in the face.

2015. He was an influential vote-getter. Barging into the newly-elected official's office with his moronic-looking son in tow, he announced expansively, "Bill, my boy says he would like a job in your department."

The official regarded the boy dubiously. "What can he do?"

"Nothing," the big shot admitted frankly.

"Oh, that simplifies it," beamed the office-holder. "Then we won't have to break him in!" — Louis Hirsch, *Readers Digest*

2016.   JOBS

What does the statesman talk about
When speaking to the mobs?
   It's jobs — just jobs.
What moves the multitude to deep
Appreciative sobs?
   It's jobs — just jobs.
It matters not who rules the State
As long as we participate
In some percentage of the gate
   And jobs.

Why is it that we wink our eye
When some official robs?
   It's jobs — just jobs.

And though they loot our noble land
We grin and think it simply grand,
For we should worry while they hand
    Out jobs.
                — NEWMAN LEVY

2017. It appears that three men went for a long walk, a doctor, an architect and a politician, and they fell to discussing as to whose profession was the oldest. Said the doctor: "My profession is the oldest since God created Eve out of Adam's rib and in fact, performed a surgical operation." Said the architect: "My profession is still older, since God, just like any architect, in creating the world, made it out of chaos." "Ah," joined in the politician, "but who made the chaos?"

2018.   COUNSEL FOR CANDIDATES

My boy, if office you would seek
Acquire a pleasing way to speak,
For if you have a rasping voice
You'll never be the people's choice;
And should you grate upon the ear
You'll finish sadly in the rear,
For folks who hark to radios
Won't vote for talkers through the nose.

Time was but few could hear or see
The men who would their favorites be.
They read about them in the press;
Disputed of them, more or less,
And oft mistook for common sense
What then was flowery eloquence.
So Lincoln, ugly, gaunt and thin,
Upon his merits had to win.

But things are different today.
'Tis not so much what statesmen say,
But how they say it. Do they look
Like pictures in a fashion book?
Have they the sort of chin or nose which
Pleases folks at picture shows?
And have they glamor? Will they go
On film and disc and radio?

Get glamor! Glamor, such as can
Attract the moving picture fan.
At work or at your favorite sport
Remember you must make a "short."
And if you are not good to see,
At ballot time you'll beaten be.
Not all the wisdom you enjoy
Will not outrun a glamor boy. — EDGAR A. GUEST

2019. In Washington a sightseer observed: "A good politician must also be an acrobat."

"How do you figure that?" queried his pal.

"Well," explained the first fellow, "They've got to straddle a fence, keep their fingers on the nation's pulse, point with pride and look to the future while keeping both ears to the ground!"

2020. Potomac fever: that hideous disease which causes one to swell without growing.

2021. The tree of liberty will not survive too much grafting.

2022. Webster's Biographical Dictionary, which lists the lives of all kinds of people, from Moses to John Kieran, finds it necessary to state in the Explanatory Notes: "It should be noted that the word Politician is used in the Dictionary in the general meaning of 'a person engaged in politics' and has no derogatory implications."

— *P. M.*

2023. The true joy of life is not in realization, but in anticipation. So, the good man waiteth patiently for his riches in Heaven, and the hungry politician for a change of administration.

2024. He was one of those politicians whose greatest asset is his lie-ability.

2025. Said the successful lawyer, "When I was an infant, my good folks were undecided what I would become when I grew up, and they struck on a plan. They gave me an apple, a prayer book, and a dollar bill; representing farming, the clergy and banking, to see which one I'd take to. I ate the apple, read the prayer book, and put the dollar bill in my pocket. They decided I was a born politician!"

2026. How a minority, reaching majority, seizing authority, hates a minority!
— L. H. Robbins

2027. The three major parties in the United States
 — the Democratic Party
 — the Republican Party
 — the cocktail party

2028. Some politicians repair their fences by hedging.

2029. Back in Cleveland's and McKinley's day 83 out of every 100 registered voters went to the polls. (No hard roads, no cars, widely separated voting places!) In 1916, 72 out of 100 voted. In 1936, that number had shrunk to 57 out of every 100. In 1948, just 50 out of every 100 registered voters took the "trouble" to vote! . . . Of the 5,000,000 registered voters in Illinois, only 1,400,-000 "bothered" about voting Primary Day! (1952)

2030. Whenever a man has cast a longing eye on offices, a rottenness begins in his conduct.
— Thomas Jefferson

2031. The conduct of a wise politician is ever suited to the present posture of affairs. Often by foregoing a part he saves the whole, and by yielding in a small matter secures a greater.
— Plutarch, *Lives*

2032. When I was a boy I was told that anybody could become President; I'm beginning to believe it.
— Clarence Darrow

2033. A politician thinks of the next election; a statesman of the next generation.

2034. Politician: a man who divides his time between running for office and running for cover.

2035. A politician is a man who stands for what he thinks others will fall for.

2036. Political war: one in which everyone shoots from the lip.
— Raymond Moley

2037. During his first campaign for mayor of New York City in 1929, La Guardia charged the popular Jimmy Walker with all sorts of corruption, and Walker never answered a single charge. "Why should I make his campaign for him?" he said to me. "I won't build him up. It would be fun, though, to ask him one question — what was he doing in Waterbury on July 16, 1928?"

"Was he there at that time?" I asked.

"I dunno," Walker replied. "But if I asked that question he could deny he was there until he was blue in the face. A lot of suckers would still believe there was something very fishy about him and Waterbury." — WILLIAM R. CONKLIN, *We Saw it Happen*

2038. Political economy: two words that should be divorced on grounds of incompatibility.

2039. Public sentiment is everything. With public sentiment, nothing can fail; without it nothing can succeed.

— ABRAHAM LINCOLN

2040. A candidate for the Kentucky legislature was running shortly after a no-squirrel-hunting bill had been passed. The bill provoked a storm of opposition and the candidate was urged by his advisers to duck any mention of it.

During the course of the campaign he was at a meeting where a question concerning the legislation in question was directed to him. As he started to answer his advisers paled and motioned him to keep still. "No," he whispered, "I can handle this." Then, turning to his audience, he took this firm position: "Some of my friends are for this law. And some of my friends are against this law. I want you folks to know that I always stand with my friends!"

2041. To find money growing on trees first takes a lot of grafting.

2042. A statesman is a politician who is held upright by equal pressure from all directions. — ERIC A. JOHNSTON, Pres. of the National Chamber of Commerce

2043. True glory lies in noble deeds, and in the recognition, alike by leading men and by the nation at large, of valuable services rendered to the State. — CICERO, *Philippica*

2044. A statesman is an ex-politician who has mastered the art of holding his tongue.

2045. Mugwump: a man who sits on a fence with his mug on one side and his wump on the other. — IRVING STONE, *They Also Ran*

2046. Practical politician: a man who shakes your hand before election and your acquaintance afterwards.

2047. Better vote for a poor man who believes as you do than a good man who believes in the opposite principles, for the good man can do more harm by reason of his greater efficiency and his wrong belief than the poor man can do when he is trying his best to do what you believe is right.

popularity

2048. Popularity is exhausting. The life of the party always winds up in a corner with an overcoat over him.
— WILSON MIZNER

posterity

2049. The lowest possible state to which I could sink would be one in which, before I died, I could say — I do not care whether the world is better for my having lived. The sin against the Holy Ghost is the sin against posterity. Any man who has planted a tree and knows that it will grow up and be pleasant to others in years hence is experiencing in a small way what is one of the strongest emotions in humanity. This is a noble emotion. It is noble when a man lays out gardens, levels terraces and plants woods for no other benefit than for his successors. — GEORGE BUCHANAN, *Passage Through the Present*

poverty — See also *Wealth*

2050. The poorest man in the world is the one who is always wanting more than he has.

2051. It is a toss up whether it is worse to be old and bent or young and broke.

2052. There is only one class in the community that thinks more about money than the rich, and that is the poor. The poor can think of nothing else. That is the misery of being poor.

— OSCAR WILDE

2053. "Can I lead a good Christian life in New York City on $15 a week?" a young man once asked Dr. S. Parkes Cadman.
"My boy," was the reply, "that's all you can do."

— WALTER WINCHELL

2054. Poverty does not mean the possession of little, but the non-possession of much.   — *Antipater*

praise

2055. To find out a girl's faults, praise her to her girl friends.

— BENJAMIN FRANKLIN

2056. If with pleasure you are viewing
        Any work a man is doing
And you like him, or you love him, say it now!
Don't withhold your approbation
        'Till the parson makes oration
And he lies with snowy lilies o'er his brow.
For no matter how you shout it
        He won't really care about it
He won't know how many tear drops you have shed.
If you think some praise is due him
        Now's the time to hand it to him
For he cannot read his tombstone when he's dead!

More than fame and more than money
        Is the comment kind and sunny
And the hearty warm approval of a friend;
Oh! it gives to life a savor
        And strengthens those who waver
And gives one heart and courage to the end.
If one earns your praise — bestow it!
If you like him — let him know it!
        Let the words of true encouragement be said!

Let's not wait 'till life is over,
   And he lies beneath the clover
For he cannot read his tombstone when he's dead.
— Author Unknown

2057. Praise is not only gratifying — it is the source of fresh energy which can be measured in the laboratory.

Dr. Henry H. Goddard, in his years at the Vineland Training School in New Jersey, used the "ergograph," an instrument devised to measure fatigue. When an assistant said to a tired child at the instrument, "You're doing fine, John," the boy's energy-curve soared. Discouragement and fault-finding were found to have a measurable opposite effect.
— Gretta Palmer

2058. It is necessary to praise the moon as well as the sun. The sun shines in the daytime when it is light anyway, but the moon comes out and gives some light at night when it's dark.

2059. To refuse praise is to seek praise twice.
— La Rouchefoucauld

2060. It is better to say something good about a bad man, than something bad about a good man.

2061. The man who wants credit for everything he does, seldom does anything deserving credit.

2062. Be moderate in praising a man when he is present, but give him full credit when he is absent.
— The Talmud

2063. Eulogy: praise that's too much and too late.
— Des Moines Register

prayer

2064. Lord, when we are wrong, make us willing to change. And when we are right, make us easy to live with.

2065. *Mrs. Dixon:* "What did you use to open that can of peaches?"

Kennet: "A can opener, of course. Why?"

Mrs. D.: "From the fragments of language I heard I thought you were opening it with prayer."

2066. Mr. Gridell, the office correspondent, was invited to dinner the other day and his host asked him to say grace. It was a new experience for Gridell but he was not to be found wanting. "Dear Lord," he began, "We thank Thee for all Thy favors of recent date. We trust that we may continue to merit Your confidence and that we may be favored with many more blessings from You in the near future. Yours very truly, Amen."

2067. This quaint prayer hangs outside the door of the Refectory of the Cathedral at Chester, England.

Give me a good digestion, Lord,
And also something to digest;
Give me a healthy body, Lord,
With sense to keep it at its best.
Give me a healthy mind, Good Lord,
To keep the good and pure in sight,
Which, seeing sin, is not appalled
But finds a way to set it right.

Give me a mind that is not bored,
That does not whimper, whine or sigh;
Don't let me worry over much
About the fussy thing called "I."
Give me a sense of humor, Lord,
Give me the grace to see a joke,
To get some pleasure out of life
And pass it on to other folk.

2068.   A WORLD-WIDE PRAYER

May peace return among men
Co-operation unite them
Friendship bind them
Love rule them
Justice prevail among them
Self-control strengthen them
Righteousness exalt them
Service ennoble them
Brotherhood enfold them
The past be forgiven them
The future be sanctified for them.

2069. The day returns and brings us the petty round of irritating concerns and duties. Help us to play the man, help us to perform them with laughter and kind faces; let cheerfulness abound with industry. Give us to go blithely on our business all this day, bring us to our resting beds weary and content and undishonored, and grant us in the end the gift of sleep. — ROBERT LOUIS STEVENSON

2070. An elderly man was in the habit when entering church, of bowing his head on the back of the pew in front of him for a long time. This excited the interest of a youngster who asked him just what he did during that time. The old man replied, "Lad, that's a fair question and demands a fair answer. I don't know what other people do when they bow their heads, but I always count forty!"

preaching

2071. Aunt Becky was punctuating the Negro preacher's sermon with "Amen! Amen! . . . Praise de Lawd! . . ." as he lit into every sort of sin from murder to shooting craps. Then the parson moved on against snuff-dipping, and Aunt Becky exclaimed to her neighbor indignantly, "Dar now! He's done stopped preachin' and gone to meddlin'!" — MRS. CHARLES ALLAN, *Progressive Farmer*

precaution

2072. The stitch is lost unless the thread be knotted. — *Italian Proverb*

2073. When your neighbor's house is on fire, carry water to your own. — *Italian Proverb*

precedent

2074. A precedent embalms a principle. — DISRAELI, speech of Feb. 22, 1848

prejudice — See *Discrimination*

present, the

2075. To change my opinion today, does not mean to say that I know less today than I knew yesterday.

2076. No matter what looms ahead, if you can eat today, enjoy the sunlight today, mix good cheer with friends today, enjoy it and bless God for it. Do not look back on happiness — or dream of it in the future. You are only sure of today; do not let yourself be cheated out of it. — HENRY WARD BEECHER

2077. In every today walks a tomorrow. We have a right to look to you, young men, to tell us what is the tomorrow that walks in today. Not to create a tomorrow out of your own imaginings, nor to insist that we shall always live in today; but to find the tomorrow that is in today, and to teach us how to find it for ourselves.

— Reprinted by permission of Dodd, Mead & Company from *Problems of Life* by LYMAN ABBOTT

2078. Very few men live at present, but are providing to live another time. — JONATHAN SWIFT

2079. Reflect upon your present blessings, of which every man has many, not on your past misfortunes, of which all men have some. — CHARLES DICKENS

2080. The psychologist William Moulton Marston asked 3,000 persons: "What have you to live for?"

He was shocked to find that 94 percent were simply enduring the present while they waited for the future; waited for "something" to happen; waited for children to grow up and leave home; waited for next year; waited for another time to take a long-dreamed-about trip; waited for someone to die; waited for tomorrow without realizing that all anyone ever has is today because yesterday is gone and tomorrow never comes. — DOUGLAS LURTON, *The Power of Positive Living* (McGraw-Hill)

2081. One today is worth two tomorrows.

— BENJAMIN FRANKLIN

2082. Many of us are waiting for a public announcement that the old world has been laid to rest and that a brand new world will be inaugurated as of a specific date. Few realize the obvious truth that the future is now. No visible chalkline of demarcation exists between the present and the future. In the present are mingled the dying echoes of the past and the first lusty cries of the nascent future.

— PIERRE VAN PAASSEN, "The Future Is Now!" *Redbook*

2083. Today is the tomorrow you worried about yesterday.

2084. Yesterday is a cancelled check; tomorrow is a promissory note; today is ready cash — spend it . . . wisely. — *Typo Graphic*

pretense

2085. Many of us live expensively to impress our friends who live expensively to impress us.

pride

2086. The most pleasing argument for admitting Alaska as a state is that it would make Texas the second biggest state in the Union.

2087. No one with a good catch of fish goes home by way of the back alley.

2088. I like to see a man proud of the place in which he lives. I like to see a man who lives in it so that his place will be proud of him. — ABRAHAM LINCOLN

principle

2089. He that hath principle is inspired.

printing

2090.
THE PRINTER
It may be sad, but still 'tis true,
There's one thing all us humans do,
And that is, blame the printer.
He does his best, without our help,

For all we do is stand and yelp,
Then cuss, and blame the printer.

We write our manuscript by pen.
To read it is beyond our ken,
Yet we expect the printer
To dope it out and get it right.
We think not of his time or sight;
If wrong — we blame the printer.

We hold our stuff until the last,
Then try to rush it through so fast
The printer gets snowed under.
But still we camp upon his trail,
And prod him on with woeful tale,
Or rant and roar like thunder.

He shoots it through, the proof we get, —
Hell's bells! the job is not right yet.
We chop that proof to splinters.
It takes two days, before he knows
Just what each hieroglyphic shows —

A dumb lot are those printers.
The job's delivered. Some relief!
To know we're through with rush and grief,
We ought to thank the printer.
But no! The poor gink's out of luck —
He overcharged us one whole buck.
Once more we damn the printer.

— Edson S. Dunbar

procrastination — See also *Delay*

2091. Most people put off until tomorrow that which they should have done yesterday. — Edgar W. Howe

profession

2092. WHAT MAKES A PROFESSION

"If there is such a thing as a profession as a concept distinct from a vocation it must consist in the ideals which its members maintain, the dignity of character which they bring to the performance of their duties, and the austerity of the self-imposed ethical standards. To constitute a true profession there must be ethical tradition so potent as to bring into conformity members whose personal standards of conduct are at a lower level, and to have an elevating and ennobling effect on those members. A profession cannot be created by resolution or become such overnight. It requires many years for its development, and they must be years of self-denial, years when success by base means is scorned, years when no results bring honor except those free from the taint of unworthy methods."

— Author Unknown

progress

2093. This clipping appeared in a Boston newspaper published three quarters of a century ago: "A man about forty-six years of age, giving the name of Joshua Coppersmith, has been arrested in New York for attempting to extort funds from ignorant and superstitious people by exhibiting a device which he says will convey the human voice any distance over metallic wires so that he will be heard by the listener at the other end. He calls the instrument a 'telephone' which is obviously intended to imitate the word 'telegraph' and win the confidence of those who know the success of the latter instrument without understanding the principles on which it is based. Well-informed people know that it is impossible to transmit the human voice over wires as may be done with dots and dashes and signals of the Morse Code, and that, were it possible to do so, the thing would be of no practical value. The authorities who apprehended this criminal are to be congratulated, and it is hoped that his punishment will be prompt and fitting, that it may serve as an example to other conscienceless schemers who enrich themselves at the expense of their fellow creatures."

2094. The very essence of progress is the elevation of punishment from the base rank of vengeance to the exalted level of justice.

— R. H. MARKHAM, The Goal in Sight

2095. Steam interferes with the comfort of traveling, philosophized Samuel Brock, who died in 1862. It destroys every salutary distinction in society and overturns by its whirligig power the once rational gentlemanly, and safe mode of getting along on a journey.

Talk of ladies on board a steamboat or in a railroad car! There are none. To restore herself to her caste, let a lady move in select company at five miles an hour. — Donald G. Mitchell, *American Land and Letters* (Charles Scribners & Sons)

2096. Progress consists of swapping old troubles for new.

2097. The longer I live the more keenly I feel that whatever was good enough for our fathers is not good enough for us.
— Oscar Wilde

2098. Science is wonderful, but so many startling things happen these days that it's hard to keep up with them. We have nothing but warm sympathy for the youngster who came home from school and announced excitedly to his mother: "They've got a magic record player at school! You don't have to plug it in or even use electricity to make it play. All you do is wind up a crank!"

2099. Progress: a state of human development where a man pays a laundry for destroying his shirts and collars.

2100. To face tomorrow with the thought of using the methods of yesterday is to envision life at a standstill. Even that which we now do well must be done better tomorrow. — James F. Bell

2101. Some people are like what the school boy said about the mule —"awfully backward about going forward."
— *Religious Telescope*

2102. Mandy positively refused to ride on the merry-go-round at the county fair. To her protesting friends, she declared: "No indeed! Ah don't travel on dat thing. De other day I seen Rastus Green get on an ride, til Ah was dizzy watching him. When he gets off, I sez to him, 'Rastus yo' done spent yo' money, but whar yo' been?' "
— *Christian Science Monitor*

2103. All progress is based upon a universal innate desire on the part of every organism to live beyond its income.
— Samuel Butler

promise

2104. We must not promise what we ought not, lest we be called upon to perform what we cannot. — ABRAHAM LINCOLN

2105. Some persons make promises for the pleasure of breaking them. — WILLIAM HAZLITT

2106. *Father:* "Didn't you promise me to be a good boy?"
Son: "Yes, Father."
Father: "And didn't I promise you a thrashing if you weren't?"
Son: "Yes, Father, but as I've broken my promise, you needn't keep yours."

prophesy

2107. Don't ever prophesy; for if you prophesy wrong, nobody will forget it; and if you prophesy right, nobody will remember it. — JOSH BILLINGS

psychiatry

2108. "My family thinks there's something wrong with me," a woman complained to the psychoanalyst, "simply because I like buckwheat cakes."

"But there's nothing wrong about liking buckwheat cakes," the doctor murmured, puzzled, " I like them myself."

"Oh, do you?" The woman was delighted. "You must come up some day. I have seven trunks full." — *Readers Digest*

2109. The psychiatrist had just signed up with the Army, and announcing his departure to one of his patients, he slipped in a little boasting. "You see, I come from a fighting family. My great-great-grandfather fought in the Revolutionary War; my great grandfather fought in the Civil War; my grandfather fought in the Spanish-American War; my father in the first World War, and now I'm leaving to fight in the second World War."

The patient was unimpressed. "What's the matter with your family? Can't they get along with anybody?"
— J. N. BAKER, *Readers Digest*

2110. They are telling of the time when Queen Marie visited America, and asked to meet Dr. Adolpf Meyer, the psychiatrist at Johns Hopkins. "Dr. Meyer," an intermediary introduced, "I want you to meet the Queen of Romania." The psychiatrist's professional reply was: "How long does she think she's been queen?"

2111. The Journal of the American Medical Association reports this incident at the Mayo Clinic: A lady psychiatrist was questioning a patient and asked: "What would you say would be the difference between a little boy and a dwarf?". . . . The patient thought a while and said: "Well, there might be a lot of difference."

"What for instance?" asked the psychiatrist encouragingly.

"Well," replied the patient, "the dwarf might be a girl."

2112. The teacher in an extremely modern progressive school, asked a new seven-year-old girl pupil, "Are you a little boy or a little girl?" The pupil answered, "I'm a little boy." The teacher alarmed at this answer, called for the mother and proceeded to tell her that the little girl was psychologically confused and that she was decidedly a problem child.

Later on at home, her mother called her child aside and said to her: "Sheila, why did you say you were a little boy?" Sheila answered: "When anybody asks me a dumb question, I always give a dumb answer."

2113. Anybody who would go to a psychiatrist ought to have his head examined.

2114. Psychiatrist: a man who doesn't have to worry as long as other people do.

2115. The paranoid's classic golden rule:

"Believe — and act on the belief — that others want to do to you what you would like to do to them."

— B. BRICKNER, *Is Germany Curable?*

2116. Mad money: the fee charged by a psychiatrist.

psychology

2117. Mass psychology: doing it the herd way.

2118. Psychologist: a man who, when a good-looking girl enters a room, watches everybody else.

public speaking – speakers – audience

2119. I remember my lesson from the horse and buggy days: The longer the *spoke* the bigger the *tire*.

2120. A long-winded lecturer had been holding forth for over an hour, except for brief pauses from time to time to gulp a hasty drink of water. Finally, during one such "intermission", an old man in the audience leaned toward his neighbor and announced in a loud whisper: "First time I ever saw a windmill run by water!"
— Readers Digest

2121. Lady leaving a lecture hall: "What a complete waste of time that was — although I will admit it was quite educational."
— BILL GOLD, The Washington Post

2122. A speaker talked loud and long, then asked brightly, "Are there any questions?" A hand shot up. The speaker nodded.
"What time is it?" the listener inquired.
— KENNY NICHOLS, All About The Town (Danner)

2123. A minister noticing only one man in his audience went down from the pulpit and talked to him, asking what he should do under the circumstances and whether or not he should go ahead with his sermon just the same. The man replied: "I'm not very smart but if I were shepherd of a flock and I found only one sheep, I'd feed him." So the minister returned to the rostrum and proceeded to go through his whole sermon. When finished, he again went down to the same man and asked him how he had done. The man replied: "I'm not very smart, but if I found only one sheep in my flock, I wouldn't throw off the whole load."

2124. You can't usually tell whether a man is a finished speaker until he sits down.

311

2125. On the audience-reaction cards passed out at a movie pre-view, one question read: "Should anything be cut?"

One irate moviegoer wrote: "Yes, several things should be cut. The throats of the writer, director, producer and star."

— ERSKINE JOHNSON, NEA

2126. While I was editor of Southern Agriculturist, I spoke at many meetings. At a country church in Arkansas, after I got well into my speech and began talking loudly and waving my arms freely, a baby started to fret and fuss. When the embarrassed mother got up to take it out, I halted and said, "Never mind the baby, lady. It's not bothering me one bit."

"The baby may not be bothering you," the mother retorted, "but you sure are bothering the baby!" — J. E. STANFORD, *Farm and Ranch*

2127. It was an interminable speech, but finally he wound up, "I want land reform. I want housing reform, I want educational reform, I want —" Just then a bored voice in the audience interrupted: "Chloroform." — *Readers Digest*

2128. Public speakers should speak up so that they can be heard, stand up so that they can be seen and shut up so that they can be enjoyed.

2129. Chief Justice Warren, when governor of California began a political address thus: "Ladies and gentlemen, I'm pleased to see this dense crowd here tonight." A voice from the back shouted, "Don't be too pleased. We ain't all dense!"

— Sacramento (Calif.) *Shopping
News Times*

2130. Speaking at a large political gathering, the late Alfred E. Smith ignored a particularly cantankerous heckler. Finally the man yelled, "Go ahead, Al — tell 'em all you know! It won't take long!"

Smiling amiably, Smith replied: "I'll tell them all we both know. It won't take any longer." — DONALD E. BURROWS, *The Saturday
Evening Post*

2131. Once when Harry Collins Spillman was introduced at a meeting in an auditorium, he began: "I am delighted to have the privilege of speaking to you today in this magnificent auditorium. I presume you know the meaning of the word auditorium. It is derived from two Latin words — audio, to hear, and taurus, the bull."

— G. LYNN SUMNER, *We Have
With Us Tonight* (Harpers)

2132. The more you say, the less people remember.
— François Fenelon

2133. The best test of a sermon is depth — not length.

2134. After a fulsome introduction by an effusive lady, Alfred Hooper, the mathematician, wooed his audience back to good humor with this story: An Italian farmer, bringing a calf to market, was stymied by the calf's refusal to cross a bridge over a creek. Cajoling and prodding made no impression whatever. Finally a motorist drove up and let out a loud blast with his horn. The panic-stricken calf made a wild leap over the bridge's railing and was promptly drowned in the whirling current below. The philosophical farmer summed up the situation in one sentence: "Too bigga da honk for so smalla da calf!"
— Bennett Cerf

2135. Little Tommy, seated on his father's lap, was thumbing the pages of an illustrated Bible when suddenly he came upon a picture of Daniel about to enter the lion's den. Tommy was truly perplexed for the picture portrayed Daniel all wreathed in smiles. To help him solve his dilemma, Tommy turned to his father with this all-important query: "Dad," he said, "I don't quite understand this picture. Here is Daniel about to enter the lion's den and he seems to be quite happy about it."

"Well, my son," came the reply, "That's probably because he realizes that when the feasting is over he won't be called upon to say anything."

2136. I met my friend Jones on the street a short while ago and we exchanged ideas. Now my mind is a blank.

2137. My speech will be like the latest Paris fashion: Long enough to cover the subject and short enough to be interesting.

2138. I really don't know where to begin — usually when I begin to talk on this subject I don't know where to stop.

2139. We feel somewhat like the speaker who got on the platform and opened his remarks with the statement that a few hours before there were two who knew what he was going to say, the Lord and himself. "Now," he said, "the Lord only knows."

2140. My friends: (I know you too well to call you gentlemen).

2141. A chauffeur-driven Cadillac pulled up in front of the auditorium, stopped with a jerk and out came our speaker of the evening.

2142. Rev. Harry Emerson Fosdick gave this most whimsical response to a flattering speech of introduction:

"Once," said Dr. Fosdick, "rumor went abroad that Miss Lucretia Sproggs, the perennial spinster, was at last engaged to be married. Shortly thereafter, her minister met her on the street and congratulated her heartily."

" 'O dear,' said Lucretia; 'there isn't a word of truth to it, but thank God for the rumor!'

"And so I say 'There isn't a word of truth in the kind remarks of the Chairman," said Dr. Fosdick, "but thank God for the rumor!"

2143. You know, as I look at you fellows I am reminded of the story they tell of the distinguished United States Senator who was in the habit of speaking before all sorts of groups, and invariably he would pose this question before the audience: He used to say, "Ladies and gentlemen, why are we here?" He had occasion to address the inmates of a mental hospital in Ohio; and he finally said, "Ladies and gentlemen, why are we here?" One of the inmates arose and probably in his only lucid interval in seven years, said, "Well, because, Mister, we're not all there."

2144. A local official, as chairman, was presenting a visiting representative from the general office. Preliminaries and the introductory speech took so long that when the honored guest finally gained the floor he looked at his watch, which now allotted him five minutes and said:

"I am reminded of a little girl who put a nickel up on the counter for a candy bar.

"But we have no nickel bars," said the clerk.

"May I please have a soda pop?"

"But they are seven cents."

Puzzled, the girl made a final attempt by ordering a popsicle. When told they were also seven cents, she reached the sidewalk before the clerk could remind her of the nickel on the counter.

"That's all right," she said, "I can't buy anything with it anyway."

— GUSTAVE LARSON, "Talk Takes
Time," *Future*

2145. The American Congress is strange," a Russian actor once reported after sitting in the spectator's gallery of the House of Representatives. "A man gets up and speaks and says nothing. Nobody listens — then everybody disagrees."

— Liberty

2146. Walking with a friend one day, Fritz Kreisler passed a large fish shop where a fine catch of codfish, with mouths open and eyes staring, were arranged in a row. Kreisler suddenly stopped, looked at them, and clutching his friend by the arm, exclaimed:

"Heavens! That reminds me — I should be playing at a concert!"

— Quoted by permission from The Orchestra Speaks, BERNARD SHORE, Longmans Green & Co., 1938

2147. A certain South African tribe considers long speeches injurious both to the orator and his audience. To protect both, there is an unwritten law that every public speaker must stand on one leg while addressing his hearers. As soon as his other foot touches the ground, his speech is brought to a close, by force if necessary.

— Quote

2148. A preacher who had written his sermon carefully found himself at the church without his manuscript. "As I have forgotten my notes," he began his sermon, "I will rely on the Lord for guidance. Tonight I will come better prepared." *— Religious Digest*

2149. "Freedom of speech" does not give a person the right to shout "Fire" in a crowded theatre.

— JUSTICE OLIVER WENDELL HOLMES

2150. In the preliminary correspondence (before a visit to a town) Elbert Hubbard rarely failed to mention that his fee for lecturing was, say, $200 — but to lecture and to be a guest at a private house was $250. He charged $50 extra when obliged to receive "entertainment." — FELIX SHAY, *Elbert Hubbard of East Aurora*

2151. Rabbi Charles Shulman used to tell this story about being invited to address his Sisterhood meeting on the subject of Confucius. He thought his group was becoming very high brow and intellectual. When he got to the meeting he was greeted by the president who said: "Oh, Rabbi, we're so glad you were able to come. We've planned a Chinese afternoon with Chop Suey and Mah Jong and now with you here to talk on Confucius, that rounds out the program very nicely."

2152. After an introduction such as that just accorded me, I just can't wait until I hear what I have to say.

2153. "If we want to be saved we had better get on the ball . . . ."
(Then tell the story of the golfer who missed the ball several times and each time hit a nest of ants. Finally after hitting a nest, one ant was heard to say to another, "If we want to be saved we had better get on the ball.")

2154. The community dinner was over at last and the patient guests who had listened to the long address of the principal speaker breathed a deep sigh of relief.

"The speaker was all right," the toastmaster's wife whispered, "but it seems to me that he didn't put enough fire into his speech."

"I feel the opposite way," answered the toastmaster. "In my opinion he didn't put enough of his speech into the fire."

2155. A speaker who does not strike oil in ten minutes should stop boring.

2156. A young boy was asked what different forms of punishment we had in this country. His answer was: In the United States many people are put to death annually by *elocution*.

2157. At an Advertising Club luncheon the principal speaker was exceedingly long winded. The chairman, becoming annoyed by the ever-increasing disorder, gave a tremendous thump on the table with his gavel. Off flew the gavel head, coming to rest swiftly and surely upon the bald cranium of a very bored man, who without a groan, slid under the table. Upon being told that the victim was regaining consciousness the speaker went on again.

"My Gawd," said the stricken one upon opening his eyes, "I still hear his voice; hit me again."

2158. Sir Joshua Stamp, in a speech at the Chicago Club, expressed a hope that he wasn't talking too long. "I wouldn't like to be in the position of the parson," he explained, "who in the midst of an interminable sermon, suddenly stopped to chide: 'You know I don't mind a bit having you look at your watches to see what time it is, but it really annoys me when you put them up to your ears to see if they are still running.' " — *The Laughten Library* (Maxwell Drake)

2159. The jawbone of an ass is just as dangerous a weapon today as it was in Sampson's time.

2160. It is reputed that Mr. Disraeli when he was once asked by a new member whether he advised him to take part often in debate replied:

"No, I do not think you ought to do so, because it is much better that the House should wonder why you do not speak than why you do."

2161. What can be more pathetic than an empty speaker pouring himself forth to a full house? — JOHN ANDREW HOLMES

2162. As some Englishmen would put it, our village barber shop was the original Town Meeting of the Air. — JOHN ANDREW HOLMES

2163. The most popular way nowadays to read a book is to hear a reviewer who hasn't read it either. — JOHN ANDREW HOLMES

2164. When a sermon at length comes to an end, people rise and praise God, and they feel the same way after many other speeches. — JOHN ANDREW HOLMES

2165. A certain University of North Carolina professor found himself in somewhat of a dilemma recently when he received an invitation from a local Post of the American Legion to make a Memorial Day address. The invitation read as follows: "You are invited to be one of the speakers at our Memorial Day meeting. The program includes a talk by the Mayor, recitation of Lincoln's Gettysburg Address by a high school boy, your talk, and then the firing squad."

2166. "After-dinner" speeches in Japan come before the meal. The custom not only relieves the speaker's nervous tension but also limits the length of the speech, as the serving of the meal interrupts a long-winded orator.

2167. When columnist Merryle Stanley Rukeyser got up to speak at a luncheon of the Pittsburgh Advertising Club, he asked the president, "How long shall I speak?"

The president told him cheerfully, "Take as long as you like — we all leave at 1:30."

2168. It's too bad those talkers who speak "straight from the shoulder" can't speak from a little higher up.

2169. If you are the speaker and someone in the audience says he cannot hear what you are saying just tell him that the words of the wise are softly spoken.

2170. Clarence Darrow once participated in a panel discussion on religion in Orchestra Hall, Chicago. In all there were four participants. One had for his subject "Why I am a Catholic"; another, "Why I am a Jew"; the third, "Why I am a Protestant", and the theme of Mr. Darrow's discourse was "Why I am an Agnostic".

Curtain time was 8:15 o'clock but there was a slight delay in getting started. Backstage the four panelists were waiting for the "go" sign to take their places on the platform. A reporter for the Chicago Tribune approached Mr. Darrow, whose every spoken word was deemed newsworthy, and in an appealing tone of voice implored, "Mr. Darrow, do you have an advance copy of your speech? I have an early edition to make and can't stay for the entire evening, and both my city editor and I will be grateful to you if you can give us the benefit of some advance copy." Barely lifting his eyes, Mr. Darrow bent forward as he reached into the back pocket of his trousers and brought forth a blank pad of paper which he handed to the reporter. One brief look was enough. "Why, Mr. Darrow," he said, "that's the same speech you made last week."

2171. The celebrated English clergyman and wit, Sidney Smith, was discussing the relative importance of two prominent men. "There is the same difference between their tongues," he observed, "as between the hour and the minute hand on a clock. The one goes twelve times as fast, the other signifies twelve times as much."

— Christian Science Monitor

2172. Years ago, when I first came to New York, Mark Twain gave a dinner in my honor. There were some thirty distinguished guests present, and as the dinner progressed, I became panicky.

"Don't you feel well?" asked Mr. Clemens.

"I'm scared to death," I said. "I know that I shall be called upon to speak and I'm sure I shan't be able to rise from my chair. When I stand up, my mind sits down!"

"Eddie," said my host, "it may help you if you keep one thing in mind — just remember they don't expect much!"

I have never since been self-conscious when I get to my feet.

> — MAJOR EDWARD BOWES, *Readers Digest*

2173. When I was invited to speak here tonight, I knew exactly how Androcles felt . . . Androcles, you know, was the fellow who made quite a reputation, fighting man-eating lions for the edification of the Caesars. One Roman Emperor noted that the gladiator's system seemed to consist of whispering in the lion's ear, whereupon the beast would demonstrate a complete loss of appetite, and slink away spiritless and defeated. Androcles was summoned to the royal box, and the Emperor asked, "How come?"

Androcles answered, "It's this way, sire. I merely tell him, "As soon as you've finished your dinner, you'll be asked to say a few words.' It gets them every time."

2174. Speeches are like steer horns — a point here, a point there and a lot of bull in between.

2175. *At a Testimonial Dinner:*

Honored guest: (After hearing many nice things said about him) "I know now how a pancake feels when it is immersed in a lot of sweet maple syrup."

2176. The minister's speech was like God's wisdom — It surpassed all understanding and like God's mercy, it was everlasting.

2177. The orator said: When I get through with my speech, there's usually a great awakening.

2178. As we grow older, our bodies get shorter and our anecdotes longer.

> — ROBERT QUILLEN

2179. The retirement of Max Mason as president of the Rocke-feller Foundation reminded a University of Chicago official of a story Mr. Mason told on himself when he was president of the University. He was an overnight guest at an Indiana home in a town where he was scheduled to speak before a large community gathering. He ate sparingly at dinner, expressing his appreciation of the excellent fare, but explaining that he never could speak well after eating heartily.

As he was retiring that night he heard the voices of his host and hostess in the next room. The wife had asked her husband how he liked the speech. His answer came distinctly through the thin walls:

"He might as well have 'et'," he said.

2180. Trying to give a friend a definition of "oratory," a Negro elucidated thus. "If you says black am white, dat's foolish. But if you says black *am* white, an' bellers like a bull an' pounds de table with both fists, dat's oratory."   *— Readers Digest*

2181. A minister was delivering a sermon during the course of which one of the members of his congregation fell asleep. The min-itser was anxious to awaken him and reclaim his attention by re-questing him to lead in the singing of the next hymn, so he said, "Mr. Smith, will you lead?" Startled out of his slumber, Mr. Smith woke with a start and exclaimed, "But I just dealt."

2182. *Judge:* "I am a man of few words and short sentences . . ."

2183. *Judge:* "I am a man of few words but long sentences . . ."

2184. The reason there are so few good talkers in public is that there are so few good thinkers in private.

2185. *Minister: (who has a cut on his face)* "As I was shaving this morning I was thinking of my sermon and as a result I cut my face."

Member of the Congregation: "The next time you shave think of your face and cut your sermon."

2186. It is better to keep one's mouth closed and be thought a fool, than to open it and remove all doubt. — ELBERT HUBBARD

2187. It's all right for you to have a train of thought if you also have a terminal.

2188. *Church notice in Seattle, Washington:*
"Come early — if you want a back seat."

2189. Most after dinner speakers are men. Women can't wait that long.

2190. As to your employment of language, the great aim is to be simple, and in a measure, conversational; and then let eloquence come of itself. If most people talked as well in public as in private, public meetings would be more interesting.
— THOMAS WENTWORTH HIGGINSON,
Study and Work

2191. The following paragraph is the standard test given applicants for jobs as radio announcers. Read it clearly and without mistakes in twenty seconds and you have an above-average diction!
I bought a batch of baking powder and baked a batch of biscuits. I brought a big basket of biscuits back to the bakery and baked a basket of big biscuits. Then I took the big basket of biscuits and the basket of big biscuits and mixed the big biscuits with the basket of biscuits that was next to the big basket and put a bunch of biscuits from the basket into a box. Then I took the box of mixed biscuits and a biscuit mixer and the biscuit basket and brought the basket of biscuits and the box of mixed biscuits and the biscuit mixer to the bakery and opened a tin of sardines. — *Facts*

2192. When all is said and done — too many people just keep on talking.

2193. Every orator has his moment. The trouble is too many of them stretch their moment into hours.

2194. Accustomed as I am to public speaking, I know the futility of it.

2195. Swans sing before they die; 'twere no bad thing should certain persons die before they sing. — SAMUEL T. COLERIDGE

2196. I am reminded of the story of the itinerant preacher who always complained that he made his best speeches on the way home. All that he had forgotten to tell his audience came to his mind then and his horse usually got the best part of the speech.

2197. *Chairman:* It's getting late. I've always had the feeling that a meeting such as this should always end on the *same* day it begins.

2198. According to one who should know, too many after-dinner speeches make people dull. The truth is that too many dull people make after-dinner speeches.

2199. The long-winded speaker who tells his audience that he is speaking not only to the present generation but also to posterity is usually waiting for his audience to assemble before he sits down.

2200. Toastmaster: the punk that starts things off.

2201. Speeches are like babies — easy to conceive, hard to deliver.

2202. Lecture: an occasion when you numb one end to benefit the other.

2203. Orator: a man who is willing to lay down your life for his country.

2204. Oratoreador: an orator who specializes in throwing the bull.

2205. Oratory: eloquence accompanied by a Prince Albert.

2206. Radio announcer: a man who talks until you have a headache, then tries to sell you something to relieve it.

2207. To be positive is to be mistaken at the top of your voice.

2208. Immortal words of Robert (Bob) Benchley:
"Before I make a speech, I want to say something."

2209. How does your voice sound to others? If you cup your ears with both hands, pressing the ears forward slightly, and speak, you'll have a pretty good idea. And you will be surprised how different your words sound. Radio performers often test themselves this way just before a program. — LOUIS PAINE BENJAMIN, *Ladies Home Journal*

2210. After dinner speaker: a fellow who rises to the occasion — and then stands too long.

2211. A good inspiring sermon helps people in several ways. Some rise from it greatly strengthened. Others wake from it refreshed.

2212. Second wind: what a public speaker acquires when he says, "And, in conclusion." — *Cincinnati Enquirer*

2213. What many orators lack in depth they make up for in length. — BARON DE MONTESQUIEU

2214. Banquet: a 50¢ dinner served in sufficient number to enable a caterer to charge $5.00 for it.

2215. After dinner speaker: the guy who starts the bull rolling.

2216. Good speech: a beginning and a conclusion placed not too far apart.

publishing

2217. Editor: the fellow who makes a long story short.

2218. Tabloids: fast reading for the slow-thinking. — P. J. THOMAJAN

pullman

2219. Recalling the tale of the new porter on the crowded Pullman, who roused the conductor's curiosity by hanging a red lantern on a berth. "Ah just follows the rules, boss," he explained. "Rule 19 says to hang out a red light when the rear end of a sleeper is exposed."

2220. A passenger on a New York–Chicago limited train, upon looking under his berth in the morning found one black shoe and one tan shoe. He called the porter's attention to the error. The porter scratched his woolly head in bewilderment.

"Well, if dat don't beat ebberything!" he said. "Dat's de second time dis mornin' dat dat mistake's happened."

punctuality

2221. Did you ever stop to figure out how much time we lose by being on time?

2222. With some, punctuality is the art of guessing how late the other fellow is going to be.

2223. I owe all my success in life to having been always a quarter of an hour before hand. — LORD NELSON

2224. A gentleman in business on Broadway, New York, was greatly annoyed by the tardiness of one of his skilled office staff. Calling him into the office one morning he said:— "Mr. Smith, I get here at 8:30 every morning and look over my mail; at 9 o'clock I look out of the window and see young Mr. Rockefeller on his way to the office; at 9:30 Mr. Schwab passes; at 10 I see Mr. Vanderbilt going by; at 10:30 Mr. Gould passes by on the way to his office; and at 11 you come in. Now tell me: — Who the heck are you? ? ?"

2225. Once there was a man who put on a big spurt to catch his train — but he missed it. A bystander who had seen his final brave and nearly successful effort said, "Well, if you had just run a little faster you would have made it."

"No," the man replied, "it wasn't a case of running faster, but of starting sooner." — C. J. KETLER, *Nalaco*

2226. I believe in punctuality, though it makes me very lonely. — EDWARD V. LUCAS

2227. Punctuality is the politeness of kings. — LOUIS XVIII

2228. *Husband to wife:* "Congratulations. This is the earliest you've ever been late."

2229. Punctuality: the art of arranging to keep an appointment just in time to be indignant at the tardiness of the other party.

2230. Napoleon once invited his marshals to dine with him and to discuss important matters. As they did not arrive at the moment appointed, he began to eat without them. They appeared just as he was rising from the table. "Gentlemen," said he, "dinner is now over, and we will immediately proceed to business."

2231. The customer had waited half an hour for the fish he had ordered. At last the waiter appeared.
"Your fish will be here in five minutes," he said.
Another quarter of an hour passed and then the customer summoned the waiter. "Say," he inquired, "what kind of bait are you using?"

quarrelsome

2232. An unfailing mark of the blockhead is a chip on the shoulder.

reading — See also *Books*

2233. If we encounter a man of rare intellect, we should ask him what books he has read. — RALPH WALDO EMERSON, *Letters and Social Aims*

2234. It is absurd to have a hard-and-fast rule about what one should read and what one shouldn't. More than half of modern culture depends on what one shouldn't read. — OSCAR WILDE

2235. Reading is to the mind what exercise is to the body. — STEELE, *The Tatler*

reform

2236. Reforms come from below. No man with four aces howls for a new deal.

regret

2237. Make it a rule of life never to regret and never to look back. Regret is an appalling waste of energy; you can't build on it; it's only good for wallowing in. — KATHERINE MANSFIELD,
Bliss and Other Stories (Knopf)

relative

2238. Attending a church bazaar, Abraham Lincoln tendered a $20 bill to pay for a bunch of violets. The lady at the booth, making no attempt to return any change, gushed, "Oh thank you, Mr. President."

Lincoln reached down from his great height, and gently touched the lady on the wrist, saying, "And what do you call this?"

"Why, Mr. President, that is my wrist. What did you think it was?"

"Well," drawled Lincoln, "I thought it might be your ankle. Everything is so high around here."

2239. Small town: any town smaller than the one you live in.

2240. The king and queen of Holland visited England some time ago. Throughout the trip the royal pair spoke English to their hosts, although during one of Juliana's many speeches a number of Britons had to be reassured that this was so. Speaking slowly and precisely at London's Guildhall of the friendly relations between Britain (the big neighbor) and Holland (the small), Juliana said: "Big is reflected in small as big; small is reflected in big as small, and in that lies their bond and mutual appreciation; as big is not big without small, and small is not small without big; and in their inter-connection they offer a profusion of possibility."

2241. The difference between a groove and a grave is only a matter of depth.

2242. We can all perceive the difference between ourselves and our inferiors, but when it comes to a question of the difference between us and our superiors we fail to appreciate merits of which we have no proper conceptions.

2243. Despite its high mountains and great ocean depths, the surface of the earth is relatively smooth. If the earth were reduced to a sphere a foot in diameter, it would be smoother than the average bowling ball.
— Readers Digest

2244. The one-eyed person is a beauty in the country of the blind.
— Arabian Proverb

religion

2245. A great Archbishop once asked the actor, Betterton, this question: "Can you tell me why actors can make people feel as if all that transpires on the stage is reality, while we in the church seem to give people the impression that what we are talking about is imaginary?" The actor said, "Why really, I don't know. Unless we actors speak of things imaginary as if they were real; while you in the pulpit speak of things real as if they were imaginary."
— JOHN D. BANKS, "The Gardener, I Presume?," Pulpit Digest

2246.   THE CREED OF A LIBERAL

We believe in man, in his slow, ascendant progress, in the autonomy of his spirit and in the primacy of his claims over the claims of all forms of human organization.

We believe in freedom — the fullest measure of freedom compatible with the fullest measure of responsibility.

We believe in authority — but only in authority sanctioned by reason and consent.

We believe that the only tools of social progress are education, experimentation and cooperation.

We believe that to be well-governed is not as important as to be self-governed. Hence, we reject all manner of millenniums proffered to us at the spearpoint of dictatorship.

We believe that all truth is made manifest through the contact and clash of diverse opinions and that the very motive power of progress in the free exchange of ideas and the exercised privilege of non-conformity.

We believe in tolerance but not in indifference, in enthusiasm but not in fanaticism, in convictions but not in obsessions, in independence but not in isolation, in conflict but not in hate.
— RABBI ABBA HILLEL SILVER

2247. Did you ever think of your prayers as being like radar? They are just that. We send our prayers into the unseen and the answers that come back give us the safest guidance to be found anywhere. — *The Exposition*

2248. Religion is a journey, not a destination.

2249. A fortune awaits the person who will design a church without any front pews.

2250. A great teacher once said: "The only way to save religion is to allow religion to save you."

2251. A soldier, in a camp hundreds of miles away from his wife, wrote her:
"I like to think that we are never really alone, because I can take God with me and leave Him there with you." — *Quote*

2252. "I see in your church convention," said the old farmer, "that you discuss the subject, how to get people to attend church. I have never heard a single address at a farmer's convention on how to get the cattle to come to the rack. We spend our time in discussing the best kind of feeds." — *Christian Advocate*

2253. If absence makes the heart grow fonder, then a lot of folks sure do love the church.

2254. There is a vast difference between saying prayers and — praying.

2255. I never told my own religion nor scutinized that of another. I never attempted to make a convert nor wished to change another's creed. I have judged of others' religion by their lives, for it is from our lives and not from our words that our religion must be read. By the same test must the world judge me.
— THOMAS JEFFERSON

2256. Too many persons regard religion as a trolley car on which they ride only as long as it is going their way.
— *Progressive Farmer*

2257. In spite of my fervor, devotion and piety the Saturday for the picnic was not nice. It was cold and miserable.

I took it up with my mother one day while she was ironing. "Why," I asked, "does the Lord not make a nice day when I pray for a nice day?"

"Oh," my mother said easily, "suppose some poor farmer prayed for rain on the same day? Do you not suppose he needs rain as much as you need sunshine?" — ROBERT FONTAINE, *The Happy Time* (Simon & Schuster)

2258. In the eighth century, B. C., in the heart of a world of idolatrous polytheists, the Hebrew prophets put forth a conception of religion which appears to me to be as wonderful an inspiration of genius as the art of Phidias or the science of Aristotle. "And what doth the Lord require of these but to do justly, and to love mercy, and to walk humbly with thy God?" If any so-called religion takes away from this great saying of Micah, I think it wantonly mutilates, while if it adds thereto I think it obscures the perfect ideal of religion.
— THOMAS HUXLEY

2259. Prayer is not only worship; it is also an invisible emanation of man's worshiping spirit — the most powerful form of energy that one can generate. The influence of prayer on the human mind and body is as demonstrable as that of secreting glands. Its results can be measured in terms of increased physical buoyancy, greater intellectual vigor, moral stamina, and a deeper understanding of the realities underlying human relationships.

If you make a habit of sincere prayer, your life will be very noticeably and profoundly altered. Prayer stamps with its indelible mark our actions and demeanor. A tranquillity of bearing, a facial and bodily repose, are observed in those whose inner lives are thus enriched. Within the depths of consciousness a flame kindles. And man sees himself. He discovers his selfishness, his silly pride, his fears, his greeds, his moral obligation, intellectual humility. Thus begins a journey of the soul towards the realm of grace.
— DR. ALEXIS CARREL

2260. If a man has peace with the universe, peace with his own soul and peace with his fellowmen, that man has religion.
— J. WILLIAM LLOYD

2261. There are many religions, but there is only one morality.
— RUSKIN, *Lectures in Art*

329

religion

2262. When any church will inscribe over its altar, as its sole qualification for membership, the Savior's condensed statement of the substance of both law and Gospel, "Thou shalt love the Lord thy God with all thy heart, and with all thy soul and thy neighbor as thyself," that church will I join with all my heart and all my soul.
— ABRAHAM LINCOLN

2263. Science has not found a substitute for God.
— HENRY DRUMMOND, *The New Evangelism*

2264. A man has no right to call himself a Christian unless the virtues of Christianity are in his life. I do not ask for degree, but I do ask that they be there. If you have a plant in a pot for ten years that has never put out a leaf or shown the least symptoms of life, what reason have you to believe it is alive at all? It looks uncommonly like a bit of dead stick. — ALEXANDER MACLAREN

2265. Judaism is the religion of the partial answer. Those who approach life demanding an absolute answer will always be disillusioned infants. No teacher of Israel ever guaranteed to explain the ways of God completely to man, but every teacher of Judaism has maintained that life rooted in a denial of God is more mysterious, more completely inexplicable. — RABBI JOSHUA LOTH LIEBMAN

2266. It is only the fear of God that can deliver us from the fear of man. — WITHERSPOON

2267. Most people have some sort of religion, at least they know which church they're staying away from. — JOHN ERSKINE

2268. I learned a good lesson in religion from an agnostic. It was Elbert Hubbard who preached: Remember the week day to keep it holy. — WILLIAM K. HOLLANDER

2269. Let us have faith that right makes might, and in that faith let us dare to do our duty as we understand it.
— ABRAHAM LINCOLN

2270. Atheist: a man who has no invisible means of support.
— JOHN BUCHAN

2271. If men are so wicked with religion, what would they be without it? — BENJAMIN FRANKLIN

2272. Great men are they who see that the spiritual is stronger than any material force; that thoughts rule the world.
— RALPH WALDO EMERSON

2273. WHO DOES GOD'S WORK WILL GET GOD'S PAY

Who does God's work will get God's pay
However long may seem the day,
However weary be the way.

Though powers may thunder "Nay!"
No human hand God's hand may stay,
Who does God's work will get His pay.

God hurries not, nor makes delay,
Who works for Him will get His pay,
Some certain hour, some certain day.

He does not pay as others pay
In gold or land or raiment gay,
In goods that perish and decay.

But God's high wisdom knows a way,
And this is sure, let come what may,
Who does God's work will get God's pay.
— *Author Unknown*

2274. A man, when asked to explain what God is, replied: "I know if I'm not asked."

2275. Men will wrangle for religion; write for it; fight for it; die for it; anything but live for it.   — CHARLES C. COLTON

repetition

2276. If fifty million people say a foolish thing, it is still a foolish thing.
— ANATOLE FRANCE

reputation

2277. "Good name in man and woman, dear my lord,
Is the immediate jewel of their souls:
Who steals my purse steals trash; 'tis something, nothing;
'T was mine, 't is his, and has been slave to thousands;

But he that filches from me my good name
Robs me of that which not enriches him
And makes me poor indeed."
— OTHELLO, Act iii, Sc. 3

2278. Associate with men of good quality, if you esteem your own reputation; for it is better to be alone than in bad company.
— GEORGE WASHINGTON, *Social Maxims*

2279. How many people live on the reputation of the reputation they might have made! — OLIVER WENDELL HOLMES, *The Autocrat of the Breakfast Table*

2280. To enjoy a good reputation, give publicly, and steal privately.
— JOSH BILLINGS

2281. You probably wouldn't worry about what people think of you if you could know how seldom they do! — OLIN MILLER

2282. The way to gain a good reputation is to endeavor to be what you desire to appear. — SOCRATES

resourcefulness — See *Ingenuity*

respect

2283. The way to procure insults is to submit to them. A man meets with no more respect than he exacts.
— HAZLITT, *Characteristics*

responsibility

2284. Responsibility develops some men and ruins others.

2285. Colleague: someone who is called in at the last moment to share the blame.

2286. Some men grow under responsibility, others only swell.
— *Readers Digest*

retreat

2287. It makes no difference if I burn my bridges behind me, since I never retreat. — FIORELLO H. LA GUARDIA

retribution

2288. He who pelts every barking dog must pick up many stones.

revenge

2289. In revenge, haste is criminal.
— SIR FRANCIS BACON, *Moral and Historical Works*

righteousness

2290. There are two classes of people, the righteous and the unrighteous. The classifying is done by the righteous.
— *The Sign*

rumor

2291.   RUMOR
Actual evidence I have none,
But my aunt's charwoman's sister's son
Heard a policeman on his beat
Say to a housemaid in Downing Street
That he had a brother, who had a friend,
Who knew when the war was going to end.
— REGINALD ARKELL

salesmanship

2292. "Don't you know," said the commissioner, "that you can't sell life insurance without a state license?"

"Boss, you sure said a mouthful. I knew I couldn't sell it, but I didn't know the reason."

2293. One traveling man to another in Thompson's restaurant: "What's the matter, Bill? You are only eating crackers and milk. Are you on a diet?"

"No, on commission."

2294.   You don't buy coal, you buy heat;
          you don't buy circus tickets, you buy thrills;
          you don't buy a paper, you buy news;
          you don't buy spectacles, you buy vision.
          you don't buy printing, you buy selling.

2295. *Boss:* "Shame on you. Do you know what we do with office boys who tell lies?"

Boy: "Yes, sir. When they get old enough, the firm sends them out as salesmen."

2296. The successful salesman sells his goods on their merit — not on knocking his competitor.

2297. The salesman, seeking employment, called on a "cloak-and suiter." "Tell you what," the boss told him. "I've got one suit in the house I can't sell. It's purple, green and yellow. If you can make that sale, you've not only got a job — you become a life-time employee." The boss then went out to lunch.

On his return, he noticed his new salesman's clothes had been ripped to tatters and his face and hands were scratched. But a beautific smile adorned his face. "What's with you?" asked the boss. . . . "Well, I sold it! — I sold the suit!" exclaimed the salesman through bleeding lips. "Congratulations, but did you have to get into a fight to make the sale?" — "Oh, no," was the reply, "the customer was perfectly delighted — but his Seeing Eye dog fought like the devil!"

2298. It takes less effort to keep an old customer satisfied than to get a new customer interested.

2299. An impressive young man who, incidentally, is sure to be blacklisted by the door-to-door salesman's guild, called on a prospective customer.

"Here is just what you've been looking for. It's only fifty cents and it stops petty annoyance, prevents drafts, and saves time," he said, displaying a neatly printed sign: No Salesmen Allowed.

334

"I'll take it," said the customer, both pleased and amused.

"I'm sure you'll find it effective," he said, "but before you put it up let me show you —" and with a disarming grin he opened a sample case full of the usual assortment of kitchen gadgets.

— ROY G. LOUGHARY, *Readers Digest*

2300. *Brown (who recently got a job as a commercial traveler):* Since I started this traveling business I'm my own boss.

Friend: How's that?

Brown: Well, I'm not taking orders from anybody.

2301. Some salesmen electrify their prospects; others merely gas them.

2302. A youthful graduate of a New England university applied for a job as a bond salesman at a financial house which specialized in South American securities.

"I'm the best bond salesman in the country, for I have hundreds of rich friends," he boasted.

As his references were of the best and he had an engaging personality he soon was hired, and sent out to peddle an issue of municipal bonds of some jazzy city near the equator in the territory assigned to him. The first week ended without any orders being sent in. So did the second — and the third. At the end of the fourth week, as not a single bond had been sold, the head of the banking house sent for him.

"You told me you were the best bond salesman in the world," said the banker, when he had him on the carpet. "Why, you haven't sold a thousand dollar bond."

"I know — and I made a mistake when I told you I was the best bond salesman in the world," replied the youth. "I'm the second best salesman though."

"How do you get that way?" demanded the banker.

"The fiscal agent who sold you those bonds is the best salesman in the world."

2303. An automobile dealer recently set up in his sales room a number of nude manikins — one representing each salesman. As each salesman sold a car, an article of apparel was put on his manikin; the contest concluded with a banquet at which each guest wore the amount of clothing he won during the contest. The tactful

335

dealer, to avoid embarrassment, announced that he would attend the dinner dressed in the same manner as the man who won the fewest number of points. — HAROLD W. DONAHUE

2304. Good salesmanship consists in selling goods that won't come back to customers who will.

2305. One real-estate operator rents his apartment houses by having two identical apartments vary as much as ten percent in price. One sort of customer always notices the difference, compares the two apartments, and rushes to rent the cheaper one before anyone else notices the apparent mistake. On the other side, with equal frequency, bobs up the customer ready to pay the ten dollar difference in order to have the highest-priced suite on the floor.

— From *Showmanship in Business*
by GOODE & KAUFMAN (Harper)

2306. *Joe:* "I traveled as a salesman the entire summer, and only received two orders."
Sympathetic one: "Too bad; who gave you those?"
Joe: "Every one — Get out, and stay out!"

2307. People will buy anything that's one to a customer.

— SINCLAIR LEWIS

2308. Sales managers might well subject their men to the "match test." Give each individual a pad of safety matches; ask him to light one and hold it between thumb and forefinger. Then ask the salesman to state the essential virtues of his product before the match burns down to the point where he must drop it. This provides a period of sixty to ninety seconds. It forces quick concentration on essentials; indicates which men follow the main line, which are likely to be sidetracked. — DR. GEORGE W. CRANE,
Psychology Applied (Hopkins, 1952)

2309. Sales resistance: the triumph of mind over patter.

2310. A super salesman is one who can sell a double-breasted suit to a man with a Phi Beta Kappa key.

sarcasm

2311. Several years ago Firestone, Ford, Edison and Burroughs were touring through West Virginia. A light on their car went bad, and they stopped at a little crossroads store in the Buckhannon section. Mr. Ford went into the store to make the purchase.

"What kind of automobile lights do you have?" said Ford.

"Edison," replied the merchant.

"I'll take one," said Ford, "and by the way, you may be interested to know that Mr. Edison is out in my car."

"So?" said the merchant.

When the light was put in, it was found that a new tire was needed, so Ford went back into the store and asked what kind of tires the merchant had.

"Firestone," was the reply.

"By the way, you may be interested to know that Mr. Firestone is out there in my car, and that I am Mr. Ford — Henry Ford."

"So?" said the merchant and let drive a long squirt of tobacco juice against the wall.

While the merchant was putting on the tire, Burroughs, who had white whiskers, leaned out of the car and said, "Good evening, sir."

The merchant looked up at him with a grin full of sarcasm and said:

"If you try to tell me that you are Santa Claus, I'll be damned if I don't crown you with this wrench."

2312. At the death of Edward MacDowell, the composer, a certain lady whose ambition exceeded her talent undertook to write an elegy in his honor, and played it before Josef Hofmann, the pianist. Hofmann listened politely, but his soul twisted in torment. When she had finished:

"It's quite nice," the pianist murmured defensively, "but don't you think it would have been better if . . . if . . ."

"If what?" asked the composer.

"If you had died and MacDowell had written the elegy."

2313. Once when Clarence Darrow was a fledgling lawyer beginning his career, he was opposed in court by a veteran attorney who, during the course of the trial repeatedly and insultingly referred to Darrow as "that beardless youth."

At length Darrow rejoined: "My opponent seems to condemn me for not having a beard. Let me reply with a story. The King of Spain once dispatched a youthful nobleman to a court of a neighboring king, who received the visitor with the outraged complaint: 'Does the King of Spain lack men, that he sends me a beardless boy?' To which the ambassador rejoined, 'Sir, if my King had supposed you imputed wisdom to a beard he would have sent you a goat.' " Darrow won the case.

2314. *Joe E. Lewis ribbing Lou Breese:* "I have heard," confided Joe, "that when Lou went on the radio recently he was responsible for the sale of a quarter-million radios. I sold mine, my brother-in-law sold his . . ."

satisfaction

2315. He's the kind of a fellow — well, his father wanted a girl, his mother wanted a boy — and they were both satisfied.

2316. I will study how to give account of my little, rather than how to make it more. — Bishop A. C. A. Hall

2317. "It doesn't do any good to scold the janitor about our cold rooms."
"Yes, it does. I get all warmed up when I talk to him."

2318. "And if I take the job I'm to get a raise in salary every year?"
"Yes, provided, of course, that your work is satisfactory."
"Ah! I thought there was a catch somewhere."

2319. If you don't get everything you want, think of the things you don't get that you don't want.

2320.
I thought I was abused
Because I had no shoes
Until I met a man
Who had no feet.
— *Old Arabian Proverb*

science

2321. In all science error precedes the truth, and it is better it should go first than last. — HORACE WALPOLE

2322. Perfume: chemical warfare.

2323. Professor Vaillant of Paris lost both his arms through undue exposure to X-rays in years of experimentation. This case is merely one of many that show how the men of the laboratories may be as truly heroes and martyrs to the cause of science as were pioneer experimenters with airplanes or explorers of remote wildernesses.

2324. Science is wonderful. It has taught man everything — that is, nearly everything — except to keep his shirt from bulging; to shave without cutting himself and to refrain from arguing with a woman.

secret

2325. Secret: something that is hushed about from place to place.

2326. Millinery secret: one that should be kept under your hat.

2327. Trade secrets: what women do.

2328. It's a great kindness to trust people with a secret. They feel so important while telling it. — ROBERT QUILLEN

self

2329. It is as impossible for a man to be cheated by anyone but himself, as for a thing to be and not to be at the same time.
— RALPH WALDO EMERSON

2330. The only gift is a portion of thyself . . . Therefore the poet brings his poem; the shepherd, his lamb; the farmer, corn; the miner, a gem; the sailor, coral and shells; the painter, his picture; the girl, a handkerchief of her own sewing.
— RALPH WALDO EMERSON, *Essays*

self-acclaim

2331. A loud and objectionable bore had been talking for hours about himself and his achievements.

"I'm a self-made man, that's what I am — a self-made man," he said.

"You knocked off work too soon," came a quiet voice from the corner.

2332. Orville Wright, at a dinner in Dayton, was reproached for not taking up the challenge of the Smithsonian Institution that it was Langley, not the Wrights, who was the first to fly. "The trouble with you, Orville," said a banker, "is that you are too taciturn. You don't assert yourself enough. You should pressagentize more."

"My dear friend," Orville Wright answered, "the best talker and the worst flyer among the birds is the parrot."

self-appraisal

2333. Some times we class those who are one-and-a-half witted with the half-witted because we appreciate only one-third of their wit.

2334. Before a man can wake up and find himself famous he has to wake up and find himself.

2335. Before you flare up at anyone's faults, take time to count ten — ten of your own.

2336. If someone betrays you once, it's his fault. If he betrays you twice, it's your fault. — RUMANIAN PROVERB, *Ladies' Home Journal*

2337. It is needless to find fault with yourself — plenty of people will do it for you.

self-blame

2338. A little girl did not dust the furniture to suit grandmother; and grandmother made her do it again — once, twice, three times and still grandmother was not satisfied. Finally, the child looked up and said, "Grandmother, that dust is not on the furniture; it is on your glasses."

— G. S. NICHOLS, *They Shall See God* (Pastor)

2339. *Neighbor:* "Did I bring your snow shovel back last winter?"
Indignant householder: "No, you did not."
Neighbor: "Now, what'll I do? I wanted to borrow it again."

2340. *Has it occurred to you . . .*
That other people may find it difficult to get on with you?
That you were young yourself once?
That others have a right to their own opinions?
That what you do and say helps to shape other lives?
That home is where you ought to be at your best, not your worst?
That you can begin again?
That you might have tried harder?

self-destruction

2341. Senator Henry Cabot Lodge, commenting on the ineffectiveness of some Congressional investigating committees, remarked that they reminded him of a certain Si Hoskins. "Every day," he said, "Si sat near a dam with a gun on his knee. Seeing him one day, I asked, 'What are you doing, Si?'

" 'I'm paid to shoot the muskrats, sir. They're undermining the dam.'

" 'There goes one now!' I yelled. 'Why don't you shoot?'

"Si puffed a tranquil cloud from his pipe and said, 'Do you think I want to lose my job?' "

— *Readers Digest*

self-esteem

2342. The minute you get the idea you're indispensable, you aren't.

2343. The pompous young minister, who had been appointed to help the pastor of a large New York church, was annoyed that he was to be called "assistant minister." He felt that "associate minister" was a title more befitting his ability. He aired his grievance

to an older colleague, who listened attentively, then said, "My dear boy, what does it matter either way? They'll both be abbreviated into Ass."
— THOMAS H. WARNER, *Church Management*

2344. Too many fellows think they can push themselves forward by patting themselves on the back.

2345. The graveyards are full of people the world could not do without.
— ELBERT HUBBARD

2346. The six-year-old son of a well-known insurance man has inherited his father's self-confidence and gift of gab. One evening the father came home to find sonny with a ball and bat. "Hi, Dad!" shouted sonny. "Watch me! I'm hitting 'em a mile!"

The boy tossed the ball up, took a swing and missed. "Strike one!" he shouted gleefully. "But watch this one, Dad. Boy, oh, boy, am I going to knock the cover off this one!"

Again he tossed the ball in the air, took a poke at it, missed. "Strrrike two!" he intoned. "Whata you know! Well, it only takes one to hit it. Am I going to clout this one!"

Carefully he took his stance, carefully he tossed his ball, mightily he swung his bat — and missed.

"Strrrrike three!" he announced. "And out." Then, exultantly, "Gee, Dad, am I a pitcher!"
— CLAIRE MACMURRAY, *Cleveland Plain Dealer*

2347. There is no greater self-protection from all that is low, ordinary, and inferior than the cultivation of a lofty estimate of one-self and one's possibilities. All the forces within you will then work together to help you realize your ideals, for the life always follows the aim; we always take the direction of the life purpose.
— O. S. MARDEN

2348. They're telling of a young Hollywood actor who leaped into fame during the past year. He came home a few nights ago to find his wife weeping bitterly. She said the eternal triangle was going to break up their home.

"Nonsense, my dear!" exclaimed the new star. "I'm world famous today, and yet I've never so much as looked at another woman. How can you say there's a triangle?"

"But there is a triangle, sobbed the wife. "And a vicious triangle, too. Both you and I are in love with you!"
— *Pictorial Review*

selfishness

2349. Selfishness is not living as one wishes to live; it is asking others to live as one wishes to live. And unselfishness is letting other people's lives alone, not interfering with them. Selfishness always aims at creating around it an absolute uniformity of type. Unselfishness recognizes infinite variety of type as a delightful thing, accepts it, acquiesces in it, enjoys it. — OSCAR WILDE

2350. The same people who can deny others everything are famous for refusing themselves nothing.
— LEIGH HUNT, *Table Talk*

2351. Too many of us conduct our lives on the cafeteria plan — self-service only.

2352. No man can live happily who regards himself alone, who turns everything to his own advantage. Thou must live for another if thou wishest to live for thyself. — SENECA

selflessness

2353. Abundance consists not only alone in material possession, but in an uncovetous spirit. — SELDON

2354.

Our dreams paint many pleasures,
    Sometimes the dreams come true;
Our hearts try many treasures —
    Sometimes retain a few
But the fairest flowers of living
    Bloom for us when we find
The garden that is giving
    For love of humankind.

Then wealth is dedication;
    Wisdom, the light to lead;
Then power is obligation —
    To serve is to succeed;
Then health becomes a holding
    In trust, to spend at will,

A fund for the enfolding
And succor of the ill.

Today, in tones faint-sounding,
From matin to evensong,
"Give of your life abounding!"
The weak call to the strong;
And they who heed the crying
Shall but increase their store —
They draw on a source undying
Forever and evermore.

— *Anonymous*

2355. LESS OF ME

Let me be a little kinder,
Let me be a little blinder,
To the faults of those about me,
Let me praise a little more;
Let me be when I am weary
Just a little bit more cheery —
Let me serve a little better
Those that I am striving for.

Let me be a little braver
When temptation bids me waver,
Let me strive a little harder
To be all that I should be;
Let me be a little meeker
With the brother who is weaker
Let me think more of my neighbor,
And a little less of me.

self-mastery

2356. A gray-haired old woman was waiting for an 8th Avenue bus. She was very large and crippled with rheumatism. Her arms were loaded with packages.

As the bus door opened, a man waiting behind her offered a helping hand. The old woman smiled and shook her head. "I'd best manage alone," she said. "If I get help today — I'll want it tomorrow."

2357. No man is such a conqueror as the man who has defeated himself.

— HENRY WARD BEECHER

2358. I count him braver who overcomes his desires than him who conquers his enemies; for the hardest victory is the victory over self.
— ARISTOTLE

self-praise

2359. Hollywood actor Jack Carson has his own definition of a fan club:

A group of people who tell an actor he's not alone in the way he feels about himself.
— JAMES HARRIS

self-restraint

2360. Self-restraint: feeling your oats without sowing them.

self-training

2361. The safest principle through life, instead of reforming others, is to set about perfecting yourself.
— B. R. HAYDON, *Table Talk*

2362. PROMISE YOURSELF

To be so strong that nothing can disturb your
    peace of mind.
To talk health, happiness and prosperity to
    every person you meet.
To make all your friends feel that there is
    something in them.
To look at the sunny side of everything and
    make your optimism come true.
To think only of the best, to work only for
    the best and to expect only the best.
To be just as enthusiastic about the success
    of others as you are about your own.
To forget the mistakes of the past and press
    on to the greater achievements of the future.
To wear a cheerful countenance at all times and
    give every living creature you meet a smile.

345

> To give so much time to the improvement of your-
>   self that you have no time to criticize others.
> To be too large for worry, too noble for anger,
>   too strong for fear, and too happy to permit
>   the presence of trouble.
> — CHRISTIAN D. LARSON

service

2363. Cast thy bread upon the waters; for thou shalt find it after many days.   — *Old Testament, Ecclesiastes xi 1*

2364. In the kingdom of God the reward of a great service is the opportunity to render a still greater service.
> — Reprinted by permission of Dodd,
> Mead & Company from *Problems
> of Life* by LYMAN ABBOTT

signs

2365. "There sure is one sign I'd like to see on every mail box."
"What one?"
"Post no bills."

silence

2366. A smoothly running engine makes little noise, and yet produces great power.

2367. Many a man won't shut his trap until he has his foot in it.
> — HOWARD W. NEWTON, *Redbook*

2368. Never, never do great thoughts come to a man while he is discontented or fretful. There must be quiet in the temple of his soul before the windows of it will open for him to see out of them into the infinite. Quiet is what heavenly powers move in. It is in silence that the stars move on, and it is in quiet that our souls are visited from on high.   — MOUNTFORD

2369. When you are in company, talk often, but not long; in that case if you do not please, at least you are sure not to tire your hearers.
> — LORD CHESTERFIELD

2370. Silence is one of the hardest arguments to refute.

2371. The best way of answering a bad argument is to let it go on.
— SIDNEY SMITH

2372. Silence never makes any blunders. — H. W. SHAW

2373. The unspoken word is your slave; the spoken word is your master.

2374. Few men have ever repented of silence.
— PATRICK HENRY

2375. It is better for a man to keep his mouth shut and be thought a fool than to open it and remove all doubt.

2376. Silence never shows itself to so great an advantage as when it is made the reply to calumny and defamation, provided that we give no just occasion for them. — JOSEPH ADDISON, *The Tatler*

2377. Blessed is the man who, having nothing to say, abstains from giving us wordy evidence of the fact.
— GEORGE ELIOT, *Theophrastus Such*

2378. If you don't say anything, you won't be called on to repeat it. — CALVIN COOLIDGE

2379. I have never been hurt by anything I didn't say.
— CALVIN COOLIDGE

2380. Abuse is often of service. There is nothing so dangerous to an author as silence. His name, like a shuttlecock, must be beat backward and forward, or it falls to the ground.
— SAMUEL JOHNSON

2381. Most of us know how to say nothing. Few of us know when.

simplicity

2382. Nothing is more simple than greatness; indeed, to be simple is to be great. — RALPH WALDO EMERSON

sincerity

2383. A man in earnest finds means, or, if he cannot find, creates them.
— WILLIAM ELLERY CHANNING
Address, Boston, Mass.
September 1838

2384. Many a man would reach a greater height if he had more depth.

2385. You will never get me to support a measure which I believe to be wrong, although by doing so I may accomplish that which I believe to be right. — ABRAHAM LINCOLN

2386. We are not sent into this world to do anything into which we cannot put our hearts. — JOHN RUSKIN

2387. Sincerity is impossible unless it pervade the whole being; and the pretence of it saps the very foundation of character.
— JAMES RUSSELL LOWELL, *My Study Windows*

2388. A pure heart and a pure mind are all that God requires of man, let his piety choose what form it will, so long as it is genuine.
— CARL H. CORNILL

slander

2389. Mud thrown is ground lost.

smiles

2390. The man who borrows troubles will never lend smiles.

2391. A smile is not only woman's best cosmetic but it likewise serves as a non-verbal compliment to her companion.
— DR. GEORGE W. CRANE,
Psychology Applied

2392. Smile and conserve your energy — it requires the use of about thirty-six muscles to smile and of ninety-seven to frown. So frown and work overtime, or smile and shorten the working day.

348

smoking

2393. Having read so much about the bad effects of smoking he decided to give up reading.

social reform

2394. There once lived in England a devotee of beauty. Regarding beauty as the visible revelation of God, he devoted himself with the apostle's fervor to the task of arousing the British public to a love of beautiful things. But in the midst of his career he turned aside to become a Social reformer. We find him trying to reclaim slums, organizing a gang of street sweepers. To many this seemed an unaccountable shift. To Ruskin's mind the two were intimately associated. He had learned that a people cannot lift their souls to the clouds while their feet are stuck in the mire of hunger and overwork.

society

2395. Society is a partnership in all science; a partnership in all art; a partnership in every virtue and in all perfection. As the ends of such a partnership cannot be obtained in many generations, it becomes a partnership not only between those who are living, but between those who are living, those who are dead and those who are to be born. — EDMUND BURKE

solitude

2396. A somewhat weary-looking gentleman boarded the train, settled himself, and got out a largish sign which he carefully hung on his coat. "Listen," it read, "I think Hitler is crazy, Washington's full of Reds, business is going to pick up in the spring, we ought to get out of the Philippines, and I don't believe in the third term. Wake me up at Spokane."

2397. Many people live alone and like it, but most of them live alone and look it. — GELETT BURGESS

2398. No company is preferable to bad company because we are more apt to catch the vices of others than their virtues, as disease is far more contagious than health. — C. C. COLTON

2399. Solitude is often the best society.

source

2400. Cleanse the fountain if you would purify the streams. — A. BRONSON ALCOTT

specialization

2401. "Yes, you may put me down for a member. I already belong to a dozen organizations and I might as well join one more," said a man to a friend.

His small son, overhearing the remark, asked innocently, "Do all these things you belong to, father, know that you belong?"

The child's questions set the man thinking. He saw clearly that he was frittering away his energy trying to be in everything and counting for nothing in anything.

He dropped out of most of the organizations, put his whole heart into the few he considered the most worthwhile, and soon became a force and an outstanding figure. There was no longer any question as to whether or not he belonged.

speech

2402. When the great Rabbi Gamaliel, one of the wisest, told his servants: "Bring me something good," the servants brought a tongue. The Rabbi said: "Go to the market, bring me something bad." Again the servants brought a tongue, saying: "A tongue, my master, may be the source of either good or evil. If it is good, there is nothing better. If it is bad, there is nothing worse." — *The Talmud*

2403. Originally freedom to speak was deemed a gift from heaven. A century later Judge Holmes and Judge Brandeis gave the concept a new connotation. No longer was it the right to speak — rather it was the right to hear. For only by the free flow of ideas does society become enriched. — MORRIS L. ERNST,
The Best Is Yet

2404. Mason-Dixon line: a geographical division between "you all" and "youse guys".

2405. Frankage: the only known method of sending hot air through the mails.

2406. A good line is the shortest distance between dates.

2407. Talk is cheap because the supply always exceeds the demand.

2408. Table talk, to be perfect, should be sincere without bigotry, differing without discord, sometimes grave, always agreeable, touching on deep points, dwelling most on seasonable ones, and letting everybody speak and be heard. — LEIGH HUNT, *Table Talk*

2409. Gum chewer's mouth: that which goes without saying.

2410. When you have spoken the word, it reigns over you. When it is unspoken, you reign over it. — *Arabic Proverb*

2411. All noise is waste. So cultivate quietness in your speech, in your thoughts, in your emotions. Speak habitually low. Wait for attention and then your low words will be charged with dynamite.
— ELBERT HUBBARD

speech-making — See *Public Speaking*

spelling

2412. Two ladies stopped at a livery stable and asked for a gentle horse to drive.

The liveryman brought out one saying: "This horse is perfectly gentle so long as you don't let the rein get under his tail."

Within a few hours they returned.

"How did you get along?" asked the liveryman.

"Oh, we got along just fine. Had a couple of showers while we were out, but we took turns holding the umbrella over the horse's tail."

sportsmanship

2413. PLAYING THE GAME

So you played the game
And you lost, my lad?
And you're battered and bleeding too
And you hopes are dead
And your heart is lead
And your whole world's sad and blue.
And you sob and cry
In your grief and your pain
For the hopes that had to die
But the game is through
And it's up to you
To laugh, though you want to cry.

For someone there must be to lose, my lad
It's sad but it's always true
And day by day in the games you play
It's sure sometimes to be you.
So grit your teeth to the pain, my lad
For you battled the best you could
And there's never shame, in the losing game
When you lose like a real man should.

For after all, life is a game, my lad
And we play it as best as may
We win or lose as the Gods my choose
Who govern the games we play.
But whether we win or lose, my lad
At the end when the battle's through
We must wait with a smile
For the after while
And the chances that will come anew.

— *Author Unknown*

2414. And when that One Great Scorer comes
to mark against your name,
He writes not that you won or lost —
But how you played the game.

— GRANTLAND RICE

352

2415. A MAN'S PRAYER

Let me live, Oh Mighty Master,
  Such a life as men shall know,
Tasting triumph and disaster,
  Joy — and not too much of woe:
Let me run the gamut over,
  Let me fight and love and laugh,
And when I'm beneath the clover
  Let this be my epitaph:

Here lies one who took his chances
  In the busy world of men;
Battled luck and circumstances
  Fought and fell and fought again;
Won sometimes, but did no crowing,
  Lost sometimes, but didn't wail,
Took his beating, but kept going,
  Never let his courage fail.

He was fallible and human,
  Therefore loved and understood
Both his fellow men and women,
  Whether good or not so good;
Kept his spirit undiminished,
  Never lay down on a friend,
Played the game until it was finished,
  Lived a sportsman to the end.
                              — *Author Unknown*

2416.
            He lost the game;
              No matter for that —
            He kept his temper,
              He swung his hat
            And cheered the winners —
              A better way,
            Than to lose his temper
              And win the day.
                              — *Anonymous*

stability

2417. Horse sense is stable thinking coupled with the ability to say nay (neigh).

2418. Trees often transplanted seldom prosper.
— *Arabian Proverb*

statistics

2419. Facts are stubborn, but statistics are more pliable.

2420. A statistician is a man who draws a mathematically precise line from an unwarranted assumption to a foregone conclusion.

2421. There are three kinds of lies: lies, damned lies and statistics.
— BENJAMIN DISRAELI

2422. "We always take statistics with a grain of salt in our family," says Miss Frances Perkins, former Secretary of Labor. "My great-grandfather, who lived to be 104, was an eccentric old fellow, and at the age of 99 had a great argument with the town bootmaker as to how a pair of shoes was to be made.

" 'Look here, Mr. Perkins,' said the shoemaker, finally becoming impatient, 'why do you make such a fuss about a pair of shoes? You are 99. Do you think you'll ever live to wear them out?"

"My great-grandfather looked at him severely. 'My man,' he said, 'don't you know that very few people ever die after the age of 99? Statistics prove it!' "

2423. He uses statistics as a drunken man uses lamp-posts — for support rather than for illumination. — ANDREW LANG

status quo

2424. Let sleeping dogs lie. — WALPOLE

2425. A rather elderly man with a long beard was asked by his little grandchild what he did with the beard when he went to sleep at night. He answered that he didn't know because he had not paid any attention to it. Then when he went to sleep that night, he tried to find the answer. First he put the beard over the sheet but was uncomfortable; then he put it under the sheet and was still uncomfortable. He kept that process up all night without comfort and finally in sheer desperation exclaimed: "Here, I've had this beard for sixty years and it never gave me any trouble or concern and now by one little question, the whole situation has been disturbed."

stenographer

2426. Typewriter: a machine used by stenographers and which can't spell either.

2427.

THE TYPISTE'S HOLIDAY
My tYpust is io hor vacution,
    My trpist's away fo r a week,
My trpudt us in hwr vacarion,
    Wgile thse damu kews ploy hudge and seek.
            Chorus:
Oy, breng boxk, bting bzek,
    Brung beej mu blnnie ti my, tp mr;
B)&ng blxj, b6icx,
    Pping bozk m% beinino-o-mx CH¼ helk?

2428. One secretary to another:
"If I can't spell the words in the first place how does he expect me to find them in the dictionary?"

2429. During a hold-up in Chicago a young male stenographer was hit by a bullet. Thinking he was mortally wounded, he whispered to a friend:
"Write to Mamie. Give her my love, and tell her my last thoughts were of her. Carbon copies to Sadie, Peggy and Kathleen."

2430. He was so ungrammatical – in dictating to his secretary he ended his sentence with a proposition.

2431. Sure Sign: "How do you know that Chaucer dictated to a stenographer?"
"Just look at the spelling."

strife

2432.

GOOD TIMBER
The tree that never had to fight
For sun and air and light
That stood out in the open plain,
And always got it's share of rain,

Never became a forest king
But lived and died a scrubby thing.

The man who never had to toil,
Who never had to win his share,
Of sun and sky and light and air,
Never became a manly man
But lived and died as he began.

Good timber does not grow in ease;
The stronger wind, the tougher trees.
The farther sky, the greater length;
The more the storm, the more the strength;
By sun and cold, by rain and snows,
In tree or man good timber grows.

Where thickest stands the forest growth
We find the patriarchs of both,
And they hold converse with the stars
Whose broken branches show the scars
Of many winds and much of strife —
This is the common law of life.

— *Author Unknown*

stupidity

2433. Pat and Mike were working on the line. A train appeared unexpectedly round a curve.

Mike jumped from the track, but Pat dropped his shovel and took to his heels in front of the train.

The engineer whistled, but Pat kept running and finally rolled off the rails just as the train was about to run him down.

"Why didn't ye git off the track ye fool?" demanded Mike.

"Well, ye see," panted Pat, "it was better runnin' on the track."

2434. A girl entered the manager's office to apply for a job, and when asked if she had any particular talents, stated that she had won several prizes in crossword puzzles and slogan contests.

"That sounds good," the manager told her, "but we want somebody who will be smart during office hours."

"Ah," she explained brightly, "this was during office hours."

style — See *Dress*

subtlety

2435. Senator Vandenburg once presented a Senate secretary with his picture inscribed:

"With all the affection that the law allows."

2436. After being badly outplayed during the first half of a football game, members of the team of Texas A. and M. College sat dejectedly around the locker rooms waiting for a tongue-lashing from their coach, Dana X. Bible. He entered on the signal for the second half, looked slowly around at each player, and turned to the door. Then he paused, looked back and said, "Well, girls, shall we go?" They won the game. — STANLEY GUNN, *Readers Digest*

2437. James was considered rather a Don Juan and was quite accustomed to being questioned about affairs of the heart.

John was in trouble. He had fallen in love, but with his clumsy tongue he feared to risk a compliment to the lady of his choice.

"Ah," said James, "you want to be subtle. It won't be any good to say, 'What pretty legs you have'. She'll only be offended."

"Ah, I couldn't think of saying that!" said John.

"No," replied the sage, "but you might say, 'Your new hat is simply lovely, but no one will ever notice it until you lengthen your skirts' !"

2438. President Coolidge when told that Senator Borah went out horse-back riding every day remarked that it was difficult for him to believe that because he couldn't picture Borah going in the same direction as his horse.

2439. The sweetly cynical managing editor of the Boston Advertiser once gave me a valuable lesson in reporting. Some too-sweeping condemnation in my copy attracted his notice. "That won't do," he said. "You may believe, and it may be true, that every member of the Umteenth Ward Young Men's Political Reform Association is an incurable ass, but don't write it. Say: 'Every member, with one solitary exception is an incurable ass.' Then no member of the Association will feel personally offended."

— EDWARD P. MITCHELL, *Memoirs of an Editor*

2440. Hitler's father and mother were so proud of him when he was a child that they decided to get married.

2441. *Annoyed girl to date:* "Let's go someplace where we can each be alone."

2442. A Dutchman was dining in the restaurant car of a German train, and when the waiter approached with the usual "Heil Hitler!" he made no reply. The waiter was annoyed. "Every time I say, 'Heil Hitler!' to you," he snapped, "you must say 'Heil Hitler' to me."

"Hitler? He doesn't mean a thing in Holland," remarked the Dutchman.

"Maybe not now," said the waiter, "but one day you'll get our Fuhrer in Holland, too."

"Perhaps so," smiled the Dutchman. "We already have your Kaiser."

2443. An Irishman, inviting a friend to his wedding anniversary, explained how to find him in the apartment house where he lived. "Come to the seventh floor," he said, "and where you see the letter D on the door, push the button with your elbow and when the door opens put your foot against it."

"Why do I have to use my elbow and my foot?" asked his friend.

"Well, for heaven's sake!" exclaimed the Irishman. "You're not coming empty-handed, are you?" — *Readers Digest*

2444. An Australian, returning to his London club after many years, found only an elderly and grim-looking man in the lounge. Said the Australian, "Excuse me, sir, I know I'm a stranger but I'm feeling lonely and I wonder would you have a drink with me?"

Old Boy: "Don't drink; tried it once, didn't like it."

The Australian mooned around a bit, and thought he'd try again. "Sorry to barge in, sir, but I wonder if you'd smoke a cigar with me."

Old Boy: "No thanks, don't smoke; tried it once, didn't like it."

The Australian, wandering off once more, noticed the billiard room, and decided to make a final approach. "Pardon me, sir, but perhaps you'll have a game of billiards with me."

Old Boy: "Sorry, don't play. Tried it once, didn't like it . . . But, look here — my son will be along soon. He will enjoy a game with you, I know."

Australian: "Your only child, I'm sure, sir!"

358

2445. *He:* May I call you by your first name?

   She: Yes, if I can call myself by your last name.

2446. Walking down St. James's Street one day Disraeli met Lady Sebright in her brougham. Lady Sebright congratulated him on his earldom, on which Dizzy, with gracious gravity and a flourish of his hat, replied: "Of what avail or value are dignities to me, so long as Sir John Sebright continues to exist?"

> — MARGOT OXFORD, *More or Less*
> *About Myself* (Dutton)

2447. "Sometimes my father takes things apart to see why they don't go," said the girl to her boy friend. "So what?" he asked. "So you'd better go," she said.

success — See also *Failure*

2448. Asked for the secret of his popularity, a successful business-man said:

   "I made it a practice to be game — but not everybody's."

2449. You can't climb the ladder of success with cold feet.

2450. He has achieved success who has lived well, laughed often and loved much; who has enjoyed the trust of pure women, the respect of intelligent men and the love of little children; who has filled his niche and accomplished his task; who has left the world better than he found it, whether by an improved poppy, a perfect poem, or a rescued soul; who has never lacked appreciation of earth's beauty or failed to express it; who has always looked for the best in others and given them the best he had; whose life was an inspiration; whose memory a benediction.   — BESSIE ANDERSON STANLEY
> *Brown Book Magazine* (1904)

2451. Success depends on three things: who says it, what he says, how he says it: and of these three things, what he says is the least important.   — VISCOUNT JOHN MORLEY

2452. The men whom I have seen succeed best in life have always been cheerful and hopeful men, who went about their business with a smile on their faces, and took the changes and chances of this mortal life like men, facing rough and smooth alike as it came.

> — CHARLES KINGSLEY

2453. The man who starts out with the idea of getting rich won't succeed: you must have a larger ambition. There is no mystery in business success. If you do each day's task successfully, stay faithful within the natural operations of commercial law, and keep your head clear, you will come out all right. — JOHN D. ROCKEFELLER

2454. A successful man is one who has tried, not cried; who has worked, not dodged; who has shouldered responsibility not evaded it; who has gotten under the burden, not merely stood off looking on, giving advice and philosophizing on the situation. The result of a "down with the ship in storm and tempest" attitude is better than to paddle away to Paradise in an Orthodox canoe. To have worked is to have succeeded — we leave the results to time. Life is too short to gather the harvest — we can only sow.

2455. The mind is master of the man, and so "they can who think they can." — NIXON WATERMAN

2456. Yesterday I saw an honest-to-goodness bumble bee in a florist's window. Of all places for him to be in, I thought. He must be happy. And yet I fancied he was not. Too many flowers for a bee must be like too much success for a man. It makes him restless — and unhappy. The keenest joy in life is in the effort toward a goal — not in the winning itself. — *Anonymous*

2457. Meet success like a gentleman and disaster like a man. — LORD BIRKENHEAD

2458. There is no philosophy by which a man can do a thing when he thinks he can't.

2459. Going! Climbing! Building! Creating! That's fun, that's living. Arriving is the end.

2460. Every man should make up his mind that if he expects to succeed, he must give an honest return for the other man's dollar. — EDWARD H. HARRIMAN

2461. It is doubtful if anyone ever made a success of anything who waited until all the conditions were "just right" before starting.

2462. There is no future in any job. The future lies in the man who holds the job.
— DR. GEORGE W. CRANE
Psychology Applied

2463. Too many people quit looking for work when they find a job.

2464. You can hardly make a success without making enemies.

2465. Whenever you are asked if you can do a job, tell 'em, "Certainly, I can!" Then get busy and find out how to do it.

2466.   The heights by great men reached and kept,
         Were not attained by sudden flight —
         But they, while their companions slept,
         Were toiling upward in the night.
— HENRY WADSWORTH LONGFELLOW

2467. Success is to succeed. To succeed is to be successful. To succeed it is necessary at all times for a man to keep his expenses within his income, to learn to labor truly, attend to business, and do today's job today. The way to get ahead in this world is to do whatever work you are doing well, then you will be picked to do some other job that is not being done well.   — SAMUEL VAUCLAIN

2468. The law of success: more bone in the back and less in the head.

2469. People are always blaming their circumstances for what they are. I don't believe in circumstances. The people who get on in this world are the people who get up and look for the circumstances they want, and if they can't find them, make them.
— GEORGE BERNARD SHAW

2470. Nothing splendid has ever been achieved except by those who dared believe that something inside them was superior to circumstance.   — BRUCE BARTON, *Readers Digest*

2471. A retired industrial tycoon, talking to his listless grandson, said, "Why don't you go out and look for a job? Why, when I was your age, I was working for $3 a week. At the end of five years, I owned the store."

"You can't do that now," was the lackadaisical reply. " They have cash registers."
— OLGA J. FERT,
Louisville Courier-Journal

2472. The way for a young man to rise is to improve himself every way he can, never suspecting that anybody wishes to hinder him.
— ABRAHAM LINCOLN

2473. Let none falter, who thinks he is right, and we may succeed (Dec. 26, 1839). And on Nov. 5, 1855 — Always bear in mind that your own resolution to succeed is more important than any other one thing.
— ABRAHAM LINCOLN

2474. Success is a bright sun that obscures and makes ridiculously unimportant all the little shadowy flecks of failure.
— HAROLD HELFER,
The Kiwanis Magazine

2475. People would feel a lot less sensitive about failure if they remembered it just doesn't matter, except as a guidepost for oneself.
— HAROLD HELFER,
The Kiwanis Magazine

2476. The man who says "It can't be done" is interrupted by the man who is doing it.

2477. The only difference between stumbling blocks and stepping stones is the way you use them.

2478. The law of worthy life is fundamentally the law of strife. It is only through labor and painful effort, by grim energy and resolute courage, that we move on to better things.
— THEODORE ROOSEVELT

2479. The great trouble today is that there are too many people looking for someone else to do something for them. The solution of most of our troubles is to be found in everyone doing something for himself.
— HENRY FORD

2480. If a man can write a better book, preach a better sermon, or make a better mouse trap than his neighbor, though he builds his house in the woods, the world will make a beaten path to his door.
— RALPH WALDO EMERSON

2481. Only the game fish swims upstream.
— JOHN TROTWOOD MOORE

2482. Many men owe the grandeur of their lives to their tremendous difficulties.
— C. H. SPURGEON

2483. Far better it is to dare mighty things, to win glorious triumphs, even though checked by failure, than to take rank with those poor spirits who neither enjoy much nor suffer much, because they live in the gray twilight that knows neither victory or defeat.
— THEODORE ROOSEVELT

2484. It is not miserable to be blind; it is miserable to be incapable of enduring blindness.
— JOHN MILTON

2485. Our greatest glory is not in never failing, but in rising every time we fail.
— CONFUCIOUS

2486. The probability that we may fail in a worthy cause is not sufficient justification for our refusing to support it.
— ABRAHAM LINCOLN

2487. Replying to the tributes paid to him at a testimonial dinner, Herbert Bayard Swope said: "I cannot give you the formula for success, but I can give you the formula for failure — Try to please everybody."

2488. Our greatest glory consists not in never falling, but in rising every time we fall.
— RALPH WALDO EMERSON

2489. The difficult is that which can be done immediately; the impossible that which takes a little longer. — GEORGE SANTAYANA

2490. The big things you can see with one eye closed. But keep both eyes wide open for the little things. Little things mark the great dividing line between success and failure.

2491. Good and bad luck is but a synonym, in the great majority of instances, for good and bad judgment. — CHATFIELD

2492. Show me a thoroughly satisfied man — and I will show you a failure.
— THOMAS A. EDISON

2493. THE TEN COMMANDMENTS OF SUCCESS

1. *Work Hard.* Hard work is the best investment a man can make.
2. *Study Hard.* Knowledge enables a man to work more intelligently and effectively.
3. *Have Initiative.* Ruts often deepen into graves.
4. *Love Your Work.* Then you will find pleasure in mastering it.
5. *Be Exact.* Slipshod methods bring slipshod results.
6. *Have the Spirit of Conquest.* Thus you can successfully battle and overcome difficulties.
7. *Cultivate Personality.* Personality is to a man what perfume is to the flower.
8. *Help and Share with Others.* The real test of business greatness lies in giving opportunity to others.
9. *Be Democratic.* Unless you feel right towards your fellowmen you can never be a successful leader of men.
10. *In All Things Do Your Best.* The man who has done his best has done everything. The man who has done less than his best has done nothing. — CHARLES M. SCHWAB

2494. Better to do a little well than a great deal poorly.

2495. Life's greatest adventure is in doing one's level best.
— ARTHUR MORGAN

2496. The difference between success and failure is only ten cents. The business man who takes in a dollar and spends only 95¢ is on the road to financial independence, but the fellow who spends $1.05 when he has only a dollar in the bank is headed for the rocks.

2497. There may be splinters on the ladder of success, but you don't notice them until you slide down.

2498. If you cannot win, make the one ahead break the record.

2499. The man at the top is usually someone who has been in the habit of going to the bottom of things.

2500. It is never a sign of weakness when a man in high position delegates authority; on the contrary, it is a sign of his strength and of his capacity to deserve success. — WALTER LIPPMANN

2501. If you haven't received a raise, ask yourself — not your boss — why.

2502. A man may fail many times, but he isn't a failure until he begins to blame somebody else. — JOHN BURROUGHS

2503. Begin — to begin is half the work. Let half still remain; again begin this, and thou wilt have finished. — AUSONIUS

2504. The secret of success is constancy of purpose. — BENJAMIN DISRAELI

2505. How can you keep a determined man from success? Place stumbling-blocks in his way, and he uses them for stepping stones. Imprison him, and he produces the "Pilgrim's Progress." Deprive him of eyesight, and he writes the "Conquest of Mexico."

2506. The most important single ingredient in the formula of success is knowing how to get along with people. — THEODORE ROOSEVELT

2507. The only time you mustn't fail is the last time you try. — CHARLES F. KITTERING

2508. Before you can score you must first have a goal. — GREEK PROVERB

2509. David Sarnoff, reminiscing about his early years in the radio industry, mentioned the strong competition he had had to face. "But I'm grateful to my enemies," he said. "In the long-range movement toward progress, a kick in the pants sends you further along than a friendly handshake." — LEONARD LYONS, *Readers Digest*

2510. Almost everybody thought that Marshal Joffre had won the first battle of the Marne, but some refused to agree. One day a newspaper man appealed to Joffre: "Will you tell me who did win the battle of the Marne?" "I can't answer that," said the Marshal. "But I can tell you that if the battle of the Marne had been lost the blame would have been on me." — *Newsweek*

2511. An assistant rushed into William S. Knudsen's office one day, very upset because a certain report was missing. How could they act?

"There are two kinds of reports," Knudsen said calmly. "One says you can't do it. The other says it has been done. The first kind is no good. The second kind you don't need."
— FDSON BLAIR, *Barron's Weekly*

2512. Defeat never comes to any man until he admits it.
JOSEPHUS DANIELS

2513. Defeat isn't bitter if you don't swallow it.

2514. A motto to express the ideal of maximum service and efficiency: "Make sure you are underpaid." — V. ORVAL WATTS

2515. "If I were to draw up ten commandments for those earnestly seeking to fight successfully the battle of life," said B. C. Forbes, founder of *Forbes Magazine,* "They would read:
First — study
Second — sweat
Third — keep accounts
Fourth — save systematically
Fifth — take out life insurance
Sixth — buy your own home
Seventh — invest in sound securities, or launch your own business
Eighth — educate your children
Ninth — travel
Tenth — give generously."

2516. If you do the best and the most you can today, don't worry about tomorrow. — B. C. FORBES, founder of *Forbes Magazine*

2517. An Irishman was seeing his son off on the steamer to a new land where the lad was to seek his fortune. "Now Michael, my boy," he said, as they parted, "remember the *three bones* and ye'll always get along all right."
A stranger standing nearby overheard the remark and asked what three bones he referred to.
"Sure, now," said the Irishman, "and wouldn't it be the *wishbone,* the *jawbone,* and the *backbone?* It's the wishbone that keeps you going after things, and it's the jawbone that helps you find out how to go after them if you're not too proud to ask a question when there's something you don't know; and it's the backbone keeps you at it till you get there." — *Religious Telescope*

2518. Worse than a quitter is the man who is afraid to begin.

2519. Columbus doesn't deserve as much credit for discovering America as he does for having tried.

2520. It ain't no disgrace for a man to fall, but to lie there and grunt is.
— Josh Billings

2521. It is far better to acknowledge failure and to make a new beginning than to let pride bar the way to possible future success.

2522. If people could only concentrate on their work as whole-heartedly as they concentrate on their worries, success would be assured.

2523. When success turns a man's head he faces failure.

2524. Some think they have made a success of life, when all they've made is just a lot of money.

2525. If you have tried to do something and failed, you are vastly better off than if you had tried to do nothing and succeeded.

2526. Some men succeed because they are destined to, but most men because they are determined to.

2527. But study alone is not enough; the ambitious man must think. If he is not succeeding, he takes account of himself and, by thinking, tries to find out what he can do to become successful, to get ahead. He analyzes his own situation; he tries to find out what is wrong; he seeks advice, but he depends upon himself and his own thinking. He can help himself in a way that no one else can help him.
— Judge Elbert H. Gary

2528. Your success and happiness lie in you. External conditions are the accidents of life. The great enduring realities are love and service. Joy is the holy fire that keeps our purpose warm and our intelligence aglow.

Resolve to keep happy, and your joy and you shall form an invincible host against difficulty.
— Helen Keller

2529. Don't be afraid of opposition. Remember a kite rises against, not with, the wind. — HAMILTON MABIE, *Parade*

2530.
Success is speaking words of praise
In cheering other people's ways,
In doing just the best you can
With every task and every plan.
It's silence when your speech would hurt.
Politeness when your neighbor's curt.
It's deafness when the scandal flows,
And sympathy with others' woes.
It's loyalty when duty calls,
It's courage when disaster falls,
It's patience when the hours are long;
It's found in laughter and in song;
It's in the silent time of prayer,
In happiness and in despair
In all of life and nothing less
We find the thing we call success.
— *Author Unknown*

2531. The victory of success is half won when one gains the habit of work.

2532. Success is getting what you want; happiness is wanting what you get.

2533. About all there is to success in life — is making promises and keeping them. Promises to others. Promises to yourself.

2534. To fail at all is to fail utterly. — JAMES RUSSELL LOWELL

2535. The winds are always on the side of the ablest navigators.
— EDWARD GIBBON, *Decline and Fall of the Roman Empire*

2536. Leaving business at the office sounds like a good rule, but it is one that can easily be carried too far because, to my mind, a man who intends to make a success should be collecting ideas and tips, and mapping out programs during every waking hour. Dismissing business after office hours has a nice sound, but I have found that often the business does not come back after the recess!
— JOHN H. PATTERSON

2537. The secret of success in life is known only to those who have not succeeded. — JOHN C. COLLINS

2538. He who shoots best may sometimes miss the mark; but he that shoots not at all can never hit it. — FELLTHAM

2539. A life of ease is a difficult pursuit. — WILLIAM COWPER

2540. There are two kinds of men who never amount to much: those who cannot do what they are told, and those who can do nothing else. — CYRUS H. K. CURTIS

2541. The road to success is filled with women pushing their husbands along. — THOMAS R. DEWAR

2542.
We must not hope to be mowers,
    And to gather the ripe gold ears,
Unless we have first been sowers
    And water the furrows with tears.
It is not just as we take it,
    This mystical world of ours;
Life's field will yield as we make it,
    A harvest of thorns or of flowers.
— GOETHE

2543. It is very easy to succeed in spite of poverty. It is difficult to succeed in spite of wealth. — ARTHUR BRISBANE

2544. Success: making more money to meet obligations you wouldn't have if you didn't make so much money.

2545. A snob is one who in climbing the ladder of success kisses the feet of the one ahead of him and kicks the head of the one following him.

2546. Success: the degree to which other people envy you.

2547. Successful man: one who earns more than his wife can spend.

2548. Successful woman: one who finds such a man.

2549. If you build castles in the air, your work need not be lost; that is where they should be. Now put the foundations under them.

— HENRY DAVID THOREAU

2550. There's a difference between rising to the top and going up in the air.

2551. Not the senses I have but what I do with them is my kingdom.

— HELEN KELLER

2552. You can do more than strike while the iron is hot; you can make the iron hot by striking.

— C. C. COLTON

suffering

2553. Suffering is really a revelation. One discerns things one never discerned before. One approaches the whole of history from a different standpoint. What one had felt dimly, through instinct, about art, is intellectually and emotionally realised with perfect clearness of vision and absolute intensity of apprehension.

— OSCAR WILDE

superlative

2554. *Superlatives All!*
The greatest sin — fear.
The best day — today.
The greatest deceiver — one who deceives himself.
The greatest mistake — giving up.
The most expensive indulgence — hate.
The cheapest, stupidest and easiest thing to do — finding fault.
The worst bankrupt — the soul that has lost its enthusiasm.
The cleverest man — one who always does what he thinks is right.
The best part of anyone's religion — gentleness and cheerfulness.
The meanest feeling — jealousy.
The best gift — forgiveness.

— DR. FRANK CRANE

surprise

2555. Traditionally brought-up young lady, looking at a fig tree for the first time: "But I thought the leaves were bigger than that!"

2556. A certain English Professor was one day unexpectedly caught by his wife in the act of embracing one of his servants.

"Why, Professor," she exclaimed, "I'm surprised!"

"Oh, no, my dear," came the reply, "it is I who am surprised, you're astonished."

2557. At Columbia College they still remember the time the late Professor Raymond Weaver gave his first class in English literature their first quiz. A whistle of joy went up from the group, which had been trying to make things hard for the new instructor, when Weaver wrote on the blackboard, "Which of the books read so far has interested you least?"

But then Weaver wrote the second and last question: "To what defect in yourself do you attribute this lack of interest?"

– JOSEPH WOOD KRUTCH,
The Nation

2558. The townsman was buying a fountain pen for his son's graduation gift.

"It's to be a surprise, I suppose," said the clerk.

"I'll say it is," said the father. "He's expecting a convertible coupe."

– HAROLD L. SPENCE,
Holdrege (Neb.) Citizen

sympathy

2559. Groucho Marx, buying a frankfurter, "Give me the bottom one – I'm always for the underdog."

2560. Sympathy with pain is not the highest form of sympathy. . . . Anyone can sympathize with the sufferings of a friend, but it requires a very fine nature . . . to sympathize with a friend's success. . . . Sympathy with joy intensifies the sum of joy in the world. . . . Sympathy with pain does not really diminish the amount of pain.

– OSCAR WILDE

system

2561. He was a director of unbounded enthusiasm, but faintly balanced by experience. Having invented a completely new office system, he went abroad to recuperate. His first question on his return was, "How is the system working?"

"Splendidly," said the manager, rubbing his chin.
"I thought you'd like it," said the director.
"And how's the business?"
"We gave that up," said the manager, "to attend to the system."

2562.   *Manager:* "I am afraid you are ignorant of our efficiency system, Smith."
Smith: "Perhaps so, sir, but somebody has to get the work done."

tact

2563.   Social tact: the ability to make your guests feel at home, though you wish they were.

2564.   Tact is the knack of making a point without making an enemy.

2565.   Grant graciously what you cannot refuse safely, and conciliate those you cannot conquer.   — C. C. COLTON

taxes

2566.   Taxpayer: a person who has the government on his payroll.

2567.   Taxation: the process by which money is collected from the people to pay the salaries of the men who do the collecting. The surplus is used to pay the salaries of the men the people elect to decide how much shall be collected from them.

2568.   Federal aid: a system of making money taken from the people look like a gift when handed back.

2569.   Income-tax expert: someone whose fee is the amount he saves you in making out your tax return.   — *Readers Digest*

2570.   When the tax investigator asked the suspected party why he did not list all his sources of income, the culprit replied, "Well, I guess I was in a listless mood."

2571. Dean Swift proposed to tax beauty, and to leave every lady to rate her own charms; he said the tax would be cheerfully paid and very productive. — FREDERICK SAUNDERS

2572. The one thing that hurts more than paying an income tax is not having to pay an income tax. — THOMAS R. DEWAR

television

2573. Television is a kind of radio which lets people at home see what the studio audience is not laughing at.

2574. Television: something to put on a radio so that folks can see things are really as bad as they heard they were.
— MORTON THOMPSON, *Joe the Wounded Tennis Player*

2575. Television: Vidiot's delight.

2576. Alan Young tells about the man who stared into the mirror and, noting his bloodshot eyes, resolved never to go to a bar again. "This television," he muttered, "is wrecking my eyes!"
— ERSKINE JOHNSON

2577. The phone rang in Lapidus' apartment.
"This is the Radio Survey," announced the voice at the other end. "May we inquire what program you listened to last night."
"Absolutely," replied Lapidus. "Last night I was entertained by Phil Baker."
"I am sorry," argued the Survey Specialist, "but you must be mistaken. Phil Baker doesn't go on the air until tomorrow night."
"Tomorrow night!" repeated Lapidus, in amazement. "Well, no wonder I couldn't get him so clearly!"

temptation

2578. *Passenger:* "Madam, pardon me, but you're standing on my foot."
Lady: "Why don't you put your foot where it belongs?"
Passenger: "Don't tempt me, lady — don't tempt me."

2579. An old French theory:
The only way to handle temptation successfully is to yield to it.

theory

2580. At the air-training base a group was called up for a swimming test. "How about you, Mac?" demanded the instructor. "Can you swim?"

"Sure!" replied the gob. To prove it he splashed the length of the pool in an old-fashioned dog-paddle.

"You call that swimming?" bawled the instructor.

"Well," observed the sailor mildly, "that's what kept me up when the Hornet went down." — SERVICE CHUCKLES,
American Magazine

thought

2581. You are today where your thoughts have brought you; you will be tomorrow where your thoughts take you. You cannot escape the result of your thoughts.

2582. Most folks have presence of mind. The trouble is absence of thought. — HOWARD W. NEWTON

thoughtfulness

2583. It is related that when James A. Garfield decided to go to college he favored Yale, but also wrote to the presidents of Brown and Williams colleges. Yale's president made a formal reply and the president of Brown did the same. But the president of Williams took an extra second to add this line, "We shall be glad to do what we can for you." As a result of that line, Williams college received the honor of graduating a president of the United States and having as its own president, Harry A. Garfield, son of President Garfield.

thrift

2584. What this country needs is a non-skid coin, guaranteed not to slip thru the fingers.

2585. Thrift is a habit. A habit is a thing you do unconsciously or automatically, without thought. We are ruled by our habits. When habits are young, they are like lion cubs, soft, fluffy, funny, frolicsome little animals. They grow day by day. Eventually they rule you. Choose ye this day the habit ye would have to rule over you. The habit of thrift is simply the habit which dictates that you shall earn more than you spend. In other words, thrift is the habit that provides that you shall spend less than you earn. Take your choice.

— ELBERT HUBBARD

2586. A well-to-do-man was asked the secret of his success. "Surely," said the questioner, "you must have been tempted to indulge in extravagances."

"Oh, yes," agreed the opulent one, "but a long time ago I worked out a four-question formula that has saved me a lot of money. First, before I buy, I ask myself, 'Do you really want it?' Usually I can answer 'Yes' to that one!

"Then I ask, 'But do you need it?' That cuts short a good many proposed purchases.

"The next question is, 'Can you afford it?' That's a real stopper!

"And finally I ask, 'But can't you get along without it?' The few items that survive after that are pretty essential!"

2587. Men do not realize how great a revenue economy is.

— CICERO

2588. The trouble with most of us is that in retrenching we don't want to take the "me" out of economy.

2589. Thrift is a wonderful virtue — especially in an ancestor.

2590. The best way to double your money is to fold it once and put it back in your pocket.

2591. Economy: a way to spend money without getting any fun out of it.

2592. Without care and method, the largest fortune will not, and with them almost the smallest will, supply all necessary expenses.

— LORD CHESTERFIELD (advice to his son)

2593. Buy what thou hast no need of, and ere long thou shalt sell thy necessaries. — BENJAMIN FRANKLIN,
Poor Richard's Almanac

2594. Miser: one who's perfectly content to let the rest of the world go buy.

2595. A Scotchman went to town for a holiday, and a friend met him later wandering down the street with a pair of trousers over his arm. "Where are ye goin', Sandy?"
And he replied: "Oh, A'h'm lookin' for the 'Aberdeen Free Press.' "

2596. One of the difficult tasks in this world is to convince a woman that even a bargain costs money. — EDGAR W. HOWE

2597. The hardest ups and downs in life are keeping expenses down and keeping appearances up.

2598. This is the story of the man who ate beef tongue and ox tail soup in order to make both ends meet.

2599. So often we rob tomorrow's memories by today's economies. — JOHN MASON BROWN, *Morning Faces*

time

2600. Spring: when boys begin to feel gallant and girls begin to feel buoyant.

2061. People who have half an hour to spend usually spend it with someone who hasn't.

2602. There is many a slip 'twixt the cup and the lip. — WILLIAM HAZLITT, *English Proverbs*

2603. 20th century stuff:
Rome was not built in a day; but Gary (Indiana) was.

2604. We are always complaining that our days are few, and acting as though there would be no end to them. — SENECA

2605. Leo McCarey, who produced successfully the religious film, "Going My Way," answering critics who warned that his next picture, "Bells of St. Mary's," would be repetitious:

"This is a story people have been telling for 2,000 years. I don't think another hour and forty minutes of it will hurt."

— ALYCE CANFIELD, *Liberty*

2606. Time goes, you say? Ah no!
Alas, Time stays, *we* go.

— HENRY AUSTIN DOBSON,
The Paradox of Time

2607. *Orchestra Drummer:* "I'm the fastest man in the world.'
Violinist: "How's that?"
O. D.: "Times flies, doesn't it?"
V.: "So they say."
O. D.: "Well, I beat time."

2608. When Theodore Roosevelt was visiting in Germany, he sent to find out if he could call upon the Kaiser as he had never met him before. The Kaiser said he could give up only half an hour of his time. Roosevelt sent back word that he was sorry that he could only spare fifteen minutes.

2609. I spent a year in that town, one Sunday.

— WARWICK DEEPING

2610. Time: the stuff between pay days.

2611. Time: the arbitrary division of eternity.

2612. Money lost can be replaced but time lost is gone forever.

2613. You will never "find" time for anything. If you want time you must make it.

— CHARLES BUXTON

toasts

2614.   We come into this world naked and bare
We go through this world with sorrow and care
We go out of this world, we know not where
But if we're good fellows here, we'll be
thoroughbreds there.

377

2615.   Here's to Solomon and David
              And their merry, merry, lives,
          With their many, many, lady friends
              And many, many, wives.
          But when old age came creeping with
              Its many, many qualms,
          Solomon wrote the proverbs
              And David wrote the Psalms

2616. May you live all the days of your life.   — SWIFT

2617. Let us wipe out the past, trust in the future and rejoice in the glorious Now.

2618.   Here's to God's first thought, Man!
          Here's to God's second thought, Woman!
          Second thoughts are always best,
          So here's to Woman!

2619. Famous was the toast given by Benjamin Franklin when he was dining, as the American emissary, with the English Ambassador and the French Minister, at Versailles. The story was first published in 1797.

"George the Third," proposed the British Ambassador, "who, like the sun in its meridian, spreads a luster throughout and enlightens the world."

"The illustrious Louis the Sixteenth," proposed the French Minister, "who, like the moon, sheds his mild and benignant rays on and influences the globe."

"George Washington," thereupon proposed witty Benjamin Franklin, "commander of the American armies, who, like Joshua of old, commanded the sun and the moon to stand still, and they obeyed him."

2620. At a banquet of firemen, recently, the chief proposed this toast: "The Ladies! Their eyes kindle the only flame which we cannot extinguish, and against which there is no insurance."

2621. Here's to woman — ah, that we could fall into her arms without falling into her hands.   — AMBROSE BIERCE

2622. To our friends, who know the worst about us but refuse to believe it.

tolerance – See also *Discrimination*

2623. How shall we ever learn toleration for what we do not believe? The last lesson a man ever learns is, that liberty of thought and speech is the right for all mankind; that the man who denies every article of our creed is to be allowed to preach just as often and just as loud as we ourselves. – WENDELL PHILLIPS, *Speeches, Lectures and Letters*

traffic – See also *Automobile*

2624. If you want to live to see ninety, don't look for it on the speedometer.

2625. Before a Pennsylvania-Columbia game at Baker Field during Prohibition, a "happy" group of Penn students who had somehow driven all the way from Philadelphia with no visible scars were maneuvering a topless jalopy up and down the sidewalks, brandishing a jug and cheering for Penn. At the approach to the field a Manhattan cop stopped them, reached into the car and took out the keys. Too nonplussed to protest, the boys obeyed his order to get out, meekly followed him across the street to a stationery store. "Gotta dime?" he asked. They produced a dime and the cop bought a stamped envelope.

"Let's see yer drivers' licenses." The boys handed them over. The cop put the keys and licenses in the envelope, wrote the owner's name and address on it. Then he walked outside, dropped the whole thing in the mailbox – and went back to directing traffic.
– TOM O'REILLY, *Town & Country*

2626. When a woman driver gives you more than half the road, chances are she's walking. – FRANKLIN P. JONES

2627. Shifting for oneself is considered a virtue by everybody except automobile designers. – *Wall Street Journal*

2628. What we need is an automobile brake that will get tight when the driver does. – ANDREW MEREDITH

2629. A driver may be color blind but he can still tell which is the green light; it's the one that's on such a short time.

— RICHARD ARMOUR

2630. A pessimist is a woman driver who's sure she can't park her car in a tight place. An optimist is a man who thinks she won't try.

— BILL BERTOLOTTI, quoted by Earl Wilson

2631. Putting motors in the rear will concentrate all of the noise in the back seat.

— *Bluebird Briefs*

2632. Some time ago, the champion safety driver of one of the largest bus companies of the world was given a banquet and a medal. He had completed half a million miles without an accident.

When called on for his speech, he rose bashfully and said: "I ain't much of a hand at making speeches. I suppose you want to know how I got away so long without no accidents? I got just one rule. I drive like the other fellow was crazy."

2633. A man's automobile and the way in which he drives it are merely projections of his personality.

2634. As my friend and I were driving downtown, we were hailed by a traffic cop. "Hey, you!" he shouted, "pull over."

We did. The next day the judge fined my friend $25 for speeding. She was anxious to keep her husband from learning of the incident. And so, since he regularly examined her checkbook, she marked the stub; "One pull-over — $25."

— *Readers Digest*

2635. Fellows who drive with one hand are usually headed for a church aisle. Some will walk down it, some will be carried.

— *Business Briefs*

2636. If all the cars in America were placed end to end on a long hill, some fool would try to pass them.

2637. "Tell me, Jack, does Elsie know much about automobiles?"

"I should say not. Why she asked me the other day if I cooled my car by stripping the gears."

2638. Most automobile accidents occur on Saturday and Sunday. It's a great life if you don't week-end.

2639. Care may kill people, but don't care kills more.

2640. The Bingville board of selectmen had held many sessions and finally formulated a set of auto laws that was the pride of the county. So the constable felt no worriment when he stopped a motorist.

"Ye're pinched for violatin' the auto laws," he pronounced.

"Which one?" inquired the traveler.

"Durned if I know but ye certainly hain't come all the way down Main Street without bustin' one of them."

— *The American Legion Magazine*

2641. THE MOTORISTS' PRAYER

Grant me a steady hand and watchful eye,
That no man shall be hurt when I pass by.
Thou gavest Life: I pray no act of mine
May take away or mar this gift of Thine.
Teach me to use my car for others' need
Nor ever miss, through any love of speed,
The beauties of Thy world — and thus I may
With joyous heart and courtesy go my way. — *Anonymous*

2642. *Traffic Cop:* "Hey you! Is that your car?"

"Well, officer, since you ask me, considering the fact that I still have fifty payments to make, owe three repair bills and haven't settled for the new tire, I really don't think it is."

2643. *Judge:* "How far were you from this spot when these cars collided?"

Witness: "Twenty-two feet and nine inches."

Judge: "How do you know it was exactly?"

Witness: "Because I measured it, thinking some fool might ask me the distance."

2644. *To a reckless driver:*

Not so fast careless pest
Want a lily on your chest?

2645. If you have plans for tomorrow, be careful today.

2646. A woman should hold on to her youth, but not when he's driving.

— *Readers Digest*

2647. It was the dear old lady's first ride in a taxi, and she watched with growing alarm the driver continually putting his hand outside the car as a signal to following traffic. At last she became exasperated.

"Young man," she said, "you look after that car of yourn and watch where you are going. I'll tell you when it starts raining."

2648. *Auto prospect:* You have shown me that your new car can go seventy miles an hour, but will such a car last?

Agent: My dear friend, don't let that worry you. Anyone who drives seventy miles an hour will not need a car very long.

2649. Proof that they had automobiles in Biblical times: These freely-translated passages in the Bible:

      1. Moses went up to heaven on high.

      2. The children of Israel came upon a ford.

2650. Each year our manners become cruder as our gasoline becomes more refined.

2651. A popcorn farmer from Terre Haute, Indiana, states that one firm alone employs thirty-three trucks to deliver popcorn to taverns to stimulate thirst in customers.

2652. When we get a gentleman at the wheel, we need not fear the monster under the hood.

2653. For every accident caused by high speeding, there are a thousand caused by low breeding.

2654. Some people have a veneer that comes off easily with a little alcohol.   — PAUL HARRISON, *N. Y. World-Telegram*

2655.

    If every one who drives a car could lie a month in bed,
    With broken bones and stitched-up wounds, or fractures of
        the head,
    And there endure the agonies that many people do,
    They'd never need preach safety any more to me or you.

    If every one could stand beside the bed of some close friend,
    And hear the doctor say, "No hope," before that fatal end,

And see him there unconscious, never knowing what took place,
The laws and rules of traffic I am sure we'd soon embrace.

If everyone could meet the wife and children left alone
And step into the darkened home where once the sunlight
    shone,
And look upon "The Vacant Chair" where Daddy used to sit,
I'm sure each reckless driver would be forced to think a bit.

If everyone who takes the wheel would say a little prayer,
And keep in mind those in the car depending on his care,
And make a vow, and pledge himself to never take a chance,
The great crusade for safety then would suddenly advance.

— Author Unknown

2656.   A fool there was and he took a chance —
              They carried him off in an ambulance!

2657.   Lose a minute and save a life.

2658.   It's better to be last in the traffic lane than first in the
funeral procession.

2659.   Take chances and the chances are that you won't have
many chances left to take.

2660.   He who sitteth upon a Throne
                 Or in a Presidential Chair,
                 Hearing the complaints of the multitude.
                 Hath nothing on him
                 Who sitteth behind the Wheel
                 of the Family car
                 With his Wife in the Back Seat

2661.   Statistics show that an average of over 39,000 persons are
killed by gas annually. Sixty inhale it; forty light matches in it, and
38,900 step on it.

2662.   The American may not be the most uncivil citizen on two
feet but he certainly is the prize terror on four wheels.

2663.   Epitaph: He walked on the suicide of the road.

2664. Traffic Sign in a Pennsylvania village:
Slow. No Hospital — *Readers Digest*

2665. Life may begin at 40 but death begins at 50.

2666. Children should be seen and not hurt.

2667. One push on the horn is worth two on the brake.

2668. Whoever originated the popular belief that when two automobiles cross paths, one has a technical, arbitrary, irrevocable right of way, should be held responsible for many traffic accidents.

There is no such thing as an unqualified right of way of one motorist over another. It is utter foolishness to insist that one has the right of way at an intersection simply because he arrives there first; or because he has read somewhere that the motorist on the right has the privilege of proceeding first.

2669. Advice to motorist: Just because you see its tracks is no sign that a train has just passed.

2670. The growing problem of automobile fatalities will not be solved around the drafting board, but rather around the family table.

2671. The truck ahead of us made a left turn and we followed. Immediately the traffic officer whistled. "I was just following that truck," I explained.

"That was a newspaper truck. Don't you know that newspaper trucks have the right o' way?"

"Sorry, officer, I didn't know that."

"Ain't you ever heard of Freedom o' the Press? Now git goin' before I give you a ticket!" — *Readers Digest*

2672. Safety slogan used in Los Angeles during Christmas and New Year's season: "Don't let death take your holiday."

2673. Watch out for the fellow behind the man in front.

2674. Do not depend on the other fellow because he may be depending on you.

2675. In Detroit, it takes a thousand nuts to complete an automobile, but it takes only one nut to scatter it all over the road.

2676. Wide roads won't prevent accidents, so long as they continue to fill up with narrow people.

2677.   I hate the chap who tries to beat the traffic light
           But if he happens to be me — Well that's all right!
         I loathe the car that in a jam, twists out and in;
           But if I'm sitting at the wheel, I slyly grin.
         At drivers who lean on their horns I rave and shout
           But when some fool gets in my way I honk him out.
         I grow indignant at the chance another takes;
           But I drive 60 miles an hour and trust my brakes.
         I wonder, is it possible they cannot ever see
           That traffic laws were made for them and not at
             all for me?
                                                — L. N. HALE

2678. The right of way is not worth dying for.

2679. The safety test may remove from the streets the rattle trap, but will not remove the rattle brain.

2680.   The life of the highway is just what you make it
           For you and the others who ride.
         It is a great life. Will you live it or take it?
           Each moment it's yours to decide.
         So figure the distance by miles safely driven,
           And carry a good-judgment spare;
         Take a tankful of patience to help you keep livin';
           And measure your pleasure with care.
                                                — *Anonymous*

2681. Sign on florist's truck:
"Drive carefully — The Next Load May Be Yours!"

2682. Be extra considerate to pedestrians — this may include your parents, your children, the fellow who is going to save your life one day, people who have just fallen wonderfully in love with each other, and, on occasions, yourself . . .

2683. Remember that side streets are a good deal like trees. Some sap is apt to be running out of them.

2684. To avoid that run down feeling — cross the streets carefully.

2685. The motorcycle cop finally caught up with the huge limousine. He ordered the driver — a beautiful showgirl — to pull over to the curb.

"Sixty miles an hour!" growled the cop. "Don't you know we have speed limits in this town?"

The showgirl looked extremely innocent.

"Why, officer," she protested, "I was only going thirty."

"Only thirty, eh?" snapped the cop. "Then why is it I had to go over sixty miles an hour to catch up with you?"

The girl shrugged haughtily.

"Look here, my man," she cried, "What are you trying to do — compare a cheap motorcycle to my limousine?"

2686. Good brakes on cars are no protection against bad breaks in behavior.

2687. DRIVER'S DECALOGUE

Composed by Bishop George Craig Stewart, Episcopal Church, Evanston, Illinois.

1. Thou shalt keep "safety first" ever before thee.
2. Thou shalt not make of thyself a dangerous nuisance, nor the likeness of anyone that grabbeth the road beside; the road ahead and cutteth in and out of the line.
3. Thou shalt not take the laws of the state in vain for the cop and the judge will not hold him guiltless that taketh the laws in vain.
4. Remember thy brakes and tires and take curves slowly.
5. Honor the red lights and the green lights that thy days may be long in the land which the Lord thy God giveth thee.
6. Thou shalt not kill.
7. Thou shalt not stop abruptly.
8. Thou shalt not steal — past a street car loading and unloading.
9. Thou shalt not flash big lights against thy neighbor.
10. Thou shalt not shove it, thy neighbor's car, nor his fenders, nor his bumpers, nor his locks, nor his glass, nor anything that is thy neighbor's.

2688. *Traffic cop, (producing notebook):* "Name, please."
Motorist: "Aloysius Alastair Cyprian."
Traffic cop, (putting book away): "Well, don't let me catch you again."

2689. A motorist was picked up unconscious after a crash and was being carried to a nearby filling station. Opening his eyes on route, he began to kick and struggle desperately to get away. Later he explained that the first thing he saw was a "Shell" sign and "some guy was standing in front of the 'S'."

2690. Women drivers can be very healthy and still take a turn for the worse.

2691. Women drivers would be as good as men, but for one thing: Fenders.

2692. *Friend:* "So you fined Miss Sweetly $5 for speeding. Is she appealing?"
Judge: "Oh, very, but we couldn't let that affect our decision, you know!"

2693. In Springfield, Ohio, a truck driver charged with drunken driving and who had knocked down a pedestrian was fined $150 and sentenced to "spend as much time in jail as the victim spends in the hospital."
— *Readers Digest*

2694. A taxi driver, weaving in and out of traffic at a fast clip, burst out laughing. "What's so amusing?" asked his fare.

"Aw," he said, "I was thinking of the two preachers and the cab driver who went up to heaven at the same time. St. Peter asked the first minister, 'Who are you and what have you done?'

" 'I'm a Baptist minister and I've preached for twenty-five years.'

" 'Well, stand over to one side there,' ordered St. Peter. He then put the question to the second clergyman. 'I've been a Methodist pastor for twenty-five years.'

" 'Stand to one side,' said St. Peter. 'What about you?' he asked the last man.

" 'I'm a taxi driver,' the cabbie answered. 'Been one for about fifteen years.'

" 'Pass through the gates,' intoned St. Peter.

" 'Why have you allowed that man to go before us?' the preachers protested.

" 'Because,' said St. Peter, 'in fifteen years he has scared more hell out of people than you both have in half a century.' "

— Readers Digest

2695.   YOU BET YOUR LIFE

Do you speed when the sign says "Beware!"?
Do you take chances when you should take care?
    You bet your life!
Do you make blunders you never should make?
What are you betting, man? What is the stake?
    You Bet Your Life!
You gain a second — or maybe a minute —
    You bet your life!
Sometimes there may not be anything in it —
    You bet your life!
If you would bet, you should figure the cost;
Too late to argue with Fate when you've lost!
Too late to claim that you've been double crossed!
    You Bet Your Life!

2696. Texas highway sign: This is God's country. Don't drive like hell.

2697. Pedestrian: a man with a son in high school and only one car in the family.

2698. Today we put a premium on agility rather than civility.

2699. Even the speeder can't do thirty days in less time than that.

2700. It is better to have one foot on the brake than six feet under the ground.

2701. "Pickled" drivers make "traffic jams."

2702. Coffin linings cost more now. As a matter of economy, one should pay more attention to the brake linings.

2703. The only time that liquor makes a man go straight is when the road curves.
— EVERETT M. RENSBURG

2704. The more patient pedestrians, the fewer pedestrian patients.

2705. Pedestrian: a guy with three good tires.

2706. Let the other fellow have the right of way; you take the right way.

2707. Truck driver: a man who has the opportunity to run into so many nice people.

2708. Roadhog: a fellow who meets you more than half way.

2709. Some years ago when the author of this volume was presiding as Judge over the Chicago Automobile Safety Court, he participated in a Safety Program on a radio broadcast. The following letter, which appeared as an editorial in the Tribune of Eufaula, Alabama, was included in his address on that occasion. Thereafter, he received many comments from his listening audience, but none more touching and effective than the one from Mrs. R. Both letters follow below:

"Dear Driver:

Today my daughter, who is 7 years old, started to school as usual. She wore a dark blue dress with a white collar. She had on black shoes and wore blue gloves. Her cocker spaniel, whose name is Coot, sat on the front porch and whined his canine belief in the folly of education as she waved good-bye and started off to the hall of learning.

Tonight we talked about school. She told me about the girl who sits in front of her, the girl with yellow curls, and the boy across the aisle who makes funny faces. She told me about her teacher, who has eyes in the back of her head, and about the trees in the schoolyard, and about the big girl who doesn't believe in Santa Claus. We talked about a lot of things — tremendously vital, unimportant things; and then we studied spelling, reading, arithmetic — and then to bed.

She's back there now — back in the nursery sound asleep, with 'Princess Elizabeth' (that's a doll) cuddled in her right arm.

You guys wouldn't hurt her, would you? You see, I'm her daddy.

When her doll is broken or her finger is cut or her head gets bumped, I can fix it — but when she starts to school, when she walks across the street, then she's in your hands.

She's a nice kid. She can run like a deer and darts about like a chipmunk. She likes to ride horses and swim and hike with me on Sunday afternoons. But I can't be with her all the time; I have to work to pay for her clothes and her education. So please help me look out for her. Please drive slowly past the schools and intersections — and please remember that children run from behind parked cars.

Please don't run over my little girl." — H. K. L.

"Dear Judge Braude:

I have just heard you read the letter addressed to 'Dear Driver.' I am glad *you* can say 'Dear Driver' because I can't. Sometimes when I think of these monsters they appear as something between a leopard and an elephant — they sneak up quietly with great speed, like a leopard, but suddenly become as huge and impossible to stop as an elephant.

You see, I am a mother. I have a daughter, too. If she is a wee bit late getting home from school I become so horribly frightened I think death would be preferable to the awful torture I must endure. I even dislike letting her go out to play, because, as you say, I cannot be with her. But, of course, she must go out to play — "all the other kids do." At night I am afraid to pray that God will watch her and keep her from harm because that is what I used to do when we had our daughter and our son.

Now we don't have him any more because I let him go out to play once too often, and one of your 'dear drivers' cut him down. Less than ten minutes after he went out to play some of my neighbors brought one of his little shoes up to my apartment. You should see what being hit by a car can do to a pair of shoes. I didn't recognize that shoe. He had on his play shoes; we were saving his 'new shoes' for special occasions. He was buried in them!

Honestly, Judge Braude, it takes much strength to look at a child whom you have bathed; the one whose little hands and face and knees sometimes got so black that you wondered if they would ever scrub clean again; and whose clothes you worried so over; and got up many times during the night so see if he was covered, and you wondered what you would do if his fever went up much farther, knowing your

390

purse wouldn't stetch to include many doctor's calls; and looking at those golden curls and that so fair skin, wondering (in your own secret heart) how anything so beautiful happened to come to you.

Honestly, it is hard to enter the portals of a place marked "Funeral Home" and walk down quiet empty aisles to a small white casket and look at that child of white marble. You feel, alternately, too utterly crushed to weep, and then you feel 'this can't be so; it's only a hideous nightmare, and soon I shall awaken and see him again.' But you never *do!* You go quietly, if limply, through the whole dreamlike ordeal because you are conventional and civilized and you know other parents have gone through the same thing. You say to yourself 'if they can, I can.' Sometimes you feel you just can't go on and that you must abandon yourself to wild grief. But somehow you don't.

Then sets in 'the rest of your life'; the common everydays and you wonder how you will be able to bear them. A very large chunk has been cut out of your heart, and believe me it does not heal. And somehow you know that it will never heal,' — that life can never again be completely happy for you and that you never again will be quite free. Tears well up at most unexpected times and places, but you fight to restrain them at all costs because you know that even a beast hides his cuts and bruises from the world and licks his wounds away from the light of day.

And oh! those nights! You witness that accident ten thousand times. Your body aches because you can't drive from your mind's eye those wheels going over that tiny body, and you pray God it didn't hurt him too much. You wish that you could have borne the pain for him — you will, the rest of your life.

Then you think and think; wondering if there is something you can do to help a cause about which something *must* be done. *Something must be done,* because each day children or parents, or both, are being cut down. Such needless slaughter in a world already saturated with grief, bloodshed and death. Why, each year an army killed right here at home on our own soil! Something must be done. 'Your' little girl and my little girl must not be sacrificed. It would be more than I could bear, it seems, to lose another.

This is the first letter I have ever written to some one I do not know, but because my boy is always on my mind, and the letter you read fitted in — well, here it is — unplanned and perhaps poorly done.

Let me know if there is anything I can do or any way in which

I can be of service in the cause of 'safety.' I have no money, but I am strong and willing to work, so please inform me if there is anything I can do along these lines. Please do not use my name, though, will you? I am simply writing as one friend to another.

Mrs. R.————"

translate

2710. A translator is to be like his author; it is not his business to excel him. — SAMUEL JOHNSON, *Lives of the Poets*

travel

2711. The best cure for restlessness for far places is to go there and find them full of people who would like to get back home again.

2712. Upper berth: where you rise to retire and get down to get up.

2713. Seasickness: traveling across the ocean by rail.

2714. Suitcase: something you sit on while waiting for the train.

2715. "My husband is particularly liable to seasickness, captain," remarked a lady passenger. "Could you tell him what to do in case of an attack?"

"Tain't necessary, mum," replied the captain, "He'll do it."

2716. Traveler: one who usually returns brag and baggage.
— *Des Moines Register*

2717. "If you go to London," Gertrude Lawrence is reported to have told an American friend, "there's one place you must be sure of visiting."

"Where is that?" asked the friend.

"Paris," said Miss Lawrence. — B. A. YOUNG, *Punch*

truth

2718. Truth is a thing immortal and perpetual, and it gives to us a beauty that fades not away in time, nor does it take away that freedom of speech which proceeds from justice, but it gives to us the knowledge of what is just and lawful.   — EPICTETUS

2719.   There are three sides to every story:
  1. Your side
  2. My side
  3. The Truth

2720.   A lie is a poor substitute for the truth, but the only one so far discovered.

2721.   Some people have tact; others tell the truth.

2722.   "You have heard what the last witness said," persisted counsel, "and yet your evidence is to the contrary. Am I to infer that you wish to throw doubt on her veracity?"
  The polite young man waved a deprecating hand. "Not at all," he replied, "I merely wished to make it clear what a liar I am if she's speaking the truth."

2723.   "Did you ever see one of those machines that can tell when a person is not telling the truth?"
  "Did I ever see one? I married one!"

2724.   All truth is safe and nothing else is safe; and he who keeps back the truth, or withholds it from men, from motives of expedience, is either a coward or a criminal, or both.   — MAX MULLER

2725.   "I want an explanation and I want the truth."
  "Make up your mind. You can't have both."

2726.   The only answer to error is a statement of truth, and not forceful suppression.

2727.   An offended and angry patient strode into the room of the Sanatorium gossip.
  "Look here," she cried, "you have been telling lies about me."
  "That's right," replied the nosy one. "I know it, but what would you do if I told the truth?"

2728. Truth it not only violated by falsehood; it may be equally outraged by silence.

2729. No man has a good enough memory to be a successful liar. — ABRAHAM LINCOLN

2730. Nothing is more criminal, mean, or ridiculous, than lying. It is the production either of malice, cowardice or vanity; but it generally misses of its aim in everyone of these views; for lies are always detected sooner or later. — LORD CHESTERFIELD

2731. If one tells the truth, one is sure sooner or later to be found out. — OSCAR WILDE

2732. An error is the more dangerous in proportion to the degree of truth which it contains. — AMIEL

2733. Neurotic: A person who, when you ask how she is, tells you.

2734. Withholding the truth suggests falsehood. — LEGAL MAXIM

2735. Martinelli, the famous opera singer was approached by two newspaper reporters who sought to interview him about his smoking habits.

"Tobacco! Cigarettes! Cigars! Bahhh!" said the singer. "I would not think of it."

"But, sir," one of the reporters interposed, "I remember that you recently endorsed a cigarette in an ad and said that it did not irritate your throat."

"Yes, yes, of course I gave the endorsement. I did do that. How could it irritate my throat? I have never smoked."

2736. Legend: a lie that has attained the dignity of age.

2737. If a crooked stick is before you, you need not explain how crooked it is. Lay a straight one down by the side of it, and the work is well done. Preach the truth, and error will stand abashed in its presence. — SPURGEON

2738. No boy can tell me two lies running; he gives himself away by his manner. But little girls look at me with starry eyes and take me in every time. Ladies with whom I have discussed this question say that it is merely a matter of sex — they are equally unable to detect boys in untruths. — CANON PETER GREEN, quoted in *Medley*

2739. "Billy, do you know what happens to little boys who tell lies?"

"Sure, they ride for half fare."

2740. Falsity binds and enslaves; truth makes men free.

2741. Epigram: a half truth so stated as to irritate the person who believes the other half.

2742. A man who won't lie to a woman has very little consideration for her feelings. — OLIN MILLER

turnabout

2743. Zoo: a place devised for animals to study the habits of human beings. — OLIVER HERFORD

2744. Emerging from the theater one night when New York was bathed in a ground-soaker, Adele Longmire, the actress, hailed taxis in vain. At last an ancient cab hove into sight, and as she hailed it the driver first glared at her, then laughed, and wouldn't stop. She pursued him till he was halted by a traffic light and climbed in, threatening to report him for his lofty behavior.

"Well," he confessed, "youse look like a regular dame, so I'll tell you. It's like dis. When de weather's nice, all youse snooty people toin up your noses at dis old bus for dose new shiny wagons. So when a rainy night comes along, I allus rides around and laff my head off at youse. Costs me ten bucks, but it's worth it!" — GEORGE ROSS, *N. Y. World Telegram*

2745. One of the reasons why you can buy an electric light bulb today for 15 cents that in 1931 would have cost 40 cents, and would have delivered only half the present quantity of light, is the joke old-timers in General Electric's lamp division used to play on new engineers. They were assigned the "impossible" task of frosting bulbs on the inside. Such a bulb would diffuse more light with less absorption, but everyone knew it couldn't be done, and each perspiring neophyte forgave the snickers greeting his failure.

One day, however, Marvin Pipkin was initiated. And he not only found a way to frost bulbs on the inside, but developed an etching acid which gave minute rounded pits instead of sharp depressions, thus materially strengthening each bulb. No one told him it couldn't be done, and he took it so seriously that he did it.

— *Christian Science Monitor*

2746. When in America, Dr. Wu Ting-fang, the grand old man of the Chinese diplomatic service in his day, was questioned sweetly by an American:

"What 'nese' are you — Japanese, Javanese, Chinese?"

Replying that he was Chinese, he asked in turn: "and what 'kee' are you — monkey, donkey, or Yankee?"

— L. Z. YUAN, *Shanghai Evening Post and Mercury*

2747. At a dinner some years ago in honor of the newly elected president of the University of Chicago, Dr. Robert M. Hutchins, a visiting educator who did not know the young president remarked to the lady at his side, "So that is the new president!"

"I beg your pardon, but do you know who I am?" the lady asked stiffly. The visiting dean admitted that he did not. "Well," she remarked icily, "I am Mrs. Hutchins."

The stranger was stricken dumb for a moment, then said, "I'm sorry. Do you know who I am?" Mrs. Hutchins shook her head.

"Thank God," the dean responded weakly.   — MILTON BACON

2748. Chauncey Depew, asked what kind of exercise he took, answered: "I get my exercise acting as pallbearer to my friends who exercise."   — *Readers Digest*

2749. "I'm sure you will like Jack," said the oldest daughter, just home from college. "He's a fine young man."

"Has he got any property?" demanded her father.

"Oh, you men are so curious," sighed the girl. "Jack asked me the same thing about you."

2750. When the German delegation came to Marshal Foch at the end of the War to ask for armistice terms, the Frenchman picked up a paper from his desk and read a set of conditions. "But — there must be some mistake," the leader of the German officers stammered in dismay. "These are terms which no civilized nation could impose on another!"

"I am very glad to hear you say so," replied Foch gravely. "No, gentlemen, these are not our terms. They are the terms imposed on Lille by the German commander when that city surrendered.

> — SIR BASIL THOMSON, *The Scene
> Changes* (Doubleday, Doran)

2751. *Boss:* "Sir, what does this mean? Someone just called up and said that you were sick and could not come to work today."

Clerk: "Ha, ha! The joke's on him. He wasn't supposed to call up until tomorrow."

typical

2752. A woman came to an Ozark town looking for a "Hillbilly." At last she pointed out a dirty, bewhiskered man after a long and disappointing afternoon of watching a crowd of average-looking farmers at their Saturday buying. "There now!" she exclaimed to her hostess. "Isn't he typical?"
> — EVERETT and OLGA WEBBER,
> *In Them Hills, Holiday*

tyranny

2753. Where law ends, tyranny begins.
> — WILLIAM PITT, speech Jan. 9, 1770

2754. Rebellion to tyrants is obedience to God.
> — (Inscription on a cannon near which the ashes
> of Pres. John Bradshaw were lodged, on top
> hill near Martha Bay in Jamaica)

unanimity

2755. One day a rent collector knocked three times at a certain house without getting a reply. Becoming enraged, he went back a fourth time, and in response to his knock an urchin opened the door.

"Where were you all day?" demanded the collector.

"I was out," replied the boy.

"Where is your father?"

"He's out."

"Where is your mother?"

"She's out."

"Well," said the collector, "I will just go in and sit at the fire until someone of them returns."

"But the fire's out, too," quickly responded the boy.

understanding

2756   IF I KNEW YOU

If I knew you and you knew me;
    if both of us could clearly see,
And with an inner sight divine,
    the meaning of your heart and mine.
I'm sure that we should differ less;
    And clasp our hands in friendliness;
Our thoughts would pleasantly agree,
    If I knew you and you knew me.

If I knew you and you knew me,
    as each one knows his ownself, we
Could look each other in the face,
    and see therein a truer grace.
Life has so many hidden woes,
    So many thorns for every rose,
The "Why" of things our hearts would see
    If I knew you and you knew me.
                     — *Author Unknown*

2757.   People, like boats, toot loudest when they're in a fog.

2758.   It is better to understand a little than to misunderstand a lot.   — ANATOLE FRANCE

2759.   I never could understand how a person speaking only English thought it funny to hear broken English spoken by a foreigner who could speak 10 other languages, too.
                     — GRACIE ALLEN

2760.   I have found you an argument; I am not obliged to find you an understanding.   — DR. JOHNSON, *Boswell's Life of Johnson*

2761. From the summit of power men no longer turn their eyes upwards, but begin to look about them.

— LOWELL, *Among My Books*

2762.   IF WE KNEW EACH OTHER BETTER

If we knew each other better,
We would praise where now we blame,
We would know each bears his burden
Wears some hidden cross of shame.
We would feel the heartaches bitter
They so long alone have borne,
If we knew each other better,
We would praise instead of scorn.

If we knew each other better,
You and I and all the rest,
Seeing down beneath the surface
To the sorrows all unguessed,
We would quit our cold complaining
And a hand of trust extend;
If we knew each other better
We would count each one a friend.

We can know each other better
If we take the time to try,
Little deeds of loving kindness
Make a better by-and-by;
Just a look of understanding
Brings a touch with all mankind;
We can know each other better —
Yes, — seeking, we shall find. — ANNETTE DENSTED

vanity

2763. Horace Greeley was accused of being a self-made man who worshipped his creator.

— IRVING STONE, *They Also Ran*

variety

2764. A variety of nothing is better than a monotony of something.

— JEAN PAUL RICHTER

virtue

2765. Thank God every morning when you get up that you have something to do that day which must be done, whether you like it or not. Being forced to work, and forced to do your best, will breed in you temperance and self-control, diligence and strength of will, cheerfulness and content, and a hundred virtues which the idle never know.
— CHARLES KINGSLEY

2766. She is chaste who was never asked the question.
— WILLIAM CONGREVE

vision – foresightedness

2767. An American, visiting in France came upon a scene where a large church was being erected. He approached three stone masons, one after the other. Of each he asked this question: "What are you doing?" The first replied: "I'm cutting stone." The second said: "I'm cutting stone for seven francs a day." The third responded: "I'm helping to build a great cathedral."

2768. Some years ago, in a Federal courtroom in New York, a sardonic district attorney presented to a jury a glass gadget which looked something like a small electric light bulb. With masterly scorn he accused the defendant of claiming that by use of this "worthless" device, the human voice would some day be transmitted across the Atlantic. He said that gullible investors had been persuaded by such preposterous claims to buy stock in a company and urged prison terms for the defendant and his partners. Two of the associates were convicted, but the inventor got off with a severe lecture from the judge.

The defendant in this case was Lee de Forest; the "worthless glass bulb" was the audion tube, greatest single invention of the 20th century and the foundation of today's four billion dollar electronics industry.
— HARLAND MANCHESTER, *His Gadget the World* (Argosy)

2769. You must scale the mountains if you would view the plain.
— CHINESE PHILOSOPHER

2770. If you keep your eyes so fixed on heaven that you never look at the earth, you will stumble into hell. — AUSTIN O'MALLEY

2771. He was so narrow-minded he could see through a keyhole with two eyes.
— ESTHER FORBES

2772. "I will not permit thirty men to travel 400 miles merely to agitate a bag of wind," said President White of Cornell University, in 1873, when the University of Michigan challenged Cornell to a football game to be played at Cleveland, with thirty men on a side.
— JOHN McCARTHY, *The Commentator*

2773. A task without a vision is drudgery. A vision without a task is a dream. A task with a vision is victory.

2774. "I hope you are not afraid of microbes," apologized the paying teller as he cashed the school teacher's check with soiled currency.

"Don't worry," said the young lady. "A microbe couldn't live on my salary."
— *The Seamen's Journal*

war – peace

2775. A man began to lose his hair. It got thinner and thinner until finally he had but one hair left. He brushed that hair and combed it and shampooed it. One morning he woke up and looked down upon his pillow and there was the hair. He exclaimed: "My God! I'm bald." It is that way with war. It comes on gradually over many years. We wake up and find ourselves at war, but the roots of that war lie way back in the motives and habits and institutions of mankind.
— JOY ELMER MORGAN, "Foundations of World Order." Reprinted from *School and Society*, Aug. 11, 1945, with permission of William W. Brickman, Editor; Stanley Lehrer, Managing Editor

2776. All great wars create as many problems as they settle.
— ROBERT STRAUSZ-HUPE, *The Balance of Tomorrow* (Putman)

2777. Man is a wonderful fellow, learning from the other animals the way he does. He studies the hawk and the vulture and flies through the air with the greatest of ease. He learns from the crab with its shell and the skunk with its tear gas. He considers the ways of the squirrel and becomes a hoarder; the ways of the snake in the grass and the shark and the crocodile, the mole and the hedgehog,

and makes himself terrible on land and sea and underneath both . . . .
About the only creature left in nature for him to learn something
useful from is the dove.   *— New York Times Magazine*

2778. It cost about 75 cents to kill a man in Caesar's time. The
price rose to about $3,000 per man during the Napoleonic wars; to
$5,000 in the American Civil War; and then to $21,000 per man in
World War I. Estimates for the future wars indicate that it may cost
the warring countries not less than $50,000 for each man killed.
    — SENATOR HOMER T. BONE

2779. We believe that the really impractical people in this world
are those who resign themselves to wars on an inevitable, recurrent,
and ever more destructive basis. People who called themselves hard-
headed realists have proved on former occasions that the thirteen
colonies could never be united, that modern industry could not
function without child labor, that education of all the children of
all the people was an impious and scandalous notion, that chattel
slavery could not be destroyed because it was divinely approved, that
no gentleman could ever adjudicate a personal quarrel except with a
pistol at forty paces, and that the flying machine was a physical
impossibility, the steamboat a dreamer's folly, and the telephone a
passing fad.   *— Education and the People's Peace*

2780. Two U.S. Indians were talking things over between air
raids in a Saipan foxhole during World War II.
"The way I figure," one said, "when they smoked the pipe of peace
in 1918, nobody inhaled."

2781.   Green and yellow are the fields of peace,
       Red in the time of war
   Black are the fields when the cannons cease
      And white forevermore.

2782. It is a biological principle that it is easier to stop a seed
from growing than to kill a poisonous plant after it has attained its
full growth. Could we not apply the knowledge of science toward the
eradication of future conflicts? — H. H. STEVENS, "Begin with German
       Youth," *Religious Digest*

402

2783. Overheard in a defense plant during World War II:
"If this war continues, some of the war workers may be so worn out they'll begin to look like the photos on their badges."
— *Louisville Courier-Journal*

2784. The best way to end a war is not to begin it.

2785. The thing that makes war inevitable is the conviction that it is inevitable.

2786. The motto of some countries today:
Business as usual during altercations.

2787. Very frequently a fight for what is right degenerates into a quarrel for what is left.

2788. It also takes two to make up after a quarrel.
— NATE COLLIER, *Peoria Star*

2789. Ocean: huge body of water surrounded entirely by rumors of everlasting peace.

2790. War: a monster which will destroy us unless we destroy it.
— VISCOUNT JAMES BRYCE

2791. Peace: a short pause between wars for enemy identifications.
— CLEMENS KIRCHNER

waste

2792. *He:* "The tunnel we just passed through cost a million dollars."
Fair one: "It was an absolute waste of money so far as you are concerned."

weakness

2793. There are two kinds of weakness; that which breaks and that which bends.
— LOWELL, *Among My Books*

wealth – See also *Poverty*

2794. Most people believe that because a man has made a fortune his views on any subject are valuable. I have always believed that most large fortunes are made by men of ordinary ability who tumbled into a lucky opportunity and could not help getting rich, and in most cases, others, given the same chance, would have done far better with it. Hard work and attention to business are necessary, but they rarely result in achieving a large fortune. Do not be fooled into believing that because a man is rich he is necessarily smart. There is ample proof to the contrary.　　　— JULIUS ROSENWALD

2795. I congratulate poor young men upon being born to that ancient and honorable degree which renders it necessary that they should devote themselves to hard work.　　— ANDREW CARNEGIE

2796. He who multiplies riches multiplies cares.
　　　　　　　　　　　　　　　　— BENJAMIN FRANKLIN

2797. "I'm glad to find you as you are," said the old friend. "Your wealth hasn't changed you."
　"Well," replied the candid millionaire, "it has changed me in one way. I'm now eccentric where I used to be impolite, and delightfully witty where I used to be rude."

2798. A man is rich according to what he gives, not what he has.
　　　　　　　　　　　　　　　　— HENRY WARD BEECHER

2799. Money is an article which may be used as a universal passport to everywhere except Heaven, and as a universal provider of everything except happiness.　　　— *Wall Street Journal*

2800. Riches are not an end of life, but an instrument of life.
　　　　　　　　　　　　　　　　— HENRY WARD BEECHER

2801. A good name is better than riches.
　　　　　　　　　　　　　　　— CERVANTES, *Don Quixote*

2802. Poverty is not essentially a lack of money; nor is the mere lack of money poverty. Rather, poverty is the lack of ability, in any given set of circumstances, to get whatever is necessary for comfortable living. . . .
　The millions of world citizens who have never known much about money would be little better off if they received a weekly pay-check.

In fact, stories have come out of the South Pacific to the effect that some of the natives see no point in cashing the army checks they receive. These natives are penniless — poor from our point of view — and don't know it. — EDWARD H. FAULKNER, "Uneasy Money," *University of Oklahoma Press*

2803. The money that men make lives after them.
— SAMUEL BUTLER

2804. How easy it is for a man to die rich, if he will but be contented to live miserable. — HENRY FIELDING

2805. Some people lose their health getting wealth and then lose the wealth regaining health.

2806. Fortune does not make men, it only unmasks them.
— RICCOBONI

2807. Wealth is the smallest thing on earth, the least gift that God has bestowed on mankind. — MARTIN LUTHER, *Of the Nature of the World*

2808. A man can no more make a safe use of wealth without reason, than he can of a horse without a bridle. — SOCRATES

2809. He started as poor as the proverbial church mouse twenty years ago. He has now retired with a fortune of $50,000.00. This money was acquired through economy, conscientious effort to give full value, indomitable perseverance, and the death of an uncle who left him $49,999.50.

2810. Wealth may be an excellent thing, for it means power, it means leisure, it means liberty. — JAMES RUSSELL LOWELL, *Democracy and Other Addresses*

2811. Riches are no menace if we do not divorce dollars from sense.

2812. Many speak the truth when they say that they despise riches, but they mean the riches possessed by other men.
— C. C. COLTON

will power — See also *Determination*

2813. Will power: the ability to eat *one* salted peanut.
— *Readers Digest*

wisdom

2814. A wise man is he who does not grieve for the thing which he has not, but rejoices for those which he has. — EPICTETUS

2815.	Wisdom is knowing what to do next.
Skill is knowing how to do it and
Virtue is doing it.

2816. A man should never be ashamed to own he has been in the wrong, which is but saying, in other words, that he is wiser today than he was yesterday. — JONATHAN SWIFT

2817. The man who questions opinions is wise; the man who quarrels with facts is a fool. — FRANK A. GARBUTT

2818. Wise men always know more than they tell but fools tell more than they know.

2819. If a man will begin with certainties, he will end with doubts; but if he will be content to begin with doubts, he will end in certainties. — FRANCIS BACON

2820. A wise man will desire no more than he can get justly, use soberly, distribute cheerfully and leave contentedly.

wit and humor

2821. Charles Lamb once had the misfortune of being seated next to a very garrulous and very senseless woman at a dinner party. She chattered and chattered incessantly and then, discovering that the author was paying no attention to her whatever, rebuked him by saying: "You seem to be none the better for what I am telling you."

"No, madam," he answered, "but this gentleman on the other side of me must be — for it all went in one ear and out the other."

2822. An Englishman, according to popular legends, gets three laughs from a joke — first, when the joke is told; second, when it is explained to him; third, when he understands it.

The Frenchman gets only the first two — he never sees the point.

The German gets only one — he won't wait for an explanation.

And the American gets none at all, because he's heard the joke before.

2823. PUNS

When someone asked Henry Erskine "Is punning the lowest form of wit?" he answered, "Yes, it is, and therefore the foundation of all wit."

And when Killigrew said he could make a pun on any subject, King Charles said, "Make one on me," to which the ready-witted Killigrew answered, "Ah, but the King is no subject."

A gentleman who squinted very badly asked the troubled Talleyrand how things were going. He answered, "Why, as you see, sir," (which was bad indeed).

Thomas Hood liked a pun and his favorite one was about the solicitous undertaker who was seeking to "Urn a lively Hood."

William Walsh's favorite was about a would-be masher of middle age, who was looking at a house. He asked the pretty servant-girl whether she was to let with the establishment. "No, sir," was the answer; "please, sir, I am to be let alone." Here is a pun which hits with both its barrels; each of its two meanings speaks a volume.

> — Adapted from an article by
> M. N. in *High Points*

2824. A jest loses its point when he who makes it is the first to laugh. — SCHILLER, *Fiesco,* Act i., Scene 7

2825. IT'S A POOR JOKE —

When some woman blushes with embarrassment.

When some heart carries away an ache.

When something sacred is made to appear common

When a man's weakness provides the cause for laughter.

When profanity is required to make it funny.

When a little child is brought to tears.

When everyone can't join in the laughter.

woman – women

2826. THE 7 AGES OF WOMAN

In her infancy she needs love and care.
In childhood she wants fun.
In her teen age she wants excitement.
In her twenties she wants romance.
In her thirties she wants admiration.
In her forties she wants sympathy.
In her fifties she wants cash.

2827. A woman admiring a friend's unusual piece of jewelry remarked: "I love it, it's so modern! It makes you look as though someone had cared for you recently."

2828. The Kinsey report proved just one thing: women like to talk.

2829. A woman may race to get a man a gift but it always ends in a tie. — EARL WILSON

2830. One of the most charming women in society, a peeress, remarked to H.R.H., the Prince of Wales:
  "I wish I could go into business. I should like to decorate houses."
  "By living in them Lady . . . ?" asked the prince.

2831. The difference between conversation and gossip is this: when three women stand at a street corner talking to each other, that's conversation. When one of them leaves that's gossip.

2832. There are many times where a woman would gladly drop her husband if she did not feel morally certain that some other woman would come right along and pick him up.
— HELEN ROWLAND, *Guide to Men*

2833. When Beau Brummell was asked the secret of his success with women, he answered: "Oh, I merely treat the charwomen like duchesses, and the duchesses like charwomen."
— MARGERY WILSON, *Your Life*

2834. Nature has given women so much power that the law has very wisely given them very little. — SAMUEL JOHNSON

2835. There's nothing strange in the fact that the modern girl is a live wire. She carries practically no insulation.

2836. *Harvard graduate:* "The members of my class who have married have had an average of a little less than two children."

Vassar graduate: "Isn't that remarkable? The married women of my class have averaged almost three. I wonder what that proves?"

Harvard graduate: "Oh, not much. Simply that women have more children than men."

2837. The only kind of letters women love to receive are those which never should have been written.

2838. A man likes you for what he thinks you are; a woman, for what you think she is. — IVAN PANIN

2839. In Europe, every woman is every other woman's instinctive enemy. In America, women band together in clubs, crowd happily to lectures, and, so far as I can see, actually seem to like each other. — C. E. M. JOAD, *The London Mercury*

2840. Three women can keep a secret if two are dead.

2841. A good woman inspires a man, a brilliant woman interests him, a beautiful woman fascinates him — the sympathetic woman gets him. — HELEN ROWLAND

2842. Modern girls adore spinning wheels — but they like four of them, and a spare.

2843. They say that it takes a man about two minutes to decide on a new hat — a woman about two hours. That is why woman's hats are so expensive. It is the overhead time charge.

2844. A lady approached Congressman John Allen, of Mississippi, one day and held out her hand. "Now confess, Mr. Allen," she said, "that you've forgotten all about me."

He had. He knew her face, but his memory would serve him no further. But with a low bow he replied, "Madam, I've made it the business of my life to try to forget you." — O. HENRY

2845. Womankind is divided into two classes — the careless ones who lose their gloves, and the careful ones who lose only one glove.
— This Week

2846. The easiest way to change a woman's mind is to agree with her.

2847. *Patron:* "Have you a book called, 'Man, the Master of Woman'?"
Assistant librarian: "You'll find the fiction on those shelves right over there."

2848. Some girls' clothes are fitting and proper; others are just fitting.

2849. She always makes a hit with men but never a home run.

2850. Womankind suffers from three delusions: marriage will reform a man; a rejected lover is heartbroken for life; and if the other women were only out of the way, he would come back.
— Myrtle Reed

2851. In the French Parliament, one of the Deputies, making a speech urging the improvement of the legal status of women, cried: "After all, there is very little difference between men and women!"
With great accord, the entire Chamber of Deputies rose and shouted as one man: "Vive la difference!"

— Reprinted from The Art of Conversation by Milton Wright. Published by the McGraw-Hill Book Company, Inc., New York, N. Y., Copyright 1936, by the McGraw-Hill Book Co., Inc.

2852. What every man in his heart of hearts desires is a woman to whom he can safely tell everything, to whom he can turn in his weariness, to whom he can take his defeats and failures, the lost things, the lamps that are gone out, the hopes that are ashes, the springs that spring no more, the secret, sordid things that eat him up, that drag him down. *— Alfred Edye, Mainly About Women* (Goeffrey Dies, Ltd.)

2853. What passes for woman's intuition is often nothing more than man's transparency. *— George Jean Nathan*

2854. It is surprising how often a woman is holding the ladder a man climbs to success.

2855. Physicians say one million women are overweight. These of course, are round figures.

2856. Women's styles may change, but their designs remain the same.
— OSCAR WILDE

2857. A horse is usually a horse; but a woman can also be a nag.

2858. *Q.* Why don't women achieve as much as men do?
A. Women have no wives.
— PROFESSOR MARJORIE NICHOLSON,
Barnard College (in response to
question on radio Q and A
program)

2859. Modern women fall into two classes: those who make a home for a man and those who make a man for a home.
— EARL WILSON

2860. The weaker sex is the stronger sex because of the weakness of the stronger sex for the weaker sex.

2861. Life has a way of evening up things. For every woman who makes a fool out of some man there's another who makes a man out of some fool.

2862.   WOMAN:
CHEMICAL COMPOSITION AND PROPERTIES
Species: A member of the human family.
Occurrence: Can be found wherever man exists. Seldom occurs in the free or native state. Quality depends on the state in which it is found, the combined state is to be preferred.
Physical Properties: All colors and sizes. Always appears in disguised condition. Surface of face seldom unprotected by coating of paint or film of powder (composition immaterial).
Chemical Properties: Extremely active. Possesses a great affinity for gold, silver, platinum and precious stones of all kinds. Violent reaction when left alone by men. Ability to absorb all sorts of expensive food at any time. Undissolved by liquids, but activity is greatly increased when saturated with spirit solutions. Sometimes yields to pressure. Turns green when placed next to a better appear-

ing sample. Ages very rapidly. Fresh variety has great magnetic attraction.

Note: Highly explosive and likely to be dangerous in inexperienced hands.

2863. At a large banquet Lady Astor once remarked that men were vainer than women and, meeting with stormy opposition declared herself ready to substantiate her statement. Steering the conversation to men's fashions, she suddenly said in a loud voice: "It's a pity that the most intelligent and learned men attach least importance to the way they dress. Why right at this table the most cultivated man is wearing the most clumsily knotted tie!"

As if on a given signal, every man in the room immediately put his hand to his tie to straighten it.   — *L'Humeur* (Paris)

2864. All women love brutal men — if their husbands are kind.

2865. The Manu moral code which governs the lives of 250,-000,000 Hindus condones lying only when saving a life and when paying a compliment to a woman.

2866. Women without principle draw considerable interest.

2867. Arguing with a woman is like trying to read a newspaper in a high wind.

2868. People who wish they were as "strong as a horse" or as "contented as a cow" may be surprised to learn which mammal actually lives the longest. It is not the horse, not the cow, not the hippopotamus, not even the durable elephant. The longest-living mammal today is woman. The average girl can expect to live fully seventy-one years. The mighty elephant, once ranked as the longest-living mammal, now lags far behind with its sixty-year life span. The hippo has an expectancy of forty; the horse twenty to twenty-five; and the cow averages from nine to fifteen years. Even men live longer than elephants these days, an average of sixty-five years.

The turtle, which is not a mammal, lives at least a century longer than human beings. But the turtle can't brag about its advanced age and women probably won't, so we men are safe.

   — CEDRIC ADAMS, *Minneapolis Tribune*

2869. A woman will never forgive a man if she is wrong.

2870. You can never tell about a woman, and if you can, you shouldn't.

2871. The only way a man can get the better of a woman in an argument is to let her keep on talking after she has won it.

2872. Differentiation between the sexes:
Women prefer shopping on the sunny side of the street, while men prefer to do their business on the shady side.

2873. I have heard Lincoln say he thanked God that he was not born a woman, because he could not refuse any request if it was not apparently dishonest. — HERNDON, *The Life of Lincoln*

2874. A woman's face is her fortune — and sometimes it runs into a nice little figure.

2875. Women have a wonderful instinct about things. They can discover everything except the obvious. — OSCAR WILDE

2876. Women have a much better time than men in this world; there are far more things forbidden them. — OSCAR WILDE

2877. There is only one real tragedy in a woman's life. The fact that her past is always her lover, and her future invariably her husband. — OSCAR WILDE

2878. Women are pictures; men are problems: if you want to know what a woman really means, look at her, don't listen to her. — OSCAR WILDE

2879. All women become like their mothers — that is their tragedy. No man does. That is his. — OSCAR WILDE

2880. When a man has a birthday, sometimes he takes a day off; when a woman has one, she takes at least a year off.

2881. If men knew all that women think, they'd be twenty times more daring. — ALPHONSE KARR

2882. Our vocabulary is defective; we give the same name to woman's lack of temptation as to man's lack of opportunity.

— AMBROSE BIERCE

2883. Is it because they have been trying to fill men's shoes that experts tell us women's feet are two sizes larger than they were twenty years ago?

2884. Strange it is, but we never hear of a self-made woman.

2885. To have the last word with a woman — apologize.

2886. In telling her age a woman is often shy in more ways than one.

2887. Brigands demand your money or your life; women require both.

— SAMUEL BUTLER

2888. Being a woman is a terribly difficult trade, since it consists principally of dealing with men.

— JOSEPH CONRAD

2889. It is a characteristic of good wives that they feel and resent an injury to their husbands much more than they do one done to themselves. Women's feeling are aroused only when we have regained the guiding-rope which seemed to slip out of our hands.

— BISMARCK, from collection by
von Poschinger

2890. Women forgive injuries, but never forget slights.

— THOMAS C. HALIBURTON

2891. When a man does good work out of all proportion to his pay, in seven cases out of nine there is a woman at the back of the virtue.

— RUDYARD KIPLING, *Plain Tales
from the Hills*

2892. If God made woman beautiful, he made her so to be looked at — to give pleasure to the eyes which rest upon her — and she has no business to dress herself as if she were a hitching post, or to transform that which should give delight to those among whom she moves, into a ludicrous caricature of a woman's form.

— TIMOTHY TITCOMB, *Lessons in Life*

2893. The cruelest revenge of a woman is to remain faithful to a man.

— JACQUES BOSSUET

2894. Woman: a person who can hurry through a drug store aisle 18 inches wide without brushing against the piled up tinware and then drive home and still knock off one of the doors of a 12-foot garage.

2895. Woman: a person who will spend $20 on a beautiful slip and then be annoyed if it shows.

2896. Give a woman an inch and she thinks she's a ruler.

2897. There is no such thing as a dangerous woman; there are only susceptible men.
— JOSEPH WOOD KRUTCH

2898. Women are meant to be loved, not to be understood.
— OSCAR WILDE

2899. Women resist in order to be conquered.
— *Italian Proverb*

2900. A bad girl: nothing but a good girl found out.

2901. Chemical warfare: the eternal conflict between blondes and brunettes.
— *Purdue Engineer*

2902. Intuition: suspicion in skirts.

2903. Water works: a woman's tears.

2904. Counter irritant: the woman who shops all day and buys nothing.
— *Milwaukee Journal*

2905. Do right and fear no man. Don't write and fear no woman.

2906. A coquette is a woman without a heart, who makes a fool of a man who has no head.

2907. Debutante: a bareback with greenbacks.

2908. Thirty is a great age for a woman . . . young enough for an interesting future; old enough for an interesting past.

2909. Woman is like your shadow. Follow her, she flies; flee her, she follows. — *Chinese Proverb*

2910. Why is the word "tongue" feminine in Greek, Latin, Italian, Spanish, French, and German? — Austin O'Malley

2911. I wish Adam had died with all his ribs in his body. — Dion Boucicault

2912. One woman's poise is another woman's poison. — Katherine Brush

2913. Feminine wile: keeping a man at arm's length by a hair's breadth.

words

2914. When the report went around that Rudyard Kipling was getting a shilling a word for his writings, some Oxford students set about a "rag." They sent him a shilling, accompanied by this message:

"Please send us one of your words."
And right back came the unexpected answer:
"Thanks."

2915. Language is the apparel in which your thoughts parade before the public. Never clothe them in vulgar or shoddy attire. — Dr. George W. Crane, *Psychology Applied*

2916. "Mamma," shrieked the little boy, watching his toy train in operation, "it's faster than hell, ain't it?"

"Willie," exclaimed the modern mother, "how many times do I have to tell you never to use that vulgar word 'ain't?' "

2917. A synonym is a word you use when you can't spell the other one.

work — See also *Labor*

2918. An old negro went to the office of the commissioner of registration in a Missouri town and applied for registration papers.

"What is your name?" asked the official.

"George Washington," was the reply.

"Well, George, are you the man who cut down the cherry-tree?"

"No suh, I ain't de man. I ain't done no work for nigh onto a year."

worry

2919. Many of us worry about things that won't happen. We're like the patient in a mental hospital who stood with his ear to the wall, listening intently. "Sh!" he whispered, beckoning an attendant. The attendant pressed his ear to the wall. "I can't hear anything," he reported. "No," replied the patient, "it's been like that all day!"

2920. Don't worry over possible mishaps of tomorrow, for thou knowest not what a day may bring forth. Tomorrow thou mayest not exist, and hence will have worried over a world to which thou dost not belong. — *The Talmud*

2921. Worry doesn't pay. A lot of folks I know have acquired gray hair from worrying about getting gray hair.

2922. Worry is interest paid on trouble before it falls due.

2923. Never worry because the tide is going out. It always comes back.

writing

2924. Manuscript: something submitted in haste and returned at leisure. — Oliver Herford

youth

2925. The future alone can in some measure redeem the dead. As a seventeen year old miner's son said recently: "The last generation let us down. We must see to it that we don't let down the next."
— Mary Seaton, "Billy Turner, War's Child," *Free World*

2926. The old believe everything; the middle-aged suspect everything; the young know everything.

2927. When I was a boy of fourteen, my father was so ignorant I could hardly stand to have the old man around. But when I got to be twenty-one, I was astonished at how much the old man had learned in those seven years. — MARK TWAIN

2928.   IN DEFENSE OF YOUTH
We call them wrong! God pity us, the blind,
Imputing evil as our grandsires did,
When we explored new realms with feet and mind,
Uncovering what old fogies damned and hid!
The dreams, the wanton fantasies are there
As you and I once knew them, loved them till
We came to staleness and to foolish fear
Lest something change, be different, jolt our will!
'Tis life they seek, not sin, no sordid thing,
But joy in 'ealth and beauty, and in all
The urge of thrilling bodies that would sing
And freely dance with laughter at earth's call.
Let's laugh with them, full knowing that when tried
By Truth and Duty, Youth is on God's side!
                              — ROBBINS WOLCOTT BARSTOW

2929. Physically, the adolescent is like a house on moving day — a temporary mess. — JULIUS E. WARREN, "Are High Schools of Any Value?," *Quote*

2930. The happy people of this world are never free. It is only youth which really wants freedom, or those who have set up a defensive mechanism against life, since to live is also to suffer. The older and wiser know that nothing is of value unless it can be shared, and that the eternal cry of the human heart is to belong to someone else. It is its escape from loneliness, its support in weakness, a solace to its pride. Even youth should think twice before it asks for freedom. Surely to be happy is better than to be free; and to be kind to all, to like many and love a few, to be needed and wanted by those we love, is certainly the nearest we can come to happiness.
                              — MARY ROBERTS RINEHART

2931. The older generation thought nothing of getting up at six in the morning. . . . We can assure you the younger generation doesn't think much of it either.

2932. If I could get to the highest place in Athens I would lift up my voice and say: "What mean ye, fellow citizens, that ye turn every stone to scrape wealth together, and take so little care of your children, to whom ye must one day relinquish all? — SOCRATES

2933. A man is not old until regrets take the place of dreams.
— JOHN BARRYMORE

2934. Policeman Jones had a late night beat. Strolling along a street at three o'clock in the morning, he noticed a man sitting on the front steps of a house.

"What are you doing here at three a.m.?" he asked.

"I've lost my key," was the answer, "and I'm waiting for my children to come home and let me in."

2935. Youth is not a time of life — it is a state of mind. It is a temper of the will, a quality of the imagination, a vigor of the emotions. It is a freshness of the deep springs of life. Youth means a predominance of courage over timidity, of the appetite of adventure over the love of ease.

Nobody grows old by merely living a number of years. People grow old by deserting their ideals.

2936. Youth is glorious, but it isn't a career.
— From an Editorial in the *St. Louis Post-Dispatch*

2937. Bert Lahr told Ruth Chatterton he wanted to play a romantic lead opposite her. "But Bert, you have gray hair," objected Miss Chatterton.

"Well," snorted the comedian, "just because there's snow on the roof don't think there's no fire inside!"   — *The Woman*

2938. Obstinacy in children is like a kite; it is kept up just as long as we pull against it.   — MARCELENE COX, *Ladies Home Journal*

2939. A friend of mine (he happens to be the president of a big bank) has a six-year-old son who is beginning to ask embarrassing questions. When the father took him to the circus recently, the lad was fascinated by some of the Ubangi savages. Their black skin, showing above their costumes, for some reason interested him more than anything else. In fact, he could not take his eyes off one of the big-lipped belles.

Pulling his father aside, he asked:

"Are they black all over, father?"

"Yes, my son," replied the banker.

"Gee, pop, you know everything," came back the lad.

— *Source Unknown*

2940. The child's point of view was aptly expressed in a recent essay by a boy. "The world," he wrote, "is full of people who keep saying, 'I was a boy myself once,' but who never show any signs of it."

— JOHN A. F. WATSON, *Spectator*

2941. A child asked a man to pick a flower for her. That was simple enough. But when she said, "Now put it back," the man experienced a baffling helplessness he never knew before. "How can you explain that it cannot be done?" he asked. "How can one make clear to young people that there are some things which when once broken, once mutilated, can never be replaced or mended?"

— MARCIA BOROWSKY, "Education for the New World Order," *Quote*

2942. Up to sixteen, a lad is a Boy Scout. After that he is a girl scout.

2943. On an NBC television broadcast, Lewis B. Hershey, as Draft Director was discussing the question of when a boy becomes an adult. "A boy becomes an adult," he said, "three years before his parents think he does — and about two years after he thinks he does."

2944. Two small boys put their hands side by side.

"Hah! Mine's dirtier'n yours," said one.

"Well," said the other, "You're a year older'n me."

2945. Youth is past when the sensation of adventure is ended, when instead of the boundless expectation and curiosity that penetrates all the corners of existence, a man is content to take things as they are, when eagerness gives way to a complacency and questioning to the cynicism of experience. The man devoid of curiosity is the man who in the end attains to nothing. — *The Living Age*

420

2946. Youth is not a time of life — it is a state of mind. . . . You are as young as your faith, as old as your doubt; as young as your self confidence, as old as your fear; as young as your hope, as old as your despair.

2947. Who touches a Boy, by the Master's plan
    Is shaping the course of the future man.
Father or mother or teacher or priest,
    Friend or stranger or saint or beast,
Is dealing with one who is living seed,
    And may be the man whom the world shall need.
*   — Author Unknown*

2948. We can report only the fascinating title of an essay which was being written in a school notebook one morning on a Van Cortlandt express. It was: "Do Adolescents Need Parents?" Age of the essayist: about seventeen. — From *Pleasures of Publishing*
(Columbia University Press)

2949. I am not young enough to know everything.
— J. M. BARRIE

2950. Following the birth of his third son, Leonard Lyons, columnist mused: "Before I got married I had three theories about bringing up kids. Now I have three kids — and no theories."
— IRVING HOFFMAN, *Hollywood Reporter*

2951. You cannot do much for a boy if you make up your mind that all boys are bad.

2952. Only the young die good.   — OLIVER HERFORD

2953. The schoolmaster deserves to be beaten himself who beats nature in a boy for a fault.   — THOMAS FULLER

2954.   IF I HAD A BOY
If I had a boy, I would say to him, Son,
Be fair and be square in the race you must run,
Be brave if you lose and be meek if you win,
Be better and nobler than I've ever been,
Be honest and fearless in all that you do,
And Honor the name I have given to you.

If I had a boy, I would want him to know,
We reap in this life just about as we sow,

And we get what we earn, be it little or great,
Regardless of luck and regardless of fate,
I would teach him and show him, the best that I could,
That it pays to be honest and upright and good.

I would make him a pal and a partner of mine,
And show him the things in this world that are fine,
I would show him the things that are wicked and bad,
For I figure this knowledge should come from his Dad,
I would walk with him, talk with him, play with him, too,
And to all of my promises strive to be true.

We would grow up together and I'd be a boy,
And share his trouble and share his joy,
We could work out our problems together and then,
We would lay out our plans when we both would be men.
And Oh! what a wonderful joy it would be,
No pleasure in life could be greater for me.

— FRANK CARLETON NELSON

2955. Morning: the time when the rising generation retires and the retiring generation rises.

2956. As I approve of a youth that has something of the old man in him, so I am no less pleased with an old man that has something of the youth. — CICERO

2957. Hold fast to your illusions — they'll keep you young and happy.

2958. To be able to play with the kids and enjoy it, is a sure sign that you are still young.

2959. Ask the young; they know everything. — *Chinese Proverb*

2960. WHAT IS A BOY?

Between the innocence of babyhood and the dignity of manhood we find a delightful creature called a boy. Boys come in assorted sizes, weights and colors, but all boys have the same creed: To enjoy every second of every minute of every hour of every day and to protest with noise (their only weapon) when their last minute is finished and the adult males pack them off to bed at night.

Boys are found everywhere — on top of, underneath, inside of, climbing on, swinging from, running around, or jumping to. Mothers love them, little girls hate them, older sisters and brothers tolerate them, adults ignore them, and Heaven protects them. A boy is Truth with dirt on its face, Beauty with a cut on its finger, Wisdom with bubble gum in its hair, and the Hope of the future with a frog in its pocket.

When you are busy, a boy is an inconsiderate, bothersome, intruding jangle of noise. When you want him to make a good impression, his brain turns to jelly or else he becomes a savage, sadistic jungle creature bent on destroying the world and himself with it.

A boy is a composite — he has the appetite of a horse, the disposition of a sword swallower, the energy of a pocket-size atomic bomb, the curiosity of a cat, the lungs of a dictator, the imagination of a Paul Bunyan, the shyness of a violet, the audacity of a steel trap, the enthusiasm of a fire cracker, and when he makes something he has five thumbs on each hand.

He likes ice cream, knives, saws, Christmas, comic books, the boy across the street, woods, water (in its natural habitat), large animals, Dad, trains, Saturday mornings, and fire engines. He is not much for Sunday School, company, schools, books without pictures, music lessons, neckties, barbers, girls, overcoats, adults or bedtime.

Nobody else is so early to rise, or so late to supper. Nobody else gets so much fun out of trees, dogs, and breezes. Nobody else can cram into one pocket a rusty knife, a half-eaten apple, 3 feet of string, an empty Bull Durham sack, 2 gum drops, 6 cents, a sling shot, a chunk of unknown substance, and a genuine supersonic code ring with a secret compartment.

A boy is a magical creature — you can lock him out of your work shop, but you can't lock him out of your heart. You can get him out of your study, but you can't get him out of your mind. Might as well give up — he is your captor, your jailer, your boss, and your master — a freckled-face, pint-sized, cat-chasing, bundle of noise. But when you come home at night with only the shattered pieces of your hopes and dreams, he can mend them like new with the two magic words — "Hi Dad!"

— ALAN BECK

2961. WHAT IS A GIRL?

Little girls are the nicest things that happen to people. They are born with a little bit of angel-shine about them and though it wears thin sometimes, there is always enough left to lasso your heart —

even when they are sitting in the mud, or crying temperamental tears, or parading up the street in mother's best clothes.

A little girl can be sweeter (and badder) oftener than anyone else in the world. She can jitter around, and stomp, and make funny noises that frazzle your nerves, yet just when you open your mouth, she stands there demure with that special look in her eyes. A girl is Innocence playing in the mud, Beauty standing on its head, and Motherhood dragging a doll by the foot.

Girls are available in five colors — black, white, red, yellow, or brown, yet Mother Nature always manages to select your favorite color when you place your order. They disprove the law of supply and demand — there are millions of little girls, but each is as precious as rubies.

God borrows from many creatures to make a little girl. He uses the song of a bird, the squeal of a pig, the stubbornness of a mule, the antics of a monkey, the spryness of a grasshopper, the curiosity of a cat, the speed of a gazelle, the slyness of a fox, the softness of a kitten, and to top it all off He adds the mysterious mind of a woman.

A little girl likes new shoes, party dresses, small animals, first grade, noise makers, the girl next door, dolls, make-believe, dancing lessons, ice cream, kitchens, coloring books, make-up, cans of water, going visiting, tea parties, and one boy. She doesn't care so much for visitors, boys in general, large dogs, hand-me-downs, straight chairs, vegetables, snow suits, or staying in the front yard. She is loudest when you are thinking, the prettiest when she has provoked you, the busiest at bedtime, the quietest when you want her to show off, and the most flirtatious when she absolutely must not get the best of you again.

Who else can cause you more grief, joy, irritation, satisfaction, embarrassment, and genuine delight than this combination of Eve, Salome, and Florence Nightingale? She can muss up your home, your hair, and your dignity — spend your money, your time, and your temper — then just when your patience is ready to crack, her sunshine peeks through and you've lost again.

Yes, she is a nerve-wracking nuisance, just a noisy bundle of mischief. But when your dreams tumble down and the world is a mess — when it seems you are pretty much of a fool after all — she can make you a king when she climbs on your knee and whispers, "I love you best of all!"   ALAN BECK

preface to index

I certainly think that the best book in the world would owe the most to a good index, and the worst book, if it had but a good single thought in it, might be kept alive by it.

— HORACE BINNEY

So essential did I consider an index to be to every book, that I proposed to bring a bill into Parliament to deprive an author who publishes a book without an index of the privilege of copyright, and, moreover to subject him for his offence to a pecuniary penalty.

— LORD CAMPBELL, *Lives of the Chief Justices*

subject index

(Numbers in the index refer to selections in the text,
not to page numbers)

subject index

Language, 648, 671, 830, 1216, 1808, 1982, 2190, 2915
Lantern, 188, 929, 2219
Larceny. See also Stealing—Theft, 274, 1345
Lark, 715, 1420
Last, 880, 2658
Late—Lateness. See also Tardiness—Punctuality, 233, 341, 2197, 2228
Latin, 671, 757, 2910
Laughter, 327, 381, 991, 1220, 1366–1369, 2069, 2530, 2822, 2825
Launch—Launching ,1667
Laundry, 1613, 1986, 2099
Law—Laws, 491, 514, 631, 647, 947, 1093, 1316, 1318, 1370–1458, 1643, 1733, 1754, 2734, 2753, 2834
Lawn mower, 1675
Law suit, 1379, 1458
Lawyer, 99, 495, 1352, 1371, 1377, 1388, 1389, 1393, 1398, 1402, 1405, 1408, 1412, 1418, 1423, 1426, 1430, 1444, 1789, 2025
Laziness. See also Industry—Laggard, 789, 1459–1463, 1540, 1546, 1716, 2479, 2539
Lead, 80
Leader—Leadership, 816, 1210, 1464–1469
Leaf—Leaves, 333, 1112
Leak—Leakage, 1247
Learning. See also Education, 672, 737, 743, 745, 767, 775, 781, 1216, 1234, 1298
Leather, 1450
Lecture—Lecturing, 256, 264, 777, 2202
Leg—Legs, 1357, 1495
Legacy, 2809
Legal. See also Law—Courts—Judges —Jury, 2718
Legend, 657, 2736
Legislature—Legislator—Legislation, 654, 1239
Leisure, 1126, 1470, 1471, 2810
Lemon, 575
Lending, 194, 290, 305, 966, 969
Leniency, 1324
Lent, 588
Lesson, 859, 1169, 1170, 1216, 2268
Letters, 205, 1222, 1267, 1457, 1472, 1803, 2837
Level, 1186, 1556
Liberal—Liberalism, 1473, 2246

Liberation. See also Freedom, 945
Liberty. See also Freedom, 514, 941, 942, 950–953, 1411, 1456, 2021, 2810
Liberty, Statue of, 944
Library, 194, 631, 749, 1354, 2847
License, 1281, 1650, 2292
Lie—Liar—Lying. See also Truth, 540, 619, 754, 1025, 1051, 1216, 1389, 1498, 1603, 2024, 2295, 2720, 2729, 2730, 2865
Lie detector, 2723
Life—Living, 14, 25, 112, 115, 179, 180, 276, 285, 336, 362, 385, 390, 453, 461, 469, 477, 483, 491, 514, 570, 591, 600, 624, 661, 758, 761, 774, 976, 1327, 1361, 1474–1494, 1851, 2255, 2459, 2616, 2665, 2887
Light, 188, 1107
Lily—Lilies, 1987
Limb, 813
Limousine, 2685
Linger—Lingering, 1660
Lion, 370, 489
Liquid, 871
Listen—Listener—Listening, 466, 1066, 1083, 1110, 2145, 2878
Literature, 547, 1935
Litigation—Litigant, 1337
Listless—Listlessness, 2570
Live—Living, 278, 514, 1093, 1177, 1216, 1451, 1827
Livelihood, 741, 748, 761, 774, 1460, 1989
Lizard, 1574
Loafing, 380, 1025
Loan, 46, 160, 500, 586
Lock, 636
Lodge, 1958
Logic, 314, 1495
London, England, 567, 669, 701, 720, 1201, 2717
Lonely—Loneliness, 2226, 2930
Longevity, 461, 2869
Long-winded, 1388, 1696, 2119, 2120, 2122, 2127, 2132, 2133, 2147, 2154, 2157, 2158, 2164, 2166, 2167, 2187, 2192, 2193, 2199, 2210, 2212, 2213, 2369, 2377, 2821
Lord, The. See Diety
Los Angeles, Calif., 2672
Lose—Loser—Loss, 443, 499, 566, 592, 1523, 1917, 2413

subject index

Obligation–Obligatory, 514, 613, 2544, 2760
Observance, 1445
Observation, 464, 683, 1052, 1852–1854
Obsession, 2246
Obstacle, 611, 1855
Obstinacy, 1947, 2938
Obstruction–Obstructionist, 721, 1466, 1478
Obvious, 2875
Ocean, 1362, 2243, 2713, 2789
Oculist, 1268
Odd–Oddity, 1965
Offender. See also Criminal, 542
Offense, 362, 551, 938, 2439
Offering, 283
Office hours, 709, 2434
Officer, 237
Oil, 162, 2155
Old-age, 54, 55, 59, 61, 63, 67, 73, 76, 79, 277, 764, 835, 858, 1856, 1918, 2051, 2178, 2615, 2933
Old-fashioned, 355, 1615
Old maid, 1631, 1665, 1857–1859
Old timer, 143, 2471
Omniscient, 2939, 2959
Onion, 1987
Opera, 1839
Operation. See also Surgery, 694, 706
Opinion, 131, 639, 1409, 1860, 1861, 1911, 2075, 2246, 2817
Opportunity, 127, 461, 513, 514, 523, 602, 641, 661, 808, 1113, 1361, 1862–1877, 2364, 2882
Opposite, 1231
Opposition, 427, 610, 817, 2000, 2529
Oppression, 46
Optimism–Optimist, 93, 1878–1888, 1987, 2362, 2630
Optometrist, 1887
Orator–Oration–Oratory. See also Public Speaking, 837, 2018, 2147, 2180, 2193, 2203, 2205, 2213
Oratoreador, 2204
Ordeal, 1370, 1646
Order–Orders–Orderly, 1344, 1889, 2306
Ordinary, 596
Oriental, 571
Origins, 659, 1370, 1890–1903
Original–Originality, 1232, 1233, 1235, 1906
Ornament, 755, 1919

Orphan, 1324, 2655
Ostrich, 1864
Out-group, 652
Outlook, 1311
Overalls, 1875
Overcharge, 685, 704
Overcoat, 617
Overdraft, 1629, 1689
Overhead, 2843
Over-heated, 464
Over-privileged, 546
Oversight, 872
Overtake, 1517
Overweight, 1988, 2855
Overwork, 1054, 1117, 2394
Ownership, 1989
Oxford University, 1272
Oxygen, 808
Oyster, 1744

P

Padlock, 1813
Pain, 321, 364, 756, 797, 1917, 2560
Paint–Painting–Painter, 1589, 1995, 2330
Pair–Pairs, 1831
Pallbearer, 495, 2748
Panacea, 1907
Pancake, 2175
Parachute, 1779, 1938
Parade, 1796
Paradise, 1990
Paradox, 1192
Paranoid, 2115
Parasite, 1897, 1900, 1908
Paratrooper, 1773, 1775, 1938
Pardon, 994
Parent-Teacher Association, 1913, 1915
Parents–Parenthood, 25, 328, 333, 337, 339, 342, 386, 519–522, 626, 918, 1156, 1623, 1909–1915, 2682
Paris (France)–Parisian, 2137, 2717
Parking, 304, 413, 2630
Parliament, Houses of, 1239, 2160
Parrot, 279, 1070, 2332
Parsley, 263
Partner–Partnership, 1376
Party, 630, 1332
Passenger, 2220
Passion, 1411
Passport, 1962, 2799
Password, 1787
Past, The, 1005, 1006, 1863, 1916, 2068, 2079, 2362, 2617, 2877

450

453

Salute, 1899
Salvation, 309, 2153
Sanctuary, 657
Sand, 645, 1855, 1864
Sandwich, 1835
San Francisco, Calif., 1855
Sanitation, 159
Sanka, 1844
Santa Claus, 1678, 2311, 2709
Sap, 1577, 2683
Sarcasm, 196, 1240, 1430, 2311–2314
Satisfaction—Satisfied, 113, 409, 1338,
   2315–2320, 2492
Saturation point, 864
Savage, 1362
Saxons, 572
Sayonara, 570
Scales, 1988
Scandal, 1634, 2530
Scandal monger, 1063
Scapegoat, 669
Scare, 45
Scarlet fever, 496, 701
Scenario—Scenarist, 1149
Scarce—Scarcity, 1900
School, 503, 519, 547, 626, 643, 735,
   1918
Schoolmaster. See also Teacher, 1829
Science—Scientist, 210, 378, 525, 534,
   1247, 2098, 2263, 2321–2324,
   2395, 2782
Scissors, 216
Scold—Scolding, 2317
Score—Scoring, 1042, 2508
Scotch—Scottish—Scotland, 163, 1748,
   2595
Scoundrel, 667, 1074
Scratch—Scratching, 788
Screen, Window, 1304
Script, 1149
Scriptures. See also Bible, 181, 184
Sculptor, 586
Sculpture, 739
Seafarer, 1218
Search, 455, 875, 1886
Sea sickness, 1431, 1991, 2713, 2715
Season, 351, 1112, 1151
Seattle, Wash., 2188
Secret—Secrecy, 974, 1443, 1488,
   1664, 1865, 1928, 2325–2328,
   2537, 2586, 2840
Secretary, 1271
Sect, 650
Security, 127, 290, 523, 851
Seed, 756, 2782

Selective service, 1152
Self, 51, 132, 291, 459, 575, 948,
   1005, 1122, 1130, 1139, 1140,
   1486, 1534, 1548, 1559, 1880,
   2067, 2242, 2329, 2330, 2462,
   2501, 2557, 2677
Self-acclaim, 2331, 2332
Self-appraisal, 932, 1572, 2333–2337
Self-blame, 2338–2340, 2501
Self-centered, 738, 764
Self-condemnation, 436, 669
Self-confidence, 54, 609, 611, 798,
   2458, 2465, 2472, 2946
Self-conscious, 656, 672
Self-control, 513, 2068, 2765
Self-defense, 1407
Self-denial, 896, 2092, 2350
Self-depreciation, 1815
Self-destruction, 2341
Self-development, 860, 1191
Self-discipline, 358, 1889, 2527
Self-distrust, 936
Self-esteem, 1317, 1501, 2342–2348
Self-expression, 799
Self-government, 1075, 2246
Self-improvement, 2527
Self-interest, 344
Selfishness, 314, 344, 514, 652, 1098,
   1122, 2259, 2349–2352
Selflessness, 2353
Self-made, 2331, 2884
Self-mastery, 948, 2356–2358
Self-praise, 196, 2359
Self-protection, 2347
Self-preservation, 2341
Self-punishment, 1497
Self-reliance, 452, 1500
Self-respect, 661
Self-restraint, 2360
Self-sacrifice, 513
Self-service, 2351
Self-spite, 1518
Self-support, 281
Self-taxation, 2571
Self-training, 2362
Self-worship, 196, 2763
Senate U.S.—Senator, 1092, 2010,
   2143
Seniors, 741
Sense—Senses, 2551, 2811
Sensitivity, 106, 2475
Sentence, 536, 1324, 1329, 1416, 1434
Sentiment—Sentimental, 316
Sentry, 1771
Separation, 570

457

459

subject index

author and source index

author and source index

D

Daniels, Josephus, 2512
Darrow, Clarence, 2032
Dayton, Dorothy, 1638
De Casseres, Benjamin, 1193
Decatur, Stephen, 1535
Deeping, Warwick, 2609
De Foe, Daniel, 1188, 1317
De Gaston, ——, 929
Deluzy, Madame, 775
Democritus, 451, 755, 1334
Demoustier, ——, 1763
Densted, Annette, 2762
Depew, Chauncey M., 315
Descartes, René, 938
Dewar, Thomas R., 2541, 2572
Dickens, Charles, 508, 2079
Dillingham, Walter F., 1091
Disraeli, Benjamin, 462, 861, 1057,
    1098, 1142, 1367, 1560, 1862,
    1957, 2074, 2421, 2504
Dobie, J. Frank, 747
Dobson, Henry Austin, 2606
Donahue, Harold W., 2303
Dressler, Marie, 39
Drummond, Henry, 116, 2263
Dryden, John, 609
Dumas, Alexander, 984, 1015, 1640
Dunne, Peter Finley, 422
Duval, Evelyn Mills, 1910
Dwight, Henry, 600

E

Eddy, Mary Baker, 1791
Edison, Thomas A., 792, 1019, 2492
Edman, Irwin, 750
Edwards, Tyron, 133
Edye, Alfred, 2852
Einstein, Albert, 477
Eliot, Charles W., 785
Eliot, George, 10, 604, 1326, 2377
Ellis, Havelock, 1469
Emerson, Ralph Waldo, 363, 601, 637,
    645, 972, 1105, 1138, 1208, 1232,
    1294, 1478, 1491, 1539, 1583,
    1757, 2233, 2272, 2329, 2330,
    2382, 2480, 2488
Epictetus, 454, 948, 2718, 2814
Ernst, Morris L., 2403
Erskine, John, 801, 2267
Eunson, Dale, 757

F

Fairchild, Fred R., 828
Falvey, Hal, 1176
Faulkner, Edward H., 2802
Fears, Peggy Caroline, 1739
Felltham, Owen, 2538
Fenelon, François, 2132
Ferguson, Mrs. Walter, 1623
Fert, Olga J., 2471
Fidler, Jimmy, 1688
Field, David Dudley, 1330
Field, Marshall, 220
Fielding, Henry, 2804
Fishbein, Morris, 1280
Flammer, ——, 897
Florio, John, 1900
Foley, J. A., 810
Fontaine, Robert, 2257
Forbes, B. C., 2515, 2516
Forbes, Esther, 2771
Ford, Henry, 240, 851, 1872, 2479
Ford, Miriam Allen de, 1415
Forer, Raymond, 640
Fosdick, Harry Emerson, 358, 596,
    1107, 1518, 2142
Foster, Constance J., 632
France, Anatole, 194, 724, 927, 1439,
    2276, 2758
Franklin, Benjamin, 113, 203, 703,
    737, 919, 957, 958, 1236, 1494,
    1738, 1849, 1921, 1953, 2055,
    2081, 2271, 2593, 2796
Freedman, Ray, 507
Freeman, Frank N., 568
Frost, Robert, 1713
Froth, ——, 560
Froude, James Anthony, 826
Fuller, Thomas, 935, 2953

G

Galileo, 776
Gandhi, Mahatma, 943
Garbutt, Frank A., 2817
Garrison, Webb B., 1370
Gary, Elbert H., 2527
Gessler, Clifford, 574
Gibbon, Edward, 2535
Gibbs, Sir Philip, 305
Giles, Henry, 292
Gist, Nathan Howard, 1655
Gittelsohn, Roland B., 599
Gladstone, William E., 1319

Spaulding, C. C., 641
Spence, Harold L., 2558
Spencer, Herbert, 1704
Spring, Howard, 1499
Spurgeon, C. H., 2482, 2737
Stanford, J. E., 2126
Stanley, Bessie Anderson, 2450
Steele, Richard, 2235
Steier, Kenneth, 439
Sterne, Laurence, 425
Stevens, H. H., 2782
Stevenson, Adlai E., 1820
Stevenson, Robert Louis, 981, 2069
Stewart, George Craig, 2687
Stockton, Frank R., 360
Stone, Irving, 799, 2045, 2763
Stopes, Marie, 166
Strausz-Hupe, Robert, 2776
Summer, G. Lynn, 2131
Swift, Jonathan, 1109, 2078, 2616, 2816
Swift, Linton B., 513
Syrus, Publius, 987, 1325

T

Tacitus, Publius, 821
Taft, William Howard, 1408
Tait, William, 631
Talmage, T. DeWitt, 1365
Tarbell, Ida M., 184
Tausek, Joseph, 1495
Taylor, Jeremy, 1329
Tertullian, 1919
Thackeray, William Makepeace, 719, 1523
Thomajan, P. K., 2218
Thompson, Morton, 2574
Thomson, Sir Basil, 2750
Thoreau, Henry David, 682, 1210, 2549
Thornbury, George Walter, 931
Tiorio, ——, 473
Titcomb, Timothy, 2892
Todd, John, 1211
Trout, Robert, 1112
Twain, Mark, 848, 969, 1009, 1041, 1136, 2927
Tweedsmuir, Lord, 1956

V

Vada, Cecil de, 142
Vance, Eleanor Graham, 1912

Van Paassen, Pierre, 2082
Vauclain, Samuel, 2467
Voltaire, François de, 825, 841, 949, 1071, 1153, 1235
Von Poschinger, ——, 2889

W

Wade, H. V., 1725
Waite, John Barker, 539
Wallace, Lew, 1758
Walpole, Horace, 2321, 2424
Wanamaker, John, 222
Warner, Thomas H., 2343
Warren, Earl, 1072
Warren, Julius E., 2929
Washington, George, 1008, 2278
Waterman, Nixon, 2455
Watts, V. Orval, 2514
Watson, John A. F., 2940
Webber, Everett and Olga, 2752
Webster, Daniel, 418, 1826
Weiss, George P., 1652
Wellington, Duke of, 1957
Wellman, Francis L., 1118
Wells, H. G., 1307
Welshimer, Helen, 626
Wenley, Robert Mark, 1355
West, Robert, 896
Westcott, Cannon, 832
Wharton, John F., 469
White, William Allen, 56
Whitman, Walt, 1243
Whittier, John Greenleaf, 580
Wiggin, Kate Douglas, 1831
Wilberforce, William, 1957
Wilcox, Carlos, 877
Wilcox, Ella Wheeler, 483, 1135
Wilcox, John, 749
Wilde, Oscar, 50, 79, 312, 533, 559, 860, 989, 999, 1097, 1172, 1315, 1316, 1468, 1476, 1493, 1548, 1563, 1578, 1621, 1935, 1964, 2052, 2097, 2234, 2349, 2553, 2560, 2731, 2856, 2875–2879, 2898
Wilder, Viney, 484
Wilhelm, Donald, 1989
Williams, D. W., 856
Williams, Valentine, 1277
Wilson, Earl, 2630, 2829, 2859
Wilson, Margery, 543, 2833
Wilson, Thomas, 965
Wilson, Woodrow, 593, 942

471

author and source index

index to names and personalities referred to in the text

(Numbers in the index refer to selections in the text, not to page numbers)

K

Killigrew, Anne, 2823
Kinsey, Alfred C., 2828
Kipling, Rudyard, 2914
Knudsen, William S., 2511
Kober, Arthur, 1684
Kreisler, Fritz, 141, 2146
Kruger, Paul, 1248B
Kyser, Kay, 355

L

Lafayette, Marquis, 492
LaGuardia, Fiorello H., 2037
Lahr, Bert, 2937
Lamb, Charles, 1132, 2821
Landis, Kenesaw Mountain, 1416
Langley, Samuel P., 2332
Lawrence, Gertrude, 2717
Leacock, Stephen, 750
Lincoln, Abraham, 92, 314, 488, 748, 956, 971, 994, 1089, 1116, 1495, 2018, 2165, 2238, 2873
Linn, James Weber, 1104
Lockwood, Ralph, 1415
Lodge, Henry Cabot, 2341
Logan, John A., 1904
Longfellow, Henry Wadsworth, 1174, 1843
Longmire, Adele, 2744
Longworth, Nicholas, 1843
Louis XVI, King, 2619
Luey, Sir Henry, 1267
Luther, Martin, 1294
Lyons, Sir Joseph, 284

M

MacDowell, Edward, 2312
Madison, James, 1089
Maimonides, 281
Mann, Horace, 760
Mann, Thomas, 1984
Marie Antoinette, 1957
Marie, Queen, 2110
Marlborough, Duke of, 1848
Marshall, John, 5
Marshalov, Boris, 1083
Martinelli, Giovanni, 2735
Marx, Groucho, 1915, 2559
Mason, Max, 2179
Meyer, Adolf, 2110
Micah, 2258

Michelangelo, 1227
Moody, Dwight L., 397
Morrow, Dwight, 399, 1032
Moses, 187, 1426, 2022, 2649
Mussolini, Benito, 1899

Mc

McAfee, Mildred, 764
McCarey, Leo, 2605
McKinley, William, 2029
McNeill, Don, 72

N

Napoleon (Bonaparte), 1152, 2230
National Probation Association, 294, 519
Nazarene, The, 760
Nelson, Lord, 1152
Nero, Emperor, 669
Nineveh, 631

O

Osler, William, 701
Ouida, 550

P

Parker, Francis Wayland, 341
Parks, Bert, 1993
Perkins, Frances, 2422
Pestalozzi, Johann Heinrich, 760
Phidias, 2258
Pipkin, Marvin, 2745
Pitt, William, 1957
Plato, 760
Post, Emily, 1085

R

Ramée, Louise de la, 550
Revere, Paul, 1174
Ripley, Robert L., 1866
Rockefeller, John D., 514
Roosevelt, Franklin D., 590, 1112, 1388
Roosevelt, Theodore, 597, 1086, 1088, 2608
Rosenwald, Julius, 507
Rousseau, Jean Jacques, 760
Rukeyser, Merryle Stanley, 2167